MW00799910

Irene C. Fountas **&** Gay Su Pinnell

# The Reading Minilessons Book

## Your Every Day Guide for Literacy Teaching

## GRADE 1

**HEINEMANN**
Portsmouth, NH

**Heinemann**
361 Hanover Street
Portsmouth, NH 03801–3912
www.heinemann.com

*Offices and agents throughout the world*

©2019 by Irene C. Fountas and Gay Su Pinnell

The author and publisher wish to thank those who have generously given permission to reprint borrowed material: Please see the Credits section at the back of the book, starting on page 503.

Library of Congress Cataloging-in-Publication Data is on file at the Library of Congress.
ISBN: 978-0-325-09862-3

*Editor:* Sue Paro
*Production:* Cindy Strowman
*Cover and interior designs:* Ellery Harvey
*Illustrator:* Will Sweeney
*Typesetter:* Ed Stevens Design
*Manufacturing:* Deanna Richardson

Printed in the United States of America on acid-free paper

22  21  20  19  18  LSC  1  2  3  4  5  6

# CONTENTS

## Introduction

## 1   Management

# 2 Literary Analysis

## Fiction and Nonfiction

### General

## Style and Language

## Illustrations

# 3 Strategies and Skills

# 4 Writing About Reading

1

# The Role of Reading Minilessons in Early Literacy Learning

THE GOAL OF ALL READING is the joyful, independent, and meaningful processing of a written text. As a competent reader, you become immersed in a fiction or nonfiction text; you read for a purpose; you become highly engaged with the plot and characters or the content. Focused on the experience of reading the text, you are largely unconscious of the thousands of actions happening in your brain that support the construction of meaning from the print that represents language. And, this is true whether the print is on a piece of paper or an electronic device. Your purpose may be to have vicarious experiences via works of fiction that take you to places far distant in time and space—even to worlds that do not and cannot exist! Or, your purpose may be to gather fuel for thinking (by using fiction or nonfiction) or it may simply be to enjoy the sounds of human language via literature and poetry. Most of us engage in the reading of multiple texts every day— some for work, some for pleasure, and some for practical guidance—but what we all have in common as readers is the ability to independently and simultaneously apply in-the-head systems of strategic actions that enable us to act on written texts.

Young readers are on a journey toward efficient processing of any texts they might like to attempt, and it is important every step of the way that they have successful experiences in reading independently those texts that are available at each point in time. In a literacy-rich classroom with a multitext approach, readers have the opportunity to hear written texts read aloud through interactive read-aloud, and so they build a rich treasure chest of known stories and nonfiction books that they can share as a classroom community. They understand and talk about these shared texts in ways that extend comprehension, vocabulary, and knowledge of the ways written texts are presented and organized. They participate with their classmates in the shared reading of a common text so that they understand more and know how to act on written language. They experience tailored instruction in small guided reading groups using leveled texts precisely matched to their current abilities and needs for challenge. They stretch their thinking as they discuss a variety of complex texts in book clubs. They process fiction and nonfiction books with expert teacher support—always moving in the direction of more complex texts that will lift their reading abilities. *But it is in independent reading that they apply everything they have learned across all of those instructional contexts.* So the goal of all the reading instruction is to enable the young reader to engage in effective, efficient, and joyful independent and meaningful processing of written text *every day* in the classroom. This is what it means to grow up literate in our schools.

Independent reading involves choice based on interests and tastes. Competent, independent readers are eager to talk and write about the books they have read for themselves. They are gaining awareness of themselves as readers with favorite authors, illustrators, genres, and topics; their capacity for self-regulation is growing. The key to this kind of independent reading is making an explicit connection between all other instructional contexts— interactive read-aloud, shared reading, guided reading, and book clubs—and the reader's own independent work. Making these explicit links is the goal of minilessons. All teaching, support, and confirmation lead to the individual's successful, independent reading.

## Making Learning Visible Through Minilessons

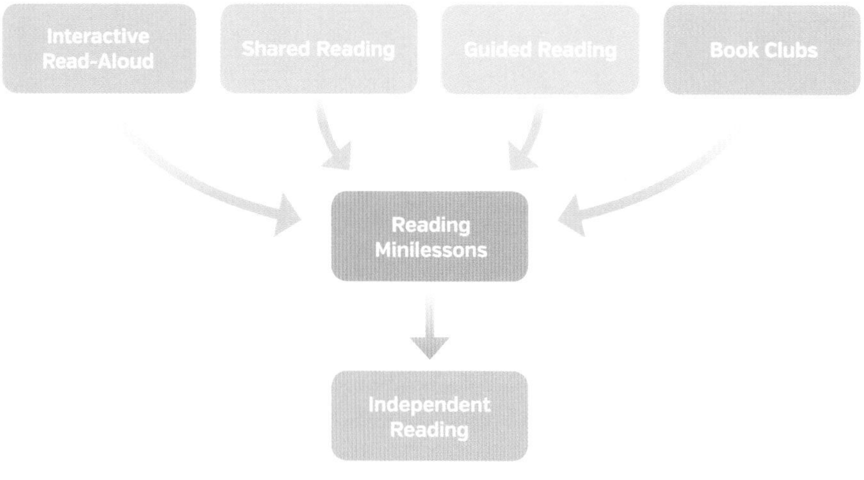

Figure 1-1: Various reading experiences supported by explicit instruction in reading minilessons lead to independent reading.

## What Is a Reading Minilesson?

A reading minilesson is a concise and focused lesson on any aspect of effective reading or classroom reading work that is important for children to explicitly understand at a particular point in time. It is an opportunity to build on all of the children's literacy experiences, make one important understanding visible, and hold the children accountable for applying it consistently in reading. Minilessons place a strong instructional frame around independent reading.

A minilesson takes only a few minutes and usually involves the whole class. It builds on shared literary experiences the children in your class have experienced prior to the lesson. You can quickly bring these shared texts to mind as powerful examples. Usually, you will teach only one focused lesson each day, but minilessons will be logically organized and build on each other. Each minilesson engages children in an inquiry process that leads to the discovery and understanding of a general principle. Most of the time interactive read-aloud books and shared reading texts that children have already heard serve as mentor texts, from which they generalize the understanding. The reading minilesson provides the link between students' previous experience with texts to their own independent reading (see Figure 1-1). It plays a key role in systematic, coherent teaching, which is directed toward each reader's developing competencies.

To help children connect ideas and develop deep knowledge and broad application of principles, related reading minilessons are grouped under "umbrella" concepts (see Chapter 3). An umbrella is the broad category in which there are several lessons that are linked to each other and all of which contribute to the understanding of the umbrella concept. Within an umbrella, the lessons build on each other (see Figure 1-2). In each lesson you create an "anchor chart" with the children. This visual representation of the principles will be a useful reference tool as young children learn new routines, encounter new texts, and draw and write about their reading in a reader's notebook.

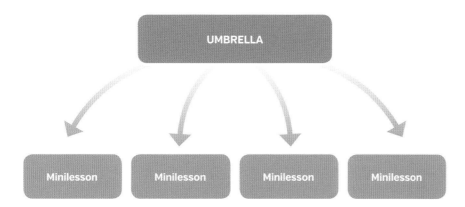

Figure 1-2: Each minilesson focuses on a different aspect of the larger umbrella concept.

Figure 1-3: The
minilessons in this book
are organized into four
sections.

## Four Types of Reading Minilessons

In this book, you will find 175 minilessons that are organized into four types:

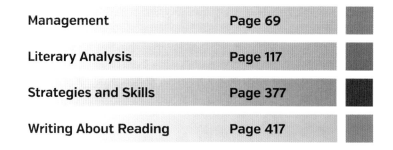

| | | |
|---|---|---|
| **Management** | **Page 69** | |
| **Literary Analysis** | **Page 117** | |
| **Strategies and Skills** | **Page 377** | |
| **Writing About Reading** | **Page 417** | |

**Management Minilessons.** These lessons include routines that are essential to the smooth functioning of the classroom and student-centered, independent literacy learning. The management minilessons are designed to support children's development of independence and self-regulatory behavior. Most of your minilessons at the beginning of the school year will focus on management. You will want to repeat any of the lessons as needed across the year. A guiding principle: teach a minilesson on anything that prevents the classroom from running smoothly.

**Literary Analysis Minilessons.** These lessons build children's awareness of the characteristics of various genres and of the elements of fiction and nonfiction texts. The books that you read during interactive read-aloud and shared reading serve as mentor texts when applying the principles of literary analysis. Through these lessons, children learn how to apply new thinking to their independent reading and how to share their thinking with others.

**Strategies and Skills Minilessons.** Young readers need to develop a robust body of in-the-head strategic actions for the efficient processing of texts. For example, they need to monitor their reading for accuracy and understanding, solve words (simple and complex), read fluently with phrasing, and constantly construct meaning. Teaching related to processing texts will best take place in guided reading and shared reading; these general lessons reinforce broad principles that every reader in your class may need to be reminded of from time to time.

**Writing About Reading Minilessons.** Throughout the first-grade year, children will have opportunities to respond to what they read in a reader's notebook in the forms of drawing and writing. These lessons introduce the *Fountas & Pinnell Reader's Notebook: Primary* (Fountas and Pinnell 2014) and help children use this important tool for independent literacy learning. First-grade children will often create drawings in response to the text, but as the year progresses, they will increase the amount of writing they do.

The goal of all minilessons is to help children to think and act like readers and to build effective processing strategies while reading continuous text independently. Whether you are teaching management lessons, literary analysis lessons, strategies and skills lessons, or writing about reading lessons, the characteristics of effective minilessons, listed in Figure 1-4, apply.

## Characteristics of Effective Minilessons

**Effective Minilessons . . .**

- have a clear rationale and a goal to focus meaningful teaching
- are relevant to the specific needs of readers so that your teaching connects with the learners
- are brief, concise, and to the point for immediate application
- use clear and specific language to avoid talk that clutters learning
- stay focused on a single idea so students can apply the learning and build on it day after day
- build one understanding on another across several days instead of single isolated lessons
- use an inquiry approach whenever possible to support constructive learning
- often include shared, high-quality mentor texts that can be used as examples
- are well paced to engage and hold students' interest
- are grouped into umbrellas to provide depth and coherence
- provide time for children to "try out" the new concept before independent application
- engage students in summarizing the new learning and thinking about its application to their own work
- build academic vocabulary appropriate to the grade level
- help students become better readers and writers
- foster community through the development of shared language
- can be assessed as you observe students in authentic literacy activities to provide feedback on your teaching
- help students understand what they are learning how to do and how it helps them as readers

**Figure 1-4:** Characteristics of effective minilessons

## Constructing Anchor Charts
## for Effective Minilessons

Anchor charts are an essential part of each minilesson in this book (see Figure 1-5). They provide a way for you to capture the children's thinking during the lesson and reflect on the learning at the end. When you think about a chart, it helps you think through the big, important ideas and the language you will use in the minilesson. It helps you think about the sequence and your efficiency in getting down what is important.

Each minilesson in this book provides guidance for adding information to the chart. Read through lessons carefully to know whether any parts of the chart should be prepared ahead or whether the chart is constructed during the lesson or left until the end. After the lesson, the charts become a resource for your students to use as a reference throughout the day. They provide a visual resource for children who need to not only hear but also see the information. They can revisit these charts as they apply the principle in reading, talking, and writing about books, or as they try out new routines in the classroom. You can refer to them during interactive read-aloud, shared reading, reading conferences, guided reading, and book clubs.

Though your charts will be unique because they are built from the ideas your students share, you will want to consider some of the common characteristics among the charts we have included in this book. We have created one example in each lesson, but vary it as you see fit. When you create charts with children, consider the following:

> **Make your charts simple, clear, and organized.** The charts you create with your students should be clearly organized. It is particularly important in first grade to keep them simple without a lot of dense text. Provide white space and print neatly in dark, easy-to-read colors. You will notice that some of the sample charts are more conceptual. The idea is conveyed through a few words and a visual representation. Others use a grid to show how the principle is applied specifically across several texts.

> **Make your charts visually appealing and useful.** Most of the minilesson charts for first grade contain visual support. For example, you will see book covers, symbols, and drawings throughout the lesson charts to support first graders in reading the words on the chart and in understanding the concept. The drawings are intentionally simple to give you a quick model to draw yourself. These visuals are particularly supportive for English language learners, who might need to rely heavily on a graphic representation of the principle ideas. You might find it helpful to prepare these drawings on separate pieces of paper or sticky notes ahead of the lesson and tape or glue them on the chart as the students construct their understandings. This time-saving tip can also make the charts look more interesting and colorful, because certain parts stand out for the children.

When you teach English language learners, you must adjust your teaching—not more teaching, but different teaching—to teach effectively. Look for this symbol to see ways to support English language learners.

ELL CONNECTION

▶ **Make your charts colorful.** Though the sample minilesson charts are colorful for the purpose of engagement or organization, be careful about the amount and types of color that you use. You may want to use color for a purpose. Color can help you point out particular parts of the chart. For example, "Look at the purple word on the chart." Color can support English language learners by providing a visual link to certain words or ideas. However, color can also be distracting if overused. Be thoughtful about when you choose to use colors to highlight an idea or a word on a chart so that children are supported in reading continuous text. Text that is broken up by a lot of different colors can be very distracting for beginning readers who are just getting used to the distinguishing characteristics of letters. You will notice that the minilesson principle is usually written in black or a dark color across the top of the chart so that it stands out and is easily recognized as the focus of the lesson.

Anchor charts support language growth in all students, and especially in English language learners. Conversation about the minilesson develops oral language and then connects that oral language to print when you write words on the chart and provide picture support. By constructing an anchor chart with your students, you provide print that is immediately accessible to them because they helped create it and have ownership of the language. After a chart is finished, revisit it as often as needed to reinforce not only the ideas but also the printed words.

 **ELL CONNECTION**

**Figure 1-5:** Constructing anchor charts with your students provides verbal and visual support for all learners.

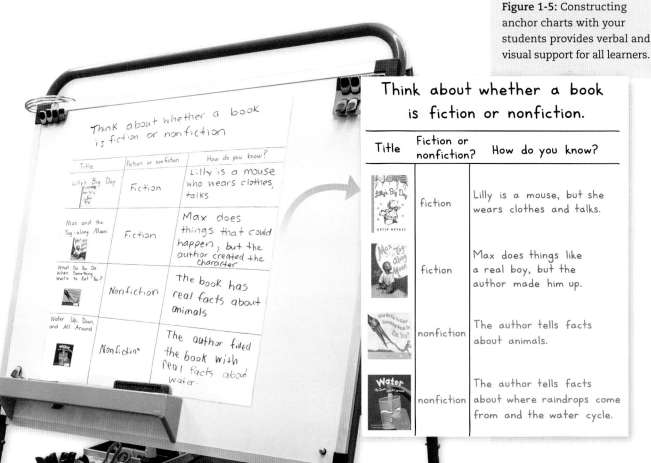

## Think about whether a book is fiction or nonfiction.

| Title | Fiction or nonfiction? | How do you know? |
|-------|------------------------|------------------|
| Lilly's Big Day | fiction | Lilly is a mouse, but she wears clothes and talks. |
| Max the Tag-along Moon | fiction | Max does things like a real boy, but the author made him up. |
| What Are You You When Something Wants to Eat You? | nonfiction | The author tells facts about animals. |
| Water Up, Down, and All Around | nonfiction | The author tells facts about where raindrops come from and the water cycle. |

A minilesson brings to children's conscious attention a focused principle that will assist them in developing an effective, independent literacy processing system. It provides an opportunity for students to do the following:

▶ Respond to and act on a variety texts

▶ Become aware of and be able to articulate understandings about texts

▶ Engage in further inquiry to investigate the characteristics of texts

▶ Search for and learn to recognize patterns and characteristics of written texts

▶ Build new ideas on known ideas

▶ Learn how to think about effective actions as they process texts

▶ Learn to manage their own reading lives

▶ Learn how to work together well in the classroom

▶ Learn to talk to others about their thinking about books

▶ Learn how to use and care for books and materials

Reading minilessons help readers build in-the-head processing systems. In the following chapters, you will explore how minilessons support children in using integrated systems of strategic actions for thinking *within*, *beyond*, and *about* many different kinds of texts and also how to use minilessons to build a community of readers who demonstrate a sense of agency and responsibility. You will also look in more depth at how minilessons fit within a design for literacy learning and within a multitext approach.

We conclude this chapter with some key terms we will use as we describe minilessons in the next chapters (see Figure 1-6). Keep these in mind so we can develop a common language to talk about the minilessons you teach.

**Figure 1-6:** Important terms used in *The Reading Minilessons Book*

### Key Terms When Talking About Reading Minilessons

| | |
|---|---|
| Umbrella | A group of minilessons, all of which are directed at different aspects of the same larger understanding. |
| Principle | A concise statement of the understanding children will need to learn and apply. |
| Mentor Text | A fiction or nonfiction text that offers a clear example of the principle. Students will have previously heard and discussed the text. |
| Text Set | A group of fiction or nonfiction or a combination of fiction and nonfiction texts that, taken together, support a theme or exemplify a genre. Students will have previously heard all the texts referenced in a minilesson and had opportunities to make connections between them. |
| Anchor Chart | A visual representation of the lesson concept, using a combination of words and images. It is constructed by the teacher and students to summarize the learning and is used as a reference tool by the children. |

# Chapter 2

## Using *The Literacy Continuum* to Guide the Teaching of Reading Minilessons

WE BELIEVE SCHOOLS SHOULD BE places where students read, think, talk, and write every day about relevant content that engages their hearts and minds. Learning deepens when students engage in thinking, talking, reading, and writing about texts across many different instructional contexts and in whole-group, small-group, and individual instruction. Students who live a literate life in their classrooms have access to multiple experiences with texts throughout a day. As they participate in interactive read-aloud, shared reading, guided reading, book clubs, and independent reading, they engage in the real work of reading and writing. They build a network of systems of strategic actions that allow them to think deeply within, beyond, and about text.

The networks of in-the-head strategic actions are inferred from observations of proficient readers, writers, and speakers. We have described these networks in *The Fountas & Pinnell Literacy Continuum: A Tool for Assessment, Planning, and Teaching* (Fountas and Pinnell 2017c). This volume presents detailed text characteristics and behaviors and understandings to notice, teach for, and support for prekindergarten through middle school, across eight instructional reading, writing, and language contexts. In sum, *The Literacy Continuum* describes proficiency in reading, writing, and language as it changes over grades and over levels.

**Figure 2-1:** Minilesson principles are drawn from the observable behaviors of proficient students as listed in *The Literacy Continuum.*

| | INSTRUCTIONAL CONTEXT | BRIEF DEFINITION | DESCRIPTION OF THE CONTINUUM |
|---|---|---|---|
| 1 | Interactive Read-Aloud and Literature Discussion | Students engage in discussion with one another about a text that they have heard read aloud or one they have read independently. | • Year by year, grades PreK–8<br>• Genres appropriate to grades PreK–8<br>• Specific behaviors and understandings that are evidence of thinking within, beyond, and about the text |
| 2 | Shared and Performance Reading | Students read together or take roles in reading a shared text. They reflect the meaning of the text with their voices. | • Year by year, grades PreK–8<br>• Genres appropriate to grades PreK–8<br>• Specific behaviors and understandings that are evidence of thinking within, beyond, and about the text |
| 3 | Writing About Reading | Students extend their understanding of a text through a variety of writing genres and sometimes with illustrations. | • Year by year, grades PreK–8<br>• Genres/forms for writing about reading appropriate to grades PreK–8<br>• Specific evidence in the writing that reflects thinking within, beyond, and about the text |
| 4 | Writing | Students compose and write their own examples of a variety of genres, written for varying purposes and audiences. | • Year by year, grades PreK–8<br>• Genres/forms for writing appropriate to grades PreK–8<br>• Aspects of craft, conventions, and process that are evident in students' writing, grades PreK–8 |
| 5 | Oral and Visual Communication | Students present their ideas through oral discussion and presentation. | • Year by year, grades PreK–8<br>• Specific behaviors and understandings related to listening and speaking, presentation |
| 6 | Technological Communication | Students learn effective ways of communicating and searching for information through technology; they learn to think critically about information and sources. | • Year by year, grades PreK–8<br>• Specific behaviors and understandings related to effective and ethical uses of technology |
| 7 | Phonics, Spelling, and Word Study | Students learn about the relationships of letters to sounds as well as the structure and meaning of words to help them in reading and spelling. | • Year by year, grades PreK–8<br>• Specific behaviors and understandings related to nine areas of understanding related to letters, sounds, and words, and how they work in reading and spelling |
| 8 | Guided Reading | Students read a teacher-selected text in a small group; the teacher provides explicit teaching and support for reading increasingly challenging texts. | • Level by level, A to Z<br>• Genres appropriate to grades PreK–8<br>• Specific behaviors and understandings that are evidence of thinking within, beyond, and about the text<br>• Specific suggestions for word work (drawn from the phonics and word analysis continuum) |

**Figure 2-2:** From *The Literacy Continuum* (Fountas and Pinnell 2017c, 3)

# Systems of Strategic Actions

The systems of strategic actions are represented in the wheel diagram shown on the inside back cover of this book. This model helps us think about the thousands of in-the-head processes that take place simultaneously and largely unconsciously when a competent reader processes a text. When the reader engages the neural network, he builds a literacy processing system over time that becomes increasingly sophisticated. Teaching in each instructional context is directed toward helping every reader expand these in-the-head networks across increasingly complex texts.

Four sections of *The Literacy Continuum* (Fountas and Pinnell 2017c)—Interactive Read-Aloud and Literature Discussion, Shared and Performance Reading, Guided Reading, and Writing About Reading—describe the specific competencies or goals of readers, writers, and language users:

*Within* the text (literal understanding achieved through searching for and using information, monitoring and self-correcting, solving words, maintaining fluency, adjusting, and summarizing) The reader gathers the important information from the fiction or nonfiction text.

*Beyond* the text (predicting, making connections with personal experience, content knowledge and other texts, synthesizing new information, and inferring what is implied but not stated) The reader brings understanding to the processing of a text, reaching for ideas or concepts that are implied but not explicitly stated.

**About** the text (analyzing or critiquing the text) The reader looks at a text to appreciate or evaluate its construction, logic, or literary elements.

*The Literacy Continuum* is the foundation for all the minilessons. The minilesson principles come largely from the behaviors and understandings in the interactive read-aloud continuum, but some are selected from the shared reading, oral and visual communication, and writing about reading continua. In addition, we have included minilessons related to working together in a classroom community to assure that effective literacy instruction can take place. In most lessons, you will see a direct link to the goals from *The Literacy Continuum* called Continuum Connection.

As you ground your teaching in support of each reader's development of the systems of strategic actions, it is important to remember that these actions are never applied one at a time. A reader who comprehends a text engages these actions rapidly and simultaneously and largely without conscious attention. Your intentional talk and conversations in the various instructional contexts should support students in engaging and building their processing systems while they respond authentically as readers and enjoy the text.

**Figure 2-3:** All of your teaching will be grounded in support of each reader's development of the systems of strategic actions (see the inside back cover for a larger version of the Systems of Strategic Actions wheel).

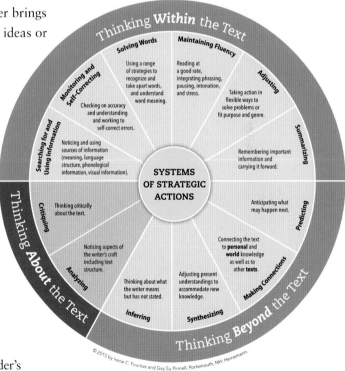

## Relationship of Intentional Talk to Reading Minilessons

*Intentional talk* refers to the language you use that is consciously directed toward the goal of instruction. We have used the term *facilitative talk* to refer to the language that supports student learning in specific ways. When you plan for intentional talk in your interactive read-aloud and shared reading experiences, think about the meaning of the text and what your students will need to think about to fully understand and enjoy the story. You might select certain pages where you want to stop and have students turn and talk about their reading so they can engage in sharing their thinking with each other. The interactive read-aloud and shared reading sections of *The Literacy Continuum* can help plan what to talk about. For example, when you read a book like *Elizabeti's School*, you would likely invite talk about how Elizabeti feels about school, notice where the story takes place, and notice and discuss the details in the illustrations. When you read a text set of folktales, including stories like *The Tale of Rabbit and Coyote* and *Mrs. Chicken and the Hungry Crocodile*, you might invite your students to comment on the funny parts of the story, on the humorous illustrations, on the repetition of language, and on how folktales share certain characteristics.

As you talk about texts together, embed brief and specific teaching in your read-aloud and shared reading lessons while maintaining a focus on enjoyment and support for your students in gaining the meaning of the whole text. In preparation, mark a few places with sticky notes and a comment or question to invite thinking. Later, when you teach explicit minilessons about concepts such as character feelings, illustrations, and text organization, your students will already have background knowledge to bring to the minilesson and will be ready to explore how the principle works across multiple texts.

In reading minilessons, you explicitly teach the principles you have already embedded in the students' previous experiences with text in these different instructional contexts. Intentional talk within each context prepares a foundation for this explicit focus. Through each interactive read-aloud and shared reading experience, you build a large body of background knowledge, academic vocabulary, and a library of shared texts to draw on as you explore specific literary principles. You will read more about this multitext approach in Chapter 9.

**Figure 2-3:** Mark a few pages to invite students to think about in the reading minilesson.

Chapter 3

# Understanding the Umbrellas and Minilessons

MINILESSONS IN THIS BOOK ARE organized into conceptual groups called "umbrellas," in which a group of principles are explored in sequence, working toward a larger concept. Within each section (Management, Literary Analysis, etc.), the umbrellas are numbered in sequence and are often referred to by *U* plus the number; for example, U1 for the first umbrella. A suggested sequence of umbrellas is presented on pages 51–52 to assist you in planning across the year, but the needs of your students always take priority.

## Umbrella Front Page

Each umbrella has an introductory page on which the minilessons in the umbrella are listed and directions are provided to help you prepare to present the minilessons within the umbrella (see Figure 3-1). The introductory page is designed to provide an overview of how the umbrella is organized and the texts from *Fountas & Pinnell Classroom*™ (FPC) *Collections* that are suggested for the lessons. In addition, we provide types of texts you might select if you are not using the *FPC Collections* referenced in the lessons. Understanding how the umbrella is designed and how the minilessons fit together will help you keep your lessons focused, concise, and brief. Using familiar mentor texts that you have read and enjoyed with your children previously will help you streamline the lessons in the umbrella. You will not need to spend a lot of time rereading large sections of the text because the students already know the texts so well.

When you teach lessons in an umbrella, you help children make connections between concepts and texts and help them develop deeper understandings. A rich context such as this one is particularly helpful for English language learners. Grouping lessons into umbrellas supports English language learners in developing shared vocabulary and language around a single and important area of knowledge.

Following the umbrella front page, you will see a series of two-page lesson spreads that include several parts.

ELL CONNECTION

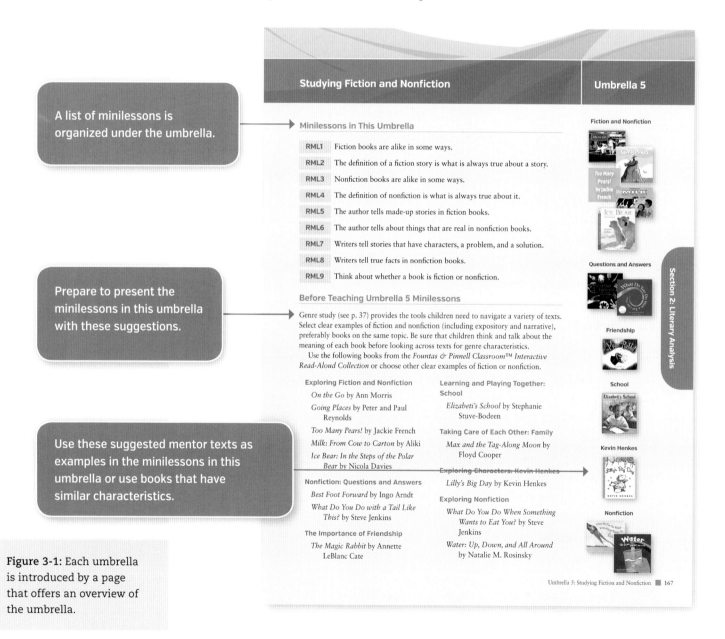

**A list of minilessons is organized under the umbrella.**

**Prepare to present the minilessons in this umbrella with these suggestions.**

**Use these suggested mentor texts as examples in the minilessons in this umbrella or use books that have similar characteristics.**

Studying Fiction and Nonfiction | Umbrella 5

**Minilessons in This Umbrella**

RML1  Fiction books are alike in some ways.
RML2  The definition of a fiction story is what is always true about a story.
RML3  Nonfiction books are alike in some ways.
RML4  The definition of nonfiction is what is always true about it.
RML5  The author tells made-up stories in fiction books.
RML6  The author tells about things that are real in nonfiction books.
RML7  Writers tell stories that have characters, a problem, and a solution.
RML8  Writers tell true facts in nonfiction books.
RML9  Think about whether a book is fiction or nonfiction.

**Before Teaching Umbrella 5 Minilessons**

Genre study (see p. 37) provides the tools children need to navigate a variety of texts. Select clear examples of fiction and nonfiction (including expository and narrative), preferably books on the same topic. Be sure that children think and talk about the meaning of each book before looking across texts for genre characteristics.

Use the following books from the *Fountas & Pinnell Classroom™ Interactive Read-Aloud Collection* or choose other clear examples of fiction or nonfiction.

**Exploring Fiction and Nonfiction**
*On the Go* by Ann Morris
*Going Places* by Peter and Paul Reynolds
*Too Many Pears!* by Jackie French
*Milk: From Cow to Carton* by Aliki
*Ice Bear: In the Steps of the Polar Bear* by Nicola Davies

**Nonfiction: Questions and Answers**
*Best Foot Forward* by Ingo Arndt
*What Do You Do with a Tail Like This?* by Steve Jenkins

**The Importance of Friendship**
*The Magic Rabbit* by Annette LeBlanc Cate

**Learning and Playing Together: School**
*Elizabeti's School* by Stephanie Stuve-Bodeen

**Taking Care of Each Other: Family**
*Max and the Tag-Along Moon* by Floyd Cooper

**Exploring Characters: Kevin Henkes**
*Lilly's Big Day* by Kevin Henkes

**Exploring Nonfiction**
*What Do You Do When Something Wants to Eat You?* by Steve Jenkins
*Water: Up, Down, and All Around* by Natalie M. Rosinsky

Fiction and Nonfiction

Questions and Answers

Friendship

School

Kevin Henkes

Nonfiction

Section 2: Literary Analysis

Umbrella 5: Studying Fiction and Nonfiction ■ 167

**Figure 3-1:** Each umbrella is introduced by a page that offers an overview of the umbrella.

# Two-Page Minilesson Spread

Each minilesson includes a two-page spread that consists of several parts. The section (for example, Literary Analysis), umbrella number (for example, U1), and minilesson number (for example, RML1) are listed at the top to help you locate the lesson you are looking for. For example, the code LA.U1.RML1 identifies the first minilesson in the first umbrella of the Literary Analysis section.

## Principle, Goal, Rationale

The **principle** describes the understanding the children will need to learn and apply. The idea of the principle is based on *The Literacy Continuum* (Fountas and Pinnell 2017c), but the language of the principle has been carefully crafted to be precise, focused on a single idea, and accessible to children. We have placed the principle at the top of the lesson on the left-hand page so you have a clear idea of the understanding you will help children construct through the example texts used in the lesson. Although we have crafted the language to make it simple and appropriate for the age group, you may shape the language in a slightly different way to reflect the way your students use language. Be sure that the principle is stated simply and clearly.

The **goal** of the minilesson is stated in the top section of the lesson, as is the **rationale,** to help you understand what this particular minilesson will do and why it may be important for the children in your classroom. In this beginning section, you will also find suggestions for specific behaviors and understandings to observe as you assess children's learning during or after the minilesson.

## Minilesson

In the Minilesson section of the lesson, you will find an example lesson for teaching the understanding, or principle. The example includes suggestions for teaching and the use of precise language and open-ended questions to engage students in a brief, focused inquiry. Effective minilessons include, when possible, the process of inquiry so children can actively construct their understanding from concrete examples, because telling is not teaching. Instead of simply being told what they need to know, the children get inside the understanding by engaging in the thinking themselves. In the inquiry process, invite the children to look at a group of texts that were read previously (for example, stories with animals that act like people). Choose the books carefully so they represent the characteristics the children are learning about. They will have knowledge of these texts because they have previously experienced them. Invite them to talk about what they notice across all the books. As children explore the text examples using your

# A Closer Look at a Reading Minilesson

The Goal of the minilesson is clearly identified, as is the Rationale, to support your understanding of what this particular minilesson is and why it may be important for the children in your classroom.

The Reading Minilesson Principle—a brief statement that describes the understanding children will need to learn and apply.

This code identifies this minilesson as the ninth reading minilesson (RML9) in the fifth umbrella (U5) in the Literary Analysis (LA) section.

Specific behaviors and understandings to observe as you assess children's learning after presenting the minilesson.

Academic Language and Important Vocabulary that children will need to understand in order to access the learning in the minilesson.

Suggested language to use when teaching the minilesson principle.

---

## RML9
### LA.U5.RML9

**Reading Minilesson Principle**
**Think about whether a book is fiction or nonfiction.**

**Studying Fiction and Nonfiction**

**You Will Need**

- three or four familiar fiction and nonfiction books such as the following:
  - *Lilly's Big Day* by Kevin Henkes, from Text Set: Kevin Henkes
  - *Max and the Tag-Along Moon* by Floyd Cooper, from Text Set: Family
  - *What Do You Do When Something Wants to Eat You?* by Steve Jenkins, from Text Set: Nonfiction
  - *Water: Up, Down, and All Around* by Natalie M. Rosinsky, from Text Set: Nonfiction
- chart paper and markers

**Academic Language / Important Vocabulary**

- fiction
- story
- nonfiction
- author
- fact

**Continuum Connection**

- Understand that fiction stories are imagined [p. 34]
- Notice and understand when a book is nonfiction [true information] [p. 37]

### Goal

Notice and understand when a book is fiction or nonfiction.

### Rationale

When you teach children to differentiate between fiction and nonfiction, they are better able to anticipate the thinking they will need to do as they read the specific genre. This allows them to better understand the text.

### Assess Learning

Observe children when they talk about the fiction and nonfiction genres. Notice if there is evidence of new learning based on the goal of this minilesson.

- Are children able to identify whether a book is fiction or nonfiction?
- Are children able to explain how they know a book is fiction or nonfiction?
- Do children use the words *fiction, story, nonfiction, fact,* and *author* to talk about fiction and nonfiction?

### Minilesson

To help children think about the minilesson principle, engage them in a discussion of the differences between fiction and nonfiction. Here is an example.

- Read and show the first two pages of *Lilly's Big Day*.

  Is this book fiction or nonfiction? What makes you think that?

- Record responses on the chart paper.

  You know this story is fiction because it tells a made-up story about a mouse.

  Now listen as I read *Max and the Tag-Along Moon*.

- Read the first few pages.

  Is this book fiction or nonfiction? What makes you think that?

- Record responses on the chart. As needed, talk about how this is an imagined story, but Max, his grandpa, and the things they do could happen in the real world.

- Show *What Do You Do When Something Wants to Eat You?*

  Think about whether this book is fiction or nonfiction.

- Read the first five pages.

  Is this book fiction or nonfiction? How do you know?

- Record responses on the chart.

**Figure 3-2:** All the parts of a single minilesson are contained on a two-page spread.

## RML 9
### LA.U5.RML9

### Have a Try

Invite the children to talk with a partner about whether *Water: Up, Down, and All Around* is fiction or nonfiction.

▶ Read pages 4–7 of *Water: Up, Down, and All Around*.

   Turn and talk to a partner about whether this book is fiction or nonfiction and how you know.

▶ Invite a few children to share. Record responses on the chart.

### Summarize and Apply

Summarize the learning and remind children to think about whether a book is fiction or nonfiction before they read.

   How does our chart help you think about whether a book is fiction or nonfiction?

   As you read today, think about whether the book you choose is fiction or nonfiction. Be ready to talk about the book when we meet after independent work time.

### Share

Following independent work time, gather children together in the meeting area to talk about fiction and nonfiction.

   Give a thumbs-up if you read a fiction book today.

   Who read a nonfiction book?

▶ Ask a few children to share how they knew their book was fiction or nonfiction.

### Extend the Lesson (Optional)

After assessing children's understanding, you might decide to extend the learning.

▶ If you keep a class reading log of books you have read aloud together, add a new column, "Fiction or Nonfiction," and have children identify the genre of each new book you read.

▶ Gather fiction and nonfiction books into a basket. Encourage children to explore the books independently or with a partner. Ask the children to discuss whether the book they chose is fiction or nonfiction and what makes them think that.

▶ Drawing/Writing About Reading Use interactive writing to write about a familiar book. Include whether the book is fiction or nonfiction and how the children know.

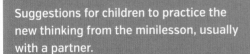

**Think about whether a book is fiction or nonfiction.**

| Title | Fiction or nonfiction? | How do you know? |
|---|---|---|
| | fiction | Lilly is a mouse, but she wears clothes and talks. |
| | fiction | Max does things like a real boy, but the author made him up. |
| | nonfiction | The author tells facts about animals. |
| | nonfiction | The author tells facts about where raindrops come from and the water cycle. |

Umbrella 5: Studying Fiction and Nonfiction ■ 185

questions and supportive comments as a guide, co-construct the anchor chart, creating an organized and visual representation of the children's noticings and understandings. (See the section on Anchor Charts in Chapter 1 for more information on chart creation.) From this exploration and the discussion surrounding it, children derive the principle, which is then written at the top of the chart.

Throughout this book, you will find models and examples of the anchor charts you will co-construct with children. Of course, the charts you create with the children will be unique because they reflect your students' thinking. Learning is more powerful and enjoyable for the children when they actively search for the meaning and find patterns. Children need to form networks of understanding around the concepts related to literacy and to be constantly looking for connections for themselves.

ELL CONNECTION

Creating a need to produce language is an important principle in building language, and reading minilessons provide many opportunities for children to express their thoughts in language and to communicate with others. The inquiry approach found in these lessons invites more student talk than teacher talk, and that can be both a challenge and an opportunity for English language learners. In our previous texts, we have written that Marie Clay (1991) urges us to be "strong minded" about holding meaningful conversations even when they are difficult. In *Becoming Literate*, she warns us that it is "misplaced sympathy" to do the talking for those who are developing and learning language. Instead, she recommends "concentrating more sharply, smiling more rewardingly and spending more time in genuine conversation." Building talk routines, such as turn and talk, into your reading minilessons can be very helpful in providing these opportunities for English language learners in a safe and supportive way.

When you ask students to think about the minilesson principle across several texts that they have previously listened to and discussed, they are more engaged and able to participate because they know these texts and can shift their attention to a new way of thinking about them. They also have some experience with the language. Using familiar texts is particularly important for English language learners. When you select examples for a reading minilesson, choose texts that you know were particularly engaging for the English language learners in your classroom. Besides choosing accessible, familiar texts, it is important to provide plenty of wait and think time. For example, you might say, "Let's think about that for a minute" before calling for responses.

When working with English language learners, value partially correct responses. Look for what the child knows about the concept instead of focusing on faulty grammar or language errors. Model appropriate language use in your responses, but do not correct a child who is attempting to use language to learn it. You might also provide an oral sentence frame to get the children's response started. Accept variety in pronunciation and intonation, remembering that the more children speak, read, and write, the more they will take on the understanding of grammatical patterns and the complex intonation patterns that reflect meaning in English.

## Have a Try

Because children will be asked to apply the new thinking independently during independent literacy work, it is important to give students a chance to apply it with a partner or a small group while still in the whole-group setting. Have a Try is designed to be brief, but it offers you an opportunity to gather information on how well students understand the minilesson principle. In many minilessons, students are asked to apply the new thinking to another concrete example from a familiar book. In management lessons, students quickly practice the new routine that they will be asked to do independently. You will often add further thinking to the chart after the students have had the chance to try out their new learning. On occasion, you will find lessons that do not include Have a Try because children will practice the routine or concept as part of the application. However, in most cases, Have a Try is an important step in reinforcing the principle and moving the students toward independence.

 **ELL CONNECTION**

The Have a Try portion of the reading minilesson is particularly important for English language learners. Besides providing repetition and allowing for the gradual release of responsibility, it gives English language learners a safe place to try out the new idea before sharing it with the whole group. These are a few suggestions for how you might support students during the Have a Try portion of the lesson:

▶ Pair children with specific partners in a way that will allow for a balance of talk between the two.

▶ Spend time teaching students how to turn and talk. (You will find a minilesson in Section Two: Literary Analysis, Umbrella 1: Thinking and Talking About Books, that helps children develop this routine.) Teach children how to provide wait time for one another, invite the other partner into the conversation, and take turns.

▶ Provide concrete examples to discuss so that children are clear about what they need to talk about and are able to stay grounded in the text. English language learners will feel more confident if they are able to talk about a text that they know really well.

▶ Observe partnerships involving English language learners and provide support as needed.

- When necessary, you might find it helpful to provide the oral language structure or language stem for how you want children to share. For example, ask students to start with the phrase "I think the character feels. . . ." Ask children to rehearse the language structure a few times before turning and talking.

## Summarize and Apply

This part of the lesson consists of two parts: summarizing the learning and applying the learning to independent reading.

The **summary** is a brief but essential part of the lesson. It provides a time to bring together all of the learning that has taken place through the inquiry and to help children think about its application and relevance to their own learning. It is best to involve the children in constructing the minilesson principle with you. Ask them to reflect on the chart you have created together and talk about what they have learned that day. In simple, clear language, shape the suggestions. Other times, you may decide to help summarize the new learning to keep the lesson short and allow time for the children to apply it independently. Whether you state the principle or co-construct it with your students, summarize the learning in a way that makes the principle generative and applicable to future texts the students will read.

After the summary, the students **apply** their new understandings to their independent reading and literacy work in the classroom. If you have literacy centers, they will apply their learning to any of their independent reading. In addition, let students know what you expect them to discuss or bring for the group sharing session so they can think about it as they read. They know they are accountable for trying out the new thinking in their own books or reflect on their participation because they are expected to share upon their return.

As you will read in Chapter 9, students engaged in independent reading might be reading books from their individual book bags or boxes, their browsing boxes, or the classroom library. When needed, plan to supply independent reading books that will provide opportunities to apply the principle. For example, if you teach the umbrella on studying folktales, make sure children have access to folktales. You will notice that in some of the lessons, children are invited to read from a certain basket of books in the classroom library to ensure that there are opportunities to apply their new learning. In some cases, the texts that provide opportunities for children to apply these concepts are not at their independent or even instructional levels. If this is the case, make sure the texts that you have placed in these baskets are familiar to the children because they have heard them read aloud. Children can also listen to audio recordings of more sophisticated texts and independently apply the minilesson principle to the audiobook.

We know that when students first take on new learning, they often overgeneralize or overapply the new learning at the exclusion of some of the other things they have learned. The best goal when children are reading any book is to enjoy it, process it effectively, and gain its full meaning. Always encourage meaningful and authentic engagement with text. You don't want children so focused and determined to apply the minilesson principle that they make only superficial connections to text, which can actually distract from the understanding of the book. You will likely find the opportunity in many reading conferences, guided reading lessons, or book club meetings to reinforce the minilesson understanding.

In our professional book, *Teaching for Comprehending and Fluency* (Fountas and Pinnell 2006), we write, "Whenever we instruct readers, we mediate (or change) the meaning they derive from their reading. Yet we must offer instruction that helps readers expand their abilities. There is value in drawing readers' attention to important aspects of the text that will enrich their understanding, but we need to understand that using effective reading strategies is not like exercising one muscle. The system must always work together as an integrated whole." The invitation to apply the new learning must be clear enough to have children try out new ways of thinking, but "light" enough to allow room for readers to expand and express their own thinking. The application of the minilesson principle should not be thought of as an exercise or task that needs to completed but instead as an invitation to deeper, more meaningful response to the events or ideas in a text.

While the children are reading independently, you may be meeting with small groups for guided reading or book clubs, rotating to observe work in literacy centers, or conferring with individuals. If you have a reading conference, you can take the opportunity to reinforce the minilesson principle. We have provided two conferring record sheets (use whichever form suits your purposes) for you to download from the Online Resources (see Figure 3-3) so that you can make notes about your individual conferences with children. You can use your notes to plan the content of future minilessons.

## Share

At the end of the independent work time, students come together and have the opportunity to share their learning with the entire group. Group share provides an opportunity for you to revisit, expand, and deepen understanding of the minilesson principle as well as to assess learning. In Figure 3-2, you will notice that in the Share section we provide suggestions for how to have children share their new learning. Often, children are asked to bring a book to share and to explain how they applied the minilesson principle in their independent reading. Sometimes we suggest sharing with the whole group, but other times we suggest that sharing take place among pairs, triads, or quads. As you observe and talk to students engaged in independent reading, shared reading, guided reading, or book clubs, you can assess whether they are easily able to apply the minilesson principle. Use this information to inform how you plan to share. If only a few students were able to apply the minilesson to their reading, you might ask only a few children to share. Or if you observe that most of the class can apply the principle, you might have them share in pairs or small groups.

As a general guideline, in addition to revisiting the reading minilesson principle at the end of independent work time, you might also ask children to share what they did in their independent literacy work that day. For example, a child might share something he noticed in the word study center or another student might tell about an all about book she made in the writing center. The Share is a wonderful way to bring the community of readers and writers back together to expand their understandings and celebrate their learning at the end of the workshop time.

**ELL CONNECTION**

There are some particular accommodations you might want to consider to support English language learners during the Share:

▶ Ask English language learners to share in pairs before sharing with the whole group.

▶ Use individual conferences and guided reading to help children rehearse the language structure they might use to share their application of the minilesson principle to the text they have read.

▶ Teach the entire class respectful ways to listen to peers and model how to give their peers time to express their thoughts. Many of the minilessons in the Management section will be useful for developing a safe and supportive community of readers and writers.

## Extending the Lesson

At the end of each lesson we offer suggestions for extending the learning of the principle. Sometimes extending the learning involves repeating the lesson over time with different examples. First graders might need to experience some of the concepts more than once before they are able to transfer actions to their independent reading. Using the questions in the Assessment section will help you to determine if you need to repeat the lesson, move on, or revisit the lesson (perhaps in a slightly different way) in the future. Other suggestions for extending the lesson include using songs or games, having students role play, and writing or drawing about reading either independently or through shared or interactive writing. In several cases, the suggestions will reference a reader's notebook. See Chapter 7 for more information about drawing and writing about reading and Section Four: Writing About Reading for minilessons that teach ways to use a reader's notebook.

# Umbrella Back Page

## Assessment and Link to Writing

Following the minilessons in each umbrella, you will see the final umbrella page that includes **Assessment** and **Link to Writing**. The last page of each umbrella, as shown in Figure 3-4, provides suggestions for assessing the learning that has taken place through the minilessons in the entire umbrella. The information you gain from observing what the children can already do, almost do, and not yet do will help inform the selection of the next umbrella you teach. (See Chapter 8 for more information about assessment and the selection of umbrellas.) For many umbrellas, this last page also provides a Link to Writing. In some cases, this section provides further suggestions for writing/drawing about reading in a reader's notebook. However, in most cases, the Link to Writing provides ideas for how students might try out some of the new learning in their own writing. For example, after learning about text features in nonfiction, you might want to teach children how to include one or more of the features, such as a table of contents or sidebar, in their own nonfiction writing.

Gain important information by assessing children's understandings as they apply and share their learning of a minilesson principle. Observe and then follow up with individuals or address the principle during guided reading.

Umbrella 5 | Studying Fiction and Nonfiction

### Assessment

After you have taught the minilessons in this umbrella, observe children talking and writing about their reading of fiction and nonfiction across instructional contexts: interactive read-aloud, independent reading and literacy work, guided reading, shared reading, and book club. Use *The Literacy Continuum* (Fountas and Pinnell 2017) to observe children's reading and writing behaviors across instructional contexts.

- What evidence do you have of new understandings related to the characteristics of fiction and nonfiction?
  - Can children identify books as fiction or nonfiction?
  - Are children able to understand the definition of fiction and nonfiction books and use academic language, such as *fiction, nonfiction,* and *topic*?
  - Can children discuss the made-up characters, places, or things in fiction?
  - Can they discuss what is real in a nonfiction book?
- In what other ways, beyond the scope of this umbrella, are children talking about genre?
  - Are children talking about whether a character seems real or not real?
  - Do they notice that some fiction stories could happen while others could not?
  - Are they noticing how illustrations give more information?
  - Are they noticing that some nonfiction books also tell a story?

Use your observations to determine the next umbrella you will teach. You may also consult Minilessons Across the Year (p. 51) for guidance.

Engage children in response to reading activities in order to link the new learning to their own writing or drawing.

### Read and Revise

After completing the steps in the genre study process, help children to read and revise their definition of the genre based on their new understandings.

- Before: Fiction books are stories that the author made up.
- After: Fiction books are stories that the author made up, and they have made-up characters, places, and things.
- Before: Nonfiction books have true information that the writer tells about a topic.
- After: Nonfiction books have facts about a topic and are about real people, animals, places, or things.

186 ■ *The Reading Minilessons Book, Grade 1*

**Figure 3-4:** The final page of each umbrella offers suggestions for assessing the learning and, in many umbrellas, a Link to Writing.

## Online Resources for Planning

We have provided examples in this book of how to engage your first-grade children in developing the behaviors and understandings of competent readers, as described in *The Literacy Continuum* (Fountas and Pinnell 2017c). However, you can modify a suggested lesson and/or construct new lessons using the goals of the continuum as needed for your particular students. The form shown in Figure 3-5 will help you plan each part of a new minilesson. For example, you can design a minilesson that uses a different set of example texts from the ones suggested in this book or you can teach a concept in a way that fits the current needs of your students. The form shown in Figure 3-6 will help you plan which minilessons to teach over a period of time so as to address the goals that are important for your students. You can find both forms at **resources.fountasandpinnell.com**.

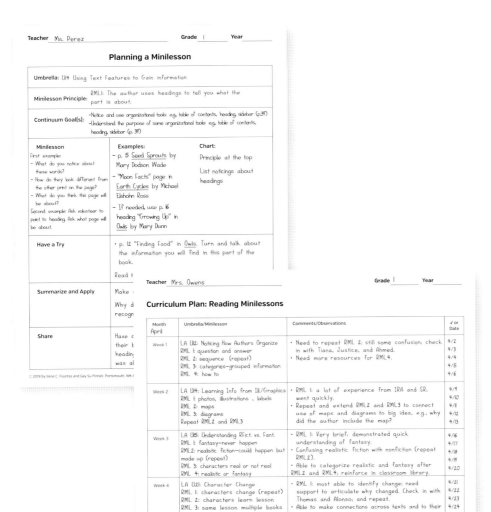

**Figure 3-5:** Use this downloadable form to plan your own minilessons.

**Figure 3-6:** Use this downloadable form to make notes about specific minilessons for future planning.

# Chapter 4

## Management Minilessons: Building a Literacy Community

MANAGEMENT MINILESSONS FOCUS ON ROUTINES for thinking and talking about reading and working together in the classroom. They allow you to teach effectively and efficiently because they create an orderly, busy classroom in which students know what is expected and how to behave responsibly and respectfully in a community of learners. They learn how the classroom library is organized, how to choose books and return them, how to use their voices in the classroom, and how to work in various organized literacy centers. You can use these minilessons to teach your young students how to use a simple list or work board to manage their own time, how to use and return materials, and how to problem solve independently. Classroom management is important in implementing a multitext approach to literacy learning. You want your students to grow in the ability to regulate their own behavior and to sustain reading and writing for increasing periods of time.

Altogether, there are twenty management minilessons for your use. Some management minilessons may need to be retaught across the year, especially as students encounter more complex situations and routines (for example, choosing books instead of reading from browsing baskets or individual book bags). Sometimes when there is a schedule change or other disruption in classroom operations, a refresher management minilesson will be needed. Any problem in your classroom should be addressed through a management minilesson.

## The Physical Space

Before students enter your classroom, prepare the physical space in a way that provides maximum support for learning. Remember that this relatively small room must support the productive work of some 20 to 30 people, 6 or 7 hours a day, 180+ days a year. Each management umbrella will help your students become acquainted with different parts of the classroom, which will make them feel secure and at home. Make sure that the classroom is:

▶ **Welcoming and Inviting.** Pleasing colors and a variety of furniture will help. There is no need for commercially published posters or slogans, except for standard references such as the Alphabet Linking Chart or colorful poetry posters. The room can be filled with the work that children have produced beginning on day one. They see signs of their learning everywhere—interactive writing, charts, drawings of various kinds, and their names. Be sure that children's names are at various places in the room—the name chart, on desks or tables, the helper's charts, and on some of the charts that you will be making in minilessons. The classroom library should be as inviting as a bookstore or a library. Place books in baskets and tubs on shelves to make the front covers of books visible and accessible for easy browsing. Clear out old, dated, or tattered books that children never choose. Clearly label the tub or basket with the topic, author, series, genre or illustrator. It can be a wonderful learning experience to create these labels with your children using interactive writing (see Figure 4-1).

▶ **Organized for Easy Use.** The first thing you might want to do is to take out everything you do not need. Clutter increases stress and noise. Scattered, hard to find materials increases student dependence on the teacher. Every work area should be clearly organized with necessary, labeled materials and nothing else. The work that takes place in each area should be visible at a glance; all materials needed for the particular activity are available. See Figure 4.2. for a list of some suggested materials to keep accessible in the different work areas, or centers, in your classroom.

▶ **Designed for Whole-Group, Small-Group, and Individual Instruction.** Minilessons are generally provided as whole-class instruction and typically take place at an easel in a meeting space that is comfortable and large enough to accommodate all students in a group or circle. It will be helpful to have a colorful rug with some way of helping students find an individual space to sit where they do not touch others. Often, the meeting space is adjacent to the classroom library so books are handy. The teacher usually has a larger chair or seat next to an easel or two so that he can display the mentor texts, make anchor charts, do interactive or shared writing, or place big books for shared

**Figure 4-1:** Whenever possible, involve the children in making the classroom their own.

reading. This space is available for all whole-group instruction; for example, the children come back to it for group share. In addition to the group meeting space, there should be designated tables and spaces in the classroom for small-group reading instruction. The guided reading table is best located in a quiet corner of the room that allows you the opportunity to scan the room to identify students who may need help staying on task independently. The table (round or horseshoe) should be positioned so the children in the group are turned away from the activity in the classroom. Students also need tables and spaces throughout the classroom where they can work independently and where you can easily set a chair next to a child for a brief, individual conference.

▶ **Respectful of Personal Space.** First-grade students do not necessarily need an individual desk, but they do need a place to keep a personal book box and other personal items such as their individual book bags (sealed plastic bags containing their independent reading books) and word study activities to take home. These containers can be placed on a shelf labeled for each student. Reader's notebooks and writer's notebooks may be stored in the same place or in groups by themselves to be retrieved easily. If students have personal poetry books (growing out of the shared reading of poetry and colorfully decorated by them), they can be placed face out on a rack for easy retrieval. Artifacts like these add considerably to the aesthetic quality of the classroom.

**Figure 4-2:** Adapted from *Guided Reading: Responsive Teaching Across the Grades* (Fountas and Pinnell 2017d)

| Yearlong Literacy Centers | Materials |
| --- | --- |
| Independent Reading | Organize books by topic, author, illustrator, genre, and series. Include colored browsing baskets geared to each guided reading group. |
| Writing Center | Pencils, paper, markers, stapler, scissors, glue, premade blank books for bookmaking, cover-up tape, sticky notes, crayons, and date stamp. |
| Word Work (ABCs) | Blank word cards, wall of high-frequency words, alphabet linking chart, magnetic letters, games, words to sort, phonogram pattern charts. |
| Listening Center | Player (e.g., iPod™, iPhone™, tablet), clear set of directions with picture clues, multiple copies of books organized in boxes or plastic bags. |
| Poetry Center (can be adjacent to the writing center so that supplies can be shared) | Personal poetry book for each student, copies of poems they have read in shared reading, glue, crayons, markers, and decorative stickers. The center may also include large-print poems, poetry cards mounted on stiff paper, small books of poems, and a class book of poems. |
| Pocket Chart | Pocket chart hanging from a rack or fastened firmly to the wall, sentence strips and individual words in a basket near the chart. |

## A Peaceable Atmosphere for a Community of Readers and Writers

The minilessons in this book will help you establish a classroom environment where children can become confident, self-determined, and kind members of the community. They are designed to contribute to an ambiance of peaceful activity and shared responsibility in the first-grade classroom. Through the management minilessons they will learn how to modulate the voice to suit various purposes (silent to outdoor). There are also lessons on keeping supplies in order and on using routines for taking turns, listening to and looking at others, and engaging in conversation. The whole tone of every classroom activity is respectful. First-grade children who enter your classroom for the first time may have some experience in a preschool or kindergarten classroom, but they may not fully understand how to work with twenty to thirty others in a small room all day every day. These minilessons are designed to help you establish the atmosphere you want. Everything in the classroom reflects the children who work there; it is their home for the year.

## Getting Started with Independent Work Time

Many of the minilessons in the Management section will be the ones that you address early in the year to establish routines that children will use to work at their best with one another and independently. In the largest umbrella in this section, Umbrella 3: Engaging in Classroom Literacy Work, you will teach children how to work independently on meaningful and productive literacy activities. The minilessons in this umbrella are designed to introduce work activities, or centers, one at a time, allowing

**Figure 4-3:** Books in the classroom library are organized in labeled bins.

children time to practice as a whole group before being expected to integrate more than one literacy task. It is possible that you will spend several days reviewing one minilesson until you feel students are able to perform the routine independently. For a beginning group of first-grade children, make independent work time relatively short and circulate around the room to help students select books, draw and write, and stay engaged. As children become more self-directed, you can increase independent work time. When you determine that they can sustain productive independent behavior, you can begin to meet with guided reading groups.

As described in our professional book, *Guided Reading: Responsive Teaching Across the Grades* (Fountas and Pinnell 2017d), we offer two options for managing this classroom literacy work in the early grades: a simple system and a work board system. You might use a combination of these approaches or start with one and then move to the other. Either way, the minilessons in Umbrella 3: Engaging in Classroom Literacy Work will help you get the children acquainted with the routines and expectations of the literacy activity. Select the minilessons that make sense for your students based on the management system you decide to use. You may decide to introduce different activities throughout the school year. The minilessons in this umbrella do not need to be taught all at once or in consecutive order.

## A Simple System: Four Activities a Day

In this system, instead of moving through centers, children work at their desks or tables on the same four or five activities every day during the time set aside for literacy and language. You can decide whether to suggest an order for the activities or allow them to choose. These four activities might include the following:

**Read a Book.** During this time, children engage in independent reading. This might include reading from their individual book bags (or boxes), from

**Figure 4-4:** A first-grade classroom accommodates many kinds of literacy activities.

a browsing box, or from the classroom library. In the first minilesson in the umbrella, you teach students how to use the classroom library or individual book bags for this reading time. In a subsequent lesson, you teach children how to read from browsing boxes since it is likely you will introduce browsing boxes a little later once guided reading is established.

**Listen to a Book.** Listening to audiobooks is a valuable and meaningful literacy activity. As children listen with a book in hand, they follow along with reading, exposing themselves to high-frequency words, to new vocabulary and language structures, and to a model for fluent reading. The listening center provides another way for children to access higher levels of text across a variety of genres. You might also incorporate writing about reading into this listening time by asking children to write or draw a brief response to the text. The minilesson that introduces the listening center (Umbrella 3: Engaging in Classroom Literacy Work) is used to teach children how to use the audio equipment and sets up the routines and procedures that need to be in place for an efficient, productive listening experience.

**Work on Words.** The word work center activity will take a little more time to prepare than some of the other activities in this simple system because you will want to connect it to your phonics lessons (see *Phonics, Spelling, and Word Study System, for Grade 1,* Fountas and Pinnell 2017e). Children can be engaged in a range of activities from simple work with the alphabet (e.g., name puzzles or sorting letters) to more complex word study (e.g., games, letter or word sorts). Use the lesson in Umbrella 3: Engaging in Classroom Literacy Work to introduce children to the routines of the word work center, including where to find supplies and visual directions for what to do during word work time and how to clean up.

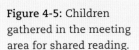
**Figure 4-5:** Children gathered in the meeting area for shared reading.

**Work on Writing.** During this time, children can work on a variety of forms of writing—cards, thank-you notes, letters, stories, alphabet books, how-to books, or all about books. They work on pieces they started in writing workshop or you might provide specific directions for writing/drawing about reading in a reader's notebook. Use the minilesson in Umbrella 3: Engaging in Classroom Literacy Work to introduce where to find directions in the writing area or center and how to access, organize, and return supplies. This writing work does not take the place of writers' workshop, in which children begin to learn through writing minilessons and to engage in the writing process.

## Using Centers and a Work Board

The other option for managing independent literacy work is to teach children how to use a work board to rotate and work independently in centers. A work board enables each child to work at her own pace. This option allows for more movement and often provides more opportunity for collaboration as children in proximity are working on the same kinds of activities. Group children and post their names in the suggested order of work you would like them to complete. You can also list options or choices for children who complete their work before others. The work board can include a variety of different literacy activities, including the four activities described in the simple system: independent reading, listening to a book, working with words, and working on writing. You will find minilessons for introducing some of the other activities in Umbrella 3: Engaging in Classroom Literacy Work. These lessons include reading and illustrating poetry in a poetry notebook; reading around the room with a pointer; assembling and reading a poem, song, or story in pocket charts; and reading with a partner. The final minilesson in the umbrella teaches children how to work independently using the work board as a tool.

English language learners can productively engage in a series of actions with the support of the work board. Take the time to "act out" each of the actions several times. Give special attention to the icon because it is the children's cue to action. Involve children in the action several times (with your support) until you are sure they can follow the steps independently. Don't just tell; show and do every step. You will find it is well worth the time it takes to do this teaching. You will see students acting with confidence and independence.

**Figure 4-6:** The four activities in the simple system from *Guided Reading: Responsive Teaching Across the Grades* (Fountas and Pinnell 2017d)

Reading Time
1. Read a book
2. Listen to a book
3. Work on words
4. Work on writing

 **ELL CONNECTION**

Reference Chapter 22 of our professional book, *Guided Reading: Responsive Teaching Across the Grades* (Fountas and Pinnell 2017d), for more detailed information on managing independent learning in the early grades. Whether you choose to use a simple system or a work board with centers, it is important for children to be engaged in meaningful, authentic reading and writing experiences. Management minilessons provide your readers with the tools and skills they need to make this time productive, collaborative, and enjoyable.

**Figure 4-7:** When children are learning to use a work board, only one or two activity choices are offered. Once children understand the routines for several activities and show that they can work independently, more icons are added.

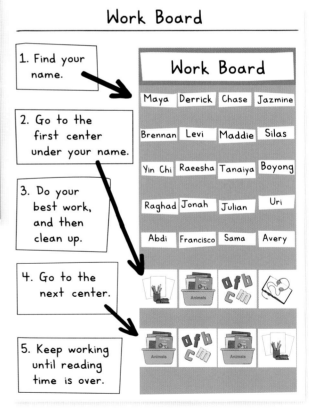

**Figure 4-8:** This chart from a management minilesson was created as children learned how to follow a work board.

# Chapter 5

## Literary Analysis Minilessons: Thinking and Talking About Books

LITERARY ANALYSIS MINILESSONS SUPPORT CHILDREN in a growing awareness of the elements of literature and the writer's and illustrator's craft. They help children learn how to think analytically about texts and identify the characteristics of fiction and nonfiction genres. Invite students to notice characters and how they change, identify problems and solutions in stories, and notice how nonfiction writers present and organize information as well as their use of graphics and other nonfiction features. Prior to each literary analysis minilesson, students will have listened to texts read aloud or have experienced them through shared reading. You will have taught specific lessons based on the text that encourage students to discuss and explore concepts and to respond in writing, art, or drama. This prior knowledge will

be accessed as they participate in the minilesson and will enable them to make the understanding explicit. They then can apply the concepts to their own reading and share what they have learned with others.

## Organization of Literary Analysis Umbrellas and the Link to *The Literacy Continuum*

There are 106 literary analysis minilessons in this book. These minilessons are divided into categories according to *The Literacy Continuum* (Fountas and Pinnell 2017c), and the order of presentation in this book follows that of *The Literacy Continuum*. The categories of fiction and nonfiction are listed below.

- Fiction and Nonfiction:
  - General
  - Genre
  - Messages and Themes
  - Style and Language
  - Book and Print Features
- Nonfiction:
  - Genre
  - Organization
  - Illustration/Graphics
  - Book and Print Features
- Fiction:
  - Genre
  - Setting
  - Plot
  - Character
  - Style and Language
  - Illustrations

As you can tell from the suggested sequence in Minilessons Across the Year (Figure 8-2), you will want to use simpler concepts (such as book title and author) before more sophisticated concepts (such as character change).

Echoes of the literary analysis minilessons reverberate across all the instruction for the year in instructional contexts for reading (interactive read-aloud, shared reading, guided reading, book clubs, and independent reading) as well as for writing. The children continue to develop their understanding of the characteristics of fiction and nonfiction texts.

# Genre Study

Within the Literary Analysis section, you will find three umbrellas that bring children through a process of inquiry-based study of the characteristics of a particular genre. Genre study gives students the tools they need to navigate a variety of texts with deep understanding. When readers understand the characteristics of a genre, they know what to expect when they begin to read a text. They use their knowledge of the predictable elements within a genre as a road map to anticipate structures and elements of the text. They make connections between books within the same genre and begin to develop a shared language for talking about genre. In our professional book, *Genre Study: Teaching with Fiction and Nonfiction Books* (Fountas and Pinnell 2012), we designed a six-step approach for learning about a variety of genres. The six broad steps are described in Figure 5-1. For this book, we have designed specific minilessons based on our *Genre Study* book to help you engage your students in the powerful process of becoming knowledgeable about a range of genres.

The first two steps of the genre study process take place before and during interactive read-aloud. Steps 3–5 are accomplished through reading minilessons. Step 6 is addressed on the last page of each genre study umbrella. In first grade, we suggest three genre studies to introduce this process and to help children develop a beginning understanding of genre. The first is a genre study of fiction and nonfiction. This umbrella utilizes a text set of fiction and nonfiction pairs (for example, Ann Morris' nonfiction book, *On the Go* and Peter and Paul Reynolds' fiction text, *Going Places*) to explore and study the difference between fiction and nonfiction. The second is a genre study of nonfiction (for example, *What If You Had Animal Teeth?* by Sandra Markle and *Surprising Sharks* by Nicola Davies). Many first

Figure 5-1: Adapted from *Genre Study* (Fountas and Pinnell 2012)

## Steps in the Genre Study Process

| | |
|---|---|
| 1 | **Collect** books in a text set that represent good examples of the genre you are studying. |
| 2 | **Immerse.** Read aloud each book using the lesson guidelines. The primary goal should be enjoyment and understanding of the book. |
| 3 | **Study.** After you have read these mentor texts, have children analyze characteristics or "noticings" that are common to the texts, and list the characteristics on chart paper. |
| 4 | **Define.** Use the list of characteristics to create a short working definition of the genre. |
| 5 | **Teach** specific minilessons on the important characteristics of the genre. |
| 6 | **Read and Revise.** Expand children's understanding by encouraging them to talk about the genre in appropriate instructional contexts (book club, independent reading conferences, guided reading lessons, and shared reading lessons) and revise the definition. |

graders love to read nonfiction books, which makes nonfiction a good choice for a genre study in first grade. The third is a genre study of folktales (for example, *Once a Mouse . . .* by Marcia Brown and *The Princess and the Pea* by Rachel Isadora), which exposes children to traditional literature.

The first step in the genre study process, **Collect**, involves collecting a set of texts. The genre study minilessons in this book draw on texts sets from the *Fountas & Pinnell Classroom™ Interactive Read-Aloud Collection*. Use these texts if you have them, but we encourage you to collect additional texts within each genre to immerse your students in as many texts as possible. Children will enjoy additional examples of the genre placed in a bin in the classroom library. You can use the texts listed in the Before Teaching section of each umbrella as a guide to making your own genre text set if you do not have access to the *Interactive Read-Aloud Collection*.

As you engage students in step 2, **Immerse,** of the genre study process, be sure that the children think and talk about the meaning of each text during the interactive read-aloud. The goal is for students to enjoy a wonderful book, so it is important for them to first enjoy and respond to the full meaning of the text before focusing their attention on the specific characteristics of the genre.

After immersing students in the books through interactive read aloud, it is time to teach minilessons in the genre study umbrella. The first minilesson in the genre study umbrella addresses step 3 in the process, **Study.** During this initial minilesson, help children notice what is common across all of the texts. As children discuss and revisit books in the genre, list their noticings on chart paper. Distinguish between what is always true about the genre and what is often true about the genre.

The second minilesson in the genre study umbrellas addresses step 4, **Define**, in the process. Teach a minilesson in which you use shared writing to co-construct a working definition of the genre based on the children's previous noticings. Help children to understand that you will revisit and revise this definition as they learn more about the genre over the next few days.

Next, as part of step 5, **Teach**, provide specific minilessons related to each of your students' noticings about the genre. In each genre study umbrella, we offer minilessons that we think would develop out of most first graders' noticings. Pick and choose the lessons that match your own students' noticings or use these lessons as a model to develop your own minilessons.

At the end of the umbrella, work with the children to **Read and Revise** the class definition of the genre based on the minilessons that have been taught. Using shared or interactive writing, make changes to the definition so it reflects children's understanding of the genre.

# Nonfiction

## Noticings:

| Always | Often |
|---|---|
| • The book is about real things. | • The author uses diagrams and labels to give information. |
| • The author teaches you facts and gives real information about something. | • The illustrator gives more information in pictures or photographs. |

**Figure 5-2:** On this anchor chart, the teacher has recorded what her class noticed was always or often true about several nonfiction texts that they had heard or read.

# Author and Illustrator Studies

Section Two: Literary Analysis also includes an umbrella of minilessons for conducting inquiry-based author and illustrator studies. Author and illustrator studies allow children to make connections to the people behind the books they love. They learn about the craft decisions an author or illustrator makes. For an author or illustrator study, be sure that the children think and talk about the full meaning of each text in interactive read-aloud before identifying characteristics specific to the author or illustrator.

Children will need plenty of opportunity to explore the texts during read-aloud time and on their own or in groups or pairs. As they become more familiar with the steps in an author or illustrator study, they learn how to notice characteristics common to a particular author's or illustrator's work. The steps in an author/illustrator study are described in Figure 5-4.

In the two minilessons in Umbrella 2: Studying Authors and Illustrators, you provide a demonstration of step 3 by working with your students to create a chart of "noticings" about an author or illustrator. In these two lessons, we model a study of Kevin Henkes and Bob Graham from the *Fountas & Pinnell Classroom™ Interactive Read-Aloud Collection*. In first grade, we have chosen to study authors who are also the illustrators of their books. You might choose to use these same popular authors or choose authors and illustrators you and your children are familiar with and love. The process described in the minilessons in this umbrella can be used throughout the year to study different authors and illustrators. Simply collect books by a particular author or illustrator and follow the steps listed in Figure 5-4. Use the same language and process modeled in the minilessons in this umbrella but substitute the authors and illustrators of your choice.

## Kevin Henkes

Noticings:

| Always | Often |
|---|---|
| • He writes about things that happen to kids in everyday life. | • His books are about friends and family. |
| • The characters in his books are animals that act like people. | |
| • The main character learns and changes by the end of the story. | |

**Figure 5-3:** This chart shows what students noticed about illustrator Bob Graham's work.

**Figure 5-4:** Minilessons address step 3 of an author/ illustrator study.

## Steps in an Author/Illustrator Study

1  Gather a set of books and read them aloud to the class over several days.

2  Take children on a quick tour of all the books in the set. As you reexamine each book, you might want to have children do a brief turn and talk with a partner about what they notice.

3  Have children analyze the characteristics of the author's or illustrator's work, and record their noticings on chart paper.

4  You may choose to read a few more books by the author and compare them to the books in this set, adding to the noticings as needed.

# Chapter 6

## Strategies and Skills Minilessons: Teaching for Effective Processing

FOR THE STRATEGIES AND SKILLS lessons, you will usually use enlarged texts that have been created for shared reading because children can see the print and the illustrations easily. These minilessons are most effective after children have begun to process print and to search for and use information from the text, self-monitor their reading, and self-correct their errors. You'll notice the children engaging in these behaviors in your shared reading lessons.

The large print is ideal for problem solving with a common example. Shared reading leads the way for children to apply strategic actions in guided reading lessons. Strategies and skills are taught in every instructional context for reading, but guided reading is the most powerful one. The text is just right to support the learning of all the readers in the group, enabling them to learn how to solve words and engage in the act of problem solving across a whole text.

The strategies and skills minilessons in this book are some general lessons that may serve as reminders and be helpful to the whole class. For example, as students engage in independent reading, they may need to realize that a reader

- looks at the illustrations and thinks what would make sense, and

- uses information from the book or sentence to understand the meaning of a word.

The minilessons in Section Three: Strategies and Skills are designed to bring a few important strategies to temporary, conscious attention so that first-grade children are reminded to think in these ways as they problem solve in independent reading. By the time students participate in these minilessons, they should have engaged these strategic actions successfully in shared or guided reading. In the minilessons, they will recognize the strategic actions; bringing them to brief, focused attention; and think about applying them consistently in independent reading.

Because the children have read continuous text in unison and individually, they have developed an internal sense of actions, like monitoring and checking, searching for and using information, and using multiple sources of information to solve words. They have experienced early foundational concepts of print (such as left-to-right directionality, word-by-word matching) through processing a text. They have a sense of how to put words together to sound like talking. The minilesson, the application, and the share help them better understand what they do and internalize the effective behaviors.

**Figure 6-1:** Children are able to see and follow print and punctuation when you use an enlarged text, such as a big book or a poetry poster, or project a text.

# Chapter 7

## Writing About Reading Minilessons: The Reading-Writing Connection

Through drawing/writing about reading, children reflect on their understanding of a text. For example, a story might have a captivating character or characters or a humorous sequence of events. A nonfiction text might have interesting information or call for an opinion. There are several kinds of writing about reading that are highly effective with first-grade students.

▶ **Shared Writing.** In shared writing you offer the highest level of support to the students. You act as scribe while the students participate fully in the composition of the text. You help shape the text, but the students supply the language and context.

| Ms. Bloom | Mouse |
|---|---|
| What she did: I put cheese in a trap. I took the mouse to the woods. | What he did: I ate the cheese. |
| How she felt: I did not want a mouse in my house. | How he felt: Ms. Bloom was kind. She fed me and took me home. |

**Figure 7-1:** In shared writing, the teacher acts as scribe.

▶ **Interactive Writing.** Interactive writing is exactly the same as shared writing in that the students participate actively in the actual composition of the text and you act as scribe. But in interactive writing, you invite students to "share the pen" at points in the text that offer high instructional value. An individual may contribute the first letter of a word, the middle, or last letter of a word. He may contribute a word part like *-ing* or quickly write a high-frequency word that has just been learned. In general, you write words that are too difficult for students to attempt and you also write words that everyone knows how to write quickly (so in this case sharing the pen would not result in new learning). It is important to move interactive writing along at a good pace and to make teaching points with precision. Don't try to have students write too much because the lesson can become tedious. Be selective.

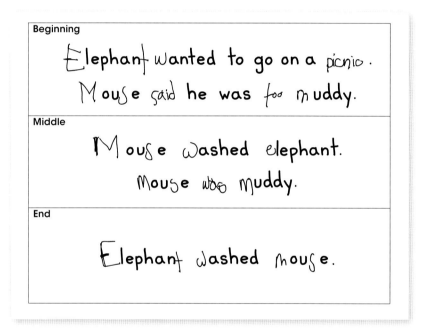

**Figure 7-2:** Interactive writing differs from shared writing only in that the teacher shares the pen with students at points that offer high instructional value.

▶ **Independent Writing.** For first-grade children, the first response is often drawing, painting, or collage. But very soon they like to add print to their works of art. This may involve labels or simple texts with approximated spellings. But soon they will begin to write simple sentences because they are immersed in language through read-aloud, shared reading, and guided reading. Keep good examples of different writing on hand (possibly in a scrapbook) for children to use as models.

In most literary analysis lessons, you will find a suggestion for extending the learning using one of these types of writing. But at any point in these minilessons, you can choose to use shared, interactive, or independent writing. When children have the opportunity to apply the new thinking through shared writing or interactive writing, they are exposed to different ways of writing about their reading. It is important at some point to encourage students to do their own writing. Of course, the early independent writing of your students will not be entirely standard spelling. They are developing new systems for writing words through approximation and their risk-taking attempts are critical to their success. If students know some easy high-frequency words, these may be accurately spelled, but you can expect them to try many others using their growing knowledge of how to say words slowly and listen for the sounds and connect them with letters.

Much of the children's independent writing will be in a reader's notebook. The Writing About Reading umbrellas, Umbrella 3: Writing About Fiction Books in a Reader's Notebook and Umbrella 4: Writing About Nonfiction Books in a Reader's Notebook, both provide inquiry-based lessons to help children make this transition to independent writing about reading. Like management minilessons, the lessons in these umbrellas might not be taught consecutively within the umbrella, but instead paired with the literary analysis lessons that support the concept students are being asked to draw or write about. For example, after you have taught a lesson on the feelings of characters, you might first extend learning by providing an interactive writing lesson in which you write about a character's feelings with your students. Once you feel they are ready, you might introduce them to writing or drawing about character feelings in a reader's notebook using the minilessons in Umbrella 3: Writing About Fiction Books in a Reader's Notebook. Through this gradual release of responsibility, children learn how to transition to writing about their reading independently as they learn how to use each section of the notebook. A reader's notebook is an important tool to support student independence and response to books. It becomes a rich collection of thinking across the years.

For English language learners, a reader's notebook is a safe place to practice a new language. It eventually becomes a record of their progress. In first grade, all children will do more drawing than writing early in the year. Drawing is key because it promotes a way to rehearse ideas. Use this opportunity to ask students to talk about what they have drawn, and then help them compose labels for their artwork so they begin to attach meaning to the English words. Eventually, the students will do more writing, but you can support the writing by providing a chance for them to rehearse their sentences before writing them and encourage

 **ELL CONNECTION**

**Figure 7-3:** Through independent writing, children develop new systems for writing words.

students to borrow language from the texts they are writing about. The writing in a reader's notebook is a product they can read because they have written it. It is theirs. They can read and reread it to themselves and to others, thereby developing their confidence in the language.

## Using a Reader's Notebook in First Grade

A reader's notebook is a place where children can collect their thinking about books. They draw and write to tell about themselves and respond to books. A reader's notebook includes

- ▶ a variety of sections for children to tell about themselves,
- ▶ a section for children to list and respond to books they have read or listened to,
- ▶ a section for children to list words they know, and
- ▶ several letter and word resources.

With places where students can draw and write about themselves as well as make a record of their reading and what they think about it, a reader's notebook thus represents a rich record of progress. To the child, the notebook represents a year's work to reflect on with pride and share with family. Children keep their notebooks in their personal book boxes, along with their bags of book choices for independent reading time. We provide a series of minilessons in Section Four: Writing About Reading for teaching students how to use a reader's notebook. As we described previously, reading minilessons in the Writing About Reading section focus on drawing and writing in response to reading.

If you do not have access to the preprinted *Reader's Notebook: Primary* (Fountas and Pinnell 2014), simply give each student a blank notebook (bound if possible). Glue in sections and insert tabs yourself to make a neat, professional notebook that can be cherished.

**Figure 7-4:** Children draw and write about themselves and share their thinking about reading in a reader's notebook.

# Chapter 8

## Putting Minilessons into Action: Assessing and Planning

As NOTED IN CHAPTER 2, the minilessons in this book are examples of teaching that address the specific bullets that list the behaviors and understandings to notice, teach for, and support in *The Literacy Continuum* (Fountas and Pinnell 2017c) for first grade. We have drawn from the sections on Interactive Read-Aloud, Shared Reading, Guided Reading, Writing About Reading, and Oral and Visual Communication to provide a comprehensive vision of what children need to become aware of, understand, and apply to their own literacy and learning. With such a range of important goals, how do you decide what to teach and when?

## Deciding Which Reading Minilessons to Teach

To decide which reading minilessons to teach, first look at the students in front of you. Teach within what Vygotsky (1979) called the students' "zone of proximal development"—the zone between what the students can do independently and what they can do with the support of a more expert other. Teach on the cutting edge of children's competencies. Select topics for minilessons that address the needs of the majority of students in your class.

Think about what will be helpful to most readers based on your observations of their reading and writing behaviors. Here are some suggestions and tools to help you think about the students in your classroom:

▸ **Use *The Literacy Continuum*** (Fountas and Pinnell 2017c) to assess your students and observe how they are thinking, talking, and writing/drawing about books. Think about what they can already do, almost do, and not yet do to select the emphasis for your teaching. Look at the Selecting Goals pages in each section to guide your observations.

▸ **Use the Interactive Read-Aloud and Literature Discussion section.** Scan the Selecting Goals in this section and think about the ways you have noticed students thinking and talking about books.

▸ **Use the Writing About Reading section** to analyze how students are responding to texts in their drawing and writing. This analysis will help you determine possible next steps. Talking and writing about reading provides concrete evidence of students' thinking.

▸ **Use the Oral Language Continuum** to help you think about some of the routines your students might need for better communication between peers. You will find essential listening and speaking competencies to observe and teach.

▸ **Look for patterns in your anecdotal records.** Review the anecdotal notes you take during reading conferences, shared reading, guided reading, and book clubs to notice trends in students' responses and thinking. Use *The Literacy Continuum* to help you analyze the records and determine strengths and areas for growth across the classroom. Your observations will reveal what children know and what they need to learn next as they build understanding over time. Each goal becomes a possible topic for a minilesson.

▸ **Consult district and state standards as a resource.** Analyze the suggested skills and areas of knowledge specified in your local and state standards. Align these standards with the minilessons suggested in this text to determine which might be applicable within your frameworks (see **fountasandpinnell.com/resourcelibrary** for an alignment of *The Literacy Continuum* with Common Core Standards).

▸ **Use the Assessment section after each umbrella.** Take time to assess student learning after the completion of each umbrella. Use the guiding questions on the last page of each umbrella to determine strengths and next steps for your students. This analysis can help you determine what minilessons to reteach if needed and what umbrella to teach next.

# A Suggested Sequence

The suggested sequence of umbrellas, Minilessons Across the Year shown in Figure 8-2 (also downloadable from the Online Resources for record keeping), is intended to establish good classroom management early and work toward more sophisticated concepts across the year. Learning in minilessons is applied in many different situations and so is reinforced daily across the curriculum. Minilessons in this sequence are timed so they occur after children have had sufficient opportunities to build some explicit understandings as well as a great deal of implicit knowledge of aspects of written texts through interactive read-aloud and shared reading texts. In the community of readers, they have acted on texts through talk, writing, and extension through writing and art. These experiences have prepared them to fully engage in the reading minilesson and move from this shared experience to the application of the concepts in their independent reading.

The sequence of umbrellas in Minilessons Across the Year follows the suggested sequence of text sets in *Fountas & Pinnell Classroom™ Interactive Read-Aloud Collection*. If you are using this collection, you are invited to follow this sequence of texts. If you are not using it, the first page of each umbrella describes the types of books students will need to read before you teach the minilessons. The text sets are grouped together by theme, topic, author, and genre, not by skill or concept. Thus, in many minilessons, you will use books from several different text sets.

The umbrellas draw examples from text sets that have been read and enjoyed previously. In most cases, the minilessons draw on text sets that are introduced within the same month or at least in close proximity to the umbrella. However, in some cases, minilessons taught later, for example in month 8, might draw on texts introduced earlier in the year.

We have selected the most concrete and instructive examples from the texts available to illustrate the minilesson principle. Most of the time, children will have no problem recalling the events of these early texts because you have read and discussed them thoroughly as a class. However, in some cases, you might want to reread these texts, or a portion of the text, quickly before teaching the umbrella so the books are fresh in the students' minds.

As you begin to work with the minilessons, you may want to follow the suggested sequence, but remember to use the lessons flexibly to meet the needs of the children you teach:

- Omit lessons that you think are not necessary for your children (based on assessment and your experiences with them in interactive read-aloud).

- Repeat some lessons that you think need more time and instructional attention (based on observation of children across reading contexts).

- Repeat some lessons using different examples for a particularly rich experience.

- Move lessons around to be consistent with the curriculum that is adopted in your school or district.

The minilessons are here for you to choose from according to the instructional needs of your class, so do not be concerned if you do not use them all within the year. Record or check the minilessons you have taught so that you can reflect on the work of the semester and year. You can do this simply by making a copy of the list or downloading it from Online Resources (Figure 8-1) for your record keeping. Visit **resources.fountasandpinnell.com** to download this online resource.

**Figure 8-1:** Download this record-keeping form to record the minilessons that you have taught.

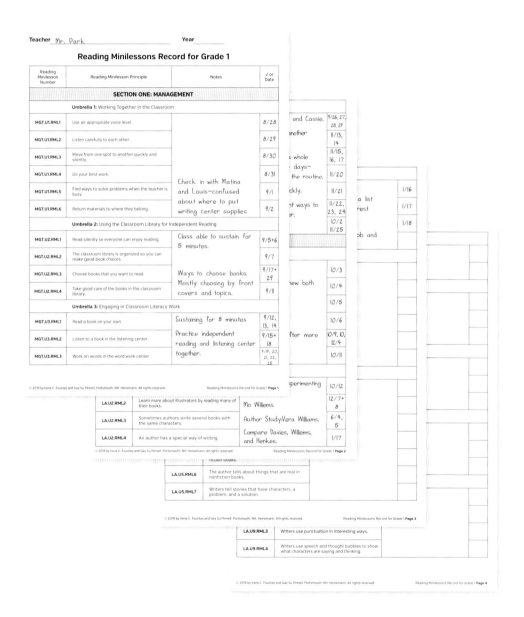

## MINILESSONS ACROSS THE YEAR

| Month | Recommended Umbrellas | Approximate Time |
|---|---|---|
| | **MGT U1:** Working Together in the Classroom | **1 week** |
| | **MGT U2:** Using the Classroom Library for Independent Reading | **1 week** |
| Month 1 | **MGT U3:** Engaging in Classroom Literacy Work RML1–4, RML10 (optional)<br>*Note: Our recommendation is to introduce children to the first four literacy activities, and if use a work board to organize independent literacy activities then also teach RML 10 (modified according to the activities you have introduced). We recommend revisiting this umbrella to introduce the rest of the literacy activities in month 4.* | **1.5 weeks** |
| | **LA U1:** Thinking and Talking About Books | **1 week** |
| | **WAR U1:** Introducing a Reader's Notebook<br>*Note: Teach the lessons in this umbrella consecutively or break them up over time in a way that makes sense for the children in your classroom.* | **1.5 weeks** |
| Month 2 | **LA U2:** Studying Authors and Illustrators, RML1<br>*Note: This first lesson introduces the process of studying an author. The lesson will take only a day, but the preparation for the author study will take about a week.We suggest repeating these minilessons whenever you conduct an author or illustrator study* | **1 day** |
| | **LA U19:** Understanding Characters and Their Feelings | **1.5 weeks** |
| | **WAR U3:** Writing About Fiction Books in a Reader's Notebook, RML1–3<br>*Note: These lessons in can be taught consecutively, or you may decide to teach them alongside the Literacy Analysis lessons that address similar behaviors.* | **1 week** |
| | **LA U4:** Getting Started with Book Clubs | **1.5 weeks** |
| Month 3 | **SAS U1:** Monitoring, Searching, and Self-Correcting | **0.5 week** |
| | **LA U5:** Studying Fiction and Nonfiction | **1 week** |
| | **LA U2:** Studying Authors and Illustrators RML1<br>*Note: If you are using Fountas & Pinnell Classroom Interactive Read-Aloud Collection, we suggest repeating RML1 to study Mo Willems as an author or combine RML1 and RML2 to study him as both author and illustrator.* | **0.5 week** |
| | **SAS U2:** Solving Words | **1 week** |
| Month 4 | **LA U20:** Knowing Characters Inside and Out | **1 week** |
| | **LA U18:** Understanding Simple Plot: Problem and Solution | **0.5 week** |
| | **WAR U2:** Using a Reader's Notebook | **1 week** |

| KEY | | |
|---|---|---|
| **MGT** | **Section One** | Management Minilessons |
| **LA** | **Section Two** | Literary Analysis Minilessons |
| **SAS** | **Section Three** | Strategies and Skills Minilessons |
| **WAR** | **Section Four** | Writing About Reading Minilessons |

**Figure 8-2:** Use this chart as a guideline for planning your year with minilessons.

| Month | Recommended Umbrellas | Approximate Time |
|---|---|---|
| **Month 5** | **MGT U3:** Engaging in Classroom Literacy Work, RML5–9, RML10 (optional)<br>*Note: We suggest introducing the remaining minilessons at the end of month 4 or beginning of month 5. The last minilesson can be repeated if necessary.* | 1.5 weeks |
| | **SAS U3:** Maintaining Fluency RMLS 1–4 | 1 week |
| | **LA U11:** Studying Nonfiction | 2 weeks |
| **Month 6** | **WAR U4:** Writing About Nonfiction Books in a Reader's Notebook | 1.5 weeks |
| | **LA U2:** Studying Authors and Illustrators, RML4<br>*Note: We recommend teaching this lesson after children have completed one or two other author studies so they have the opportunity to compare authors.* | 1–2 days |
| | **LA U3:** Giving a Book Talk | 1 week |
| | **WAR U5:** Writing Opinions About Books | 1 week |
| **Month 7** | **LA U22:** Analyzing the Way Writers Play with Language | 1 week |
| | **LA U9:** Looking Closely at Print | 1 week |
| | **LA U7:** Thinking About the Author's Purpose | 0.5 week |
| | **LA U6:** Thinking About the Author's Message | 1 week |
| **Month 8** | **LA U16:** Studying Folktales | 2 weeks |
| | **LA U2:** Studying Authors and Illustrators, RML2<br>*Note: This lesson introduces the process of studying an illustrator.* | 0.5 week |
| | **LA U17:** Thinking About Where Stories Take Place<br>*Revisit Writing About Reading and Strategy and Skills minilessons as needed* | 0.5 week |
| **Month 9** | **LA U10:** Noticing Text Resources | 1 week |
| | **LA U23:** Looking Closely at Illustrations | 1 week |
| | **LA U8:** Analyzing Writer's Craft | 1 week |
| | **LA U12:** Noticing How Authors Organize Nonfiction | 1.5 weeks |
| **Month 10** | **LA U13:** Learning Information from Illustrations/Graphics | 1 week |
| | **LA U14:** Using Text Features to Gain Information | 1 week |
| | **LA U15:** Understanding Realistic Fiction vs. Fantasy | 1 week |
| | **LA U21:** Understanding That Characters Can Change | 1 week |
| | **LA U2:** Studying Authors and Illustrators<br>*Note: If you are using Fountas & Pinnell Classroom Interactive Read-Aloud Collection, we suggest you repeat RML1 and RML2 to study to study Vera B. Williams as both author and illustrator. RML3 teaches that an author might write more than one book about the same character.* | 0.5 week |

# Chapter 9

## Reading Minilessons Within a Multitext Approach to Literacy Learning

THIS COLLECTION OF 175 LESSONS for first grade are embedded within an integrated set of instructional approaches that build an awareness of classroom routines, literary characteristics, strategies and skills, and ways of writing about written texts. In Figure 9-1, this comprehensive, multitext approach is represented, along with the central role of minilessons. Note that students' processing systems are built across instructional contexts so that students can read increasingly complex texts independently. In this chapter, we will look at how the reading minilessons fit within this multitext approach and provide a balance between implicit and explicit teaching that allows for authentic response and promotes the enjoyment of books.

In Figure 9-1, we describe how to build the shared literary knowledge of your classroom community, embedding implicit and explicit teaching with your use of intentional conversation and specific points of instructional value to set a foundation for explicit teaching in reading minilessons. All of the teaching in minilessons is reinforced in shared reading, guided reading, and book clubs, with all pathways leading to the goal of effective independent reading.

Let's look at the range of research-based instructional contexts that comprise an effective literacy design.

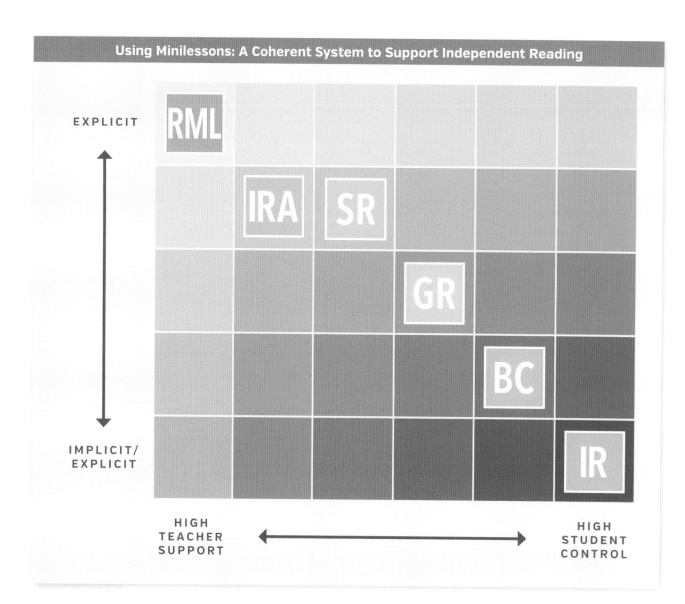

**Figure 9-1:** Implicit or explicit text experiences, supported and developed by explicit teaching in reading minilessons and reinforced in shared reading, guided reading, book clubs, and reading reading conferences lead to effective independent reading.

# Interactive Read-Aloud

Interactive read-aloud includes the highest level of teacher support for students as they experience a complex, grade-appropriate text. Carefully select sets of high-quality children's literature, fiction and nonfiction, and read them aloud to students. We use the word *interactive* because talk is a salient characteristic of this instructional context. You do the reading but pause to invite student discussion in pairs, in triads, or as a whole group at selected points. After the reading, students engage in a lively discussion. Finally, you invite students to revisit specific points in the text for deeper learning and may provide further opportunities for responding to the text through writing, drama, movement, or art.

We recommend that you read aloud from high-quality, organized text sets, which you use across the year. A text set contains several titles that are related in some conceptual way, for example:

- Author
- Illustrator
- Genre
- Topic
- Theme or big idea
- Format (such as graphic texts)

When you use books organized in text sets, you can support children in making connections across a related group of texts and in engaging them in deeper thinking about texts. All children benefit from the use of preselected sets, but these connected texts are particularly supportive for English language learners. Text sets allow children to develop vocabulary around a particular theme, genre or topic. This shared collection of familiar texts and the shared vocabulary developed through the talk provides essential background knowledge that all students will be able to apply during subsequent reading minilessons.

**ELL CONNECTION**

**Figure 9-2:** Interactive read-aloud in a first-grade class

The key to success with reading minilessons is providing the intentional instruction in interactive read-aloud that will, first, enable the children to enjoy and come to love books and, second, build a foundation of shared understandings about texts within a community of readers and writers.

If you are using *Fountas & Pinnell Classroom™*, you will notice that we have used examples from *Interactive Read-Aloud Collection* as the mentor texts in the minilessons. If you do not have the texts from *Fountas & Pinnell Classroom™*, select read-aloud texts with the same characteristics (described at the beginning of each umbrella) to read well ahead of the minilessons and use the lessons as organized and presented in this book. Simply substitute the particular texts you selected. You can draw on any texts you have already read and discussed with the children as long as the genre is appropriate for the set of minilessons and the ideas can be connected. For example, if you are going to teach a set of minilessons about characters, pull examples from fiction stories rather than nonfiction books and include engaging characters. If you are reading rich literature in various genres to your children, the chances are high that many of the types of reading behaviors or understandings you are teaching for in reading minilessons can be applied to those texts.

At the beginning of each umbrella (set of related minilessons), you will find a section titled "Before Teaching Minilessons," which offers guidance in the use of interactive read-aloud as a prelude to teaching the explicit minilessons in the umbrella. It is important to note that the texts in a text set can be used for several different umbrellas. In general, text sets are connected with each other in particular ways so children can think about concepts across texts and notice literary characteristics during read-aloud lessons. But the texts have multiple uses. When you complete reading the books in a set, you will have provided children with a rich, connected set of literacy experiences that include both explicit teaching and implicitly

**Figure 9-3:** Examples of preselected text sets from *Fountas & Pinnell Classroom™ Interactive Read-Aloud Collection*

IRA **Exploring Nonfiction**

IRA **Taking Care of Each Other: Family**

understood concepts. But, we would not label one text set for the study of illustrations and another for the study of character. Instead, we have often selected examples across sets. Rich, literary texts can be used for multiple types of lessons, so you will see many of the same, familiar texts referenced throughout the reading minilessons across umbrellas. Each time a text is used for a different focus, children have a chance to view it with new eyes and see it differently. Usually, texts are not reread in entirety. They are known from a rich and deep experience, and the result is shared literary knowledge for the class. In minilessons, they are revisited briefly with a particular focus. It is most powerful to select examples from texts that children have heard in their *recent* experience. But you can always revisit favorites that you read at the very beginning of the year, which can be referenced all year long. When texts have been enjoyed and loved in interactive read-aloud, children know them deeply and can remember them over time. Here are some steps to follow for incorporating your own texts into the minilessons:

1. Identify a group of read-aloud texts that will be valuable resources for use in the particular minilesson. (These texts may be from the same text set, but usually they are drawn from several different sets. The key is their value in teaching routines, engaging in literary analysis, building particular strategies and skills, or writing about reading.)

2. The mentor texts you select will usually be some that you have already read to and discussed with the children; but if not, read and discuss them with the goal of enjoyment and understanding. The emphasis in inter-active read-aloud is not on the minilesson principle but on enjoying and deeply understanding the text, appreciating the illustrations and design, and constructing an understanding of the deeper messages of the text.

3. Teach the reading minilesson as designed, substituting the texts you have chosen and read to the children.

Interactive read-aloud will greatly benefit your English language learners. In *Fountas & Pinnell Classroom*™, we have selected the texts with English language learners in mind and recommend that you do the same if you are selecting texts from your existing resources. In addition to expanding both listening and speaking vocabularies, interactive read-aloud provides constant exposure to English language syntax. Stories read aloud provide "ear print" for children. Hearing grammatical structures of English over and over helps English language learners form an implicit knowledge of the rules. Here are some other considerations for your English language learners:

**ELL CONNECTION**

▶ Increase the frequency of your interactive read-alouds.

▶ Choose books that have familiar themes and concepts and take into account the cultural backgrounds of all the students in your classroom.

▶ Reread texts that your English language learners enjoy. Rereading texts that children especially enjoy will help them acquire and make use of language that goes beyond their current understanding.

▶ Choose texts that are simple and have high picture support. This will allow you to later revisit concrete examples from these texts during reading minilessons.

▶ Seat English language learners in places where they can easily see, hear, and participate in the text.

▶ Preview the text with English language learners by holding a small-group discussion before reading the book to the entire class. As they hear it the second time, they will understand more and will have had the experience of talking. This will encourage the children to participate more actively during the discussion.

When you provide a rich and supportive experience through interactive read-aloud, you prepare English language learners for a successful experience in reading minilessons. They will bring the vocabulary and background knowledge developed in interactive read-aloud to the exploration of the reading minilesson principle. These multiple layers of support will pave the road to successful independent reading.

## Shared Reading

In shared reading with first-grade children, use an enlarged text, either fiction or nonfiction. Read the text to the children and then invite them to read a part of the text or the whole text in unison. Have children reread the text several times until they know it well, and then you have the option of revisiting it for different purposes (for example, to locate high-frequency words, words that start with the same letter, or punctuation) and to extend the meaning through writing, art, or drama.

Like the texts in interactive read-aloud, shared reading texts offer students the opportunity to understand and discuss characters, events, concepts, and ideas. In addition, an enlarged text offers the advantage of making print, layout, and punctuation available to the readers because all can see them clearly.

You will find that some minilessons in this book refer to shared reading examples from *Fountas & Pinnell Classroom™*. If you do not have access to these resources, you can easily use the lessons in this book by collecting your own set of shared reading books and/or using a document camera to show pages of an appropriate book. Simply substitute the texts you select.

At the beginning of each umbrella, you will find a short section titled "Before Teaching Minilessons," which will have suggestions for the teaching needed prior to your use of the umbrella. Here are some steps to follow for incorporating your own shared reading texts into the minilessons:

1. Prior to implementing a lesson, select a group of texts that are appropriate for teaching the principle. Use the examples in the lesson as a guide. The texts may be some that you have previously read and built lessons around.

2. Engage children in a shared reading of each text that is not familiar to them. Shared reading books are designed for repeated readings, so plan to reread each several times. (Use your own judgment. Sometimes two or three readings are sufficient.) Remember, the focus is on understanding and enjoying the text, not on a specific principle.

3. Revisit the text to do some specific teaching toward any of the systems of strategic actions listed in *The Literacy Continuum* (Fountas and Pinnell 2017c). As an option, give children opportunities to respond to the text through writing, art, or drama.

4. Implement the reading minilesson as designed using the texts you have used in teaching.

In lessons using shared reading texts, students have had opportunities to notice print and how it works—the directionality, the use of space, and the way letters are used to spell words. They have located individual words and noticed the use of bold and sound words. They have learned how to use the meaning, language, and print together to process the text fluently. In addition, here, too, they noticed characteristics of the genre, the characters, and the message anchors.

**Figure 9-4:** Shared reading in a first-grade class

Shared reading can also be important in reinforcing students' ability to apply understandings from the minilesson. You can revisit the texts to remind children of the minilesson principle and invite them to notice text characteristics or engage strategic actions to process them. When you work across texts, you help children apply understandings in many contexts.

Shared reading provides a supportive environment for English language learners to both hear and produce English language structures and patterns. Familiar shared reading texts often have repeated or rhythmic text, which is easy to learn. Using shared reading texts to teach strategies and skills minilessons can be particularly supportive for English language learners because they have had the opportunity to develop familiarity with the meaning, the vocabulary, and the language structures of the text. They can focus on exploring the minilesson principle because they are not working so hard to read and understand the text. Shared reading gives them the background and familiarity with text that facilitates the learning of the minilesson principle.

Shared reading is a context that is particularly supportive to English language learners because of the enjoyable repetition and opportunity to "practice" English syntax with the support of the group. Following are some suggestions you can use to support English language learners:

▶ Select enlarged texts with simple illustrations.

▶ Select enlarged texts with easy-to-say refrains, often involving rhyme and repeating patterns.

▶ Reread the book as much as needed to help children become confident in joining in.

▶ Use some texts that lend themselves to inserting children's names or adding repetitive verses.

▶ Meet in a small group so learners can get "hands-on" experience pointing to words and pictures.

## Guided Reading

Guided reading is small-group instruction using an appropriately selected leveled text that is at students' instructional level. This means that the text is more complex than the students can process independently, so it offers appropriate challenge.

Supportive and precise instruction with the text enables the students to read it with proficiency, and in the process they develop in-the-head strategic actions that they can apply to the reading of other texts. Guided reading involves several steps:

1. Assess students' strengths through the analysis of oral reading behaviors as well as the assessment of comprehension—thinking within, beyond, and about the text. This knowledge enables you to determine an appropriate reading level for instruction.

2. Bring together a small group of students who are approximately at the same level, so it makes sense to teach them together. (Ongoing assessment takes place in the form of running records or reading records so that the information can guide the emphasis in lessons and so that groups may be changed and reformed as needed.)

3. Based on assessment, select a text that is at students' instructional level and offers opportunities for new learning.

4. Introduce the text to the students in a way that will support reading and engage them with the text.

5. Students read the text individually. (Some first-grade children may still be reading quietly [whisper reading] while pointing to the words. The goal is for them to progress to silent reading without pointing.) Support reading through quick interactions that use precise language to support effective processing.

6. Invite students to engage in an open-ended discussion of the text and use some guiding questions or prompts to help them extend their thinking.

7. Based on previous assessment and observation during reading, select a teaching point.

8. Engage students in quick word work that helps them flexibly apply principles for solving words that that have been selected based on information gained from the analysis of oral reading behaviors and reinforcement of

**Figure 9-5:** Guided reading in a first-grade class

principles explored in phonics minilessons (see *The Fountas & Pinnell Comprehensive Phonics, Spelling, and Word Study Guide* [2017b] and *Phonics, Spelling, and Word Study System, for Grade 1* [2017e]).

9. As an option, you may have children engage in drawing and/or writing about the book to extend their understanding, but it is not necessary—or desirable—to write about every book.

Guided reading texts are not usually used as examples in minilessons because they are not texts that are shared by the entire class. You can, however, take the opportunity to reinforce the minilesson principle across the guided reading lesson at one or more points:

▶ In the introduction to the text, refer to a reading minilesson principle as one of the ways that you support readers before reading a new text.

▶ In your interactions with children during the reading of the text, remind them of the principle from the reading minilesson.

▶ In the discussion after the text, reinforce the minilesson principle when appropriate.

▶ In the teaching point, reinforce a minilesson principle.

**ELL CONNECTION**

In small-group guided reading lessons, students explore aspects of written texts that are similar to the understandings they discuss in interactive read-aloud and shared reading. They notice characters and character change, talk about where the story takes place, talk about the problem in the story and the ending, and discuss the lesson or message of the story. They talk about information they learned and questions they have, they notice genre characteristics, and they develop phonics knowledge and word-solving strategies. So, guided reading also gives readers the opportunity to apply what they have learned in reading minilessons.

When you support readers in applying the minilesson principle within a guided reading lesson, you give them another opportunity to talk about text with this new thinking in mind. It is particularly helpful to English language learners to have the opportunity to try out this new thinking in a small, safe setting. Guided reading can provide the opportunity to talk about the minilesson principle before the class comes back together to share. Often, they feel more confident to share their new thinking with the whole group because they have had this opportunity to "rehearse" talking about their book in the small-group setting.

## Book Clubs

For a book club meeting, bring together a small group of students who have chosen the same book to read and discuss with their classmates. The book can be one that you have read to the group or one that the children can either read independently or listen to and understand from an audio recording.

The implementation of book clubs follows these steps:

1. Preselect about four books that offer opportunities for deep discussion. These books may be related in some way (for example, they might be by the same author or feature stories around a theme). Or, they might just be a group of titles that will give children good choices.

2. Give a book talk about each of the books to introduce them to children. A book talk is a short "commercial" for the book.

3. Children read and prepare for the book club discussion. If the child cannot read the book, prepare an audio version that can be used during independent reading time. Each reader marks a place or places that he wants to discuss with a sticky note.

4. Convene the group and facilitate the discussion.

5. The students self-evaluate the discussion.

First-grade children have much to learn about participating in a book discussion group. It's likely that this is a new experience for many of them, but you will find that first graders *love* being in a book club; they prepare for it and take it seriously. They are taking the first steps toward deep, enjoyable talk with their classmates about books. In this book, one entire umbrella is devoted to teaching the routines of book clubs (see Umbrella 4: Getting Started with Book Clubs in Section Two: Literary Analysis).

A discussion among four or five diverse first-grade students can go in many directions, and you want to hear all of their ideas! They are largely focused on using the illustrations to support their responses. *Prompting Guide, Part 2, for Comprehension: Thinking, Talking, and Writing* (Fountas and Pinnell 2016) is a helpful tool, especially the section on book discussions. The section on book discussions contains precise teacher language for getting a discussion started, asking for thinking,

**Figure 9-6:** Book club in a first-grade class

affirming thinking, agreeing and disagreeing, changing thinking, clarifying thinking, extending thinking, focusing on the big ideas, making connections, paraphrasing, questioning and hypothesizing, redirecting, seeking evidence, sharing thinking, and summarizing.

To help the students learn how to hold book club discussions, consider using the fishbowl technique. Before you teach the minilesson, prepare one group of children to model the minilesson concept. During the minilesson, seat those children in the center and the rest of the children in a ring around them so that they can see and hear what is going on.

ELL CONNECTION

Book clubs offer English language learners the unique opportunity of entering into conversations about books with other children. Because they are using picture books, the images support their understanding. If they have listened to an audio recording many times, they are gaining more and more exposure to language. The language and content of the book lifts the conversation and gives them something to talk about. They learn the conventions of discourse, which become familiar because they do it many times. They can hear others talk and respond with social language, such as "I agree with _____."

## Independent Reading

In independent reading, students have the opportunity to apply all they have learned in minilessons. To support independent reading, assemble a well-organized classroom library with a range of engaging fiction and nonfiction books. Although you will take into account the levels students can read independently to assure a range of options, we do not suggest that you arrange the books by level. It is not productive and can be destructive for the students to choose books by "level." Instead, create tubs or baskets by author, topic, genre, and so forth. There are minilessons in Section One: Management to help you teach first-grade children how to choose books for their own reading (see Umbrella 2: Using the Classroom Library for Independent Reading).

Children may choose books for independent reading from a variety of sources:

- **Individual Book Bags or Boxes.** Using clear resealable bags, empty shoeboxes, or cereal boxes, help each child build an individual collection of books they want to read. Children can put their names on the bags or boxes and decorate them. These may include some books previously read in guided reading or books they have selected from the classroom library. Students can keep these individual book bags at a central place and retrieve them during independent reading time.

- **Browsing Boxes.** Place guided reading books or small versions of shared reading books that have been previously read, along with other books at lower levels, in a basket or box identified by a color or other means. You may put children's names on the browsing boxes they are assigned to, but these should be temporary. Children select books from the box to read. Children may read several during reading time.

▶ **Classroom Library.** The classroom library is filled with baskets or tubs of books that first-grade students will love. Early in the year, students may spend their time revisiting books you have read aloud to them even though they cannot read the words. They can still notice the illustrations and "tell" the story or share the information based on their understandings. Shared reading books, too, are good resources in the classroom library. In some minilessons, you might guide children to read from a particular basket in the classroom library so they have the opportunity to apply the reading minilesson to books that include the characteristics addressed in the minilesson. For example, you might have them read from a particular genre or author set.

Becoming independent as a reader is an essential life skill for all students. English language learners need daily opportunities to use their systems of strategic actions on text that is accessible, meaningful, and interesting to them. Here are some suggestions for helping English language learners during independent reading:

**ELL CONNECTION**

▶ Make sure your classroom library has a good selection of books at a range of levels. If possible, provide books in the first language of your students as well as books with familiar settings and themes.

▶ During individual conferences, help students prepare—and sometimes rehearse—something that they can share with others about the text during group share. When possible, ask them to think about the minilesson principle.

▶ Provide opportunities for English language learners to share with partners before being asked to share with the whole group.

**Figure 9-7:** Independent reading in a first-grade class

## Combining Implicit and Explicit Teaching for Independent Reading

You are about to embark on a highly productive year of literacy lessons. We have prepared these lessons as tools for your use as you help children engage with texts, making daily shifts in learning. When children participate in a classroom that provides a multitext approach to literacy learning, they are exposed to textual elements in a variety of instructional contexts. As described in Figure 9-1, all of these instructional contexts involve embedding literary and print concepts into authentic and meaningful experiences with text. There is a powerful combination of many concepts that are implicitly understood as children engage with books and the explicit teaching that brings them to conscious awareness and supports students' ability to articulate them using academic language.

In interactive read-aloud, children are invited to respond to text as they turn and talk and participate in lively discussions after a text is read. In interactive read-aloud, you support your students to think within, beyond, and about the text because you will have used *The Literacy Continuum* to identify when you will pause and invite these conversations and how you will ask questions and model comments to support the behaviors you have selected.

In shared reading, students learn from both implicit and explicit teaching. They first read and discuss the text several times, enjoying the book and discussing aspects of the text that support their thinking within, beyond, and about the text. Teachers often revisit the text with an explicit focus that supports thinking within the text (e.g., finding high-frequency words, words with the same initial letters). The embedded, implicit teaching, as well as some of the more explicit teaching that children experience, lays the groundwork for the explicit teaching that takes place in reading minilessons. Reading minilessons become the bridge from these shared and interactive whole-group reading experiences to independent reading.

**Figure 9-8:** Organize classroom library books in labeled bins so that children can find books they will enjoy reading.

Guided reading and book clubs scaffold the reading process through a combination of implicit and explicit teaching that helps children apply the reading minilesson principles across a variety of instructional-level texts. The group share reinforces the whole process. Reading minilessons do not function in the absence of these other instructional contexts; rather, they all work in concert to build processing systems for students to grow in their ability to independently read increasingly complex texts over time.

The minilessons in this book serve as a guide to a meaningful, systematic approach to joyful, literacy learning across multiple reading contexts. Children acquire a complex range of understandings. Whole-class minilessons form the "glue" that connects all of this learning, makes it explicit, and turns it over to the children to apply it to their own reading and writing. You will find that the talk and learning in those shared experiences will bring your class together as a community with a shared knowledge base. We know that you and your students enjoy the rich experiences as you engage together in thinking, talking, and responding to a treasure chest of beautiful books. Children deserve these rich opportunities—every child, every day.

Brown, Marcia. 1961. *Once a Mouse . . .* New York: Simon & Schuster.

Clay, Marie. 2015 [1991]. *Becoming Literate: The Construction of Inner Control.* Auckland, NZ: Global Education Systems.

Davies, Nicola. 2005. *Surprising Sharks.* Somerville, MA: Candlewick.

Fountas, Irene C., and Gay Su Pinnell. 2006. *Teaching for Comprehending and Fluency.* Portsmouth, NH: Heinemann.

———. 2012a. *Genre Study: Teaching with Fiction and Nonfiction Books.* Portsmouth, NH: Heinemann.

———. 2012b. *Fountas & Pinnell Prompting Guide, Part 1, for Oral Reading and Early Writing.* Portsmouth, NH: Heinemann.

———. 2014. *Reader's Notebook: Primary.* Portsmouth, NH: Heinemann.

———. 2016. *Fountas & Pinnell Prompting Guide, Part 2, for Comprehension: Thinking, Talking, and Writing.* Portsmouth, NH: Heinemann.

———. 2017a. *Fountas & Pinnell Classroom™.* Portsmouth, NH: Heinemann.

———. 2017b. *The Fountas & Pinnell Comprehensive Phonics, Spelling, and Word Study Guide.* Portsmouth, NH: Heinemann.

———. 2017c. *The Fountas & Pinnell Literacy Continuum: A Tool for Assessment, Planning, and Teaching.* Portsmouth, NH: Heinemann.

———. 2017d. *Guided Reading: Responsive Teaching Across the Grades.* Portsmouth, NH: Heinemann.

———. 2017e. *Phonics, Spelling, and Word Study System, for Grade 1.* Portsmouth, NH: Heinemann.

Isadora, Rachel. 2007. *The Princess and the Pea.* New York: Penguin.

Johnston, Tony. 1998. *The Tale of Rabbit and Coyote.* New York: Penguin.

Markle, Sandra. 2013. *What If You Had Animal Teeth?* New York: Scholastic.

Paye, Won-Ldy. 2003. *Mrs. Chicken and the Hungry Crocodile.* New York: Square Fish.

Stuve-Bodeen, Stephanie. 2002. *Elizabeti's School.* New York: Lee & Low.

Vygotsky, Lev. 1979. Mind in Society: *The Development of Higher Psychological Processes.* Cambridge, MA: Harvard University Press.

# Section 1 | Management

Management minilessons focus on routines for thinking and talking about reading and working together in the classroom. They allow you to teach effectively and efficiently and are directed toward the creation of an orderly, busy classroom in which students know what is expected and how to behave responsibly and respectfully in a community of learners. Most of the minilessons at the beginning of the school year will focus on management.

# 1 Management

## Minilessons in This Umbrella

| RML1 | Use an appropriate voice level. |
| --- | --- |
| RML2 | Listen carefully to each other. |
| RML3 | Move from one spot to another quickly and silently. |
| RML4 | Do your best work. |
| RML5 | Find ways to solve problems when the teacher is busy. |
| RML6 | Take good care of classroom materials. |

## Before Teaching Umbrella 1 Minilessons

These minilessons are designed to help you maintain a respectful, caring, and organized classroom community. Establishment of routines supports children's ability to function as responsible members of the classroom. While explicitly teaching these routines, it is also important to incorporate opportunities to read aloud and talk about books. Interactive read-aloud is a community-building experience that teaches children how to communicate thinking about books as well as carefully listen and respond to others respectfully.

Create a warm and inviting, child-centered classroom in which children can take ownership of space and materials:

▶ Designate a whole-group meeting area where the class gathers to think and learn. Use a colorful rug with a spot for each child. Or, you use individual carpet squares they can retrieve quickly and place precisely.

▶ Post a daily schedule.

▶ Find places for materials and supplies with only one type of material/supply in a labeled container.

▶ Allow opportunities for the children to browse and choose books.

▶ Set up a daily time for children to read books.

Section 1: Management

## Working Together in the Classroom

### You Will Need

- chart prepared with the title and the column headings (Silent, Soft, Normal, Loud)
- markers

### Academic Language / Important Vocabulary

- voice level

### Continuum Connection

- Speak at an appropriate volume (p. 332)

### Goal

Learn to use an appropriate voice level for the activity.

### Rationale

Explicitly teaching appropriate voice volume to children helps them to independently determine the acceptable noise level for various settings and activities, both inside and outside of the classroom.

### Assess Learning

Observe children throughout the day. Notice if there is evidence of new learning based on the goal of this minilesson.

- ▶ Can children explain why an appropriate voice level is important to consider?
- ▶ Do they accurately evaluate the level of their voices for the activity they are doing?
- ▶ Do they use the term *voice level* correctly?

## Minilesson

To help children think about the minilesson principle, engage them in a short discussion of using an appropriate voice level. Here is an example.

- ▶ Begin a voice chart to show appropriate voice levels.

    You can help each other to do your best work by thinking about a good voice level to use. The voice level means how quiet or loud your voice is. A good voice level is just right for what you are doing. For example, how would your voice sound when you work by yourself, or you read by yourself?

    Your voice would be turned off, or it would be a whisper so quiet no one could hear it. So, let's call that zero.

- ▶ Write the numeral 0 on the chart and fill in one or two routines during which children would use a 0 voice.

- ▶ Repeat this procedure for each voice level on the chart. You may need to encourage children to rethink their responses to ensure they determine the appropriate voice level for each activity. Over time, add more routines to the chart for each voice level.

## Have a Try

Invite the children to practice using a good voice level with a partner.

▶ Select an activity to engage the children in practicing using a good voice level.

> Let's practice using a good voice level for partner work. Look at the chart to help you. Turn and tell a partner your name using a good voice level.

## Summarize and Apply

Summarize the learning and remind children to think about their voice level as they work.

> What did you learn today about using different voice levels for activities you do inside and outside of the classroom? Look at the chart if you need help remembering.

> Now you are going to read a book by yourself. Which voice level will you use? Some of you know how to read silently. Some of you may need to use a whisper voice when you read. Look at the chart to remember what your voice level should be.

## Share

Following independent work time, gather children together in the meeting area to talk about using an appropriate voice level.

> Today you learned how to use a good voice level for activities inside and outside the classroom. Give me a thumbs-up if you used a level 0 voice while you were reading today.

## Extend the Lesson (Optional)

After assessing children's understanding, you might decide to extend the learning.

▶ Review and evaluate voice levels before and after an activity.

▶ Record additional activities on the chart using shared or interactive writing.

▶ Invite a few children to draw illustrations for the activities under the voice levels.

**Our Voice Level Chart**

| 0 | 1 | 2 | 3 |
|---|---|---|---|
| Silent | Soft | Normal | Loud |
| -Working by yourself<br>-Independent reading<br>-Independent writing/drawing<br>-Hallways | -Small-group work<br>-Partner work<br>-Snack | -Whole-group work<br>-Meetings<br>-Read-aloud<br>-Shared reading<br>-Interactive writing | -Outside recess |

Section 1: Management

**Working Together in the Classroom**

### You Will Need

- two children prepared to talk about a book
- chart paper and markers
- familiar book that children have heard or read
- sticky notes

### Academic Language / Important Vocabulary

- listen
- voice level

### Continuum Connection

- Look at the speaker when spoken to (p. 332)
- Speak at an appropriate volume (p. 332)
- Demonstrate respectful listening behaviors (p. 332)

## Goal

Learn expectations for listening during whole- or small-group meetings.

## Rationale

When you teach children to listen to peers during small- or whole-group instruction, you promote effective communication and collaboration and support respectful behavior in the classroom.

## Assess Learning

Observe children when they are listening during whole or small groups. Notice if there is evidence of new learning based on the goal of this minilesson.

- ▸ Can children explain why it is important to listen carefully?
- ▸ Are they able to follow the listening guidelines from the chart?
- ▸ Do they use the terms *listen* and *voice level* correctly?

## Minilesson

To help children think about the minilesson principle, engage them in a short demonstration of listening carefully. Here is an example.

- ▸ In advance, prepare two children to talk and listen to each other about a familiar book.

  > When you listen to each other, you can do your best learning. Let's watch two of your classmates listen and talk to each other about a book. Notice what the listening person is doing while the other person is talking.

- ▸ Ask the two children to come up front and have a conversation about a book both of them have read. If necessary, prompt their conversation with questions, such as *What was this book about? What did you like about the book?* The class looks on as the two children have their conversation.

  > What did you notice about how they listened to each other?

- ▸ Prompt children to notice effective listening behaviors (e.g., eye contact, voice level, responding to what the speaker says, listening quietly) and record them on the chart.

  > What did voice level sound like when they were listening?

  > You use a 0—silent—voice so you can listen carefully.

- ▸ Let children know that there are ways they can communicate to one another silently, such as giving a thumbs-up when they agree.

## Have a Try

Invite the children to practice listening with a partner.

▶ Select a familiar book from your classroom library.

> Turn and talk with a partner about this book. You can talk about the characters, what the book was about, or what you think about it. Think about your voice level, and do your best listening so you can learn from each other.

▶ After they talk with their partner, invite a few pairs to evaluate their listening based on the chart.

## Summarize and Apply

Summarize the learning and remind children to listen carefully to each other during group meetings.

> What did you learn today about listening? Look at the chart if you need help remembering.

▶ Write the principle on the chart.

> When you read independently today, put a sticky note on an interesting page to talk about when we gather for group meeting.

## Share

Following independent work time, gather children together in the meeting area to practice listening carefully.

> Turn and talk to a partner. Share the interesting page you put a sticky note on. Remember to listen carefully while your partner speaks.

▶ After a few minutes, help children evaluate their listening behaviors.

> Give a thumbs-up if you looked at your partner while she was talking.

▶ Repeat for each item on the chart.

## Extend the Lesson (Optional)

After assessing children's understanding, you might decide to extend the learning.

▶ Over several days, review the listening chart in whole and small groups. Add additional behaviors to the chart that children notice.

▶ Reinforce behaviors by noticing and pointing out the ways children are following the listening expectations.

### Listen carefully to each other.

- Look at the person who is talking.

- Think about what the speaker is saying.

- Say something to the speaker.

- Listen silently when someone else is talking.

**Reading Minilesson Principle**
# Move from one spot to another quickly and silently.

## Working Together in the Classroom

### You Will Need

- four children prepared to demonstrate transitioning
- chart paper and markers
- voice level chart from RML1

### Academic Language / Important Vocabulary

- quickly
- silently
- voice level

## Goal

Learn how to transition from one activity to another in the classroom.

## Rationale

Establishing clear expectations for transitions in the classroom increases the amount of time available for learning. These expectations additionally provide a model for how they should move outside of the classroom.

## Assess Learning

Observe children when they transition from one activity to another. Notice if there is evidence of new learning based on the goal of this minilesson.

- Are children able to articulate what to do during transition times?
- During transitions, do they move quickly and silently?
- Do they consistently follow the routines of the chart?
- Do they use the terms *quickly*, *silently*, and *voice level* correctly?

## Minilesson

To help children think about the minilesson principle, engage them in a short demonstration of moving quickly and silently. Here is an example.

- Prepare four children ahead of the minilesson to demonstrate transitioning.

    There are many different places that you work and learn in our classroom. Sometimes you work in the meeting area. Sometimes you work at your tables.

    Let's watch _____ , _____ , _____ , and _____ move from the meeting area to their tables.

- Then have the children return to the meeting area.

    What did you notice about how they moved from one place to another?

    They walked quickly but did not run, and they sat back down in their spot. What might happen if everyone ran?

    What did they do with their hands and feet when they got to their spot?

- Record responses on the chart.

    Let's look at the voice level chart we made. What voice level did you notice they used when they moved from one place to another?

- Record responses on the chart.

    Why is it important to remember how to move from one place to another?

## Have a Try

Invite the children to practice transitioning.

▶ Decide on a signal to indicate the children should transition.

> Now, you will practice moving from one place to another. When I give this signal, I'd like you to move quickly and silently to your table.

▶ Give the signal for children to move.

> Now, I'd like everyone to move from the tables back to the meeting area.

▶ Signal children to move.

> Let's look at the chart and talk about what you did when you moved from one place to another.

## Summarize and Apply

Summarize the learning and remind children how to transition.

> What did you learn about moving quickly and silently from one place to another?

▶ Write the principle on the chart.

> When you move to independent reading today, remember to walk quickly and silently. When it is time to come back to our meeting area, put your materials away carefully and walk quickly and silently.

## Share

Following independent work time, gather children together in the meeting area to talk about transitioning.

> Give a thumbs-up if you walked quickly and silently to your spot in the meeting area. Raise your hand to share one thing you will remember to do when you move.

## Extend the Lesson (Optional)

After assessing children's understanding, you might decide to extend the learning.

▶ Teach children how to self-select a spot on the rug efficiently and politely.

▶ Teach behaviors to support learning, such as eye contact and body position.

▶ If you use literacy centers or work stations, have children practice moving between centers when you introduce them.

---

Move from one spot to another quickly and silently.

- Walk quickly but do not run.

- Use a 0 level voice.

Shhh...

- Keep hands and feet in your space.

---

**Section 1: Management**

# RML4
## MGT.U1.RML4

**Reading Minilesson Principle**
## Do your best work.

### You Will Need

- four children prepared to demonstrate starting right away to work and staying focused
- chart paper and markers

### Academic Language / Important Vocabulary

- focus
- independent

## Goal

Learn to start work promptly and stay focused.

## Rationale

When you teach children to get to work promptly and to stay focused, you promote independence. Setting the foundation early to encourage independent learning frees you to provide uninterrupted learning for other children.

## Assess Learning

Observe children when they work independently as they start working and stay focused. Notice if there is evidence of new learning based on the goal of this minilesson.

- Can children articulate why it is important to get started right away? To stay focused?
- Do they understand what it means to stay focused?
- Can they self-evaluate a strength and a goal for doing their best independent work?
- Do they understand the words *focus* and *independent*?

## Minilesson

To help children think about the minilesson principle, engage them in a short demonstration of starting work right away and staying focused. Here is an example.

- In advance, prepare four children to demonstrate going to their table, taking out materials to complete a drawing, starting right away, and staying focused.

  Sometimes you have work to do with your classmates, and sometimes you have work to do by yourself. The work that you do by yourself is called independent work. It is important to do your best when you work independently. Let's watch some of your classmates doing their best work.

- Have the rest of the class observe for just enough time to see the children getting started promptly and focus on what they are doing. Then, call the four children back to the meeting area.

  What did you notice about how they worked?

- Record responses on the chart paper.

  They walked quickly and silently to their work area. They got started right away. They followed directions. They focused. That means they kept working all the time and thought about their important work. They returned their materials when they were done. Why is it important to do all of these things?

## Have a Try

Invite the children to talk about doing their best work with a partner.

▶ Reread the chart.

> As we reread the chart, think about one thing you do well and one thing you need to practice more in order to do your best independent work.

> Turn and talk to a partner about something that you do well and something you need more practice with.

▶ After they turn and talk, invite a few children to share.

## Summarize and Apply

Summarize the learning and remind the children to start their work right away and stay focused.

▶ Review the chart with the children so that they are prepared to do their best work during independent reading time.

> During independent reading time, use the chart to help you remember how to do your best work. Be prepared to say what you did well when we come together in the meeting area.

## Share

Following independent work time, gather children together in the meeting area to talk about how they did their best work.

> Give a thumbs-up if you got started with your work right away, worked quietly, and stayed focused. You stayed focused and really thought carefully about your work.

## Extend the Lesson (Optional)

After assessing children's understanding, you might decide to extend the learning.

▶ Review the routines on the chart when you introduce new activities until the routines become automatic.

▶ Provide accommodations for children who need support getting started or staying focused.

▶ Reinforce the behaviors on the chart when you see them.

**How to Do Your Best Work**

- Begin quickly.
- Follow directions.
- Stay focused.
- Work quietly.
- Put materials away.

> I did my best work!

## RML5
**MGT.U1.RML5**

**Reading Minilesson Principle**
# Find ways to solve problems when the teacher is busy.

**Working Together in the Classroom**

**You Will Need**

▶ chart paper and markers

**Academic Language / Important Vocabulary**

▶ problem solve
▶ help
▶ question
▶ ask

## Goal

Find ways to solve problems on their own when help is needed.

## Rationale

When children learn how to collaborate and problem solve independently, they gain confidence. When they can problem solve independently, you are able to work with small groups or individuals without interruption.

## Assess Learning

Observe children when they work independently. Notice if there is evidence of new learning based on the goal of this minilesson.

▶ Do children find a way to get help when you are busy?

▶ Are they able to determine what is meant by an emergency?

▶ Do they use the terms *problem solve*, *help*, *question*, and *ask* correctly?

## Minilesson

To help children think about the minilesson principle, engage them in a discussion of what to do when they need help. Here is an example.

▶ A few days before this minilesson observe when children are asking you for help. Use these observations for the discussion.

> Sometimes when you are working on your own, you want to ask me a question, but I'm busy. What are some things you can do to help yourself without asking me?

▶ Record responses on the chart paper. If children have trouble generating ideas, provide them with some scenarios to support them.

> For example, if you don't understand your work, what could you do to help figure it out? If you have done some of your work and are stuck, what could you do while you are waiting for help?

▶ Lead children to understand that they can ask each other or, as a final choice, you for help when it is needed.

> If you can't solve your problem, who else can you ask for help?

▶ Record responses on the chart.

▶ Briefly discuss what an emergency is and that it's okay to interrupt you if there is an emergency.

## Have a Try

Invite the children to act out and discuss solving problems.

▶ Invite a few children to act out one or more of the following scenarios:

- You don't know how to spell a word.
- You forgot what to do next.
- You forgot the directions for playing a game.
- Your pencil broke, and you don't have another.

Now, I'll ask a few of you to act out what to do when you need help when I am busy.

▶ After each scenario, ask children to turn and talk with a partner about how they could solve the problem without your help.

## Summarize and Apply

Summarize the learning and remind the children to think about ways they can solve problems.

What did you learn today about solving problems? Look at the chart if you need help remembering.

▶ Write the principle at the top of the chart.

Today when you are working during independent reading time and need help, think about ways you can solve your problem. When we come back together, we will share how you solved a problem.

## Share

Following independent work time, gather children together in the meeting area to talk about solving problems.

Raise your hand if you needed help while you were working today. How did you solve your problem?

## Extend the Lesson (Optional)

After assessing children's understanding, you might decide to extend the learning.

▶ When introducing a new literacy or work center, add problem-solving strategies to the routine.

▶ Revisit the chart when new independent work is introduced.

---

**Find ways to solve problems when the teacher is busy.**

Reread the directions.

Use the word wall.

Ask a classmate in a soft voice.

Ask the teacher when she is not busy.

## Working Together in the Classroom

### You Will Need

▸ prepare two children to demonstrate returning materials
▸ chart paper
▸ markers

### Academic Language / Important Vocabulary

▸ materials
▸ return

## Goal

Learn to take good care of classroom materials and supplies and return them independently.

## Rationale

When you teach children how to use and return materials, you promote independence. You also are establishing respect for the materials and a process for keeping the classroom community organized.

## Assess Learning

Observe children when they use and return classroom materials. Notice if there is evidence of new learning based on the goal of this minilesson.

▸ Do children take good care of materials?

▸ Do they return materials to where they belong?

▸ Are children able to move about the room quickly and silently when returning materials?

▸ Do they use the terms *materials* and *return* correctly?

## Minilesson

To help children think about the minilesson principle, engage them in a short demonstration of using and putting materials away. Here is an example.

▸ In advance, prepare two children to carefully get materials, use materials, and put materials back where they belong.

Let's watch _____ and _____ work at their tables.

What did you notice about how they used the materials?

▸ Record responses on the chart paper.

They used the materials carefully.

What else did you notice?

▸ Record responses on the chart.

They put the materials away. Why is it important to put your materials away when you are finished?

Did you notice how it sounded when they put the materials away? At the end of work time, return materials quickly and silently where they belong.

## Have a Try

Invite the children to talk about putting materials away with a partner.

▶ Invite two or three more children to demonstrate how to take out different materials, use them, and return them to where they belong.

> Now we'll observe _____ and _____ using materials and then returning them.

> Turn and talk to a partner. Share what you noticed about how they used the materials and what they did when they were finished.

▶ After they turn and talk, invite a few children to share what they observed. Add new observations to the chart.

## Summarize and Apply

Summarize the learning and remind the children to put materials back where they belong.

> How should you treat the materials you use?

> What should you do with materials when you are finished using them?

▶ Write the principle at the top of the chart.

> At the end of independent reading time today, think about what you will do with the materials you used. When we come back together, be ready to share what you did with the materials.

## Share

Following independent work time, gather children together in the meeting area to talk about putting materials away.

> Give a thumbs-up if you returned the materials to where they belonged when you were finished. Who would like to share what you put away and where you put it?

## Extend the Lesson (Optional)

After assessing children's understanding, you might decide to extend the learning.

▶ Use interactive and/or shared writing to label the bins that contain materials.

▶ Revisit the chart when necessary.

▶ As literacy centers or work stations are introduced, explain where materials belong, how to use them, and how to return them correctly.

---

> ## Take good care of classroom materials.
>
> * Get your materials.
>
> * Use them carefully.
>
> * Put materials back in the same place quickly and quietly.
>
>

## Assessment

After you have taught the minilessons in this umbrella, observe children working together in a variety of classroom activities.

▶ What evidence do you have that children understand how to work well as a classroom community?

- Do they listen actively when you or their classmates are speaking?
- Can they find their spot in the meeting area quickly and silently?
- Do they move from one place in the classroom to another quickly and silently?
- Do they start new work right away and stay focused as they complete it?
- Are they using other resources for help when you are busy?
- Are they returning materials and supplies and keeping the classroom clean and organized?

▶ What minilessons might you teach to maintain and grow independent work habits?

- Are children able to locate books they want to read in the classroom library?
- Are they ready to follow a work board to know what to do during independent work time?

Use your observations to determine the next umbrella you will teach. You may also consult Minilessons Across the Year (p. 51) for guidance.

## Minilessons in This Umbrella

**RML1**  Read silently so everyone can enjoy reading.

**RML2**  The classroom library is organized so you can make good book choices.

**RML3**  Choose books that you will want to read.

**RML4**  Take good care of the books in the classroom library.

## Before Teaching Umbrella 2 Minilessons

Before teaching this umbrella, provide children with opportunities to choose books from your classroom library. They will benefit from opportunities to read silently and to explore books independently and with partners. Here are some suggestions for making your classroom library an inviting and organized space for children to select and explore books:

- Organize books into tubs or baskets in a way that allows children to see the front covers and provides easy access for browsing.

- Within each tub or basket, display high-quality and interesting books that vary in size and offer a range of difficulty levels.

- Label tubs or baskets with the topic, author, series, genre, or illustrator. As much as possible, have children make the labels so that they feel ownership of the classroom library.

- If children need support, put colored dots on the tub or basket label and a dot of the same color on the back of each book so children can easily return the books.

- Provide an empty tub or basket in which children can place books if they are unsure where to return them.

- Take the children on a tour of the classroom library, so they know it is a valued and beloved space in their classroom community.

Section 1: Management

# RML1

## MGT.U2.RML1

### Reading Minilesson Principle
## Read silently so everyone can enjoy reading.

## Using the Classroom Library for Independent Reading

### You Will Need

▶ voice level chart (see p. 73)

### Academic Language / Important Vocabulary

▶ independent reading
▶ classroom library
▶ voice level

### Continuum Connection

▶ Adjust speaking volume for different contexts (p. 332)

### Goal

Learn to manage voice levels while reading independently.

### Rationale

A classroom that is fairly quiet is more conducive for reading and thinking than a noisy one, so it is important that children understand how to manage their voice levels during independent reading time. Speaking at the appropriate volume in different instructional contexts is part of being a respectful member of the classroom community. Encourage children who can read silently to do so, and remind other children to be sure to use a soft voice when they read.

### Assess Learning

Observe children when they read independently. Notice if there is evidence of new learning based on the goal of this minilesson.

▶ Do children read silently or with a whisper voice during independent reading?

▶ Are they able to self-evaluate the voice level they used during independent reading?

▶ Can children explain why it is important to read silently, or very quietly, during independent reading?

▶ Can they use the terms *independent reading, classroom library,* and *voice level*?

## Minilesson

To help children think about the minilesson principle, engage them in a discussion of what it means to read silently and why it's important. Here is an example.

▶ Help children use the first picture on the voice chart to figure out that independent reading time should be quiet (level 0), except for whisper reading, which is between 0 and 1.

> Who can point to a good voice level for independent reading, when you're reading a book on your own?

> Some of you already know how to read books silently. Some of you may need to use a whisper voice when you read. Why do you think it is a good idea to read silently or at a whisper during independent reading?

> What would happen if some people used a 2 or 3 voice?

## Have a Try

Invite the children to practice using voice levels with a partner.

▶ Have children practice managing their voice levels by greeting a partner.

> Turn to your partner and say hello using a level 2 voice.

> Did everyone use a level 2 voice? How did the classroom sound?

> A whisper is a level 1 voice. Say hello to your partner in a whisper.

> Now, use a 0 voice.

▶ After a few seconds, ask the children to evaluate how the classroom sounded.

## Summarize and Apply

Summarize the learning and remind children to read silently.

> Who can remind us why it is important to read silently or in a whisper voice during independent reading?

> Let's review where independent reading is on the chart. When else might you use a level 0 voice?

> When you read a book today, remember to read silently or with a whisper voice.

## Share

Following independent work time, gather children together in the meeting area to talk about reading silently.

> Give a thumbs-up if you read your book silently.

> Turn and talk to a partner about the voice level you used while you read and why.

## Extend the Lesson (Optional)

After assessing children's understanding, you might decide to extend the learning.

▶ Remind children to read silently or with a whisper voice before each independent reading session. Notice children who are reading silently, or with a whisper voice, and reinforce the behavior. Ask children to self-evaluate their voice levels after independent reading.

▶ Use shared or interactive writing to create a classroom sign reminding children to read silently.

**Our Voice Level Chart**

| 0 | 1 | 2 | 3 |
|---|---|---|---|
| Silent | Soft | Normal | Loud |
| -Working by yourself<br>-Independent reading<br>-Independent writing/drawing<br>-Hallways | -Small-group work<br>-Partner work<br>-Snack | -Whole-group work<br>-Meetings<br>-Read-aloud<br>-Shared reading<br>-Interactive writing | -Outside recess |

### Reading Minilesson Principle
# The classroom library is organized so you can make good book choices.

## Using the Classroom Library for Independent Reading

### You Will Need

- two sets of three books that can be categorized by topic
- two baskets
- two sets of three books that can be categorized by author or illustrator
- sticky notes
- chart paper and markers

### Academic Language / Important Vocabulary

- topic
- author
- illustrator
- classroom library
- organize

## Goal

Understand a classroom library is organized to help them easily find the book they want to read.

## Rationale

Knowing how the classroom library is organized enables children to choose books more successfully and efficiently. When children are involved in the organization of the classroom library, they develop a sense of ownership and responsibility for maintaining it. They also learn how to sort and categorize books, which supports them in making connections among texts.

## Assess Learning

Observe children when they choose books. Notice if there is evidence of new learning based on the goal of this minilesson.

- Can children explain how and why the books in the classroom library are organized?
- Can children use baskets in the classroom library to find books about a certain topic, author, or illustrator?
- Can they use the terms *topic, author, illustrator, classroom library,* and *organize*?

## Minilesson

To help children think about the minilesson principle, engage them in a discussion of how books can be organized in the classroom library. Here is an example.

- Display six books on two distinct topics (e.g., three books about animals and three books about weather). Read the titles aloud or ask volunteers to read them.

  Think about how these books are alike and different from each other. I want to put these six books into two baskets. Which books could go together in the first basket?

  What makes these books a good collection for this basket?

  Which books could go together in the second basket?

- Place books in each basket according to the children's responses. Temporarily label each basket with a sticky note.

  One way that the books in our classroom library are organized, or grouped together, is by topic, or what the book is about. What is the topic of each basket?

- Write the word *topic* on the chart, as well as the topics of the books you sorted.

## Have a Try

Invite the children to talk about grouping books with a partner.

▶ Display six books by two authors and two empty baskets. Read the titles and authors.

> Turn and talk to a partner about how these books could be grouped into the baskets.

▶ Invite a few pairs to share their thinking.

▶ Add responses and examples to the chart.

## Summarize and Apply

Summarize the learning and remind children to think about how a classroom library can be organized.

> What does the chart show about how to make good book choices?

▶ Write the principle at the top of the chart.

> When you choose a book today, think about if you want to read about a topic you like or a book by an author or illustrator you like. Use the labels on the baskets to help you find a book you want to read.

## Share

Following independent work time, gather children together in the meeting area to talk about how they found a book to read.

> Turn and talk to a partner about what book you chose today and what basket you found it in.

## Extend the Lesson (Optional)

After assessing children's understanding, you might decide to extend the learning.

▶ Continue to add to the chart as children identify other topics, authors, and illustrators in the classroom library.

▶ After teaching minilessons about genre, repeat this lesson with fiction and nonfiction books or types of fiction books (e.g., realistic fiction, fantasy).

▶ Let individuals or pairs of children make labels for baskets in the classroom library.

The classroom library is organized so you can make good book choices.

- Topic — animals, weather

- Author — Vera Williams

- Illustrator — Bob Graham

**Reading Minilesson Principle**
# Choose books that you will want to read.

## Using the Classroom Library for Independent Reading

### You Will Need

- three to four baskets of books
- a selection of four to five books from the classroom library
- chart paper and markers

### Academic Language / Important Vocabulary

- front cover
- cover illustration
- title
- author
- illustrator
- classroom library
- independent reading

## Goal

Learn how to choose a book for independent reading.

## Rationale

When you teach children ways to choose books, you help them become more independent and develop their interests and identities as readers. Thinking about the reasons they choose books helps children develop self-awareness and introspection.

## Assess Learning

Observe children when they choose books. Notice if there is evidence of new learning based on the goal of this minilesson.

- Can children identify what interests them about a particular book (title, topic, cover illustration)?
- Can children discuss ways to choose books?
- Can they explain why it is important to choose books that are interesting to them and that they want to read?
- Do they use vocabulary such as *front cover, cover illustration, title, author,* and *illustrator?*

## Minilesson

To help children think about the minilesson principle, engage them in a short demonstration of choosing books. Here is an example.

- Display three or four baskets of books from the classroom library. Ask three or four children to choose a book that they might like to read.
- While they are making their selections, suggest that the other children think about how they would choose a book. Once the children have chosen their books, ask them to share what they selected and how they made their choice.

  What made you choose that book? Why do you want to read it?

- Record children's responses on the chart.

  What are some other ways you can think of to choose books to read?

  How does the way the classroom library is organized help you choose books?

## Have a Try

Invite the children to talk about books they'd choose to read with a partner.

▸ Display the covers of four or five books from the classroom library.

> Turn and talk to a partner about which of these books you would choose and why.

▸ Ask a few pairs to share how they made their choices.

▸ Write responses on the chart.

## Summarize and Apply

Summarize the learning and remind children to think about how to choose books they want to read.

▸ Review the chart of ways to choose books.

> When you choose a book to read today, look at the chart to remind yourself of ways to find a book that you will want to read. When you're finished reading, be ready to share the reason you chose your book.

## Share

Following independent work time, gather children together in the meeting area to talk about choosing books to read.

> Give a thumbs-up if you enjoyed the book you chose. Turn and talk to a partner about why you chose the book.

## Extend the Lesson (Optional)

After assessing children's understanding, you might decide to extend the learning.

▸ As children discover more ways to choose books (e.g., teacher recommendations, book awards, series), add them to the chart.

▸ Regularly invite children to share why they chose particular books so that other children can benefit from the recommendations.

▸ **Drawing/Writing About Reading** If children are keeping a reader's notebook, have them write and draw about a book they enjoyed reading.

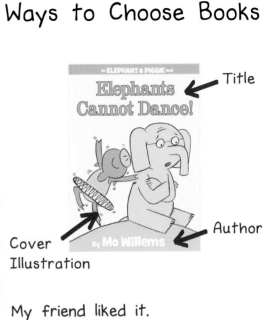

Ways to Choose Books

Title

Author

Cover
Illustration

My friend liked it.
I like funny books.

# RML4
## MGT.U2.RML4

### Reading Minilesson Principle
## Take good care of the books in the classroom library.

**Using the Classroom Library for Independent Reading**

### You Will Need

- several baskets of books
- a selection of books from the classroom library
- chart paper and markers

### Academic Language / Important Vocabulary

- classroom library
- independent reading
- pages

## Goal

Take care of the books in the classroom library.

## Rationale

When you teach children to handle books with care, you promote independence and a sense of responsibility in the classroom community. Developing a sense of responsibility will also encourage children to respect all classroom materials and supplies.

## Assess Learning

Observe children when they read books. Notice if there is evidence of new learning based on the goal of this minilesson.

- ▶ Do children hold books with two hands and turn the pages carefully?
- ▶ Can children identify other ways to take good care of books?
- ▶ Can they explain why it is important to handle books properly?
- ▶ Do they use the terms *classroom library, independent reading,* and *pages*?

## Minilesson

To help children think about the minilesson principle, engage them in a short demonstration of how to take good care of books. Here is an example.

- ▶ While children watch, select a book from the classroom library or book basket.

    Here's a book that I would like to read. Watch what I do when I hold and read my book.

- ▶ Model holding the book with two hands and turning the pages carefully.

    What did you notice that I was doing?

    Why do you think it is important to hold books with two hands and turn the pages carefully?

    Now that I have read my book, watch what I do with it.

- ▶ Model returning the book to the same place you found it.

    What did you notice about what I did?

    When you're finished reading a book from our classroom library, put it back where you found it.

    How can you take good care of the books in our classroom library?

- ▶ Write responses on the chart.

## Have a Try

Invite the children to practice taking good care of books with a partner.

▶ Hand a book to each pair of children.

Take turns showing and telling each other how to hold the book and how to turn the pages. When you finish, one partner should bring the book to me.

## Summarize and Apply

Summarize the learning and remind the children to think about how to take care of books.

Why is it important to take good care of the books in our classroom library?

Let's review the ways to take good care of books on our chart.

## Share

Following independent work time, gather children together in the meeting area to talk about taking good care of books.

Who would like to show and tell how you took good care of your book during independent reading?

## Extend the Lesson (Optional)

After assessing children's understanding, you might decide to extend the learning.

▶ Notice and praise children who handle their books carefully during independent reading to reinforce the behavior.

▶ Work with small groups of children who need additional help learning how to handle books.

▶ Have children write or draw posters for taking good care of books. Display the posters in the classroom or school library.

## Taking Good Care of Books

- Be gentle.

- Keep the book clean.

- Hold the book with 2 hands.

- Turn the pages carefully.

## Assessment

After you have taught the minilessons in this umbrella, observe children as they choose and read books from the classroom library.

▶ What evidence do you have that they understand how to use the classroom library and participate in independent reading respectively and productively?

- Do they read silently or with a whisper voice during independent reading?

- Do they understand how to find books about certain topics or by particular authors in the classroom library?

- Can children choose books they enjoy and want to read?

- Do children handle books carefully and return them to the appropriate location when they have finished reading?

- Do they understand academic terms such as *classroom library*, *independent reading*, and *voice level*?

▶ What minilessons might you want to teach next to continue to build independence in reading?

- Do children show an interest in listening to the audio version of a book?

- Are they able to read with a partner?

Use your observations to determine the next umbrella you will teach. You may also consult Minilessons Across the Year (p. 51) for guidance.

## Minilessons in This Umbrella

| RML1 | Read a book on your own. |
| RML2 | Listen to a book in the listening center. |
| RML3 | Work on words in the word work center. |
| RML4 | Write and draw in the writing center. |
| RML5 | Read a book from your browsing box. |
| RML6 | Read and illustrate a poem in your poetry notebook. |
| RML7 | Read around the room using a pointer. |
| RML8 | Read and put together a story, song, or poem in the pocket chart. |
| RML9 | Read a book with a partner. |
| RML10 | Look at your list of what to do during reading time. |

Section 1: Management

## Before Teaching Umbrella 3 Minilessons

Teaching the minilessons in this umbrella will help children learn how to work on their own, which in addition to encouraging independence will also allow you to work with small groups or individuals without interruption. These minilessons reflect a variety of literacy activities that children can learn to do by going to the center indicated by a work board or list. The minilessons can be easily modified if you prefer to have children work at their tables rather than at centers.

Each time you introduce an activity, introduce the icon for the work board that represents the activity. When children are learning to follow the work board, place the same icon across the work board for all groups. Once children understand the routines for several activities, you can place a different icon for each group and, eventually, multiple icons for each group. Whether children go to centers or work at their tables, introduce the activities one at a time and make sure children understand the routines before introducing more activities (see pp. 27–34 for more information about work boards and literacy activities).

**Reading Minilesson Principle**
# Read a book on your own.

## You Will Need

- work board prepared with the independent reading icon for each group
- two children prepared to demonstrate reading from book boxes (bags)
- individual book boxes (bags)
- chart paper and markers
- To download the following online resources for this lesson, visit **resources.fountasandpinnell.com:** independent reading icon

## Academic Language / Important Vocabulary

- icon
- work board
- independent reading
- book box/book bag

## Goal

Learn procedures for independent reading, including the use of the classroom library or individual book boxes or bags.

## Rationale

Explicitly teaching routines for independent literacy activities gives children the confidence and ability to manage tasks on their own. Children need to learn the options for where to get their independent reading books. It could be from the classroom library. Or, some teachers store the children's independent reading books in clear sealable plastic bags, while others use magazine boxes. Teaching them to manage their time and materials independently frees you to work with other children individual or in small groups (see p. 64 for more information about book boxes and bags).

## Assess Learning

Observe children during independent reading time. Notice if there is evidence of new learning based on the goal of this minilesson.

- ▶ Do children quickly and quietly retrieve and return books?
- ▶ Do they read their books silently or very quietly?
- ▶ Do they use the terms *icon, work board, independent reading,* and *book box/book bag?*

## Minilesson

To help children think about the minilesson principle, engage them in a demonstration and discussion of independent reading. Here is an example.

> Sometimes I will need to work with a group or with one of you, and the rest of you will need to work on your own. Today we will talk about how you can find out what work you need to do.

- ▶ Hold up or point to the independent reading icon on the work board.

> This picture is called an icon. This icon tells you that it is time for independent reading. When you see it, remember that it means independent reading.

> During independent reading, you will choose a book to read from either the classroom library or your book box (bag). What do you remember about using the classroom library?

- ▶ Point out where children will get the books they are to read.

> Let's watch _____ and _____ read.

- ▶ Invite the two children, who have been prepared beforehand, to retrieve a book, pretend to read it silently, and then return the book.

> What did you notice about how they got their book?

> What were their voices like when they read?

How did they put their book away?

▶ Record responses on the chart paper.

When you read from the library or your book box (bag), remember to choose a book and read it from the front to the back. What should you do with your book when you have finished reading?

## Have a Try

Invite children to talk with a partner about about the independent reading routine.

▶ Point to the independent reading icon on the work board.

Turn and talk to a partner about what you are going to do when you see this icon. Talk about the two places you can find books to read in our classroom: the library or your book box (bag).

## Summarize and Apply

Summarize the learning and remind children what to do when they see the independent reading icon.

▶ Ask a volunteer to point to the independent reading icon on the work board.

What should you do when you see this picture? During independent reading, you can read and enjoy books from the classroom library or your book box (bag).

▶ Invite children to choose a book, and provide a short period for them to read.

Today you will practice following what the icon says to do.

## Share

Following independent work time, gather children together in the meeting area to review what to do for independent reading.

▶ Review each step on the chart and invite children to give a thumbs-up if they did it.

Why is it important to put your book in the same place you found it?

## Extend the Lesson (Optional)

After assessing children's understanding, you might decide to extend the learning.

▶ Have children create labels for their own book boxes (bags).

Independent Reading

Animals

1. Quietly carry your book to your spot.

2. Read silently or with a whisper voice.

3. Read the book from front to back.

4. Carefully put the book in the same place you found it.

Section 1: Management

**Reading Minilesson Principle**

# Listen to a book in the listening center.

## Engaging in Classroom Literacy Work

### You Will Need

- work board prepared with the listening center icon for each group
- three or four children prepared to demonstrate listening to a book in the listening center
- listening device(s) (e.g., tablet, computer)
- headphones
- audiobook(s) and corresponding book(s)
- chart paper and markers
- To download the following online resources for this lesson, visit **resources.fountasandpinnell.com:** listening center icon

### Academic Language / Important Vocabulary

- icon
- work board
- listening center
- audiobook
- volume
- signal

## Goal

Learn the work board icon and routines for the listening center.

## Rationale

Listening to audiobooks allows children to engage with higher-level books than they can read on their own and provides a model of fluent reading. Teaching children how to use the listening center equipment helps them develop independence and frees you to work with other children in small groups.

## Assess Learning

Observe children as they listen to books in the listening center. Notice if there is evidence of new learning based on the goal of this minilesson.

- ▶ Do children know where to find and use audiobook equipment in the classroom?
- ▶ When listening to audiobooks in small groups, do children work well together and share the equipment?
- ▶ Can they use terms such as *icon, work board, listening center, audiobook, volume,* and *signal*?

## Minilesson

To help children think about the minilesson principle, engage them in a demonstration and short discussion of the listening center. Here is an example.

- ▶ Point to the listening center icon on the work board.

  What do you think this picture means?

  A picture that stands for something is called an icon. When you see this picture, or icon, on the work board under your name, it means that you will be listening to books.

- ▶ Show children where to find audiobooks, whether it is a listening center or a place where the supplies are stored.

- ▶ Demonstrate how to use the listening device and how to plug in headphones (if applicable). Designate a specific volume level for children to use when listening to a book in a small group.

  When you are listening in a small group, set the volume to level _____ . Why do you think it is important to not put the volume higher than this?

  Sometimes everyone can hold a copy of the book, and sometimes you will need to share a book with your partner or partners. How should you hold your book and turn the pages when you're listening to a book?

▶ Invite the three or four children, who have been prepared beforehand, to model listening to a book.

> Let's listen to the first couple of pages of the story. Watch what your classmates do.

> What did you notice your classmates doing as they listened to the book?

▶ Record responses on the chart paper.

## Summarize and Apply

Summarize the learning and remind children what to do when they see the listening center icon.

▶ Point to the listening center icon on the work board.

> What did you learn about how to listen to books in our classroom? Look at the chart to remember.

> Today, the listening picture, or icon, is under all your names, which means everyone is going to practice listening to a book.

▶ If you have more than one listening device, assign individuals or partners to each device, while the others read books as usual until a device becomes available. Alternatively, play an audiobook for the class to listen to and follow along as you show the book.

## Share

Following independent work time, gather children together in the meeting area to talk about the listening center.

> Now that you have listened to an audiobook, turn and talk to a partner about what you thought of the experience.

> How is listening to an audiobook different from reading a book?

## Extend the Lesson (Optional)

After assessing children's understanding, you might decide to extend the learning.

▶ Practice listening to audiobooks as a whole class until children understand the routine and can work independently or in small groups.

▶ When children become more accustomed to working with audiobooks, you might have them record their own dramatic read-alouds of favorite books.

---

### How to Listen to Books

1. Get what you need.

2. Turn the listening device on.

3. Make sure the volume is set to the right level.

4. Turn the pages when it is time, or when you hear a signal.

5. Turn the listening device off.

6. Put everything away.

---

**Section 1: Management**

**Reading Minilesson Principle**
## Work on words in the word work center.

### Engaging in Classroom Literacy Work

#### You Will Need

▸ work board prepared with the word work center icon for each group

▸ picture sort Materials and Directions charts prepared ahead of time

▸ two to three children prepared to demonstrate working on words in the word work center

▸ picture sort materials (one set for each child)

▸ chart paper and markers

▸ To download the following online resources for this lesson, visit **resources.fountasandpinnell.com:** word work center icon

#### Academic Language / Important Vocabulary

▸ icon
▸ work board
▸ word work
▸ directions
▸ materials

### Goal

Learn to follow the routines and handle the supplies in the word work center.

### Rationale

Literacy activities in the word work center are an extension of your phonics lessons, providing hands-on practice, and should be updated often to support and reinforce recently learned phonics concepts. Establish the basic routines for children to work independently in the word work center or at their desks so only a brief introduction to the specific task will be required during the phonics lesson.

### Assess Learning

Observe children when they work in the word work center. Notice if there is evidence of new learning based on the goal of this minilesson.

▸ Do children understand how to find materials in the word work center?

▸ Are they able to follow the directions independently?

▸ Do they handle their materials properly and return them to the appropriate place?

## Minilesson

To help children think about the minilesson principle, engage them in a demonstration and short discussion of the word work center. Here is an example.

▸ Prepare a materials chart with these materials: picture card sheet, picture sort sheet, glue stick, scissors. Also, prepare a directions chart for the activity with these steps: Cut out the picture cards. Say the word shown in the picture out loud. Think about the beginning sound of the word. Glue the picture card in the correct column on the chart.

▸ Point to the word work center icon.

> What do you think this picture, or icon, means? This icon stands for the word work center. What do you think you will do in the word work center?

▸ Show children the word work center or where the word work materials are stored.

> What do you notice about the word work center?

> The materials in the word work center are neatly organized and labeled so you can find and return them easily. The word work center will always have two charts. One chart tells you what materials you need, and the other tells you how to do the activity.

> Today, the word work center activity is sorting pictures by the beginning sound. Look at the materials chart. What will you need for this activity?

> Let's read the directions for the activity.

▶ Invite the two or three children, who have been prepared, to demonstrate the activity.

> What did you notice _____ and _____ do as they did the activity?

▶ Record responses on the chart paper.

## Summarize and Apply

Summarize the learning and remind children what to do when they see the word work icon.

> What will you do when you see the word work center icon under your name? Remember to look at the chart to remember.

▶ Give all children the opportunity to do the picture sort activity. Remind them to check the Directions chart if they forget what to do.

## Share

Following independent work time, gather children together in the meeting area to talk about the word work center.

> Give a thumbs-up if you completed your picture sort sheet.

> Turn and talk to a partner about what you will remember to do the next time you go to the word work center.

## Extend the Lesson (Optional)

After assessing children's understanding, you might decide to extend the learning.

▶ As children become accustomed to working in the word work center, teach the class routines for new word work activities (e.g., games such as lotto and bingo).

▶ Differentiate the word work activities based on the needs of the children.

---

Word Work Center

1. Read the materials chart.

2. Gather the materials.

3. Read the directions chart.

4. Do the activity.

5. Return the materials to the same place you got them.

---

**Section 1: Management**

# RML4
## MGT.U3.RML4

# Write and draw in the writing center.

### Engaging in Classroom Literacy Work

#### You Will Need

- work board prepared with the writing center icon for each group
- writing center materials (e.g., paper, stapler, markers, folders)
- directions for writing prompt
- chart paper and markers
- To download the following online resources for this lesson, visit **resources.fountasandpinnell.com:** writing center icon

#### Academic Language / Important Vocabulary

- icon
- work board
- writing center
- directions
- materials
- folder
- writing prompt

## Goal

Learn how to handle materials and follow routines in the writing center.

## Rationale

Writing center activities are separate from the writing children do in writers' workshop and might include creating cards, thank-you notes, stories, alphabet books, how-to books, or all-about books. When you explicitly teach children how to choose materials, write, and put materials away, you build their ability and confidence to work independently.

## Assess Learning

Observe children when they work in the writing center. Notice if there is evidence of new learning based on the goal of this minilesson.

- ▶ Do children use the writing center materials appropriately?
- ▶ Do children stay on task during writing center time?
- ▶ Do they understand the vocabulary related to the writing center?

## Minilesson

To help children think about the minilesson principle, engage them in a short discussion of the writing center. Here is an example.

- ▶ Point to the writing center icon on the work board.

    What do you think you will do when you see this icon?

    This icon stands for the writing center.

- ▶ Point to the materials in the writing center.

    What do you see in the writing center?

    What do you notice about how the materials are arranged? The materials are organized and labeled to help you find what you need. You will also need your writing folder.

- ▶ Use prompts such as the following to help children learn about the writing center.

    - *Why do you think there is a stapler in the writing center? You can use the stapler to add more pages to your book.*

    - *What do you think the markers are for? You can use the markers to add illustrations to your book.*

    - *How can you take good care of the materials in the writing center?*

    - *What do you think you do when you finish working in the writing center?*

▶ If you plan to provide a list of types of writing or of writing prompts, show children where to find these. Also, show children where to put their work in their writing folders.

## Summarize and Apply

Summarize the learning and remind children what to do when they see the writing center icon.

> Let's make a chart so you will remember what to do when you see the writing center icon.

▶ Show and read the directions sheet for a writing center activity (e.g., make a card for your family). Instruct children to retrieve writing supplies from the writing center and return to their tables to do the activity.

## Share

Following independent work time, gather children together in the meeting area to talk about using the writing center.

> Now that you have spent time on a writing center activity, is there anything else you want to add to the chart to make time at the writing center better?

## Extend the Lesson (Optional)

After assessing children's understanding, you might decide to extend the learning.

▶ Use interactive or shared writing to create a list of different kinds of writing children can choose from during writing time (e.g., cards, poems, letters, alphabet books).

▶ Consider integrating social studies or science content into writing center activities.

▶ **Drawing/Writing About Reading** Periodically offer writing center activities that give children opportunity to respond in writing to books read during interactive read-aloud.

**Using the Writing Center**

1. Read the directions for the writing activity.

2. Get writing materials from writing center.

3. Use the stapler to add pages to the book.

4. Make illustrations with markers.

5. Take good care of materials.

6. Put work in your folder.

7. Return materials.

My Writing Folder

**Reading Minilesson Principle**
# Read a book from your browsing box.

**Engaging in Classroom Literacy Work**

## You Will Need

- work board prepared with browsing box icon
- three children, who read at about the same instructional level, prepared to demonstrate using a browsing box
- browsing boxes (see pages 64–65)
- chart paper and markers
- To download the following online resources for this lesson, visit **resources.fountasandpinnell.com:** browsing box icon

## Academic Language / Important Vocabulary

- icon
- work board
- independent reading
- browsing box

## Goal

Learn the routine for reading books from a browsing box during independent reading.

## Rationale

A browsing box contains books children have read before or new texts you know will be accessible to a group of children. Teaching children how to use a browsing box provides them with an option for choosing books and reading independently. Reading new books and rereading familiar books support comprehension and fluency and build reading stamina.

## Assess Learning

Observe children when they read from browsing boxes. Notice if there is evidence of new learning based on the goal of this minilesson.

- Are children able to choose and read books from their browsing boxes?
- Do they return the books to the correct browsing boxes, placing them upright, and facing forward?
- Do they understand vocabulary related to the browsing box?

# Minilesson

To help children think about the minilesson principle, engage them in a demonstration and short discussion of browsing boxes. Here is an example.

- Point to the browsing box icon on the work board.

   This is the browsing box icon. When you see this icon under your name, what do you think you will do?

   Your browsing box has some books you have already read and some new books you may enjoy reading.

- Point out the location of the browsing boxes in the classroom. Invite three children, who have been prepared, to find their browsing box, choose a book, and start to read.

   Notice how they choose a book from the browsing box, and watch what they do next.

   What did you see your classmates do? What did they do with their books when they finished reading?

- Record responses on the chart paper.

   When you are finished reading your book, return it to the same box, upright, and facing forward. If there is still time, you may choose another book to read.

## Have a Try

Invite children to talk with a partner about the browsing box routine.

> Turn and talk to a partner about what you will do when you see the browsing box icon under your name on the work board.

## Summarize and Apply

Summarize the learning and remind children what to do when they see the browsing box icon.

> What did you learn to do when you see the browsing box icon under your name on the work board? Look at the chart to remember.

> For reading time today, choose a few books to read from your browsing box. If you finish your books before the time is up, you may choose more to read.

▶ Place browsing boxes around the room to avoid congestion.

# Browsing Boxes

1. Look for your browsing box.

2. Choose one or more books to read.

3. Return the book to the same browsing box.

4. Place it upright and facing forward.

5. If there is time, choose more books to read.

## Share

Following independent work time, gather children together in the meeting area to talk about browsing boxes.

> Turn and talk to a partner about the books you read from your browsing box and what you thought of them. Is there anything you would do differently next time you read from your browsing box?

## Extend the Lesson (Optional)

After assessing children's understanding, you might decide to extend the learning.

▶ Have children read books from their browsing boxes with a partner.

▶ **Drawing/Writing About Reading** Have children write or draw responses to books from their browsing boxes in a reader's notebook. They can also keep a log of the books they have read in a reader's notebook (see Section Four: Writing About Reading for minilessons on using a reader's notebook).

**Reading Minilesson Principle**
# Read and illustrate a poem in your poetry notebook.

Engaging in Classroom
Literacy Work

## You Will Need

- work board prepared with the poetry notebook icon
- enlarged version and a small version of a familiar poem
- enlarged version and small versions (for the class) of a second familiar poem
- poetry notebooks
- glue sticks and crayons
- chart paper and markers
- To download the following online resources for this lesson, visit **resources.fountasandpinnell.com:** poetry notebook icon

## Academic Language / Important Vocabulary

- icon
- work board
- poetry notebook
- poem
- illustration
- materials

## Goal

Learn the routine for using a poetry notebook.

## Rationale

Teaching children how to use a poetry notebook provides them with the opportunity to revisit and respond to familiar poems. This engagement with familiar poems supports comprehension, builds reading vocabulary, and promotes fluency.

## Assess Learning

Observe children when they use a poetry notebook. Notice if there is evidence of new learning based on the goal of this minilesson.

- Are children able to follow the instructions for using a poetry notebook?
- Do they complete the task and return the materials properly?
- Do they understand vocabulary related to the poetry notebook?

## Minilesson

To help children think about the minilesson principle, engage them in a demonstration and a short discussion of poetry notebook. Here is an example.

- Display an enlarged version of a poem children have read during shared reading.

  Let's reread this poem together. After we read a poem, like this, you can keep a small version in your poetry notebook to reread later.

- Show children where to find the poetry notebooks and the materials.

  You will find small copies of the poems we have shared in this bin. Watch how I put this poem in my poetry notebook.

- As you demonstrate how to use a poetry notebook, record the steps children notice on the chart paper.

- Demonstrate how to take a copy of the poem out of the bin and glue it in the notebook.

  What did you see me do?

- Demonstrate illustrating the poem.

  What did I do after I glued the poem in my poetry notebook?

  In your poetry notebook, you can make an illustration that shows how the poem makes you feel or think. After you finish drawing, read the poem to yourself first and then to a partner.

## Have a Try

Invite children to talk with a partner about using a poetry notebook.

▶ Read another familiar poem.

> Turn and talk to your partner about how you would put this in your poetry notebook. Tell what you would draw for an illustration.

## Summarize and Apply

Summarize the learning and remind children what to do when they see the poetry notebook icon.

> Now it is your time to use your poetry notebook. What will you do? Look at the chart to remember.

▶ Have work board groups retrieve the supplies they need and work at their tables.

## Share

Following independent work time, gather children together in the meeting area to talk about using a poetry notebook.

> Who would like to share the illustration you made for the poem in your poetry notebook?

> Is there anything you would do differently the next time you work in your poetry notebook?

## Extend the Lesson (Optional)

After assessing children's understanding, you might decide to extend the learning.

▶ Teach children how to compose poems in a poetry notebook.

▶ Have children highlight certain kinds of words in their poetry notebook poems (e.g., rhyming words, words that begin with the same consonant cluster).

▶ As students become comfortable with a routine, add a second routine for children to do during independent work time.

### How to Use a Poetry Notebook

1. Get your materials.

2. Take a small copy of the poem from the bin.

3. Glue the poem in your notebook.

4. Draw a picture for the poem.

5. Read the poem to yourself.

6. Read the poem to a partner.

7. Put away your materials.

**Section 1: Management**

**Reading Minilesson Principle**
# Read around the room using a pointer.

## Engaging in Classroom Literacy Work

### You Will Need

- work board prepared with the read around the room icon
- two children prepared to demonstrate reading around the room
- bins for long and short pointers
- charts to read on the walls
- chart paper and markers
- To download the following online resources for this lesson, visit **resources.fountasandpinnell.com:** read around the room icon

### Academic Language / Important Vocabulary

- icon
- work board
- pointer

## Goal

Learn the routine for reading around the room with a pointer.

## Rationale

When children read texts posted around the classroom, such as poems, anchor charts, and name charts, they practice and reinforce early reading behaviors. These reading behaviors include voice-print matching, noticing new things about the way print works, and developing an increased awareness of classroom print resources.

## Assess Learning

Observe children when they read around the room with a pointer. Notice if there is evidence of new learning based on the goal of this minilesson.

- Do children handle pointers appropriately?
- Do they use the pointers to point under the words?
- Do children use an appropriate voice level when reading around the room?
- Do children take turns reading around the room with their partner?
- Can they use vocabulary such as *icon, work board,* and *pointer*?

## Minilesson

To help children think about the minilesson principle, engage them in a demonstration of reading around the room with a pointer. Here is an example.

- Guide children to notice the different kinds of print around the room.

    Look at the walls around our classroom. What do you notice on the walls?

- Have children watch as you use a pointer to read around the room. Place the pointer under each word and read a variety of print out loud in a soft voice.

    What did you notice about what I did?

    What voice level did I use when I read around the room?

    Why is that a good voice level for this activity?

- Point to the read around the room icon on the work board.

    When you see this icon, you will use a pointer to read all the words around the classroom.

- Show children where the pointers are kept.

    When do you think you should use a long pointer?

    When should you use a short pointer?

## Have a Try

Invite children to watch a demonstration on reading around the room.

▶ Invite the prepared pair of children to demonstrate. Direct them to take turns reading and watching their partner read around the room.

> What did you notice about what _____ and _____ did?

> How should you handle the pointers?

## Summarize and Apply

Summarize the learning and remind children what to do when they see the read around the room icon.

> Let's make a chart so that you will remember what to do when you see the icon for reading around the room.

> Now, you will have time to practice reading around the room with a partner. Take turns reading quietly. If you forget what to do, read the chart we made together.

### Read Around the Room

- Get a pointer.
- Read the wall to your partner.
- Your partner reads the wall to you.
- Point under the words.
- Read in a soft voice.
- Put the pointer in the bin.

## Share

Following independent work time, gather children together in the meeting area to talk about reading around the room with a pointer.

> Give a thumbs-up if you followed the directions on the chart.

> What will you do the next time to make your reading around the room even better?

## Extend the Lesson (Optional)

After assessing children's understanding, you might decide to extend the learning.

▶ Once children are comfortable with the routine of reading around the room, include it with other activities on the work board.

▶ Have children go on a reading around the room scavenger hunt. They carry a clipboard and look for and record specific types of words found on the walls (e.g., two words that begin with the same consonant cluster, a word that ends with *-ing*, two words that rhyme).

Section 1: Management

**Reading Minilesson Principle**

## Read and put together a story, song, or poem in the pocket chart.

**Engaging in Classroom Literacy Work**

### You Will Need

- work board prepared with the pocket chart icon
- an enlarged version of a familiar poem or chart
- pocket chart with the same poem written on sentence strips
- the enlarged poem, pocket chart, and sentence strips for each group
- chart paper
- directions for using the pocket chart written on strips of colored paper
- glue stick or tape
- To download the following online resources for this lesson, visit **resources.fountasandpinnell.com:** pocket chart icon

### Academic Language / Important Vocabulary

- icon
- work board
- pocket chart
- sentence strips
- poem
- story
- song

### Goal

Learn how to use a pocket chart to rebuild and reread stories, songs, and poems.

### Rationale

When children rebuild a familiar story, poem, or song, they must look carefully at the text and think about how it fits together. Early literacy concepts are reinforced as children search for and use different sources of information, such as meaning, syntax, and visual information to reassemble the text.

### Assess Learning

Observe children when they use pocket charts to rebuild a story, poem, or song. Notice if there is evidence of new learning based on the goal of this minilesson.

- Do children know what to do when they see the pocket chart icon?
- Do they follow the directions on the chart?
- How well do the children work together as partners or in small groups?
- Do they understand vocabulary related to the pocket chart?

## Minilesson

To help children think about the minilesson principle, engage them in a demonstration of using a pocket chart and sentence strips to rebuild a poem. Here is an example.

- Display an enlarged version of a familiar poem. Read it aloud. Then, show children the same poem made with sentence strips in a pocket chart.

  **What do you notice about this poem?**

- Have children watch as you demonstrate how to use a pocket chart. Read the poem in the pocket chart. Take the sentence strips out and mix them up. Read each sentence strip. Pick up the first sentence strip of the poem and place it in the first pocket of the chart. Read aloud the sentence, checking it with the original poem.

  **What did you see me do?**

- Invite a different child to put each sentence into the chart until the poem is complete.

  **Who would like to find the next sentence in the poem and place it in the pocket chart?**

  **What do you think you should do once all the sentence strips are back in the pocket chart?**

  **How can you check that you placed them in the correct order?**

▸ Show the pocket chart icon on the work board.

> When you see this icon, it is your job to read a poem, story, or song in a pocket chart. You will work with a partner or small group.

## Have a Try

Invite children to watch how to use a pocket chart.

▸ Have a pair of children model the process of using a pocket chart while the rest of the class watches.

## Summarize and Apply

Summarize the learning and remind children what to do when they see the pocket chart icon.

> I have the directions for using a pocket chart on strips of paper. Let's see if you can put them in order. The chart will help you remember how to use the pocket chart.

> Now you will have time to use a pocket chart with your group. Each group will have a poem and pocket chart. Take turns choosing a sentence strip and placing it in the pocket chart.

▸ If you have only one pocket chart, have groups lay the sentence strips out on a table instead of placing them in a pocket chart.

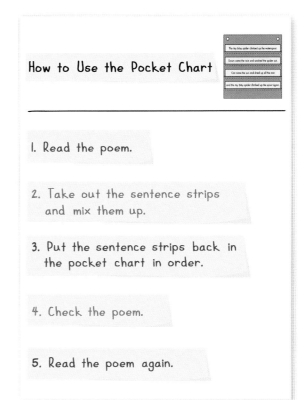

How to Use the Pocket Chart

1. Read the poem.

2. Take out the sentence strips and mix them up.

3. Put the sentence strips back in the pocket chart in order.

4. Check the poem.

5. Read the poem again.

## Share

Following independent work time, gather children together in the meeting area in their groups to talk about using the pocket chart.

> Turn and talk with your group about what you all did well when you used your pocket chart. Then talk about something that you would do differently the next time.

▸ Invite a few groups to share.

## Extend the Lesson (Optional)

After assessing children's understanding, you might decide to extend the learning.

▸ Instead of using sentence strips, use single-word cards to construct a familiar poem, story, or song. Omit words and have children choose the missing words from a word bank (e.g., "Humpty Dumpty sat on a _____ , Humpty Dumpty had a great _____.").

**Reading Minilesson Principle**
# Read a book with a partner.

**Engaging in Classroom Literacy Work**

## You Will Need

▶ work board prepared with the partner reading icon

▶ two children prepared to demonstrate partner reading

▶ chart paper and markers

▶ To download the following online resources for this lesson, visit **resources.fountasandpinnell.com:** partner reading icon

## Academic Language / Important Vocabulary

▶ icon

▶ work board

▶ partner reading

### Goal

Learn the icon and routine for partner reading.

### Rationale

Partner reading fosters good reading habits and collaborative learning. It adds to the overall enjoyment of reading and builds confidence in readers. Learning the routine for partner reading enables children to work and problem solve on their own and frees you to work with small groups or individual children.

### Assess Learning

Observe children when they read with a partner. Notice if there is evidence of new learning based on the goal of this minilesson.

▶ Do children work well with their partners?

▶ Can children self-evaluate their reading behaviors?

▶ Do they understand the terms *icon, work board,* and *partner reading*?

## Minilesson

To help children think about the minilesson principle, engage them in a demonstration and short discussion of partner reading. Here is an example.

▶ Point to the partner reading icon on the work board.

This icon has two books. What might that mean?

This is the partner reading icon. When you see it, you know you will be reading with a partner.

▶ Have the two children prepared to model partner reading each choose one book from their browsing box and sit together in the middle of the meeting area.

▶ Record responses on the chart paper as the children learn the routine for partner reading.

What do you notice about how _____ and _____ are sitting?

When you are reading with a partner, sit close to each other, elbow to elbow, and with your legs crisscrossed.

▶ Ask the two children to decide who is going to read first.

How should _____ hold her book, so _____ can see it?

▶ Invite the first child to start reading. After a few pages, give a signal to stop.

What did you notice about the voice level _____ used when she was reading?

Why is it a good idea to use a quiet voice when you are partner reading?

What did you notice _____ doing while his partner read?

When your partner is reading to you, listen carefully, look at the pictures, and follow along with the words in the book.

What do you think the partners should do after the first person has finished reading? When one partner has finished reading, it is the other partner's turn to read. Keep taking turns reading until the time is up.

## Summarize and Apply

Summarize the learning and remind children what to do when they see the partner reading icon.

▶ Point to the icon for partner reading on the work board.

This icon stands for partner reading. What do you do when you see this icon? Look at the chart to remember.

Now everyone will have a chance to read with a partner.

▶ Send pairs of children to their browsing boxes to choose books and start reading.

## Share

Following independent work time, gather children together in the meeting area to talk about partner reading.

Now that you have read with a partner, turn and talk to your partner about what you did well as you and your partner read together.

Now, turn and talk about something you will do differently next time.

▶ Invite a few pairs to share.

## Extend the Lesson (Optional)

After assessing children's understanding, you might decide to extend the learning.

▶ Teach variations of partner reading. For example, partners can take turns reading each page, they can each read the part for a character, or they can ask each other questions.

▶ Teach children how to talk about books with their partners. Use shared writing to make a list of suggested language (e.g., I'm wondering . . . ; This part reminds me of . . . ; I'm thinking . . . ; I'm noticing . . . ; I can't believe . . . ; I think the character . . .).

▶ **Drawing/Writing About Reading** Have children work with a partner to create a written or drawn response to a shared book.

---

**Partner Reading**

1. Sit next to your partner.

2. Hold the book in the middle so you can both see it.

3. Read the book to your partner in a quiet voice.

4. Take turns reading your book.

5. Put your books away.

# RML10

## MGT.U3.RML10

### Reading Minilesson Principle
## Look at your list of what to do during reading time.

## Engaging in Classroom Literacy Work

### You Will Need

- icons for two activities you have prepared
- work board prepared with two icons under each group
- directions and materials for the activities at the two work centers
- prepare a chart paper to mimic a work board or prepare labels to affix to your work board
- markers
- To download the following online resources for this lesson, visit **resources.fountasandpinnell.com:** work board icons

### Academic Language / Important Vocabulary

- icon
- work board
- center

## Goal

Learn to follow a work board to complete more than one independent literacy activity.

## Rationale

Teaching children how to use the work board (or a simple list) allows them to manage their learning independently while you meet with small groups. Knowing how to move from one activity to another without being signaled helps children learn how to self-regulate and determine when a task is complete.

## Assess Learning

Observe children when they use the work board to complete literacy activities. Notice if there is evidence of new learning based on the goal of this minilesson.

- Are children able to follow the order of activities on the work board?
- Do children work independently, stay on task, and know when to move on?
- Do they use the terms *icon, work board,* and *center*?

## Minilesson

To help children think about the minilesson principle, engage them in a short discussion of using the work board during literacy activities. Here is an example.

- Display the work board.

  What do you think you should do first when you look at the work board?

  The work board has everyone's name on it. The first thing to do is find your name.

- Record responses on the chart paper or add the label to your work board.

  Look at the two icons under your group's names. Why are there two?

  They tell you the two activities you will do during reading time.

- Invite the children to identify each icon, summarize its meaning, and point to the center or materials.

- Point to the first group listed on the work board.

  Raise your hand if you are in this group. Where will you go first?

- Repeat the questions for each group.

  How will you know when you are finished with an activity?

  What will you do before you start the next activity?

- Add labels to a sketch of a work board to summarize what children will do first, next, and last.

## Have a Try

Invite children to practice following the work board routine.

> Let's practice moving from center to center. Find your name on the work board and walk quietly to your first center. When you get there, talk quietly with your group about what you will do at the center.

> Now pretend you are finished at your first center, and you have cleaned up. What do you do next?

▶ Invite children to move to their next center. When children have demonstrated that they know how to rotate through the centers, invite them back to the meeting area.

## Summarize and Apply

Summarize the learning and remind children to read the work board during reading time.

▶ Review the chart before beginning the activity.

> Now you are going to work in centers during reading time. Use the work board and the chart we made to help you know what to do.

## Share

Following independent work time, gather children together in the meeting area to talk about using the work board.

> Now that you have used the work board to know what to do, what went well for you? What would you do differently the next time?

## Extend the Lesson (Optional)

After assessing children's understanding, you might decide to extend the learning.

▶ As children become more comfortable with centers and using the work board, continue to add new centers to the classroom and corresponding icons to the work board.

▶ Once you start guided reading groups or other small-group teaching, explain to the children how they will leave a center and return to it.

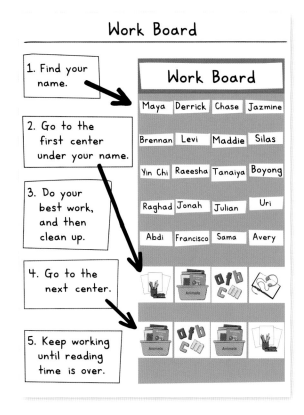

Section 1: Management

## Assessment

After you have taught the minilessons in this umbrella, observe children as they participate in independent literacy work activities.

▶ What evidence do you have that children understand how to work independently using the work board?

- How are children following the directions for each new activity?
- Do children use supplies appropriately and put them back where they belong?
- Do children understand how to work productively with partners and in small groups?
- Are children using appropriate voice levels for each activity?
- Do children stay focused at each center and move through the centers at an appropriate pace?
- How are they self-assessing whether a task is complete?
- How well can children problem solve independently?
- Do they use vocabulary such as *icon*, *center*, and work *board*?

▶ What minilesson might you teach to maintain and grow independent work habits?

- Do children know how to locate books to read in the classroom library?
- Can they transition from one activity to another quickly and quietly?

Use your observations to determine the next umbrella you will teach. You may also consult Minilessons Across the Year (p. 51) for guidance.

# Section 2 | Literary Analysis

Literary analysis minilessons support children in a growing awareness of the elements of literature and the writer's and illustrator's craft. They help children learn how to think analytically about texts and to identify the characteristics of fiction and nonfiction genres. The books that you read during interactive read-aloud and shared reading can serve as mentor texts when applying the principles of literary analysis.

## Minilessons in This Umbrella

**RML1**  The title tells what the book is about.

**RML2**  The author wrote the book. The illustrator created the pictures.

**RML3**  Think about the books you read and share your thinking with others.

**RML4**  Turn and talk to share your thinking.

**RML5**  When you read, mark places you want to talk about.

**RML6**  Read the book again to enjoy it and learn more.

## Before Teaching Umbrella 1 Minilessons

Many first graders have a rich knowledge of books; understand academic language, such as *author*, *illustrator*, and *title*; and have had experience talking about books. Some understand interactive read-aloud as a social experience and can use routines for listening and interacting. If that is the case for your entire group, you may not need these minilessons. For children who have not had enough experience to understand these concepts fully nor use academic language, this umbrella will be helpful.

To prepare for this umbrella, read and discuss picture books with simple plots that reflect the experiences of first graders. Use the following books from the *Fountas & Pinnell Classroom™ Interactive Read-Aloud Collection* text sets or choose books that your first graders can relate to from your classroom library.

**Learning and Playing Together: School**

*First Day Jitters* by Julie Danneberg

*Elizabeti's School* by Stephanie Stuve-Bodeen

*Jamaica's Blue Marker* by Juanita Havill

**The Importance of Friendship**

*The Magic Rabbit* by Annette LeBlanc Cate

**Taking Care of Each Other: Family**

*A Birthday Basket for Tía* by Pat Mora

*Papá and Me* by Arthur Dorros

*The Relatives Came* by Cynthia Rylant

**Having Fun with Language: Rhyming Texts**

*The Day the Goose Got Loose* by Reeve Lindbergh

As you read aloud and enjoy these texts together, help children

• think about the title and predict what the book is about, and

• provide evidence for thinking.

**School**

**Friendship**

**Family**

**Rhyming Texts**

**Reading Minilesson Principle**
## The title tells what the book is about.

### You Will Need

- two or three books whose titles clearly indicate the book's content, such as the following:
  - *Elizabeti's School*, by Stephanie Stuve-Bodeen, from Text Set: School
  - *A Birthday Basket for Tía* by Pat Mora, from Text Set: Family
  - *Papá and Me* by Arthur Dorros, from Text Set: Family
- chart paper and markers

### Academic Language / Important Vocabulary

- title
- front cover
- title page

### Continuum Connection

- Notice a book's title and its author on the cover and title page (p. 36)

### Goal

Locate the title on the front cover and the title page and use it to predict what the book will be about.

### Rationale

Children begin constructing their understanding of a book when they read the title on the front cover. When you teach children to think about the title before reading the book, you support their comprehension and provide them ways to select books independently.

### Assess Learning

Observe children when they talk about the title of a book. Notice if there is evidence of new learning based on the goal of this minilesson.

- ▶ Can they identify the title on the front cover and the title page?
- ▶ Can they say how the title helped them know what the book is about?
- ▶ Do children use the terms *title, title page,* and *front cover* in conversation?

## Minilesson

To help children think about the minilesson principle, engage them in a short discussion about book titles. Here is an example.

- ▶ Show the front cover of *Elizabeti's School*.

    Can someone point to the title on the front cover of this book?

    Is there another place in the book where you might find the title?

    You can also find the title on the title page.

- ▶ Show children the title page.

    Let's talk about what this story was about and how the title helped you know what the book was going to be about.

- ▶ Record responses on the chart.
- ▶ Show the front cover of *A Birthday Basket for Tía*.

    Does anyone remember what the title of this book is?

    The title of this book is *A Birthday Basket for Tía*.

    Who would like to show where to find the title page?

    What happened in this story?

- ▶ Record responses on the chart.

    How did the title help you get ready to read the book?

## Have a Try

Invite the children to identify and talk about the title of *Papá and Me*.

▸ Show the cover of *Papá and Me*.

Where is the title of this book? What is it?

Turn and talk to a partner about how the title helps you know what the story might be about.

▸ Ask a few partners to share and record responses on the chart.

## Summarize and Apply

Summarize the learning and remind children to think about the title of the book before they read.

Why is it a good idea to think about the title before you read a book?

Sometimes, the title tells what the book will be about.

▸ Write the principle at the top of the chart.

When you read today, notice the title on the front cover and title page. Use it to think what the book might be about.

## Share

Following independent work time, gather children together in the meeting area to talk about the title of a book.

Give a thumbs-up if you found the title on the front cover. On the title page.

Show your partner the title of the book. Turn and talk to your partner about how the title helped you know what the book is about.

## Extend the Lesson (Optional)

After assessing children's understanding, you might decide to extend the learning.

▸ During interactive read-aloud, shared reading, and guided reading, have children think about the title before they read. Point out that sometimes the meaning of the title isn't obvious until the end of the book.

▸ **Drawing/Writing About Reading** Show children how to record the books they read in a reader's notebook. Consider introducing the Books I Read section of *Reader's Notebook: Primary* (Fountas and Pinnell 2014). See Section Four: Writing About Reading for minilessons on using a reader's notebook.

---

### The title tells what the book is about.

| Title | What the Book Is About |
|---|---|
|  | • Elizabeti goes to school for the first time. |
|  | • The niece puts presents in a basket for Tía. |
|  | • The boy and his dad like to do things together. |

**Reading Minilesson Principle**

# The author wrote the book. The illustrator created the pictures.

## Thinking and Talking About Books

### You Will Need

- one or two familiar texts by an author/illustrator and one or two texts with different author and illustrator, such as the following:
  - *The Magic Rabbit* by Annette LeBlanc Cate, from Text Set: Friendship
  - *First Day Jitters* by Julie Danneberg, from Text Set: School
  - *The Day the Goose Got Loose* by Reeve Lindbergh, from Text Set: Rhyming Texts
- chart paper with three columns, labeled *Book*, *Author*, and *Illustrator*
- markers
- highlighter tape (optional)

### Academic Language / Important Vocabulary

- front cover
- author
- writer
- illustrator
- create

### Continuum Connection

- Understand that an illustrator created the pictures in the book (p. 36)
- Notice a book's title and its author and illustrator on the cover and title page (p. 36)

### Goal

Identify the author and illustrator of a book and understand what they do.

### Rationale

Children need to be able to identify key information on a book and use academic language to talk with each other about books. As children begin to self-select books, they are often drawn to favorite authors and illustrators. When they recognize favorite authors and illustrators, it helps them choose books they enjoy.

### Assess Learning

Observe children when they they talk about the author and illustrator of a book. Notice if there is evidence of new learning based on the goal of this minilesson.

- ▶ Are children able to identify the author and illustrator?
- ▶ Are children able to notice words that tell them who the author and illustrator are?
- ▶ Do they use the terms *author* and *illustrator* correctly?

## Minilesson

To help children think about the minilesson principle, engage them in a short discussion of identifying a book's author and illustrator and what they do. Here is an example.

- ▶ Show the front cover of *The Magic Rabbit*.

  What other information do you notice on the cover besides the title?

  You noticed the name of the author. What does the word *author* mean?

  This book has pictures, too. What do you call the person who drew the pictures?

  The person who drew the pictures is the illustrator. If you see only one name on a book that has illustrations, what do you think that means?

  Because Annette LeBlanc Cate wrote the words and drew the pictures, I'll write her name under *author* and *illustrator*.

- ▶ Record Annette LeBlanc Cate on the chart under *author* and *illustrator*.

  Let's look at *First Day Jitters*. This book has two names. It says Julie Danneberg, Illustrated by Judy Love. Who is the author?

  Who is the illustrator?

- ▶ Record responses on the chart.

  How did you know who wrote the book and who drew the pictures?

- ▶ Invite children to use highlighter tape over the words *illustrated by* on the book and the chart.

## Have a Try

Invite the children to work with a partner to identify a book's author and illustrator.

▶ Show and read the front cover of *The Day the Goose Got Loose*.

> Who are the author and illustrator of this book? Turn and talk about how you know who wrote the words and who made the pictures.

▶ Invite a child to use highlighter tape on the words *by* and *pictures by* on the book. Add to the chart.

## Summarize and Apply

Summarize the learning and remind children to identify the author and illustrator before they read.

> How does the chart help you know who wrote a book and who drew the illustrations? Sometimes one person writes the words, and another creates the pictures, and sometimes the same person does both.

> When you read today, notice the name of the author and illustrator of the book. Bring the book when we meet after independent reading time.

| | The author wrote the book. The illustrator created the pictures. | |
|---|---|---|
| **Book** | **Author** | **Illustrator** |
| The Magic Rabbit | Annette LeBlanc Cate | Annette LeBlanc Cate |
| First Day Jitters | Julie Danneberg | illustrated by Judy Love |
| the day the goose got loose | by Reeve Lindbergh | pictures by Steven Kellogg |

## Share

Following independent work time, gather children together in the meeting area to talk about a book's author and illustrator.

> Turn to a partner and show the name of the author and illustrator of the book you read. Point to the words that helped you know who the author and illustrator are. Did anyone find other words that tell who the author and illustrator are?

## Extend the Lesson (Optional)

After assessing children's understanding, you might decide to extend the learning.

▶ Continue noticing the author and illustrator during interactive read-aloud and shared reading. As you encounter other ways the author and illustrator are introduced on the front cover, add to the chart.

▶ **Drawing/Writing About Reading** Teach children to record the author's name in a reader's notebook. See Section Four: Writing About Reading for minilessons on using a reader's notebook.

**Reading Minilesson Principle**
# Think about the books you read and share your thinking with others.

## Thinking and Talking About Books

### You Will Need

- two or three favorite familiar texts, such as the following:
  - *The Magic Rabbit* by Annette LeBlanc Cate, from Text Set: Friendship
  - *The Relatives Came* by Cynthia Rylant, from Text Set: Family
  - *The Day the Goose Got Loose* by Reeve Lindbergh, from Text Set: Rhyming Texts
- chart paper and markers
- sticky notes

### Academic Language / Important Vocabulary

- opinion
- thinking

### Continuum Connection

- Give reasons (either text-based or from personal experience) to support thinking (p. 34)
- Express opinions about a text (e.g., interesting, funny, exciting) and support with evidence (p. 34)
- Articulate why they like a text (p. 34)

## Goal

Express one's thinking about a text and support opinions with evidence from the text and/or from personal experience.

## Rationale

Children at this age are learning that reading is thinking and they can explain their thinking by giving examples from the book. As they share their thinking about books, they learn that other people can agree or disagree. They develop their identities as readers as they articulate their thoughts and deepen their understanding and appreciation of texts.

## Assess Learning

Observe children when they they talk about their thinking about a book. Notice if there is evidence of new learning based on the goal of this minilesson.

- ▶ Are children able to talk about a part of a story they thought was interesting?
- ▶ Are children thinking in different ways about a book?
- ▶ Do they understand the terms *opinion* and *thinking*?

## Minilesson

To help children think about the minilesson principle, engage them in a discussion of talking about their thinking about a book. Here is an example.

▶ Show the cover of *The Magic Rabbit*. Refresh the children's memory of the story.

> The magician and rabbit were best friends that got separated, and then the rabbit found his way back home. Turn and talk to a partner about a part of the story you thought was interesting. Tell your partner why you thought the part was interesting.

▶ Invite partners to share their thinking. As children share, record on the chart paper the different ways they are thinking about books (e.g., thinking about characters, the problem, interesting illustrations, funny parts).

> You are thinking a lot of things about this book. When you share your thinking, you are sharing your opinion and what the story meant to you.

▶ Show the cover of *The Relatives Came*.

> Remember how the relatives crowded together for a long visit? Who would like to share an interesting or funny part of this book?

▶ Invite a few children to share the part they want to talk about and ask to tell why they think the part is interesting or what it means. Record responses on the chart and then summarize the thinking the children shared.

## Have a Try

Invite the children to share their thinking about *The Day the Goose Got Loose* with a partner.

▸ Show the cover of *The Day the Goose Got Loose*. Quickly go through the book to remind the children of the story.

> Remember the trouble the goose caused on the farm? Turn and talk to a partner about what you are thinking about this story.

▸ Ask a few children to share with the group and add new ideas to the chart.

## Summarize and Apply

Summarize the learning and remind children to think about what they want to talk about as they read a book.

> What are some things you can think about while reading? Look at the chart to remember.

▸ Write the principle at the top of the chart.

> When you read today, think about the book. Mark a part with a sticky note you want to talk about. Be ready to share your thinking when we come back together.

## Share

Following independent work time, gather children together in the meeting area to share their thinking about a book.

> Turn and talk to a partner to share your thinking about the book you read.

## Extend the Lesson (Optional)

After assessing children's understanding, you might decide to extend the learning.

▸ During interactive read-aloud and shared reading, ask children to share their thinking about a book. Be sure they ground their thinking in the text.

▸ **Drawing/Writing About Reading** Use interactive writing to record children's thinking about a book you have read aloud to them. For example, write about an interesting part of the book and why it is interesting.

Think about the books you read and share your thinking with others.

You might think and talk about:

How characters remind you of other characters

The problem

Where the story takes place

Illustrations

Interesting or funny parts

The ending

This book is funny because...

## RML 4
### LA.U1.RML4

**Reading Minilesson Principle**
# Turn and talk to share your thinking.

## Thinking and Talking About Books

### You Will Need

- a child prepared to demonstrate turn and talk
- two favorite, familiar texts, such as the following:
  - *Elizabeti's School* by Stephanie Stuve-Bodeen, from Text Set: School
  - *Papá and Me* by Arthur Dorros, from Text Set: Family
- chart paper and markers

### Academic Language / Important Vocabulary

- turn and talk
- listen
- signal
- voice level
- eye contact

### Continuum Connection

- Look at the speaker when being spoken to (p. 332)
- Engage actively in conversational routines: e.g., turn and talk (p. 332)

## Goal

Develop guidelines for turn and talk based on experiences talking about books.

## Rationale

Turn and talk is a routine that provides all children an opportunity to express their thinking verbally and engage in conversation with others. It helps children develop thinking and listening skills. Establishing clear guidelines for the routine gives every child numerous opportunities to share.

## Assess Learning

Observe children when they turn and share their thinking about books. Notice if there is evidence of new learning based on the goal of this minilesson.

- Do children actively listen to one another when they turn and talk?
- Do they take turns, make eye contact, and use body language that shows they are listening?
- Are they able to monitor voice level?
- Do they understand the terms *turn and talk, listen, signal, voice level,* and *eye contact*?

## Minilesson

To help children think about the minilesson principle, engage them in a demonstration and a discussion of the turn and talk routine. Here is an example.

- Ask the prepared child to talk with you about an interesting part in *Elizabeti's School*.

  _____ is my partner, and we are going to turn and talk about interesting parts in *Elizabeti's School*. While we turn and talk, notice what we are doing with our bodies and voices.

- Hold a brief conversational about *Elizabeti's School* with your partner.

  What did you notice about the way we turned and talked with each other?

- Record children's responses on the chart paper to create guidelines for turn and talk.

  What did we do with our eyes (ears, bodies, voices)?

  How does this help you turn and talk?

- Record responses on the chart.

  When you read books, you often turn and talk to a partner to share your thinking. Today you are going to think about what helps you to do your best thinking and listening when you turn and talk.

## Have a Try

Invite the children to discuss how they will know it is time to stop sharing.

▶ Involve children in a discussion of how they will know that it is time to stop sharing and turn their attention back to you.

## Summarize and Apply

Summarize the learning and remind children to think about what they want to talk about with a partner as they read.

▶ Review the chart.

> What do you need to do when you turn and talk with a partner? Look at the chart to help you remember.

▶ Write the principle at the top of the chart.

> When you read today, think of an interesting part of the story so that you can share it with a partner after independent work time.

## Share

Following independent work time, gather children together in the meeting area to talk about the routine of turn and talk.

> Turn and talk to a partner about an interesting part of your book.

▶ Ask children to use a thumbs-up or thumbs-down to evaluate their turn and talk against the chart.

## Extend the Lesson (Optional)

After assessing children's understanding, you might decide to extend the learning.

▶ Use turn and talk regularly during whole- and small-group instruction (e.g., in interactive read-aloud, shared reading, and guided reading).

▶ Continue to review guidelines as you use turn and talk. Ask children to self-assess regularly based on the guidelines.

### Turn and talk to share your thinking.

Look at your partner.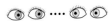

Wait for your partner to finish.

Use a soft voice.

Listen carefully to your partner's thinking.

Turn your body toward your partner, knee to knee.

Stop talking at the signal.

Section 2: Literary Analysis

## RML5
### LA.U1.RML5

**Reading Minilesson Principle**
# When you read, mark places you want to talk about.

## Thinking and Talking About Books

### You Will Need

- a familiar fiction book, such as *Jamaica's Blue Marker* by Juanita Havill, from Text Set: School
- one fiction book for each pair of children
- sticky notes

### Academic Language / Important Vocabulary

- notice
- interesting
- wondering
- question

### Continuum Connection

- Use evidence from the text to support statements about the text (p. 34)

### Goal

Identify places in a book they want to talk about with others.

### Rationale

Teaching children how to mark pages while reading encourages them to think about what they want to talk about with other readers. It prepares them for the conversation, so they have more time to share their thinking with others.

### Assess Learning

Observe children when they mark pages in a book. Notice if there is evidence of new learning based on the goal of this minilesson.

- ▶ Are children able to identify pages that they would like to talk about and explain why they chose them?
- ▶ Can children mark pages with sticky notes?
- ▶ Do children refer back to the marked pages when talking with a partner?
- ▶ Do they understand the terms *notice, interesting, wondering,* and *question*?

## Minilesson

To help children think about the minilesson principle, model how to mark pages to talk about. Here is an example.

- ▶ Show the cover of *Jamaica's Blue Marker*. Start reading from the beginning, and stop after reading page 2.

    I wonder why Jamaica doesn't want to share her markers with Russell. I'm going to put a sticky note on this page so I can find it again later.

- ▶ Continue reading and stop after page 6.

    I think it's interesting that Russell says he doesn't have to listen. I wonder why he thinks this. I'd like to think and talk more about this later.

- ▶ Add a sticky note.

    What did you notice me do as I was reading? Why did I put sticky notes in the book? I put sticky notes in the book so I will know what pages I want to talk about when I share my thinking with others.

    What are some reasons why you might want to talk about a page in a book?

- ▶ Record children's responses on the chart paper.

## Have a Try

Invite the children to practice using sticky notes with a partner.

▶ Have partners work together to practice applying a sticky note to a page in a book. Provide each pair of children with a book and four sticky notes.

> Work with your partner to place the sticky notes in your book.

▶ Engage children in a discussion about the best way to place a sticky note on a page so that the important part of the page is still visible and the note sticks out.

▶ Have the children remove the sticky notes, keeping them for their independent literacy work, and return the books.

## Summarize and Apply

Summarize the learning and remind children to mark places they want to talk about after they read.

> Talk about what you learned today about using a sticky note to mark a place in your book. Look at the chart if you need to remember.

▶ Write the principle at the top of the chart.

> When you read today, use the sticky notes to mark two pages you would like to talk about with a partner. Bring your book when we come back together.

## Share

Following independent work time, gather children together in the meeting area to talk about why they marked pages in a book.

> Turn and talk to a partner about the pages you marked in your book. Tell why you put sticky notes on those pages.

## Extend the Lesson (Optional)

After assessing children's understanding, you might decide to extend the learning.

▶ During independent reading, encourage children to mark pages to talk about.

▶ **Drawing/Writing About Reading** If you haven't already, show children how to draw and write about books in a reader's notebook. Have them write about the pages they marked with sticky notes. See Section Four: Writing About Reading for specific minilessons on using a reader's notebook.

---

### When you read, mark places you want to talk about.

- You wonder why a character does or says something.

- You have a question about the story or the characters.

- You notice something interesting or surprising.

- You don't understand something.

- The story reminds you of something you've seen or heard before.

**Section 2: Literary Analysis**

# RML6
## LA.U1.RML6

### Reading Minilesson Principle
## Read the book again to enjoy it and learn more.

**Thinking and Talking About Books**

**You Will Need**

- a familiar fiction book, such as *First Day Jitters* by Julie Danneberg, from Text Set: School

**Academic Language / Important Vocabulary**

- illustrator
- reread
- notice
- learn
- think

**Continuum Connection**

- Gain new information from both pictures and print (p. 34)

## Goal

Understand what it means to reread and why it is important.

## Rationale

When children are explicitly taught to reread, they can use rereading as a way to further enjoy and think about books and to learn more. This reading strategy supports children when reading more complex test and content-related texts.

## Assess Learning

Observe children when they can use rereading as a way to further enjoy and think about books and to learn more. Notice if there is evidence of new learning based on the goal of this minilesson.

- ▶ Are children willing to reread books or parts of books?
- ▶ Do they talk about the new things they noticed after rereading?
- ▶ Do they understand the terms *illustrator, reread, notice, learn,* and *think*?

## Minilesson

To help children think about the minilesson principle, engage them in a demonstration of rereading with a discussion of the benefits of rereading. Here is an example.

- ▶ Read aloud *First Day Jitters*. Pause after reading page 3.

    I wonder why Sarah says she's not going to school.

- ▶ Continue reading to the end of the book, allowing children to make comments when appropriate.

    I love this book, so I am going to read it again and enjoy it a second time.

- ▶ Start rereading the book from the beginning, and pause after page 3.

    I notice Sarah's body under the covers looks very long. I wonder if the illustrator did this as a clue that Sarah is a grown-up.

- ▶ Pause after a page anywhere in the middle.

    I notice that the illustrator never really shows us what Sarah looks like. I didn't notice this the first time I read the book. What did you notice about the second time I read the book?

    When I read the book again, I noticed things that I didn't notice the first time.

    When you read a book again, it's called rereading. Why might rereading a book be a good idea?

- ▶ Record responses on the chart paper.

## Have a Try

Invite the children to talk with a partner about how rereading can help them enjoy a book or learn more.

▶ Partner the children and give each pair a book.

> With your partner, talk about how rereading a book can help you enjoy it and learn more from it.

## Summarize and Apply

Summarize the learning and remind children to think about what they learned when they reread their book.

> What did you learn about rereading books today?

> You learned that you can reread a book to enjoy it and learn more.

▶ Write the principle at the top of the chart.

> After you read a book today, reread it and think about what new things you notice. Be ready to talk about your book when we come back together.

## Share

Following independent work time, gather children together in the meeting area to talk about rereading a book.

> Turn and talk to a partner about what new things you noticed when you reread a book today.

## Extend the Lesson (Optional)

After assessing children's understanding, you might decide to extend the learning.

▶ Remind children to use sticky notes when they reread to help them remember what they want to talk about with a partner.

▶ **Drawing/Writing About Reading** If you have not already done so, show children how to record their thinking in a reader's notebook after rereading books. See Section Four: Writing About Reading for specific minilessons on using a reader's notebook.

Read the book again to enjoy it and learn more.

- You can enjoy it again.

- You can learn more from the book.

- You can notice new things.

- You can think about the book more.

> Wow! I learned something new when I reread.

## Assessment

After you have taught the minilessons in this umbrella, observe children as they talk and write about their reading across instructional contexts: interactive read-aloud, independent reading and literacy work, guided reading, shared reading, and book club. Use *The Literacy Continuum* (Fountas and Pinnell 2017) to observe children's reading and writing behaviors across instructional contexts.

▶ What evidence do you have of new understandings related to thinking and talking about texts?

- Can children identify the title, author, and illustrator on the front cover of a book?
- Are children able to follow the guidelines for turn and talk?
- Are they able to express their thinking about books in oral language?
- Do children mark pages in books that they want to talk about?
- Are children willing to reread books?
- Do they use vocabulary such as *author, illustrator, title, title page,* and *front cover* when they talk about books?

▶ In what other ways, beyond the scope of this umbrella, are they thinking and talking about books?

- Do children recognize familiar authors and illustrators?
- Do they engage in conversations about interesting parts of books outside an instructional setting?

Use your observations to determine the next umbrella you will teach. You may also consult Minilessons Across the Year (p. 51) for guidance.

## Link to Writing

After teaching the minilessons in this umbrella help children link the new learning to their writing or drawing about reading.

▶ If you haven't already, introduce the Books I Like to Read section of *Reader's Notebook: Primary* (Fountas and Pinnell 2014) or have children set up a section in a notebook to record books they have read. Children can record their favorite titles and authors and draw and write about interesting parts of books. See Section Four: Writing About Reading for minilessons on using a reader's notebook.

**Kevin Henkes**

## Minilessons in This Umbrella

| RML1 | Learn more about authors by reading many of their books. |
| RML2 | Learn more about illustrators by reading many of their books. |
| RML3 | Sometimes authors write several books with the same characters. |
| RML4 | An author has a special way of writing. |

**Bob Graham**

## Before Teaching Umbrella 2 Minilessons

When children study an author or illustrator, they learn what to expect when reading a text by a familiar author or illustrator. They develop an understanding of the distinguishing characteristics of the author or illustrator and develop the tools they need to make connections and predictions. An author or illustrator study supports them in noticing and appreciating the author's or illustrator's craft—a foundation for thinking analytically and critically about texts (see p. 39). These minilessons do not need to be taught in order but can be used throughout the year.

Use the following texts from the *Fountas & Pinnell Classroom™ Interactive Read-Aloud Collection* or choose other books by a single author or illustrator.

**Vera B. Williams**

**Kevin Henkes: Exploring Characters**

*Chrysanthemum*

*Julius: The Baby of the World*

**Bob Graham: Exploring Everyday Life**

*The Silver Button*

*How to Heal a Broken Wing*

*"Let's Get a Pup," Said Kate*

**Vera B. Williams: Celebrating Family and Community**

*A Chair for My Mother*

*Something Special for Me*

*Music, Music for Everyone*

**Nicola Davies: Exploring the Animal World**

*Big Blue Whale*

*One Tiny Turtle*

**Mo Willems: Having Fun with Humor**

*I Am Invited to a Party!*

*Don't Let the Pigeon Drive the Bus!*

**Nicola Davies**

As you read aloud and enjoy these texts together, help children

- make connections among texts by a single author or illustrator, and

- begin to recognize what makes an author's or illustrator's work distinctive.

**Mo Willems**

Section 2: Literary Analysis

## RML1
### LA.U2.RML1

**Reading Minilesson Principle**
# Learn more about authors by reading many of their books.

**Studying Authors and Illustrators**

### You Will Need

- two or three books by the same author, such as the following from Text Set: Kevin Henkes:
  - *Chrysanthemum*
  - *Julius: The Baby of the World*
- chart paper and markers
- a basket of familiar books by the same author

### Academic Language / Important Vocabulary

- author
- character
- story

### Continuum Connection

- Recognize that an author or illustrator may write or illustrate several books (p. 34)
- Connect texts by obvious categories: e.g., author, character, topic genre, illustrator (p. 34)

## Goal

Understand an author usually writes several books, and there are often recognizable characteristics across the books.

## Rationale

When you guide children to recognize the various features in texts by the same author, the children will begin to make connections between texts and to understand writing a book is a process of decision making. When children learn to recognize and appreciate an author's style and recognize the kinds of decisions authors make, they know to look for more of that author's books when they make choices about what to read.

## Assess Learning

Observe children when they talk about an author's books. Notice if there is evidence of new learning based on the goal of this minilesson.

- Do children notice ways books by the same author are alike?
- Can they describe the characteristics of a familiar author's books?
- Do they use the terms *author*, *character*, and *story* in conversation?

## Minilesson

To help children think about the minilesson principle, engage them in a discussion of an author's style. Here is an example.

- Show the covers of several books by Kevin Henkes.

  These books are all by Kevin Henkes.

  What do you remember about Kevin Henkes' books?

  What kinds of events does he write about?

  Look at the covers. What kinds of characters does Kevin Henkes write about?

  What happens to the characters at the end of the stories?

- Write the author's name on the chart paper. Below it, write *Noticings* and create sections labeled *Always* and *Often*.

  We've just talked about Kevin Henkes' books. You probably have noticed some things that he always writes about or that he often writes about. What kinds of things does he always write about? Record responses on the chart.

  What are some things that he often, or sometimes, writes about?

- Record responses on the chart paper.

## Have a Try

Invite the children to talk about the chart with a partner.

▶ Have children turn and talk with a partner about one of the noticings. For example, they could talk about how one of the characters (Chrysanthemum, Julius, Lilly) acts like a person.

## Summarize and Apply

Summarize the learning and remind children to notice the author's style as they read.

▶ Review the chart.

> What did you notice today about Kevin Henkes' writing?

> In this basket are books by Kevin Henkes (or another author you may have used for this lesson). When you read during independent work time, you can choose a book from this basket. See if you notice the things we talked about, or if you notice something new. Be ready to share what you notice when we come back together.

## Share

Following independent work time, gather children in the meeting area to talk about authors' special ways of writing.

> If you read a book by Kevin Henkes today, what did you notice about his writing that we could add to our chart?

## Extend the Lesson (Optional)

After assessing children's understanding, you might decide to extend the learning.

▶ Many authors, including Kevin Henkes, have a website containing biographical information and photographs. Visit Kevin Henkes' website with your students so they learn to regard authors as real people.

▶ Encourage children to remember the characteristics they noticed in Kevin Henkes' books and to use them in their writing.

▶ As you read more books by Kevin Henkes, encourage children to talk about what they notice, and add their noticings to the minilesson chart.

### Kevin Henkes

Noticings:

| Always | Often |
|---|---|
| • He writes about things that happen to kids in everyday life. | • His books are about friends and family. |
| • The characters in his books are animals that act like people. | |
| • The main character learns and changes by the end of the story. | |

 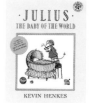

# RML2
## LA.U2.RML2

**Reading Minilesson Principle**
## Learn more about illustrators by reading many of their books.

## Studying Authors and Illustrators

### You Will Need

- two or three books by the same illustrator, such as the following from Text Set: Bob Graham:
  - *The Silver Button*
  - *How to Heal a Broken Wing*
  - *"Let's Get a Pup," Said Kate*
- chart paper and markers
- a basket of familiar books by the same illustrator

### Academic Language / Important Vocabulary

- illustrator
- illustration

### Continuum Connection

- Recognize that an author or illustrator may write or illustrate several books (p. 34)
- Connect texts by obvious categories: e.g., author, character, topic, genre, illustrator (p. 34)
- Understand that an illustrator created the pictures in the book (p. 36)

### Goal

Understand that an illustrator usually illustrates several books, and there are often recognizable characteristics across the books.

### Rationale

When you guide children to recognize the various features in illustrations by the same person, they begin to make connections between texts and to understand that illustrating a book is a process of decision making. They may also learn possibilities for making illustrations in stories they write.

### Assess Learning

Observe children when they talk about illustrators and illustrations. Notice if there is evidence of new learning based on the goal of this minilesson.

- Do children notice ways illustrations by the same illustrator are alike?
- Can children describe the characteristics of illustrations by a familiar illustrator?
- Do they use the terms *illustrator* and *illustration*?

## Minilesson

To help children think about the minilesson principle, engage them in a discussion of an illustrator's style. Here is an example.

- Show the covers of several books by Bob Graham.

  These books are by Bob Graham. He is both the author and illustrator. What does an illustrator do?

- Show illustrations from a couple of Bob Graham's books, such as *The Silver Button* (pages 9–10, 23–24) and *How to Heal a Broken Wing* (pages 1–2, 7–8), so that children can make some observations.

  What do you notice about how Bob Graham drew this illustration?

  What can you say about his illustrations?

  What materials do you think he uses to make his illustrations?

- Write the illustrator's name on the chart paper. Below it, write *Noticings* and create sections labeled *Always* and *Often*.

  Think about the illustrations that Bob Graham draws. What does he always do?

  What does he do often?

- Record responses on the chart paper.

## Have a Try

Invite the children to talk about the chart with a partner.

▶ Have children turn and talk with a partner about one of the noticings. For example, they could talk about the details they noticed in an illustration.

## Summarize and Apply

Summarize the learning and remind children to notice the illustrations as they read.

> Let's look at the chart. It shows us that Bob Graham's illustrations look like each other in many of his books. You can recognize his drawings.
>
> When you read today, you can choose a book from this basket of books by Bob Graham (or another illustrator you may have used in this lesson). See if you notice the things we talked about, or if you notice something new. Be ready to share what you noticed when we come back together.

**Bob Graham**

Noticings:

| Always | Often |
|---|---|
| • His characters look like real people. | • His illustrations are like a comic strip. |
| • His illustrations have many interesting details. | |
| • He uses watercolor paints. | |

The Silver Button — BOB GRAHAM

## Share

Following independent work time, gather children in the meeting area to talk about the illustrations in their books.

> Who read a book by Bob Graham today? What did you notice about his illustrations?

▶ Add new noticings to the chart.

## Extend the Lesson (Optional)

After assessing children's understanding, you might decide to extend the learning.

▶ Discuss Bob Graham's illustrations of people. Have children draw a picture of their own family or friends in Bob Graham's style.

▶ Show Bob Graham's illustrations alongside illustrations of another familiar illustrator (e.g., Kevin Henkes). Discuss how the two illustrators' illustrations are different and alike.

▶ Continue to add to the noticings chart for this minilesson as you read more books by Bob Graham.

Section 2: Literary Analysis

**Reading Minilesson Principle**
# Sometimes authors write several books with the same characters.

## Studying Authors and Illustrators

### You Will Need

- two or three books by the same author and about the same characters, such as the following from Text Set: Vera B. Williams:
  - *A Chair for My Mother*
  - *Something Special for Me*
  - *Music, Music for Everyone*
- chart paper and markers
- several baskets containing sets of books by the same author

### Academic Language / Important Vocabulary

- author
- character
- story

### Continuum Connection

- Recognize that an author or illustrator may write or illustrate several books (p. 34)
- Connect text by obvious categories: e.g., author, character, topic, genre, illustrator (p. 34)
- Recognize characters and report important details about them after reading (p. 35)

## Goal

Understand authors sometimes write several books with the same characters and the characters' traits are consistent across the books.

## Rationale

When you guide children to recognize that authors sometimes write several books with the same characters, they begin to make connections between books and to think more deeply about character traits and development. Often these books are part of a series. Series books allow children to "get into" a book more easily and to infer the characters' feelings and motivations.

## Assess Learning

Observe children when they talk about recurring characters in an author's books. Notice if there is evidence of new learning based on the goal of this minilesson.

- Do children notice when books by the same author are about the same characters?
- Can they talk about how a character is the same in more than one book?
- Do children use the terms *character*, *story*, and *author* in conversation?

## Minilesson

To help children think about the minilesson principle, engage them in a discussion of recurring characters written by the same author. Here is an example.

- Show the covers of *A Chair for My Mother*, *Something Special for Me*, and *Music, Music for Everyone*.

  What do you notice about these three books? What is the same about all of them?

  All these books were written by the same author, Vera B. Williams.

- Hold up *A Chair for My Mother*.

  Who are the characters in this book?

- Record responses on the chart paper.

- Hold up *Something Special for Me*.

  Who are the characters in this book?

- Record responses on the chart paper.

  What do you notice about the characters in both of these books?

## Have a Try

Invite the children to talk with a partner about the characters in *Music, Music for Everyone*.

▶ Hold up *Music, Music for Everyone*.

Turn and talk to a partner about what you notice about the characters.

▶ Invite a few children to share their thinking, and write responses on the chart.

## Summarize and Apply

Summarize the learning and remind children to notice recurring characters in books by the same author.

What did you learn about the characters in Vera B. Williams' books today? Look at the chart.

How could you tell they were the same characters? What is the same about them?

▶ Write the principle at the top of the chart.

▶ Provide children access to several baskets containing sets of books by the same author.

When you read today, choose books by the same author or a book by an author you know. Notice whether the books have the same characters.

| Sometimes authors write several books with the same characters. | |
|---|---|
| **Book** | **Characters** |
|  | Rosa, her mother, and her grandmother<br> |
|  | Rosa, her mother, and her grandmother<br> |
| 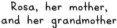 | Rosa, her mother, and her grandmother |

## Share

Following independent work time, gather children in the meeting area to talk about characters in their book.

Give a thumbs-up if you found the same characters in more than one book. Who are the characters? How could you tell they were the same in the books?

## Extend the Lesson (Optional)

After assessing children's understanding, you might decide to extend the learning.

▶ Discuss how the characters change and/or stay the same throughout a series of books by the same author. Guide children to recognize that although recurring characters have certain traits that remain consistent, they may change, grow, and learn important lessons.

▶ **Drawing/Writing About Reading** After reading aloud several books about the same characters, have children write and illustrate stories featuring those characters.

**Reading Minilesson Principle**
# An author has a special way of writing.

## Studying Authors and Illustrators

### You Will Need

- four books by two different authors with clearly different writing styles, such as the following:
  - *Big Blue Whale* and *One Tiny Turtle*, from Text Set: Nicola Davies
  - *I Am Invited to a Party!* and *Don't Let the Pigeon Drive the Bus!*, from Text Set: Mo Willems
- chart paper and markers

### Academic Language / Important Vocabulary

- author
- writing

### Continuum Connection

- Recognize that an author or illustrator may write or illustrate several books (p. 34)

## Goal

Recognize an author's writing style and compare different authors' writing styles.

## Rationale

When you guide children to recognize that each author has a special writing style, they begin to think about the author's craft and further their understanding that writing a book is a process of decision making. They begin to look for connections between books by the same author and to compare authors. They also begin to think about different ways to play with language, which will help them to develop their own writing style.

## Assess Learning

Observe children when they talk about books authors' writing styles. Notice if there is evidence of new learning based on the goal of this minilesson.

- ▶ Can children make an observation about a particular author's writing style?
- ▶ Can children talk about the differences between two authors' writing styles?
- ▶ Do they use the terms *author* and *writing*?

## Minilesson

To help children think about the minilesson principle, engage them in a discussion about authors' writing styles. Here is an example.

- ▶ Show the cover of *Big Blue Whale*.

  I'm going to read a page from *Big Blue Whale* by Nicola Davies. As I read, think carefully about the words you hear.

- ▶ Read page 9.

  What can you say about the way Nicola Davies writes? For example, how does she describe things?

- ▶ Record responses in the left column of a two-column chart.
- ▶ Show the cover of *I Am Invited to a Party!* by Mo Willems. Read pages 1–10.

  What do you notice about Mo Willems' writing? How would you describe the words and sentences he uses?

- ▶ Record responses on the chart paper.

## Have a Try

Invite the children to talk with a partner about *One Tiny Turtle*.

▶ Cover *One Tiny Turtle* so the children cannot see what it is.

> As I read, think carefully about the author's way of writing.

▶ Read pages 14–15.

> Turn and talk to a partner about what you notice about the writing in this book.

> Who do you think wrote this book, Nicola Davies or Mo Willems? Tell why you think that.

## Summarize and Apply

Summarize the learning and remind children to notice the author's way of writing as they read.

> What can you say about different authors' writing by looking at this chart?

> You learned that every author has special ways of writing.

▶ Write the principle at the top of the chart.

> When you read today, think carefully about the author's writing. Think about what makes it special.

## Share

Following independent work time, gather children in the meeting area to talk about an author's special ways of writing.

> Turn and talk to your partner about what you noticed about the author's writing in the book you read.

## Extend the Lesson (Optional)

After assessing children's understanding, you might decide to extend the learning.

▶ During interactive read-aloud, encourage children to notice something distinctive, or special, that an author does with his writing.

▶ Have children practice writing in the style of familiar authors. For example, during an author study of Mo Willems, you might have children practice writing short snippets of dialogue.

| An author has a special way of writing. | |
|---|---|
| **Nicola Davies** | **Mo Willems** |
| • She writes with a lot of detail. | • He writes short, simple sentences. |
| • She describes things by comparing them to other things. | • He writes what the characters say. |
| • Her writing sounds like a poem. | • His writing sounds like real people talking. |

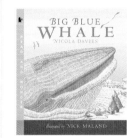 

Section 2: Literary Analysis

## Assessment

After you have taught the minilessons in this umbrella, observe children as they talk about authors and illustrators and write about their reading across instructional contexts: interactive read-aloud, independent reading and literacy work, guided reading, shared reading, and book club. Use *The Literacy Continuum* (Fountas and Pinnell 2017) to observe children's reading and writing behaviors across instructional contexts.

▌ What evidence do you have of new understandings related to making distinctions between different authors and illustrators?

- Can children describe the distinctive features of texts by authors and illustrators?
- Can they describe the features of a familiar author's writing style?
- Do they notice when several books are about the same characters?
- Can they compare and contrast two or more familiar authors or illustrators?
- Do they use academic language, such as *author* and *illustrator*?

▌ In what other ways, beyond the scope of this umbrella, are the children talking about authors and illustrators?

- Are children noticing and talking about how authors and illustrators develop characters' personalities?
- Are children looking closely at illustrations and thinking about the details?
- Do they notice the different ways authors organize books?
- Are they responding to how authors play with language, print, and punctuation?

Use your observations to determine the next umbrella you will teach. You may also consult Minilessons Across the Year (p. 51) for guidance.

## Link to Writing

After teaching the minilessons in this umbrella, help children link the new learning to their writing:

▌ After completing the author study process for a particular author/illustrator, have children make their own books in the style of that author/illustrator. For example, they can have humanlike mouse characters like Kevin Henkes or write a lyrical narrative about an animal like Nicola Davies. When they have finished their books, encourage them to talk about what features in their book were inspired by the author/illustrator studied.

## Minilessons in This Umbrella

**RML1**  A book talk is a short talk about a book you want to recommend.

**RML2**  Try to get your classmates interested in the book.

**RML3**  Learn how to give a good book talk.

**RML4**  Prepare for your book talk and practice it.

## Before Teaching Umbrella 3 Minilessons

To prepare for these minilessons, regularly model book talks, so children have exposure before they begin learning how to give book talks themselves. Students should know routines for listening to classmates and having conversations about books before starting this umbrella (see, in this section, Umbrella 1: Thinking and Talking About Books). Build a collection of books within the range of the independent reading levels of the children in the class. Organize the books into categories (e.g., genre, author, and topic). Use the following books from the *Fountas & Pinnell Classroom™ Independent Reading Collection* or choose other books children can read.

### Independent Reading

*Sea Lions* by Kate Riggs

*Mr. Putter & Tabby Walk the Dog* by Cynthia Rylant

*Josie Cleans Up* by Deborah Eaton

*Wonderful Worms* by Linda Glaser

*Socks* by Beverly Cleary

As you read aloud to the children, help them

- express and support opinions about their favorite books, and
- notice what you do when you speak to the class (e.g., make eye contact, speak at an appropriate volume and rate).

**Independent Reading**

Section 2: Literary Analysis

**Reading Minilesson Principle**

# A book talk is a short talk about a book you want to recommend.

## Giving a Book Talk

### You Will Need

- one fiction book and one nonfiction book, such as the following from *Independent Reading Collection*:
  - *Sea Lions* by Kate Riggs
  - *Mr. Putter & Tabby Walk the Dog* by Cynthia Rylant
- chart paper and markers
- three to four baskets of class favorite books, including both fiction and nonfiction selections

### Academic Language / Important Vocabulary

- book talk
- title
- author
- character
- recommend

### Continuum Connection

- Explain and describe people, events, places, and things in a story (p. 332)
- Express opinions and explain reasoning (p. 332)

## Goal

Learn that a book talk is a short talk about a book to get others excited to read it.

## Rationale

When you teach children to talk about books they enjoy with classmates, you encourage them to develop and share their opinions and expand the list of books they might enjoy reading. They also begin to develop some basic presentation skills.

## Assess Learning

Observe children when they talk about books. Notice if there is evidence of new learning based on the goal of this minilesson.

- ▶ Do children understand the purpose of a book talk?
- ▶ Do they include some of the noticings in their book talks?
- ▶ Do children use the terms *book talk, title, author, character,* and *recommend*?

## Minilesson

To help children think about the minilesson principle, engage them in a demonstration of a book talk. Here is an example.

- ▶ Show the cover of *Sea Lions*.

  I really enjoyed *Sea Lions* by Kate Riggs. It is about real sea lions and their life in the ocean. The book tells about the way sea lions look, how they act, and the place they live. My favorite thing about the book is that it has wonderful photographs. I could look at these sea lion photographs all day!

- ▶ Show a few photographs from the book.

  Now, think about what I said. What types of things did I talk about?

- ▶ As children respond, write their noticings on the chart paper in general terms that apply to all book talks.

  Do you think you would like to read *Sea Lions*? Why?

  Now, I will tell you about another book called *Mr. Putter & Tabby Walk the Dog*. Listen for any new ideas you hear to add to the chart.

- ▶ Repeat the activity with *Mr. Putter & Tabby Walk the Dog*. As you give this book talk, include the title, author, characters, setting, a summary, and why you liked the book.

  Why do you think I talked to you about these books?

  What I did is called a book talk. A book talk is a short talk about a book you think someone else would like to read. In a book talk, you recommend a book.

## Have a Try

Invite the children to talk about the book talks with a partner.

> Did these book talks get you excited to read one or both of the books? Why or why not? Turn and talk with a partner about that.

## Summarize and Apply

Summarize the learning and remind children to think about what they would say for a book talk as they are reading.

> What is a book talk? Why would you want to present a book talk?

▶ Add new noticings and review the chart.

> Choose a book you have read or heard from these baskets. Talk with a partner about what you might say in a book talk about the book. Bring the book you picked when we meet so you can share.

## Share

Following independent work time, gather children together in the meeting area in a circle to talk about what they might say in a book talk.

> As we go around the circle, I will point to each of the things on our noticings chart. Give a thumbs-up to share with us if you talked about those things with your partner.

▶ Call on a few children to share after you read each item on the chart.

## Extend the Lesson (Optional)

After assessing children's understanding, you might decide to extend the learning.

▶ In addition to oral book talks, a class blog can be created for children to add their written recommendations of books.

▶ Have children continue to give book talks as they find new favorite books they would like to share with others.

▶ **Drawing/Writing About Reading** Encourage children to make a "To Read" list of books they learn about during other children's book talks.

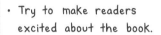

**Book Talks**

- A book talk is a short talk about a book.

- Try to make readers excited about the book.

- Say the title, characters, and place.

- Say the important things that happen.

- Tell why you liked the story.

This is a great book.

Section 2: Literary Analysis

# RML2
## LA.U3.RML2

**Reading Minilesson Principle**
# Try to get your classmates interested in the book.

## Giving a Book Talk

### You Will Need

- one fiction book and one nonfiction book, such as the following from the *Independent Reading Collection*:
  - *Josie Cleans Up* by Deborah Eaton
  - *Wonderful Worms* by Linda Glaser
- chart paper and markers
- three or four baskets of independent reading books
- sticky notes

### Academic Language / Important Vocabulary

- book talk
- excited

### Continuum Connection

- Express opinions about a text: e.g., interesting, funny, and exciting (p. 34)
- Talk about a topic with enthusiasm (p. 332)

## Goal

Share an interesting or funny part of a book to excite other readers about the book.

## Rationale

When children share thinking about what will excite someone about a book, they learn to think about the book analytically and strategically.

## Assess Learning

Observe children when they try to excite others about books. Notice if there is evidence of new learning based on the goal of this minilesson.

- ▶ Are children able think of a way to get others excited about a book?
- ▶ Do they understand the terms *book talk* and *excited*?

## Minilesson

To help children think about the minilesson principle, engage them in a short demonstration and discussion as to how to excite others about a book. Here is an example.

▶ Show the cover of *Josie Cleans Up*.

> When you give a book talk, you want to get other people excited about reading the book. Listen and notice how I try to get you excited about a book.

> I really enjoyed *Josie Cleans Up* by Deborah Eaton. It is about a girl who has a messy room. When her mom wants her to clean it up, she shoves everything into her closet. You can imagine what will happen when Josie opens her closet door!

> Turn and talk with a partner about what I did to get you excited about the book.

▶ Record responses from several children on the chart paper. Then give a short book talk on a nonfiction book. Be sure to show enthusiasm in your voice.

> You can also get your classmates excited about a nonfiction book. This book is *Wonderful Worms* by Linda Glaser. Many people don't think worms are wonderful, but I do. Did you know that worms eat dirt?

> Turn and talk with a partner about what I did to get you excited about the book.

▶ Record responses on the chart.

## Have a Try

Invite the children to talk about a book with a partner.

> Look at the list we made on the chart. Turn and talk with a partner about one thing you could tell your classmates about a book you know.

## Summarize and Apply

Summarize the learning and remind children to think about how to get their classmates excited to read the book they are reading.

> Let's read the list we made about what you can do to get your classmates interested in a book. Is there anything else you can think of?

▶ Write the principle at the top of the chart.

> Choose a book from the baskets or another book you want to read during independent work time. Use a sticky note to mark a picture, a funny part, an interesting fact—whatever you think will get others excited. Bring the book when we meet so you can share.

## Share

Following independent work time, have children sit in groups of three in the meeting area.

▶ Review the chart.

> Use the ideas on the chart to tell your group something about your book. Remember to include what will get others excited to read the book, like a funny part or an interesting part, or show a picture.

▶ After time for discussion, ask a few volunteers to share. Add new ideas to the chart.

## Extend the Lesson (Optional)

After assessing children's understanding, you might decide to extend the learning.

▶ Model how to give a book talk as often as you can: for example, during interactive read-aloud or when adding new books to the classroom library.

▶ Post the minilesson chart in the classroom and add ideas as you read other books so children can learn new ideas to include in book talks.

---

**Try to get your classmates interested in the book.**

Here's what you can do:

- Talk about a funny part.

- Show a picture.

Josie Cleans Up
by Deborah Eaton
illustrated by Renée Williams-Andriani

- Ask a question.

- Share a fact.

WONDERFUL WORMS
BY LINDA GLASER
PICTURES BY LORETTA KRUPINSKI

- Sound excited.

---

# RML3

LA.U3.RML3

## Reading Minilesson Principle
## Learn how to give a good book talk.

## Giving a Book Talk

### You Will Need

- an enjoyable book, such as *Socks* by Beverly Cleary, from *Independent Reading Collection*
- chart paper and markers
- three to four baskets of independent reading books, including both fiction and nonfiction

### Academic Language / Important Vocabulary

- book talk
- eye contact
- voice
- volume
- enthusiasm
- attention
- body language

### Continuum Connection

- Talk about a topic with enthusiasm (p. 332)
- Speak at appropriate volume to be heard, but not too loud (p. 332)
- Speak with an appropriate rate to be understood (p. 332)
- Look at the audience (or other person) while speaking (p. 332)

## Goal

Speak with a confident, clear, and enthusiastic voice and understand how to use the book and body language during a book talk.

## Rationale

When children give book talks using appropriate voice and body language, they develop, through a combination of practice and feedback, presentation skills that apply to all academic areas.

## Assess Learning

Observe children when they learn to give a book talk. Notice if there is evidence of new learning based on the goal of this minilesson.

- Are children beginning to talk about strategies for improving their presentation skills when they give a book talk?
- Do children understand the terms *book talk, eye contact, voice, volume, enthusiasm, attention,* and *body language*?

## Minilesson

To help children think about the minilesson principle, engage them in a short demonstration and discussion of presenting a book talk. Here is an example.

- As you model a book talk, emphasize eye contact, appropriate voice (e.g., speed, volume, enthusiasm), body language, and holding the book so the children can see.

  > Today when I give a book talk, notice how I use my eyes, voice, and body. We will talk about this after my book talk.

- Show the cover of *Socks* and pictures that support what you are feeling.

  > Beverly Cleary is one of my favorite authors, and she wrote this book, *Socks*. Socks is a cat who is jealous when a human baby moves into the house. I understand how Socks feels because I remember what it was like when a new baby moved into my house. This story has funny parts, like when Socks thinks the baby has a wrinkled face without fur. If you like books about animals and families, you will want to read this story!

  > Turn and talk with a partner how I used my eyes, voice, body, and the book when I gave the book talk.

- After the discussion, make a list of things the children noticed.

## Have a Try

Invite the children to talk about the book talk with a partner.

> Turn and talk to your partner about one thing that I did well during my book talk.

## Summarize and Apply

Summarize the learning and remind children to think about ways to give a good book talk.

> Look at the chart. What did you learn today about how to give a good book talk?

▶ Write the principle at the top of the chart.

> Choose a book from the baskets or one of your own you might like to share with others. When you read, think about what you could say about the book in a book talk. Bring the book when we meet.

## Share

Following independent work time, have children sit in groups of three in the meeting area.

> Show your book to the others in your group and talk about the things you would do to give a good book talk. When you talk to your group, practice how you would give a book talk. Look at the chart if you need to remember.

▶ After the discussion, ask a few volunteers to share.

## Extend the Lesson (Optional)

After assessing children's understanding, you might decide to extend the learning.

▶ Continue modeling effective presentation strategies when giving book talks and when reading aloud.

▶ Share reviews of children's books online or on the back cover of a book with the children. Talk about how the reviews are like written book talks.

Learn how to give a good book talk.

- Look at the audience.

- Make your voice not too loud and not too fast.

- Sound excited.

My book is called...

- Hold the book so everyone can see.

## Reading Minilesson Principle
# Prepare for your book talk and practice it.

## Giving a Book Talk

### You Will Need

- chart paper and markers
- class charts on book talks from RML1, 2, and 3
- three or four basket of independent reading books, including both fiction and nonfiction selections

### Academic Language / Important Vocabulary

- book talk
- steps
- prepare
- practice
- present

### Continuum Connection

- Express opinions about a text (e.g., interesting, funny, exciting) and support with evidence (p. 332)
- Talk about a topic with enthusiasm (p. 332)
- Look at the audience (or other person) while speaking (p. 332)
- Present ideas and information in a logical sequence (p. 332)

## Goal

Understand how to prepare for a book talk.

## Rationale

When children plan, prepare, and practice for a book talk, they learn important presentation skills that can be applied to other academic areas. They also learn to think about and express their opinions.

## Assess Learning

Observe children as they prepare for a book talk. Notice if there is evidence of new learning based on the goal of this minilesson.

- ▶ Are children able to talk about the steps to prepare a book talk?
- ▶ Do children understand the terms *book talk, prepare,* and *present*?

# Minilesson

To help children think about the minilesson principle, engage them in a short discussion of planning, preparing, and practicing for a book talk. Here is an example.

- ▶ Prompt the discussion so children understand that the first step is to select and read a book to share.

    What is the first thing to do before you can give a book talk?

- ▶ Create a class chart and add this as step 1.

    For step 2, think about why you liked the book. Turn and talk about why this is an important step.

- ▶ Ask volunteers to share. Add step 2 to the chart. Then show the chart from RML1.

    Look at this chart. What are the different details you can tell about the book? What should you say first? First, you should say the title and the author. Then you can say where it takes place if that's important and a little more about what happens. This can be the third step.

- ▶ Add step 3 to the chart. Then show the chart from RML2.

    For step 4, look at the chart we made that shows ways to get your classmates excited about the book. What could we write for step 4?

- ▶ Add step 4 to the chart. Finally, show the chart from RML3.

    Now, look at the chart we made about ways to use your eyes, voice, and body to give a good book talk. Why is it important to think about these things when you practice your book talk? This is step 5.

- ▶ Add step 5 to chart.

## Have a Try

Invite the children to talk with a partner about a book for a book talk.

> Turn and talk with a partner about a book you might like to talk about in a book talk.

## Summarize and Apply

Summarize the learning and remind children to think about the five steps to follow to prepare for a book talk.

▶ Review the chart.

> Today during independent work time, you and a partner will prepare for and practice giving a book talk. Choose a favorite book, one that you know and enjoy, from these baskets. Follow the steps to prepare and practice giving a book talk. Help your partner remember all the steps.

## Share

Following independent work time, gather children together in the meeting area to present a book talk.

▶ Match each pair of children with another pair.

> Give your book talk to a different pair of children. Help your partner if he needs it.

## Extend the Lesson (Optional)

After assessing children's understanding, you might decide to extend the learning.

▶ Set aside a regular time each day or week for children to present book talks.

▶ To encourage children to try some different books in the library, record several children giving book talks to use as advertisements for the books in your library.

---

### How to Prepare for a Book Talk

Step 1. Choose a book you want to share. Read it again.

Step 2. Think about why you liked the book.

Step 3. Think about the title, author, where it takes place, and what happens.

Step 4. Think about what will get kids excited to read it.

Step 5. Practice giving the book talk.

## Assessment

After you have taught the minilessons in this umbrella, observe children talking and writing about their reading across instructional contexts: interactive read-aloud, independent reading and literacy work, guided reading, shared reading, and book club. Use *The Literacy Continuum* (Fountas and Pinnell 2017) to observe children's reading and writing behaviors across instructional contexts.

> What evidence do you have of new understandings related to giving a book talk?

> - Do children understand a book talk is a short talk about a book?
> - Do they know the purpose of a book talk?
> - Are they able to apply new ideas to make their book talks better?
> - Are they able to give a book talk about a book they enjoyed?
> - Do they use academic language, such as *author, title,* and *book talk*?

> In what other ways, beyond the scope of this umbrella, are children talking about and using book talks?

> - Do children record in a reader's notebook the titles of books they want to read after a book talk?
> - Are they beginning to share their opinions about books they are reading independently?

Use your observations to determine the next umbrella you will teach. You may also consult Minilessons Across the Year (p. 51) for guidance.

## Link to Writing

After teaching the minilessons in this umbrella, help children link the new learning to their own writing:

> Have children make written versions of a book talk, which contain the essential information of a book talk and can be used to inform classmates of favorite books in the classroom or school library. The written book talks could be collected in a file, posted in the library, or gathered on a web page or in a blog.

## Minilessons in This Umbrella

**RML1**   Choose a book you would like to read and talk about.

**RML2**   Mark the pages you want to talk about.

**RML3**   Talk about your thinking in book club.

**RML4**   Learn how to have a good book club.

**RML5**   Be sure everyone has a chance to talk during book club.

**RML6**   Talk about what went well and what you want to work on to get better.

## Before Teaching Umbrella 4 Minilessons

The minilessons in this umbrella are designed to help you introduce and teach the procedures and routines to establish book clubs in your classroom. Teach these minilessons during the first few book club meetings and consider rotating each small book club for the demonstrations across several days. Book clubs are meetings with about four to six children of varying reading abilities, who come together to discuss a common text they have chosen. The goal is for the children to share their thinking with each other and build a richer meaning than one reader could gain on his or her own. In a small book club, it will be easier for children to get to know one another's point of view and for everyone to have more opportunities to talk. Also, the teacher plays a key role in scaffolding the children's responses. We suggest you read pages 62–64 before starting book clubs in your classroom.

The minilessons in this umbrella use examples from the following text sets from the *Fountas & Pinnell Classroom™ Book Club Collection* or the *Interactive Read-Aloud Collection*.

### Book Club

#### School

*Brand New Pencils, Brand New Books* by Diane de Groat

*First Grade Stinks!* by Mary Rodman

*First Day of School* by Anne Rockwell

*First Year Letters* by Julie Danneberg

### Interactive Read-Aloud

#### Understanding the Natural World: Oceans

*Sea Turtles* by Gail Gibbons

**School**

**Oceans**

Section 2: Literary Analysis

**Reading Minilesson Principle**

# Choose a book you would like to read and talk about.

Getting Started with
Book Clubs

## You Will Need

- prepare book talks for four books that children have not read or heard, such as these from the *Book Club Collection* Text Set: School:

  - *Brand New Pencils, Brand New Books* by Diane de Groat

  - *First Grade Stinks!* by Mary Rodman

  - *First Day of School* by Anne Rockwell

  - *First Year Letters* by Julie Danneberg

- chart paper and markers

- sheets of paper with the covers or titles of the four books

- sets of books for book club

## Academic Language / Important Vocabulary

- book club

- choice

- author

- illustrator

- title

## Continuum Connection

- Express opinions about a text (e.g., interesting, funny, exciting) and support with evidence (p. 34)

- Articulate why they like a text (p. 34)

## Goal

Learn how to make a good book choice for book club meetings.

## Rationale

Children will be more engaged in a book club when they actively participate in selecting the book for their discussion. Choice leads to engagement and motivation. When you teach children how to make good book choices, you make the book club meeting more enjoyable and worthwhile for all members.

## Assess Learning

Observe children when they select a book for their book clubs. Notice if there is evidence of new learning based on the goal of this minilesson.

- ▶ Can children select a book to discuss?

- ▶ How well do children problem solve when they have difficulty choosing a book?

- ▶ Are they able to articulate why they chose one book instead of another?

- ▶ Do they use vocabulary such as *choice, author, illustrator,* and *title* during book club?

## Minilesson

To help children think about the minilesson principle, engage them in learning how to choose a book for a book club meeting. Here is an example.

> What do you know about book clubs?

> People who have a book club meeting get together to talk about a book they have all read. They share their thinking about the book with each other.

> I am going to share with you four books. I want you to think about which of these books you would like to read and then talk about with friends in a book club meeting. If you choose a book that might be hard for you to read right now, I will talk with you later about how you can listen to it.

▶ Provide a short book talk for the selected books. Share the title, author, and illustrator of the book. Summarize what each book is about and talk about features that would interest the children. Show a few illustrations and, if you have time, read a page or two to give children a sense of what the book is about. The goal of book talks is to hook the children into wanting to read one of the books. Your book talk should be an advertisement for each of the books.

## Have a Try

Invite the children to talk about choosing books with a partner.

> In a moment, you are going to choose one of these books to read and talk about in a book club. How do you choose a book you like to read? Turn and talk with a partner about what you think about when you choose a book.

## Summarize and Apply

Summarize the learning and remind children to choose a book that they would like to use for book club.

> What questions can you ask yourself when you choose a book? Let's make a list.

▸ Record children's responses on chart paper. Give children the prepared list of book titles.

> Now, I want you to put your name on this paper and number the books for your three choices. Ask yourself the questions on the chart. You might not get your first choice, but sometimes you will find you will enjoy a book you didn't think you would like.

▸ Create book clubs based on the choices. List the children's names for each book club, book title, and dates the book club will meet. You might want to teach more of the minilessons in this umbrella before starting book clubs. Distribute the books. Remind children to read the book and be prepared to meet and discuss their book.

## Share

Following independent work time, gather children together in the meeting area to talk about the book they selected for book club.

> Turn and talk to your partner about which book you selected to read. Explain why you want to read this book for book club.

## Extend the Lesson (Optional)

After assessing children's understanding, you might decide to extend the learning.

▸ Confer with children about their book interests and help them to develop their reading preferences. If children use a reader's notebook, look at the kinds of books they have read and use this information to have a conversation about choosing books.

▸ Create a book club suggestion box. Encourage children to add a book title to the box when they discover a book they would like to discuss in a book club.

Choose a book you would like to read and talk about.

Which book looks interesting?

Which book sounds exciting to read?

Which book do you want to talk about?

Very interesting!

# RML2
## LA.U4.RML2

# Mark the pages you want to talk about.

## Getting Started with Book Clubs

### You Will Need

- a familiar book, such as *Sea Turtles* by Gail Gibbons, from Text Set: Oceans, from the *Interactive Read-Aloud Collection*
- sticky notes
- chart prepared with a sketch of a book with sticky note in place

### Academic Language / Important Vocabulary

- book club
- mark
- discuss

### Continuum Connection

- Use evidence from the text to support statements about the text (p. 34)

## Goal

Identify important information to discuss in preparation for book clubs.

## Rationale

When you teach children to mark pages they find interesting, and they want to discuss, they learn the importance of preparing for a discussion and develop a process for referring to important ideas and information. They also learn to look critically at a book as they determine the important parts to talk about. In this lesson, you will use a familiar interactive read-aloud book to model how to place a sticky note, and then children will practice in their book club books.

## Assess Learning

Observe children when they mark pages of the book to prepare for book club. Notice if there is evidence of new learning based on the goal of this minilesson.

- Are children able to mark pages they want to discuss in their book club meeting?
- Do children understand the terms *book club*, *mark*, and *discuss*?

## Minilesson

To help children think about the minilesson principle, engage them in a discussion of how to mark pages to discuss in a book club meeting. Here is an example.

- Show *Sea Turtles*.

    You had a lot of thinking to share when we read this book. As I show you the pages, think about a few pages you would want to discuss or talk about if you met in a small group to talk.

- Quickly review the pages of the story.
- Invite a child to come up and locate a page in the book she wants to discuss.

    How could you remember that you want to talk about this page?

    A good way to remember the page is to put a sticky note on the page.

- Have the child place a sticky note on the page.

    Put the sticky part down on the page and leave a little bit sticking over the edge. This will help you easily find the page during book club. You might number the sticky notes 1, 2, and 3 to remind you of the importance of the pages when discussing them. If you want to discuss the author and illustrator you could put a sticky note on the cover.

## Have a Try

Invite the children to practice placing a sticky note in a book with a partner.

> Take your book club book and a sticky note. Choose a page in your book to place the sticky note. Practice putting it on the page.

## Summarize and Apply

Summarize the learning and remind children to mark places while reading they want to talk about.

> What did we talk about today?

▶ Write the principle at the top of the chart.

> During independent work time today, you will read the book you will discuss during book club. Use sticky notes to mark two or three pages you want to discuss in your book club meeting.

▶ Put a pack of sticky notes in the middle of each table or give each child two to three sticky notes. Review the list of book club assignments and distribute the books.

Mark the pages you want to talk about.

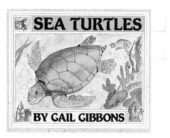

## Share

Following independent work time, gather children together in the meeting area to talk about the book pages they marked for book club.

> Turn to your partner to explain how you decided which pages to choose.

> What could you write on the sticky note to remind yourself what you want to discuss?

> If you are not sure which pages to mark, what could you do?

## Extend the Lesson (Optional)

After assessing children's understanding, you might decide to extend the learning.

▶ Encourage children to use sticky notes during independent reading to mark pages to discuss.

▶ During interactive writing, demonstrate how children can draw, write a word, or use numbers or symbols on a sticky note to remind themselves of what they want to discuss.

# RML3
## LA.U4.RML3

## Talk about your thinking in book club.

**Getting Started with Book Clubs**

### You Will Need

- four children prepared to model a book club discussion
- book club books, such as these from *Fountas & Pinnell Classroom™ Book Club Collection* Text Set: School
  - *Brand New Pencils, Brand New Books* by Diane de Groat
  - *First Grade Stinks!* by Mary Rodman
  - *First Day of School* by Anne Rockwell
  - *First Year Letters* by Julie Danneberg
- chart paper and markers

### Academic Language / Important Vocabulary

- book club
- author
- illustrator
- discuss

### Continuum Connection

- Express opinions and support with evidence (p. 332)
- Explain and describe people, events, places, and things in a story (p. 332)

## Goal

Learn how to identify important parts of a book to discuss during a book club meeting.

## Rationale

Book clubs provide children the opportunity to dig deeper into the author's intended meaning and craft as they share their thinking with other book club members. They will benefit from other's thinking and develop a richer understanding as a member of a group than they would gain alone. This minilesson uses a fishbowl to model what to talk about in a book club meeting. In the fishbowl technique, the children prepared to simulate a book club discussion sit together inside a circle and the rest of the class sits in a circle around them to observe.

## Assess Learning

Observe children talk about their thinking about the book club book. Notice if there is evidence of new learning based on the goal of this minilesson.

- Are children able to talk about their thinking about a familiar book with others?
- Do they use the terms *book club*, *author*, *illustrator*, and *discuss* in conversation?

## Minilesson

To help children think about the minilesson principle, engage them in a fishbowl experience of a book club. Each member of the club should have a copy of the book members chose to read. Here is an example.

> _____, _____, _____, and _____ are going to discuss the book they chose for their book club meeting. Be ready to talk about some of the things your classmates discuss, or talk about, in their book club meeting.

- Seat the book club members in the inside circle with you and have the book club observers, the rest of the class, in the outside circle. Lead the children on the inside circle to share their thinking about the story for about five minutes. Encourage them to take turns sharing their thinking about the author and illustrator, pages they find interesting, or pages they have comments about and showing an illustration or page to support their comments.

  > Take a minute to think about some of the things your classmates discussed in their book club. Turn and talk with a partner about something you heard the book club members discuss.

  > Let's make a list of the things you heard discussed.

## Have a Try

Invite children to talk with a partner about other book club discussion topics.

> What else could you talk about in a book club meeting?

▸ Invite children to share their noticings. When they share something specific to the book, extend it to the bigger idea. For example, if they mention the rabbit, list it as *character*. Record responses on the chart.

## Summarize and Apply

Summarize the learning and remind children to talk about their thinking in a book club.

▸ Review the chart and write the principle at the top.

▸ During independent work time, have children read their book club books. Remind them to think about what they will talk about when their book club meets.

## Share

Following independent work time, gather children together in the meeting area to talk about their thinking for book club.

> Turn and talk to your partner about something in your book that you can talk about during your book club meeting.

## Extend the Lesson (Optional)

After assessing children's understanding, you might decide to extend the learning.

▸ Post the minilesson chart where the children can see it. Continue to add to the list as children share their thinking about books.

▸ Review the chart with the list of things to talk about before each book club meeting.

▸ Share the chart with families and encourage them to have a book club at home.

---

### Talk about your thinking in book club.

- a character

- a favorite part

- an illustration

- the ending  STOP

- a funny part

- a surprising part    Wow!

- something you didn't understand    ?

---

**Section 2: Literary Analysis**

# RML4
### LA.U4.RML4

**Reading Minilesson Principle**
## Learn how to have a good book club.

## Getting Started with Book Clubs

### You Will Need

- one book club group of four children prepared to model a respectful book club discussion
- chart paper and markers

### Academic Language / Important Vocabulary

- book club
- respect
- prepare
- discuss
- voice level
- listen

### Continuum Connection

- Speak at an appropriate volume to be heard, but not too loud (p. 332)
- Refrain from speaking over others (p. 332)
- Take turns when speaking (p. 332)
- Look at the audience (or other person) while speaking (p. 332)

## Goal

Identify the routines of a book club and ways of showing respect during a discussion (e.g., showing the pages of a book, taking turns to speak).

## Rationale

A good book club meeting is one in which the members behave in ways that respect each other. Learning to respect others is an important life skill. When you teach children to take turns, ensure everyone is on the same page, take turns speaking, and look at the speaker during a book club meeting, you are teaching presentation and communication skills that they will eventually be able to transfer to other experiences throughout their lives. This lesson uses the fishbowl technique, in which one group models the desired behavior and the rest of the class, sitting in a circle around the small group, watches and listens.

## Assess Learning

Observe children during a book club meeting. Notice if there is evidence of new learning based on the goal of this minilesson.

- Are children respectful of others?
- Are they able to suggest other ways to show respect?

## Minilesson

To help children think about the minilesson principle, engage them in a fishbowl experience of a book club. Here is an example.

- Before teaching this minilesson, prepare four children to demonstrate moving to a book club and then talking respectfully with the others about a book. Conduct a short book club meeting with the group before asking the students to model for the class.

  Today you are going to watch a few of your friends moving to book club and talking about the book they have chosen. Notice how these book club members show respect for one another. Be ready to share your noticings. What do you think it means to respect one another?

- Have the prepared small group move to the book club and discuss the book for a brief period (three to five minutes). You could use the fishbowl technique.

  What did you notice about how the members of the book club showed respect for one another?

- Record responses on the chart paper. If necessary, ask questions to prompt their thinking: *When one person was speaking, what were the others doing? Did the speaker look at the book club members? What level voice did they use? Did everyone have a turn to talk? What did you notice they did with their books to make sure everyone was together? Was everyone prepared and knew what to talk about? Why is that important?*

> Was there anything else you noticed they did to make the discussion more enjoyable and respectful of all of the book club members?

▸ Invite a few volunteers to add drawings to the chart.

## Summarize and Apply

Summarize the learning and remind children to think about ways to have a book club.

▸ Review the chart.

> Why is it important to show respect for another person's thinking during book club?

> Today, if you are part of a book club, think about these things. Then after the book club, you will share how your discussion went.

▸ Meet with a book club group while the other children are engaged in independent literacy work.

## Share

Following independent work time, gather children together in the meeting area to talk about ways to have a good book club.

▸ Ask the children who participated in the book club with you that day to talk about what went well in the book club meeting. Encourage these book club members to give an example of how they showed respect to their book club members.

▸ Invite a few children to share.

## Extend the Lesson (Optional)

After assessing children's understanding, you might decide to extend the learning.

▸ Review the list of behaviors before book clubs and help children self-assess after book club.

▸ Encourage children to consider other ways to show respect and add to the chart.

▸ Remind children to show each other the same respect during other parts of the day, such as when they turn and talk with a partner or when they work in groups of three or four.

# How to Have a Good Book Club

- Listen to the speaker.

- Take turns talking.

- Look at the speaker.

- Use a level 2 voice when you talk.

- Show the page you are talking about.

- Know what you want to talk about.

**Reading Minilesson Principle**
# Be sure everyone has a chance to talk during book club.

Getting Started with
Book Clubs

## You Will Need

- one book club group of four children prepared to model a book club
- chart paper and markers

## Academic Language / Important Vocabulary

- book club
- discuss
- question
- encourage
- invite

### Continuum Connection

- Refrain from speaking over others (p. 332)
- Take turns when speaking (p. 332)
- Actively participate in the give-and-take of conversation (p. 332)

## Goal

Understand the expectations of a discussion and learn facilitative language to invite others into the discussion.

## Rationale

Children need to learn language that will invite others into a discussion, as well as respectful ways of responding. Learning how to be an active participant in a conversation is an important life skill.

## Assess Learning

Observe children's language during a book club meeting. Notice if there is evidence of new learning based on the goal of this minilesson.

- ▶ Are children able to generate a list of questions that encourage others to talk?
- ▶ Do children ask questions to provide an opportunity for everyone to talk?
- ▶ Are they able to reflect on the language they used?

## Minilesson

To help children think about the minilesson principle, engage them in a fishbowl experience of a book club. Here is an example.

- ▶ Before teaching this minilesson, prepare a group of four children to demonstrate how everyone can have an opportunity to talk during book club. Teach these children how to invite and encourage everyone in the group into the conversation before asking them to model for the class.

  _____, _____, _____, and _____ are going to discuss the book they chose in a book club meeting. Notice how your classmates and I invite or encourage others in the group to share an idea.

- ▶ Lead the discussion with the prepared group of children, while the rest of the class observes.

  Take a minute to think about what the book club members and I said to encourage each other to talk about the book and then how we responded to one another. Turn and talk with a partner about what you noticed.

- ▶ Invite children to share what they noticed.

  What questions could you ask other book club members to make sure everyone has an opportunity to speak during the book club meeting?

- ▶ Record responses on the chart paper.

  You can also say things like "Can you help me understand that?" or "Talk more about that" to invite someone to speak during the book club meeting.

## Have a Try

Invite the children to read the questions on the chart with a partner.

> With your partner, practice reading the questions we have on our chart so that you will know them when it's time for you to have a book club meeting.

## Summarize and Apply

Summarize the learning and remind children to be sure everyone has a chance to talk when they meet in their book clubs.

- ◗ Review the chart and then write the principle at the top.

  > Is there anything else you can say to invite someone to talk during book club meeting?

- ◗ During independent work time, meet with one or two book club groups to lead and facilitate the discussion and model how to invite or encourage others in the discussion.

Section 2: Literary Analysis

> **Be sure everyone has a chance to talk during book club.**
>
> What are you thinking?
>
> What did you notice?
>
> What surprised you?
>
> Who can add to that idea?
>
> What do you think about the illustrations?

## Share

Following independent work time, gather children together in the meeting area to talk about how they encouraged others in their book club.

- ◗ Ask the children who participated in a book club to share their experience with the class. Invite them to share how they made sure everyone had a chance to talk. Add any new ideas shared by the children to the chart.

## Extend the Lesson (Optional)

After assessing children's understanding, you might decide to extend the learning.

- ◗ Use the questions on the chart when you sit and talk with children about the books they are reading.

- ◗ Video or record children discussing a book. Watch the video as a group to have the children notice the questions asked to invite and encourage others to participate.

**Getting Started with Book Clubs**

**You Will Need**

▸ charts from RML1–RML5
▸ chart paper and markers

**Academic Language / Important Vocabulary**

▸ book club
▸ discuss
▸ checklist

**Continuum Connection**

▸ Take turns when speaking (p. 332)
▸ Demonstrate respectful listening behaviors (p. 332)

## Goal

Develop guidelines to self-assess the book club meeting.

## Rationale

It is important for children to learn how to reflect on their behaviors, self-assessing areas both of strength and areas for improvement. Children's sense of ownership and level of engagement in book club increase when they are a part of developing guidelines for the discussion. This summary lesson helps children look at the whole process and evaluate what behaviors result in a successful book club meeting.

## Assess Learning

Observe children when they self-assess after a book club meeting. Notice if there is evidence of new learning based on the goal of this minilesson.

▸ Are children able to identify the qualities of a good book club meeting?
▸ Can they use the guidelines effectively to self-assess a book club meeting?
▸ Do they understand the terms *book club, discuss,* and *checklist*?

## Minilesson

To help children think about the minilesson principle, engage them in a short discussion of generating guidelines for self-assessing after a book club meeting. Here is an example.

▸ Review the charts you have created with the children in the previous five minilessons.

> After you have a book club meeting, you can ask yourself questions so you can decide which parts of your meeting are working well and which parts need some work. Let's think about what you do before, during, and after a book club meeting. What questions might you ask?

▸ Record responses on the chart paper and write *yes* and *no* next to each question.

> If everyone thought about the story and marked a page in the book with a sticky note to discuss, which word would you circle? If only a few people were prepared, or no one was prepared to talk about the book, then you would circle which word? If you circle *no,* what do you think that means? Circling *no* means you and the other members of your book club are still working on the task.

## Have a Try

Invite the children to talk about having a good book club meeting with a partner.

> Turn and talk to a partner about what you think is the most important thing to remember to do to make sure you have a good book club meeting. Tell why.

## Summarize and Apply

Summarize the learning and remind children to evaluate their book club meeting.

> What should you do at the end of a book club meeting? Why should you do this?

> ▶ Write the principle at the top of the chart.

> After your book club discussion, you and your book club are going to use this list to talk about what went well and what you want to work on to get better.

> ▶ Meet with a book club during independent work time. After their discussion, guide all members to self-assess.

| Talk about what went well and what you want to work on to get better. | | |
|---|---|---|
| **Before** | | |
| Did you move quietly to the book club and get ready to start quickly? | Yes | No |
| Did everyone mark a page to talk about? | Yes | No |
| **During** | | |
| Did everyone show respect for other people's thinking? | Yes | No |
| Did everyone get a turn to talk? | Yes | No |
| **After** | | |
| Did everyone take off the sticky notes and put away the books? | Yes | No |

## Share

Following independent work time, gather children together in the meeting area to talk about their self-assessment of their book club meeting.

> ▶ Invite the book clubs you met with to share their self-assessment with the class and explain why they chose yes or no for each question.

## Extend the Lesson (Optional)

After assessing children's understanding, you might decide to extend the learning.

> ▶ If children have difficulty self-assessing, conduct a fishbowl discussion and have the children on the inside and outside of the circle assess the discussion using the guidelines. Talk about differences in opinions that might arise.

> ▶ Have children read the book club list of what to do before, during, and after before each book club and ask them to assess their experience using the list at the end of each book club.

## Assessment

After you have taught the minilessons in this umbrella, observe children as they talk and write about their reading before, during, and after book club. Use *The Literacy Continuum* (Fountas and Pinnell 2017) to observe children's reading and writing behaviors across instructional contexts.

▶ What evidence do you have of new understanding related to ways for children to talk and write about their reading before, during, and after book club?

- Do they understand the importance of book selection?
- Are children having meaningful and thoughtful conversations about books?
- Have they planned what they want to discuss?
- Do they follow the routines and show respect to their classmates during a book club meeting?
- Do children use facilitative language?
- Do they mark pages with sticky notes, sometimes with comments, to remember what they want to discuss?
- Are they able to self-assess their participation after book club?
- Do children use vocabulary such as *voice level*, *respect*, *discuss*, and *checklist* when talking about book clubs?

▶ In what other ways, beyond the scope of this umbrella, are the children talking about books and book clubs?

- Do the children show respect to others while listening to them speak?
- During independent reading, is there evidence that children are using sticky notes to indicate what they want to discuss?

Use your observations to determine the next umbrella you will teach. You may also consult Minilessons Across the Year (p. 51) for guidance.

## Link to Writing

After teaching the minilessons in this umbrella, help children link the new learning to their writing:

▶ Encourage children to get ideas from the book discussions for their writing. For example, if someone talks about another way the book could end during book club, children could write an alternative ending for the story. If they discuss the writer/illustrator's craft, they could write about what the decisions writer or illustrator made.

▶ If the book club is based on a genre study, children could create a similar book with a different topic.

## Minilessons in This Umbrella

**RML1**    Fiction books are alike in some ways.

**RML2**    The definition of a fiction story is what is always true about a story.

**RML3**    Nonfiction books are alike in some ways.

**RML4**    The definition of nonfiction is what is always true about it.

**RML5**    The author tells made-up stories in fiction books.

**RML6**    The author tells about things that are real in nonfiction books.

**RML7**    Writers tell stories that have characters, a problem, and a solution.

**RML8**    Writers tell true facts in nonfiction books.

**RML9**    Think about whether a book is fiction or nonfiction.

## Before Teaching Umbrella 5 Minilessons

Genre study (see p. 37) provides the tools children need to navigate a variety of texts. Select clear examples of fiction and nonfiction (including expository and narrative), preferably books on the same topic. Be sure that children think and talk about the meaning of each book before looking across texts for genre characteristics.

Use the following books from the *Fountas & Pinnell Classroom™ Interactive Read-Aloud Collection* or choose other clear examples of fiction or nonfiction.

### Exploring Fiction and Nonfiction

*On the Go* by Ann Morris

*Going Places* by Peter and Paul Reynolds

*Too Many Pears!* by Jackie French

*Milk: From Cow to Carton* by Aliki

*Ice Bear: In the Steps of the Polar Bear* by Nicola Davies

### Nonfiction: Questions and Answers

*Best Foot Forward* by Ingo Arndt

*What Do You Do with a Tail Like This?* by Steve Jenkins

### The Importance of Friendship

*The Magic Rabbit* by Annette LeBlanc Cate

### Learning and Playing Together: School

*Elizabeti's School* by Stephanie Stuve-Bodeen

### Taking Care of Each Other: Family

*Max and the Tag-Along Moon* by Floyd Cooper

### Exploring Characters: Kevin Henkes

*Lilly's Big Day* by Kevin Henkes

### Exploring Nonfiction

*What Do You Do When Something Wants to Eat You?* by Steve Jenkins

*Water: Up, Down, and All Around* by Natalie M. Rosinsky

**Fiction and Nonfiction**

**Questions and Answers**

**Friendship**

**School**

**Kevin Henkes**

**Nonfiction**

**Section 2: Literary Analysis**

# RML1

## LA.U5.RML1

### Reading Minilesson Principle
## Fiction books are alike in some ways.

## Studying Fiction and Nonfiction

### You Will Need

- a basket of enough familiar fiction books so that small groups each have about four books, including examples of both realism and fantasy
- chart paper and markers
- sticky notes

### Academic Language / Important Vocabulary

- fiction
- story
- character
- alike

### Continuum Connection

- Connect texts by obvious categories: e.g., author, character, topic, genre, illustrator (p. 34)
- Understand that there are different types of texts and that you can notice different things about them (p. 34)
- Understand that fiction stories are imagined (p. 34)

## Goal

Notice and understand the characteristics of fiction as a genre.

## Rationale

When children develop understandings about the fiction genre through inquiry, they form a deeper understanding of the text and genre as they notice the recurring patterns, structures, and features of that particular genre. They also develop their comprehension skills as they are able to anticipate the characteristics as they read.

## Assess Learning

Observe children when they talk about the fiction genre. Notice if there is evidence of new learning based on the goal of this minilesson.

- ▶ Do children notice ways fiction stories are alike?
- ▶ Are children able to talk about characteristics of fiction?
- ▶ Can children use the terms *fiction, story, alike,* and *character*?

## Minilesson

To help children think about the minilesson principle, engage them in a short discussion of the characteristics of fiction. Here is an example.

- ▶ Have the children form small groups. Provide several examples from the basket of realistic and fantasy fiction books to each group.

   Turn and talk with your partner about one way all these books are alike.

- ▶ Allow time for discussion.

   What did you notice about how the fiction books are alike?

- ▶ Record responses on the chart paper. If children need additional help, provide some examples of fiction and nonfiction books on similar topics to highlight the characteristics of fiction books.

- ▶ As children talk about the characteristics of fiction stories, consider providing one or more of the following prompts. Write further responses on the chart.

   What do you notice about the characters in all these stories? Are they real?

   What do you notice about where all the stories take place? Could the places be real?

   Did the story really happen?

   What is the problem in each story?

   What happens to the problem in each story?

## Have a Try

Invite the children to talk about a fiction book with a partner.

> Turn and talk to a partner about a fiction book you have read.

## Summarize and Apply

Summarize the learning and remind children to think about the genre of fiction as they read.

> Let's look at our list of how fiction stories are always alike. Is there anything else you would like to add?

> Choose a fiction story to read during independent work time today. If you notice some of the things on the chart, place a sticky note on the page. Be ready to share your book when we meet after independent work time.

## Share

Following independent work time, have children sit in the meeting area in groups of three to talk about fiction stories.

> Share the title of the fiction story you read. Show the pages you marked with sticky notes and talk about what you noticed. After each person in the group has shared, talk about how the fiction books you discussed are alike.

## Extend the Lesson (Optional)

After assessing children's understanding, you might decide to extend the learning.

▶ Encourage children to notice the features on the chart in books shared during interactive read-aloud and shared reading and to add additional noticings as more are discovered.

▶ If children notice that there are different types of fiction (e.g., animal fantasy, realistic fiction), take time to talk about what they are thinking about the books.

---

# Fiction

**Noticings:**

Always

- The story has made-up characters.

- The place where the story happens can be made-up or real.

- The story didn't really happen.

**Studying Fiction and Nonfiction**

## You Will Need

- fiction noticings chart from RML1
- chart paper and markers

## Academic Language / Important Vocabulary

- fiction
- definition

**Continuum Connection**

- Understand that fiction stories are imagined (p. 34)

## Goal

Create a working definition of the fiction genre.

## Rationale

When you work with children to construct a concise definition of a genre, summarizing the essential features, you help them think about the most important characteristics of that genre based on their knowledge at that time. The inquiry process allows them to construct their understandings so they will be able to identify books in the genre as they encounter them independently.

## Assess Learning

Observe children when they talk about the fiction genre. Notice if there is evidence of new learning based on the goal of this minilesson.

- Can children describe the characteristics of fiction stories?
- Do they understand the working definition of fiction?
- Are they able to apply the working definition of fiction?
- Do children use the terms *fiction* and *definition*?

## Minilesson

To help children think about the minilesson principle, engage them in a discussion to construct a definition for fiction. Here is an example.

- Review the fiction noticings chart from RML1 with the children.

   Think about what you have noticed that fiction stories always have. Then we will use these ideas to write a definition of fiction. Our definition will tell what is always true about fiction stories.

- Write the words *Fiction books are* on the chart paper, reading them as you write.

   How you could finish this sentence to tell about fiction stories? Use the chart to help you.

- After time for thinking, ask volunteers to provide suggestions for ways to finish the sentence. Combine children's ideas to create a definition as a whole class. Write the definition on the chart paper.

## Have a Try

Invite the children to talk about a fiction book with a partner.

> Turn and talk with a partner about a fiction book you have read. Tell how it fits the definition we just wrote.

## Summarize and Apply

Summarize the learning and remind children to think about the fiction genre as they read.

▶ Reread the definition of fiction on the chart.

> Today choose a fiction book to read during independent work time. Think about the definition of fiction and if the book you read fits this definition. Bring the book when we meet after independent work time.

## Share

Following independent work time, have children sit in a circle to talk about the fiction genre.

▶ Model by sharing a book first, and then ask for several volunteers to share their books and how they fit the definition. Review the definition and prompt the conversation as needed.

## Extend the Lesson (Optional)

After assessing children's understanding, you might decide to extend the learning.

▶ Revisit and revise the fiction definition as children gain new understandings about the fiction genre (see p. 186).

▶ When you read a fiction book in another context (e.g., interactive read-aloud or shared reading), talk with the children about how they know the book is fiction.

▶ **Drawing/Writing About Reading** If children are keeping a reader's notebook, they can draw or write about fiction books that they have read.

# Fiction

Fiction books are stories that the author made up.

## RML3
### LA.U5.RML3

**Reading Minilesson Principle**
# Nonfiction books are alike in some ways.

## Studying Fiction and Nonfiction

### You Will Need

- a basket of enough familiar nonfiction books (e.g., biographies, memoirs, narrative nonfiction, expository nonfiction, how-to texts) for small groups to have about four
- chart paper and markers
- sticky notes

### Academic Language / Important Vocabulary

- nonfiction
- topic
- fact
- alike
- illustration
- photograph

### Continuum Connection

- Understand that there are different types of texts and that you can notice different things about them (p. 37)
- Notice and understand when a book is nonfiction (true information) (p. 37)

### Goal

Notice and understand the characteristics of nonfiction as a genre.

### Rationale

When children develop understandings about the nonfiction genre through inquiry, noticing the recurring patterns, structures, and features, they form a deeper understanding of the text and genre. They also develop their comprehension skills as they are able to anticipate the characteristics as they read.

### Assess Learning

Observe children when they talk about the nonfiction genre. Notice if there is evidence of new learning based on the goal of this minilesson.

- Do children notice ways nonfiction books are alike?
- Are children able to talk about characteristics of nonfiction?
- Do children use vocabulary such as *nonfiction, topic, fact, alike, illustration,* and *photograph* to talk about nonfiction books?

## Minilesson

To help children think about the minilesson principle, engage them in a discussion of the characteristics of nonfiction. Here is an example.

- Provide several examples of nonfiction books to small groups.

  Turn and talk about what each nonfiction book is about. Then, think about the ways the nonfiction books are alike.

- Allow time for discussion.

  What did you notice about the ways the nonfiction books are alike?

- As children share, help them decide whether the characteristic is *always* or *often* a part of nonfiction books by asking other groups if the books they revisited had the same characteristics.

- Record responses on the chart paper. If children need additional help, you can provide some examples of fiction and nonfiction books on similar topics so they can notice what is unique about nonfiction.

▶ As children talk about the characteristics of nonfiction books, consider providing one or more of the following prompts:

> What types of things do the authors write about? The topic is what the author writes about.
>
> What do you notice about what the author tries to teach you?
>
> Think about the pictures (illustrations or photographs). How do they help you learn about the topic in all the books?
>
> Is there anything else you notice?

## Have a Try

Invite the children to talk about a nonfiction book with a partner.

> Turn and tell your partner about a nonfiction book you have read.

## Summarize and Apply

Summarize the learning and remind children to think about the nonfiction genre as they read.

▶ Review the chart, emphasizing both the *always* category and the *often* category.

> Today, choose a nonfiction book to read during independent work time today. If you notice some of the things on the chart as you read, place a sticky note on that page. Bring the book when we meet after independent work time.

## Share

Following independent work time, have children sit in groups of three to talk about the nonfiction genre.

> Share the title of the nonfiction books you read. Show the pages with sticky notes and talk about what you noticed. After each person in the group has shared, talk about the ways the nonfiction books you discussed are alike.

## Extend the Lesson (Optional)

After assessing children's understanding, you might decide to extend the learning.

▶ Continue to add to the chart as children read and listen to other nonfiction books.

▶ If children notice that there are different types of nonfiction (e.g., procedural, expository, biography), take time to talk about what they are thinking about the books.

### Nonfiction
**Noticings:**

| Always | Often |
|---|---|
| • The book is about real things. | • The author uses diagrams and labels to give information. |
| • The author teaches you facts and gives real information about something. | • The illustrator gives more information in pictures or photographs. |

# RML 4
## LA.U5.RML4

**Reading Minilesson Principle**
# The definition of nonfiction is what is always true about it.

## You Will Need

- nonfiction noticings chart from RML3
- chart paper and markers
- a basket of nonfiction books that children are familiar with (e.g., biographies, memoirs, narrative nonfiction, expository nonfiction, how-to texts)

## Academic Language / Important Vocabulary

- nonfiction
- definition

## Continuum Connection

- Notice and understand when a book is nonfiction (true information) (p. 37)

## Goal

Create a working definition of the nonfiction genre.

## Rationale

When you work with children to construct a concise definition of a genre, summarizing the essential features, you help them think about the most important characteristics of that genre based on their knowledge at that time. The inquiry process allows them to form their understandings so they will be able to identify books in the genre as they encounter them independently.

## Assess Learning

Observe children when they talk about the nonfiction genre. Notice if there is evidence of new learning based on the goal of this minilesson.

- Can children describe the characteristics of nonfiction books?
- Do they understand the working definition of the nonfiction genre?
- Are they able to apply the working definition of nonfiction to books they read independently?
- Do children use vocabulary such as *nonfiction* and *definition*?

## Minilesson

To help children think about the minilesson principle, engage them in a discussion to construct a definition for *nonfiction*. Here is an example.

- Review the nonfiction noticings chart from RML3 with the children.

  Our noticings chart for nonfiction is a good place to start your thinking about a definition for nonfiction books. Our definition will be true for all nonfiction books. Look at the chart and think about how we can tell about nonfiction books.

  What are some of the things nonfiction books always have?

  What are nonfiction books about?

  Authors of nonfiction books usually write about one thing, such as weather or dinosaurs. Those things are called topics. The author gives information about the topic of the book. You can tell what nonfiction books are like by thinking about what you know about nonfiction books.

- Write the words *Nonfiction books have* on the chart paper, reading them as you write.

  How you could finish this sentence in a few words? Use the nonfiction noticings chart to help you.

- Combine children's ideas to construct a definition as a whole class. Write the definition on the chart paper.

## Have a Try

Invite the children to talk about a nonfiction book with a partner.

- Turn and talk with a partner about a nonfiction book you have read and how it fits the definition.

## Summarize and Apply

Summarize the learning and remind children to think about the nonfiction genre as they read.

- Reread the definition of nonfiction on the chart.

    Our definition is what is always true about nonfiction.

    Today, choose a nonfiction book to read during independent work time. Think about the definition of nonfiction books and if the book you read fits this definition. Bring the book when we meet when independent work time is over.

## Share

Following independent work time, have children sit in a circle to talk about the nonfiction genre.

    Model by sharing the title of your book and how it fits the definition. Then ask for several volunteers to share their books. Review the definition and prompt the conversation as needed.

## Extend the Lesson (Optional)

After assessing children's understanding, you might decide to extend the learning.

- Revisit and revise the nonfiction definition as children gain new understandings about the nonfiction genre (see p. 186).

- When you read a nonfiction book in interactive read-aloud or shared reading, talk with the children about how they know the book is nonfiction.

- **Drawing/Writing About Reading** If children are keeping a reader's notebook, they can draw or write about nonfiction books that they read.

## Nonfiction

Nonfiction books have true information that the writer tells about a topic.

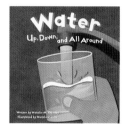

**Section 2: Literary Analysis**

**Reading Minilesson Principle**
## The author tells made-up stories in fiction books.

### Studying Fiction and Nonfiction

#### You Will Need

▶ three or four familiar books that are easily identifiable as fiction, such as the following:

- *Too Many Pears!* by Jackie French, from Text Set: Fiction and Nonfiction

- *Elizabeti's School* by Stephanie Stuve-Bodeen, from Text Set: School

- *The Magic Rabbit* by Annette LeBlanc Cate, from Text Set: Friendship

▶ chart paper and markers

#### Academic Language / Important Vocabulary

▶ fiction

▶ story

▶ character

▶ made-up

▶ author

#### Continuum Connection

▶ Understand that fiction stories are imagined (p. 34)

## Goal

Understand that the content of fiction stories is made up by the authors.

## Rationale

When children understand that fiction stories have characters, places, and things that are made up by the author, they are better able to distinguish between fiction and nonfiction books.

## Assess Learning

Observe children when they talk about the fiction genre. Notice if there is evidence of new learning based on the goal of this minilesson.

▶ Are children able to identify fiction books?

▶ Can they identify the characters, places, or things that are made up by the author?

▶ Do children use vocabulary such as *fiction*, *story*, *author*, *made-up*, and *characters* to talk about fiction?

## Minilesson

To help children think about the minilesson principle, engage them in a discussion of the characteristics of fiction. Here is an example.

▶ Begin reading *Too Many Pears!* on the page that says "Pamela liked pears for lunch" and end on the page that ends with "whipped cream."

Think about the characters and what is happening. How do you know this is a story that the author made up?

▶ Record responses on the chart paper.

You know that *Too Many Pears!* is fiction because cows don't eat pear pie and whipped cream. The author made up the story. Now think about *Elizabeti's School*.

▶ Read the first few pages of *Elizabeti's School*, and then read the author's note on the inside cover.

How do you know this is a fiction, or made-up, story?

▶ Record responses on the chart.

You know that *Elizabeti's School* is fiction because the author imagined the story. She used ideas from people she met when working in Tanzania, Africa. The things the author writes about could really happen, but she made them up for the story.

## Have a Try

Invite the children to talk with a partner about how they know *The Magic Rabbit* is fiction.

▶ Read the two-page spread of *The Magic Rabbit* that begins "Bunny hopped along."

> Turn and talk to a partner about how you know this book is fiction.

▶ After they turn and talk, invite a few children to share. Record responses on the chart.

## Summarize and Apply

Summarize the learning and remind children to think about the fiction genre as they read.

> What do authors write about in fiction books?

▶ Write the principle at the top of the chart.

> When you read today, think if the book you are reading is fiction. Be ready to share your book with a partner when we meet after independent work time.

## Share

Following independent work time, gather children together in the meeting area to talk about the fiction genre.

> Turn and talk to your partner about the book you read. Be sure to say if your book is fiction. If you read a fiction book, tell how you know it is fiction.

## Extend the Lesson (Optional)

After assessing children's understanding, you might decide to extend the learning.

▶ Continue to add to the chart as children read and listen to other fiction books.

▶ Use interactive writing to create lists of familiar fiction books.

▶ **Drawing/Writing About Reading** Have children draw and/or write about a familiar fiction book. Children could draw the characters and something that happened in the story that is made up. They can also write a few words telling what happened.

| The author tells made-up stories in fiction books. | |
|---|---|
| Book | How do you know the author made up the story? |
| **Too Many Pears!**  | Real cows don't eat pear pie with ice cream. |
| **Elizabeti's School**  | The author says she visited Tanzania, Africa, and learned ideas for this book. Elizabeti is not a real person. She is imagined by the author. |
| **A Magic Rabbit**  | A bunny walks around a city following stars to find a magician. |

Section 2: Literary Analysis

# RML6
## LA.U5.RML6

**Reading Minilesson Principle**
## The author tells about things that are real in nonfiction books.

## Studying Fiction and Nonfiction

### You Will Need

- three or four familiar books that are easily identifiable as nonfiction such as the following books from Text Set: Fiction and Nonfiction:
  - *On the Go* by Ann Morris
  - *Milk: From Cow to Carton* by Aliki
  - *Ice Bear: In the Steps of the Polar Bear* by Nicola Davies
- chart paper and markers

### Academic Language / Important Vocabulary

- nonfiction
- topic
- author
- real

### Continuum Connection

- Notice and understand when a book is nonfiction (true information) (p. 37)

## Goal

Understand that nonfiction authors write about real people, animals, places, or things.

## Rationale

When children understand that nonfiction authors tell about real people, places, and things, they are better able to distinguish between fiction and nonfiction books.

## Assess Learning

Observe children when they talk about the nonfiction genre. Notice if there is evidence of new learning based on the goal of this minilesson.

> ▶ Do children understand that the people, animals, places, or things described in nonfiction books are real?

> ▶ Do they use vocabulary such as *nonfiction*, *real*, and *author* to talk about nonfiction?

## Minilesson

To help children think about the minilesson principle, engage them in a discussion of the characteristics of nonfiction. Here is an example.

> ▶ Read a few pages of *On the Go*.
>
> > What does the author write about in this book?
> >
> > The author tells about real people, places, and things. She explains how real people around the world get from place to place.

> ▶ Record responses on the chart paper.

> ▶ Read a few pages from *Milk: From Cow to Carton*.
>
> > The topic is what the author writes about. As I read a few pages, notice the real information about the topic.

> ▶ Invite a few children to share with the group. Record responses on the chart.
>
> > The author of this book tells how real cows make milk.

## Have a Try

Invite the children to talk with a partner about what is real in *Ice Bear*.

▶ Read the page beginning with "No frost can steal" in *Ice Bear: In the Steps of the Polar Bear*.

> Turn and talk to your partner about what things the author tells about that are real.

▶ Invite a few children to share. Record responses on the chart.

## Summarize and Apply

Summarize the learning and remind children to notice the real things the author writes about as they read a nonfiction book.

> What does an author write about in a nonfiction book?

▶ Write the principle at the top of the chart.

> If you read a nonfiction book today, think about the people, animals, places, or things the author tells about that are real. Be ready to tell about your nonfiction book when we meet after independent work time.

## Share

Following independent work time, gather children in the meeting area to talk about the nonfiction genre.

> Who read a nonfiction book and would like to tell us what real things the author tells about?

## Extend the Lesson (Optional)

After assessing children's understanding, you might decide to extend the learning.

▶ Continue to add to the chart as children read and listen to other nonfiction books.

▶ Use interactive or shared writing to describe how children know a particular book is nonfiction.

▶ **Drawing/Writing About Reading** Have children draw and label a real person, animal, place, or thing from a familiar nonfiction book in a reader's notebook.

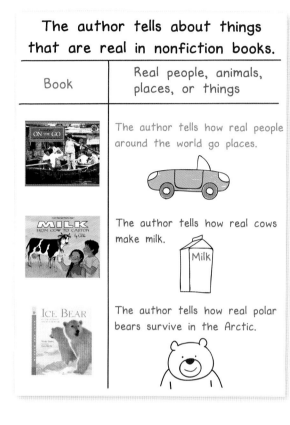

**The author tells about things that are real in nonfiction books.**

| Book | Real people, animals, places, or things |
|---|---|
| ON THE GO | The author tells how real people around the world go places. |
| MILK FROM COW TO CARTON | The author tells how real cows make milk. |
| ICE BEAR | The author tells how real polar bears survive in the Arctic. |

Section 2: Literary Analysis

**Reading Minilesson Principle**

# Writers tell stories that have characters, a problem, and a solution.

### You Will Need

- three or four fiction books that children have read recently and that have a clear narrative structure, such as the following:
  - *Lilly's Big Day* by Kevin Henkes, from Text Set: Kevin Henkes
  - *Going Places* by Peter and Paul Reynolds, from Text Set: Fiction and Nonfiction
  - *The Magic Rabbit* by Annette LeBlanc Cate, from Text Set: Friendship
- chart paper and markers

### Academic Language / Important Vocabulary

- fiction
- story
- author
- character

### Continuum Connection

- Understand that fiction stories are imagined (p. 34)
- Notice and understand a simple plot with problem and solution (p. 35)
- Recall important details about characters after a story is read (p. 35)

## Goal

Understand the important parts of a story: characters, problem, and solution.

## Rationale

When children explore the fiction genre by considering the basic structure of a story, they begin to recognize that fictional stories have characters involved in a series of events. This allows them to recognize fiction and to know what to anticipate.

## Assess Learning

Observe children when they talk about the fiction genre. Notice if there is evidence of new learning based on the goal of this minilesson.

- ▶ Do children understand the basic structure of a story, e.g., characters and a problem and solution?
- ▶ Are children able to identify the characters and important events in a story?
- ▶ Do children understand the words *fiction*, *story*, *author*, and *character*?

## Minilesson

To help children think about the minilesson principle, engage them in a discussion of the characteristics of fiction. Here is an example.

- ▶ Show *Lilly's Big Day*.

    Who is this book about? What problem does the character have?

    The most important character is Lilly. The author tells her problem and how it is solved.

- ▶ Record responses on the chart paper.
- ▶ Show *Going Places*.

    Turn and talk to your partner about who is in this story and what happens.

- ▶ Invite a few children to share with the group.

    The author tells the story of Rafael and Maya and their flying go-cart. First, the characters have a problem, and then they solve it. That's what makes the story.

- ▶ Record responses on the chart.

## Have a Try

Invite the children to talk about *The Magic Rabbit* with a partner.

▶ Show *The Magic Rabbit*.

> The stories we just looked at have characters, and the characters have a problem that they solve. Turn and talk with a partner about whether that is true for this story.

▶ Invite a few children to share. Record responses on the chart.

## Summarize and Apply

Summarize the learning and remind children to notice that fiction stories have characters, a problem, and a solution.

> Look at the chart. What is the same about these stories?

▶ Write the principle at the top of the chart.

> If you read a fiction book during independent work time today, think about the story the author tells. Bring the book so you can talk about the characters and the things that happen when we come back together.

## Share

Following independent work time, gather children in the meeting area to talk about the genre of fiction.

> Who would like to tell about the story in a fiction book they read? Did it have characters who had a problem?

## Extend the Lesson (Optional)

After assessing children's understanding, you might decide to extend the learning.

▶ Continue to add to the chart as children read and listen to more fiction books.

▶ **Drawing/Writing About Reading** Have children draw the characters and an important event from a familiar fiction book in a reader's notebook. They can also write a few words or sentences that describe what happens in the story.

| Writers tell stories that have characters, a problem, and a solution. | | |
|---|---|---|
| Title | Characters | Problem and Solution |
|  |  | Lilly wants to be a flower girl at her teacher's wedding. She helps Ginger in the wedding. |
|  |  | Rafael and Maya make a flying go-cart and win the race. |
|  |  | Bunny gets separated from Ray and finds his way back. |

**Reading Minilesson Principle**
# Writers tell true facts in nonfiction books.

## Studying Fiction and Nonfiction

### You Will Need

- three or four familiar nonfiction books with easily identifiable facts such as the following:
  - *Best Foot Forward* by Ingo Arndt, from Text Set: Questions and Answers
  - *What Do You Do with a Tail Like This?* by Steve Jenkins, from Text Set: Questions and Answers
  - *On the Go* by Ann Morris, from Text Set: Fiction and Nonfiction
- chart paper and markers
- basket of nonfiction books

### Academic Language / Important Vocabulary

- nonfiction
- author
- fact
- topic

### Continuum Connection

- Notice and understand when a book is nonfiction (true information) (p. 37)

## Goal

Understand nonfiction authors provide facts about a topic.

## Rationale

When children understand nonfiction books provide facts about a topic, they are better able to distinguish between fiction and nonfiction. This understanding prepares them to think about the new knowledge they will encounter.

## Assess Learning

Observe children when they talk about the nonfiction genre. Notice if there is evidence of new learning based on the goal of this minilesson.

- ▸ Do children understand nonfiction books contain facts about a topic?
- ▸ Are children able to identify some facts in a nonfiction book?
- ▸ Can children use vocabulary such as *nonfiction*, *fact*, *topic*, and *author* to talk about nonfiction?

## Minilesson

To help children think about the minilesson principle, engage them in a discussion of the characteristics of nonfiction. Here is an example.

- ▸ Read a few pages from *Best Foot Forward*.

  What is this book about? What facts, or true information, about animals' feet did you learn from these pages?

- ▸ Record responses on the chart paper.

  The author, Ingo Arndt, wrote about facts on this topic he is interested in. The topic is different animals' feet.

- ▸ Show *What Do You Do with a Tail Like This?*

  Listen as I read a few pages and think about what facts the author is teaching you.

- ▸ Read a few pages.

  What is the topic of this book? What facts did you learn about animal body parts from these pages?

- ▸ Record responses on the chart.

  You learned a lot of facts about animal body parts from the words and illustrations in this book.

## Have a Try

Invite the children to talk with a partner about facts in *On the Go*.

▶ Read a few pages from *On the Go*.

Think about the facts the author, Ann Morris, teaches you about her topic in these pages. Turn and talk to a partner about the facts you learned.

▶ Invite a few children to share. Record responses on the chart and review the chart.

## Summarize and Apply

Summarize the learning and remind children to notice true facts when they read nonfiction books.

What did you notice about nonfiction books today?

Authors tell facts, or true information, about a topic in nonfiction books.

▶ Write the principle at the top of the chart.

Choose a nonfiction book to read today during independent reading time. Think about the facts the author teaches you. Be ready to talk about the facts in the book when we come back together.

## Share

Following independent work time, gather children together in the meeting area to talk about facts in nonfiction books.

Who would like to share some of the facts they learned from the nonfiction book they read?

## Extend the Lesson (Optional)

After assessing children's understanding, you might decide to extend the learning.

▶ Continue to add to the chart as children read and listen to more nonfiction books.

▶ Use interactive or shared writing to list facts in nonfiction books read during interactive read-aloud.

▶ **Drawing/Writing About Reading** Have children draw a picture in a reader's notebook representing a fact they learned from reading or listening to a nonfiction book. They can also write a few words or a sentence describing what they learned.

### Writers tell true facts in nonfiction books.

| Title | Topic | Facts |
|---|---|---|
| Best Foot Forward | animal feet | • An ostrich has only two toes. <br> • A beetle has hairs on its feet. |
| What Do You Do When Something Wants To Eat You? | animal body parts | • An elephant uses its nose to give itself a bath. <br> • A hyena uses its nose to find its next meal. |
| On the Go | how people get from place to place | • People travel on foot. <br> • People ride horses. |

**Reading Minilesson Principle**
## Think about whether a book is fiction or nonfiction.

### Studying Fiction and Nonfiction

#### You Will Need

- three or four familiar fiction and nonfiction books such as the following:
  - *Lilly's Big Day* by Kevin Henkes, from Text Set: Kevin Henkes
  - *Max and the Tag-Along Moon* by Floyd Cooper, from Text Set: Family
  - *What Do You Do When Something Wants to Eat You?* by Steve Jenkins, from Text Set: Nonfiction
  - *Water: Up, Down, and All Around* by Natalie M. Rosinsky, from Text Set: Nonfiction
- chart paper and markers

#### Academic Language / Important Vocabulary

- fiction
- story
- nonfiction
- author
- fact

#### Continuum Connection

- Understand that fiction stories are imagined (p. 34)
- Notice and understand when a book is nonfiction (true information) (p. 37)

### Goal

Notice and understand when a book is fiction or nonfiction.

### Rationale

When you teach children to differentiate between fiction and nonfiction, they are better able to anticipate the thinking they will need to do as they read the specific genre. This allows them to better understand the text.

### Assess Learning

Observe children when they talk about the fiction and nonfiction genres. Notice if there is evidence of new learning based on the goal of this minilesson.

- Are children able to identify whether a book is fiction or nonfiction?
- Are children able to explain how they know a book is fiction or nonfiction?
- Do children use the words *fiction*, *story*, *nonfiction*, *fact*, and *author* to talk about fiction and nonfiction?

## Minilesson

To help children think about the minilesson principle, engage them in a discussion of the differences between fiction and nonfiction. Here is an example.

- Read and show the first two pages of *Lilly's Big Day*.

  Is this book fiction or nonfiction? What makes you think that?

- Record responses on the chart paper.

  You know this story is fiction because it tells a made-up story about a mouse.

  Now listen as I read *Max and the Tag-Along Moon*.

- Read the first few pages.

  Is this book fiction or nonfiction? What makes you think that?

- Record responses on the chart. As needed, talk about how this is an imagined story, but Max, his grandpa, and the things they do could happen in the real world.

- Show *What Do You Do When Something Wants to Eat You?*

  Think about whether this book is fiction or nonfiction.

- Read the first five pages.

  Is this book fiction or nonfiction? How do you know?

- Record responses on the chart.

## Have a Try

Invite the children to talk with a partner about whether *Water: Up, Down, and All Around* is fiction or nonfiction.

▶ Read pages 4–7 of *Water: Up, Down, and All Around*.

> Turn and talk to a partner about whether this book is fiction or nonfiction and how you know.

▶ Invite a few children to share. Record responses on the chart.

## Summarize and Apply

Summarize the learning and remind children to think about whether a book is fiction or nonfiction before they read.

> How does our chart help you think about whether a book is fiction or nonfiction?

> As you read today, think about whether the book you choose is fiction or nonfiction. Be ready to talk about the book when we meet after independent work time.

## Share

Following independent work time, gather children together in the meeting area to talk about fiction and nonfiction.

> Give a thumbs-up if you read a fiction book today.

> Who read a nonfiction book?

▶ Ask a few children to share how they knew their book was fiction or nonfiction.

## Extend the Lesson (Optional)

After assessing children's understanding, you might decide to extend the learning.

▶ If you keep a class reading log of books you have read aloud together, add a new column, "Fiction or Nonfiction," and have children identify the genre of each new book you read.

▶ Gather fiction and nonfiction books into a basket. Encourage children to explore the books independently or with a partner. Ask the children to discuss whether the book they chose is fiction or nonfiction and what makes them think that.

▶ **Drawing/Writing About Reading** Use interactive writing to write about a familiar book. Include whether the book is fiction or nonfiction and how the children know.

| Title | Fiction or nonfiction? | How do you know? |
|---|---|---|
| Lilly's Big Day | fiction | Lilly is a mouse, but she wears clothes and talks. |
| Max the Tag-Along Moon | fiction | Max does things like a real boy, but the author made him up. |
| What Do You Do When Something Wants To Eat You? | nonfiction | The author tells facts about animals. |
| Water Up-Down and All Around | nonfiction | The author tells facts about where raindrops come from and the water cycle. |

*Think about whether a book is fiction or nonfiction.*

## Assessment

After you have taught the minilessons in this umbrella, observe children talking and writing about their reading of fiction and nonfiction across instructional contexts: interactive read-aloud, independent reading and literacy work, guided reading, shared reading, and book club. Use *The Literacy Continuum* (Fountas and Pinnell 2017) to observe children's reading and writing behaviors across instructional contexts.

▶ What evidence do you have of new understandings related to the characteristics of fiction and nonfiction?

- Can children identify books as fiction or nonfiction?

- Are children able to understand the definition of fiction and nonfiction books and use academic language, such as *fiction, nonfiction,* and *topic*?

- Can children discuss the made-up characters, places, or things in fiction?

- Can they discuss what is real in a nonfiction book?

▶ In what other ways, beyond the scope of this umbrella, are children talking about genre?

- Are children talking about whether a character seems real or not real?

- Do they notice that some fiction stories could happen while others could not?

- Are they noticing how illustrations give more information?

- Are they noticing that some nonfiction books also tell a story?

Use your observations to determine the next umbrella you will teach. You may also consult Minilessons Across the Year (p. 51) for guidance.

## Read and Revise

After completing the steps in the genre study process, help children to read and revise their definition of the genre based on their new understandings.

▶ Before: Fiction books are stories that the author made up.

▶ After: Fiction books are stories that the author made up, and they have made-up characters, places, and things.

▶ Before: Nonfiction books have true information that the writer tells about a topic.

▶ After: Nonfiction books have facts about a topic and are about real people, animals, places, or things.

## Minilessons in This Umbrella

**RML1**  The author gives a message in a story.

**RML2**  The author gives a message in a nonfiction book.

**RML3**  More than one author can give the same message.

## Before Teaching Umbrella 6 Minilessons

Read and discuss fiction and nonfiction books that have a clear, easily identifiable author's message; in other words, it's clear what the author is trying to say through the medium of the story. Use the following books from the *Fountas & Pinnell Classroom™ Interactive Read-Aloud Collection* text sets or choose similar books that have a clear author's message from your library.

**The Importance of Kindness**

*Jamaica Tag-Along* by Juanita Havill

*Now One Foot, Now the Other* by Tomie dePaola

**Exploring Fiction and Nonfiction**

*Going Places* by Peter and Paul Reynolds

**Exploring Nonfiction**

*Tools* by Ann Morris

*Surprising Sharks* by Nicola Davies

**Living and Working Together: Community**

*Be My Neighbor* by Maya Ajmera and John D. Ivanko

**Journeys Near and Far**

*When This World Was New* by D. H. Figueredo

**Celebrating Diversity**

*My Name Is Yoon* by Helen Recorvits

*To Be a Kid* by Maya Ajmera and John D. Ivanko

*Whoever You Are* by Mem Fox

As you read aloud and enjoy these texts together, help children

* talk about the plot in fiction books and the information in nonfiction books,

* discuss what the author is trying to tell readers, and

* connect books that have similar messages.

**Kindness**

**Fiction and Nonfiction**

**Nonfiction**

**Community**

**Journeys**

**Diversity**

**Section 2: Literary Analysis**

# RML1
## LA.U6.RML1

**Reading Minilesson Principle**
# The author gives a message in a story.

## Thinking About the Author's Message

### You Will Need

- two or three fiction books written by different authors with different themes, such as the following:
  - *Jamaica Tag-Along* by Juanita Havill, from Text Set: Kindness
  - *Now One Foot, Now the Other* by Tomie dePaola, from Text Set: Kindness
  - *Going Places* by Peter and Paul Reynolds, from Text Set: Fiction and Nonfiction
- chart paper and markers

### Academic Language / Important Vocabulary

- author
- story
- message

### Continuum Connection

- Infer the messages in a work of fiction (p. 34)

### Goal

Understand that an author often conveys a message for the reader through a story.

### Rationale

When you teach children to think about what the author wants the reader to know by telling a story, you give them a reason to revisit the story and to think deeply about it. Thinking about the author's message also provides children insight into why an author chooses to write the story, something they can think about when they write their own stories.

### Assess Learning

Observe children when they talk about the author's message in a story. Notice if there is evidence of new learning based on the goal of this minilesson.

- Can children identify the author's message in a story?
- Do they understand the terms *author*, *story*, and *message*?

## Minilesson

To help children think about the minilesson principle, engage them in a short discussion of what an author's message is. Here is an example.

- Show *Jamaica Tag-Along* and help children recap the major events of the story.

   What happens when Jamaica wants to play ball with her brother and his friends? What happens when the little boy, Berto, wants to build a sandcastle with Jamaica? What does Jamaica learn at the end of the story? Jamaica learns a lesson at the end of this story. What do you think the author wants you to learn from reading this story?

   The author uses what the characters, in this case, Jamaica, say or do to give a message to the reader. What do you think the author's message is in this book?

- Record responses on the chart paper. Then repeat with *Now One Foot, Now the Other* to help children learn what the author's message is.

   What does Bobby's grandfather help Bobby learn when he is a baby? After his grandfather gets sick, what does Bobby help him learn how to do? What do you think the author wants you to learn about families from this story? What is his message about families?

- Record responses on the chart.

## Have a Try

Invite the children to talk with a partner about the author's message in *Going Places*.

The author gives a message in a story.

*Jamaica Tag-Along* — Treat others as you would like to be treated.

*Now One Foot, Now the Other* (Tomie dePaola) — Family members help each other in times of need.

*Going Places* — Be creative by using your imagination. It is okay to be different.

▶ Review the main events of *Going Places*.

> Turn and talk to a partner about the author's message in this story. What does the author want you to learn from reading this story?

▶ Record responses on the chart.

## Summarize and Apply

Summarize the learning and remind children to think about the author's message when they read a story.

▶ Review the chart.

> What did we talk about today?

▶ Write the principle at the top of the chart.

▶ Provide a selection of familiar fiction books for children to choose from.

> Choose a story to read today. Think about the author's message as you read. Be ready to share the author's message when we meet after independent work time.

## Share

Following independent work time, gather children together in the meeting area to talk about the author's message in a story.

> Turn and talk to your partner about the author's message in the story you read today.

## Extend the Lesson (Optional)

After assessing children's understanding, you might decide to extend the learning.

▶ When children write stories, encourage them to think about the message that they want readers to learn.

▶ **Drawing/Writing About Reading** Use interactive or shared writing to model for children how to write the message of a story in a reader's notebook.

**Reading Minilesson Principle**
# The author gives a message in a nonfiction book.

## Thinking About the Author's Message

### You Will Need

- two or three simple informational texts with a clear message, such as the following:
  - *Tools* by Ann Morris, from Text Set: Nonfiction
  - *Surprising Sharks* by Nicola Davies, from Text Set: Nonfiction
  - *Be My Neighbor*, by Maya Ajmera and John D. Ivanko, from Text Set: Community
- chart paper and markers
- selection of familiar nonfiction books

### Academic Language / Important Vocabulary

- nonfiction
- author
- message

### Continuum Connection

- Infer the significance of nonfiction content to their own lives (p. 38)

## Goal

Infer simple messages in a work of nonfiction.

## Rationale

When you teach children to think about the message in a nonfiction book, you help them to think not only about what information the author wants the reader to learn but why that information is important. Learning to look for a message in a nonfiction book will become the foundation of a critical, questioning reader later.

## Assess Learning

Observe children when they talk about the author's message in nonfiction books. Notice if there is evidence of new learning based on the goal of this minilesson.

- Are children able to identify the author's message in a nonfiction book?
- Can children talk with a partner about the messages they notice in nonfiction books?
- Can they use the terms *author*, *nonfiction*, and *message*?

## Minilesson

To help children think about the minilesson principle, engage them in a short discussion of what an author's message is in nonfiction books. Here is an example.

- Show *Tools*. Briefly recap what the book is about.

  What does the author want you to learn from this book?

  The author tells you how different tools are helpful. What is one big idea about the whole book that the author wants you to learn?

- Record responses on the chart paper. Then show *Surprising Sharks* and reread pages 24 and 27. Then read the author biography on the final page.

  Sometimes books have a note about the author that helps you understand the author's message. Why does Nicola Davies want you to learn about sharks? That is her message.

- Record responses on the chart.

## Have a Try

Invite the children to talk with a partner about the message in *Be My Neighbor*.

▶ Reread the large green text throughout *Be My Neighbor*. Encourage children to think about the message and pay attention to the photographs while they listen.

> Turn and talk to a partner about what you think the authors want you to learn from this book. What is their message about neighborhoods?

▶ Record responses on the chart.

## Summarize and Apply

Summarize the learning and remind children to think about the author's message when they read a nonfiction book.

▶ Review the chart.

> What did we talk about today?

▶ Write the principle at the top of the chart.

▶ Provide children with a selection of familiar nonfiction books to choose from.

> Choose a nonfiction book to read today and think about the author's message. You will share the author's message when we meet after independent work time.

## Share

Following independent work time, gather children together in the meeting area to talk about the author's message in the nonfiction book they read.

> Turn and talk to a partner about the author's message in the nonfiction book you read today.

## Extend the Lesson (Optional)

After assessing children's understanding, you might decide to extend the learning.

▶ Encourage children to think and talk about the author's message when discussing nonfiction books during interactive read-aloud or shared reading.

▶ **Drawing/Writing About Reading** After reading a nonfiction book, have children write or draw the author's message in a reader's notebook.

The author gives a message in a nonfiction book.

Tools help you do things.

Sharks are interesting animals and need to be protected.

Every neighborhood is special, but all neighborhoods have some of the same things.

**Reading Minilesson Principle**
# More than one author can give the same message.

### Thinking About the Author's Message

#### You Will Need

- two sets of books by different authors that have a similar message, such as the following:
  - *When This World Was New* by D. H. Figueredo, from Text Set: Journeys
  - *My Name Is Yoon* by Helen Recorvits, from Text Set: Diversity
  - *To Be a Kid* by Maya Ajmera and John D. Ivanko from Text Set: Diversity
  - *Whoever You Are* by Mem Fox, from Text Set: Diversity
- chart paper and markers

#### Academic Language / Important Vocabulary

- message
- author
- story

#### Continuum Connection

- Make connections (similarities and differences) among texts that have the same author/illustrator, setting, characters, or theme (p. 34)

## Goal

Notice the same message across multiple works of fiction and nonfiction.

## Rationale

When you teach children that some authors give the same message in different ways and through different books, you build an understanding of universal ideas and a recognition that people are connected by common ideas. Children learn to make connections from the text to themselves and from one text to another, broadening their understanding of the message and individual texts.

## Assess Learning

Observe children when they talk about the author's message. Notice if there is evidence of new learning based on the goal of this minilesson.

▶ Can children identify the author's message in fiction and nonfiction?

▶ Do children notice when two or more books have the same or a similar message?

▶ Do they use the terms *message, author,* and *story*?

## Minilesson

To help children think about the minilesson principle, engage them in a short discussion of identifying the same message by more than one author. Here is an example.

▶ Show *When This World Was New* and prompt the children to remember the important events. Recall how Danilito feels when he moves to America.

> Why is moving to America difficult for Danilito?

> Why do you think the author wants you to know what it's like to move to a new country? What is his message?

▶ Write the message on the chart paper.

▶ Show *My Name Is Yoon* and prompt the children to remember how Yoon feels about moving to a new country.

> What is difficult for her? Why does the author want you to know about moving to a new country? What do you think is her message?

▶ Note this is the same message as the first one on the chart.

> What do you notice about the author's message in both books?

> Sometimes more than one author gives the same message.

## Have a Try

Invite the children to talk about author's message with a partner.

▶ Show *Whoever You Are* and *To Be a Kid*.

Look at these two books. What do you think the authors want you to learn and think about? Turn and talk to a partner about what you think each author's message is.

What do you notice about the author's message in both books?

## Summarize and Apply

Summarize the learning and remind children to think about the author's message when they read.

▶ Review the chart.

What did you learn today about authors' messages?

▶ Write the principle at the top of the chart.

When you read during independent work time, think about the author's message. Later, we will find out if anyone's books have the same message.

## Share

Following independent work time, gather children together in the meeting area to talk about the author's message in the book they read.

Who would like to share the author's message in the book you read?

Did anyone else read a book with a similar message?

## Extend the Lesson (Optional)

After assessing children's understanding, you might decide to extend the learning.

▶ Provide children with several familiar books. Discuss the author's message in each. Have the children group the books that share a similar message.

▶ Discuss the author's message during interactive read-aloud, and encourage children to think of other books with a similar message.

▶ **Drawing/Writing About Reading** Use interactive or shared writing to add more books to the chart as children encounter more books with similar messages.

**More than one author can give the same message.**

It can be hard to get used to living in a new country.

## Assessment

After you have taught the minilessons in this umbrella, observe children as they talk and write about the author's message during their reading across instructional contexts: interactive read-aloud, independent reading and literacy work, guided reading, shared reading, and book club. Use *The Literacy Continuum* (Fountas and Pinnell 2017) to observe children's reading and writing behaviors across instructional contexts.

▶ What evidence do you have of new understandings related to the author's message?

- Can children identify the author's message in both fiction and nonfiction books?

- Do they make connections between different books with similar messages?

- Do they use academic language, such as *author, message, story,* and *nonfiction*?

▶ In what other ways, beyond the scope of this umbrella, are they talking about the author's message?

- Do children notice common messages in different books written by the same author?

- Are children beginning to realize that a book can have more than one message?

Use your observations to determine the next umbrella you will teach. You may also consult Minilessons Across the Year (p. 51) for guidance.

## Link to Writing

After teaching the minilessons in this umbrella, help children link the new learning to their own writing:

▶ When children write their own stories and nonfiction books, encourage them to think about why the topic they are writing about is important to them. What do they want their readers to learn from the book? What is their message?

## Minilessons in This Umbrella

**RML1** Authors write books to make it fun for you to read.

**RML2** Authors write books to give information.

**RML3** Authors write books to get you to think or do something.

## Before Teaching Umbrella 7 Minilessons

Read aloud and discuss both fiction and nonfiction picture books, so children have enough information to make inferences about why authors write books. Use the books suggested below from the *Fountas & Pinnell Classroom™ Interactive Read-Aloud Collection* text sets or choose fiction books with simple plots that clearly show the author tries to make readers laugh and nonfiction texts about various topics and some that get readers to think or do something. It may be important to note that all the books are fun to read but some are funny.

### Exploring Fiction and Nonfiction

*Ice Bear: In the Steps of the Polar Bear* by Nicola Davies

*Milk: From Cow to Carton* by Aliki

### Exploring Nonfiction

*Surprising Sharks* by Nicola Davies

### Mo Willems: Having Fun with Humor

*I Am Invited to a Party!* by Mo Willems

*Don't Let the Pigeon Drive the Bus!* by Mo Willems

*Knuffle Bunny: A Cautionary Tale* by Mo Willems

### Nicola Davies: Exploring the Animal World

*One Tiny Turtle* by Nicola Davies

### Asking Questions: Nonfiction

*Best Foot Forward* by Ingo Arndt

*What Do You Do with a Tail Like This?* by Steve Jenkins and Robin Page

As you read aloud and enjoy books together, help children

- express opinions about the texts (e.g., interesting, exciting, funny),
- notice humorous or entertaining parts of a story,
- understand and discuss new information learned from a nonfiction book, and
- think about why the author might have written the text.

**Fiction and Nonfiction**

**Nonfiction**

**Mo Willems**

**Nicola Davies**

**Questions: Nonfiction**

**Section 2: Literary Analysis**

# RML1
## LA.U7.RML1

**Reading Minilesson Principle**
## Authors write books to make it fun for you to read.

**Thinking About the Author's Purpose**

### You Will Need

▸ two or three books clearly written to be fun to read, such as the following from Text Set: Mo Willems:

- *Don't Let the Pigeon Drive the Bus!*
- *Knuffle Bunny: A Cautionary Tale*
- *I Am Invited to a Party!*

▸ chart paper and markers

▸ sticky notes

### Academic Language / Important Vocabulary

▸ author

▸ write

▸ funny

### Continuum Connection

▸ Understand that a writer has a purpose in writing a fiction or nonfiction text (p. 35)

▸ Express opinions about a text (e.g., interesting, funny, exciting) and support with evidence (p. 35)

## Goal

Understand that sometimes an author may write stories to entertain.

## Rationale

When children understand why an author wrote a text, it helps them to know what to expect and how to read it. Understanding that an author's purpose sometimes is to make a book fun to read allows children to enjoy the characters, the often-relatable problems, the playful language, or the engaging illustrations.

## Assess Learning

Observe children when they talk about authors who write books to entertain. Notice if there is evidence of new learning based on the goal of this minilesson.

▸ Can children tell whether a book was written to be funny?

▸ Do they provide evidence for how they know a book was written to be funny?

▸ Do they use the terms *author, write,* and *funny*?

## Minilesson

To help children think about the minilesson principle, engage them in a short discussion of authors who write to make them laugh. Here is an example.

▸ Show *Don't Let the Pigeon Drive the Bus!* Read the page before the title page and the title page, and then read the page beginning "C'mon!" through the two-page spread that says, "Let me drive the bus!"

> **What do you think about this book? What makes you laugh?**

▸ Record responses on the chart paper.

> **Now, listen to part of another book by Mo Willems, *Knuffle Bunny*.**

▸ Begin reading the page that says, "Trixie helped her daddy" through the page ending with, "Snurp."

> **Turn and talk to your partner about what you think about this book. Say what makes you think that.**

▸ After children turn and talk, guide them to think about why the author probably wrote these books.

> **You enjoyed reading these books because what the characters said and did was funny. Why do you think Mo Willems wrote these books?**

> **Mo Willems wrote these two books to make you laugh.**

## Have a Try

Invite the children to apply the new thinking about author's purpose with a partner.

> Here's another book by Mo Willems. As I read, think if Mo Willems wrote this book for the same reason he wrote the other two books.

▶ Begin reading the page that says, "What if it is a pool party?" to the end of the book.

> Turn and talk to a partner about why Mo Willems wrote this book.

▶ Invite a few children to share their thoughts. Record responses on the chart.

## Summarize and Apply

Summarize the learning and remind children to notice if the author wrote a book to make it fun to read.

> What did you learn today about why some authors write books?

▶ Review the chart and write the principle at the top.

> When you read, think about why the author wrote the book. Ask yourself, "Does the author want to make me laugh?" Use a sticky note to mark a page where the author made you laugh so you can talk about that page.

## Share

Following independent work time, gather children together in the meeting area to share how an author made a book fun to read.

> Give a thumbs-up if the author wrote the book to make you laugh.

▶ Have a few children share what made them laugh.

## Extend the Lesson (Optional)

After assessing children's understanding, you might decide to extend the learning.

▶ Teach the minilesson again using books that are fun to read for different reasons, such as familiar characters in a series book or an interesting topic in a nonfiction book.

▶ **Drawing/Writing About Reading** Invite children to draw the part of a book that indicated why the author wrote a story that is funny. They may label the illustration and/or write a sentence about why the author wrote the story.

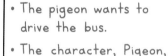

**Authors write books to make it fun for you to read.**

| Book | Why the Book Is Fun to Read |
|---|---|
|  | • The pigeon wants to drive the bus.<br>• The character, Pigeon, is funny! |
|  | • Trixie said funny words.<br>• Trixie had pants on her head! |
|  | • Gerald is funny.<br>• Piggie falls over when Elephant yells.<br>• That illustration is crazy. |

**Section 2: Literary Analysis**

## Thinking About the Author's Purpose

- two or three books clearly written to inform, such as the following:
  - *Best Foot Forward* by Ingo Arndt, from Text Set: Questions: Nonfiction
  - *Milk: From Cow to Carton* by Aliki, from Text Set: Fiction and Nonfiction
  - *What Do You Do with a Tail Like This?* by Steve Jenkins and Robin Page, from Text Set: Questions: Nonfiction
- chart paper and markers
- sticky notes

### Academic Language / Important Vocabulary

- author
- write
- information

### Continuum Connection

- Understand that a writer has a purpose in writing a fiction or nonfiction text (p. 35)
- Notice and understand when a book is nonfiction (true information) (p. 37)

## Goal

Understand that sometimes authors write to give the reader information.

## Rationale

Recognizing that an author may write a book to give information builds awareness for how to read an informational text and how that experience differs from reading a text written solely for another purpose. However, children may soon realize that some books both provide information and are funny.

## Assess Learning

Observe children when they talk about authors who write to give information. Notice if there is evidence of new learning based on the goal of this minilesson.

- ▶ Can children tell when a book was written to give the reader information?
- ▶ Do they provide evidence for their statements of how they know a book was written to give them information?
- ▶ Do they use the terms *author, write,* and *information*?

## Minilesson

To help children think about the minilesson principle, engage them in a short discussion about books written to give information. Here is an example.

> Listen to part of a book you know, *Best Foot Forward*. As I read, think about why the author wrote this book.

▶ Read pages 8–9 and 13.

> Why did the author write this book? What makes you think that?

> The author gives information about animals' feet.

▶ Record responses on the chart paper.

> Here is the book *Milk: From Cow to Carton*. As I read a bit of this book, think about why the author wrote it.

▶ Read pages 10–13.

> Turn and talk to a partner about why you think the author, Aliki, wrote this book. How do you know she wanted to give you information?

▶ Record responses on the chart.

> You learned something from both books. Ingo Arndt gave you information about different animal feet, flippers, and claws. Aliki gave you information about how milk gets from the cow to your house. When you read books like these, be sure to read carefully and pay attention to the information.

## Have a Try

Invite the children to apply the new thinking about authors writing books to give information with a partner.

▶ Show *What Do You Do with a Tail Like This?* Read the page that says, "What do you do with a nose like this?" and the next two pages.

> Turn and talk to a partner about why you think the authors wrote this book.

▶ Listen to children's comments and record responses on the chart.

## Summarize and Apply

Summarize the learning and remind children to notice when an author is giving information.

> What did you learn today about why authors sometimes write books?

▶ Review the chart and write the principle at the top.

> We talked about authors who write to give you information.

> When you read today, think about why the author wrote the book. Ask yourself, "Is the author giving me information?" Use a sticky note to mark a page that gives you new information.

## Share

Following independent work time, gather children together in the meeting area to talk about author's purpose.

> Turn and talk to a partner about the information the author gives in your book. Show some pages that helped you know.

## Extend the Lesson (Optional)

After assessing children's understanding, you might decide to extend the learning.

▶ During interactive read-aloud, talk with children about why authors write a book.

▶ **Drawing/Writing About Reading** Have children draw the part of a book that showed the author was giving information. They may label the illustration and/or write a sentence about why the author wrote the book to give information.

| Authors write books to give information. | |
|---|---|
| **Book** | **What Information the Author Gave** |
|  | • Tigers have cushioned pads on their feet. |
|  | • A cow begins to make milk when she has a baby. |
|  | • An elephant uses its nose to bathe itself. |

**Section 2: Literary Analysis**

**Reading Minilesson Principle**
## Authors write books to get you to think or do something.

**Thinking About the Author's Purpose**

### You Will Need

- two or three books clearly written to get the reader to think a certain way or to do something, such as the following:
  - *Ice Bear: In the Steps of the Polar Bear* by Nicola Davies, from Text Set: Fiction and Nonfiction
  - *Surprising Sharks* by Nicola Davies, from Text Set: Nonfiction
  - *One Tiny Turtle* by Nicola Davies, from Text Set: Nicola Davies
- chart paper
- markers
- sticky notes

### Academic Language / Important Vocabulary

- author
- write
- think

### Continuum Connection

- Understand that a writer has a purpose in writing a fiction or nonfiction text (p. 35)
- Notice when a writer is trying to persuade readers (p. 37)

### Goal

Understand that sometimes an author writes to get readers to think or do something.

### Rationale

Recognizing that an author may write to get readers to think a certain way or to do something builds awareness for how to read such a text. When children learn an author is writing to get them to think a certain way or do something, it prepares them to notice what the author wants them to do or think and then decide if the author has convinced them.

### Assess Learning

Observe children when they talk about how an author gets them to think a certain way or do something. Notice if there is evidence of new learning based on the goal of this minilesson.

- Can children tell when an author writes to get them to think a certain way or do something?
- Are they able to provide evidence for why a book was written to get them to think a certain way or do something?
- Do children notice other reasons authors write books, such as to make it fun by or to give information?
- Do they use the terms *author, write* and *think*?

## Minilesson

To help children think about the minilesson principle, engage them in a short discussion about how authors write to get them to think a certain way or to do something. Here is an example.

- Show *Ice Bear: In the Steps of the Polar Bear.*

  Listen as I read and think about why the author wrote this book.

- Read pages 26–27 and the "About Polar Bears" page.

  Why do you think Nicola Davies wrote this book?

- Children may need to be prompted to understand Nicola Davis wrote the book to get them to think about what's happening to polar bears.

  I think Nicola Davies wants us to agree with her that people should help save polar bears' homes. She wants us to think a certain way and maybe do something.

- If necessary, reread the last sentence on page 27. Record responses on the chart paper. Then show *Surprising Sharks.*

▶ Read the sentence on page 23 that starts, "Oh yes," and then read pages 24–27 and 29.

>  Why do you think Nicola Davies wrote this book?

▶ Record responses on the chart.

## Have a Try

Invite the children to apply the new thinking with a partner.

▶ Repeat with *One Tiny Turtle*. Read pages 22–27.

>  Turn and talk about why you think Nicola Davies wrote this book. Tell what makes you think that.

▶ Listen to comments and record responses on the chart.

## Summarize and Apply

Summarize the learning and remind children to think about why authors write books.

>  What did you learn today about why authors write books?

▶ Review the chart and write the principle at the top.

>  When you know an author wrote to get you to think a certain way, you can decide if you agree or disagree by focusing on the information.

>  Authors write a book to be funny, to give information, or to get you to think or do something. When you read today, think about why the author wrote your book. Use a sticky note to mark a page that helps you know why.

## Share

Following independent work time, gather children together in the meeting area to talk about how authors write to get them to think or do something.

>  Give a thumbs-up if the book you read got you to think a certain way or to do something.

▶ Ask children to share other reasons the authors wrote their books.

## Extend the Lesson (Optional)

After assessing children's understanding, you might decide to extend the learning.

▶ Talk about why authors write a book during interactive read-aloud, shared reading, and independent reading conferences. Note to the children that an author might write a book for more than one reason.

| Authors write books to get you to think or do something. | |
|---|---|
| **Book** | **What the Author Wants Me to Do** |
|  | • Help save polar bears' homes |
|  | • Understand that sharks are important and interesting creatures that only kill prey to eat |
|  | • Take care of turtles |

## Assessment

After you have taught the minilessons in this umbrella, observe children as they talk and write about their reading across instructional contexts: interactive read-aloud, independent reading and literacy work, guided reading, shared reading, and book club. Use *The Literacy Continuum* (Fountas and Pinnell 2017) to observe children's reading and writing behaviors across instructional contexts.

▶ What evidence do you have of new understandings related to author's purpose?

- Can children identify books that are written to be funny to give information, or to get them to think a certain way or do something?

- Are children able to provide evidence to explain the author's purpose?

- Do you notice children using the academic vocabulary related to author's purpose?

- Do children use their understanding of the author's purpose to help them focus on and discuss important parts of the text?

- Do they use the terms *author, write, funny,* and *information* when talking about why authors write books?

▶ In what other ways, beyond the scope of this umbrella, are they talking about author's purpose?

- Are children thinking or asking about additional author's purposes? For example, is the intention to explain how to do something (procedural), to share a memory or experience (memoir/personal narrative), to teach a moral or a lesson (folktale, fable), to express feelings or sensory images (poetry) or to share about one's life (biography)?

Use your observations to determine the next umbrella you will teach. You may also consult Minilessons Across the Year (p. 51) for guidance.

## Link to Writing

After teaching the minilessons in this umbrella, help children link the new learning to their writing:

▶ As children write informational pieces during writers' workshop, encourage them to think about their purpose for writing. What information do they want readers to know? What ideas do they want to stay with the readers?

▶ As children write personal narrative pieces during writers' workshop, encourage them to think about how they can make their writing interesting so the reader has fun reading the writing. Help them think about using engaging beginnings and endings, descriptive details, including dialogue, and interesting word choice to keep readers' attention.

## Minilessons in This Umbrella

**RML1**  Writers choose interesting words.

**RML2**  Sometimes writers compare one thing to another.

**RML3**  Writers use descriptive language to show you what they mean.

## Before Teaching Umbrella 8 Minilessons

Read and discuss fiction picture books with themes reflecting everyday life. Choose books with language that makes comparisons or is descriptive (even made-up words), figurative, and/or poetic. Use the following books from the *Fountas & Pinnell Classroom™ Interactive Read-Aloud Collection* text sets or choose other books in which the authors have made deliberate and interesting word choices.

### Poetic Language

*Mud* by Mary Lyn Ray

*Puddles* by Jonathan London

*Subway Ride* by Heather Lynn Miller

### Nicola Davies: Exploring the Animal World

*One Tiny Turtle* by Nicola Davies

### Taking Care of Each Other: Family

*The Relatives Came* by Cynthia Rylant

As you read aloud and enjoy these texts together, help children

- think and talk about the books with one another,
- notice a writer's choice of words,
- notice a writer's use of poetic, playful, or descriptive language, and
- discuss literary language.

**Poetic Language**

**Nicola Davies**

**Family**

## Analyzing the Writer's Craft

### You Will Need

- familiar books with interesting words, such as the following from Text Set: Poetic Language:
  - *Mud* by Mary Lyn Ray
  - *Puddles* by Jonathan London
  - *Subway Ride* by Heather Lynn Miller
- chart paper and markers
- sticky notes

### Academic Language / Important Vocabulary

- choose
- choice
- interesting

### Continuum Connection

- Notice a writer's use of descriptive language, including invented words and other playful forms (p. 35)
- Notice a writer's choice of interesting words (p. 35)

### Goal

Notice an author's choice of interesting words.

### Rationale

Authors choose words carefully to convey specific images to the reader and to make the reading more enjoyable. Noticing an author's choice of interesting words helps children make more precise images in their minds, appreciate the author's craft, and understand that choosing words carefully is something they can do as writers.

### Assess Learning

Observe children when they talk about interesting words in stories. Notice if there is evidence of new learning based on the goal of this minilesson.

- ▶ Can children find examples of interesting words?
- ▶ Are children able to explain how the interesting words help them?
- ▶ Do they use the terms *choose, choice,* and *interesting*?

## Minilesson

To help children think about the minilesson principle, engage them in a discussion of interesting words authors choose. Here is an example.

▶ Show the cover of *Mud*.

> Remember this book, *Mud*? Everything begins to melt, and spring begins to arrive. Listen to one part of this book.

▶ Read the page that says, "Winter will . . ."

> What do you notice about the words the writer used?

▶ Record the interesting words on sticky notes and put on the chart paper.

> This author chose particular words to help you understand more about mud and how it sounds and feels.

▶ Show the cover of *Puddles*.

> This is another book that helps you think about puddles, grass, and mud.

▶ Read the page from *Puddles* that says, "We slog through wet grass . . ."

> What do you notice about the words on this page?

▶ Record the interesting words on sticky notes and put on the chart.

> The author chose interesting words like *slog* and made-up words like *slup* to help you hear and feel what it is like to walk through the wet grass and mud. The words help you make a picture in your mind of puddles.

## Have a Try

Invite the children to apply the new thinking about authors' interesting words with a partner.

▶ Show *Subway Ride*. Begin reading on the page that says, "Doors slide open" and stop on the page ending with "clacking to the subway beat."

> Turn and talk to a partner about what you notice about the words the author chose. How do those words help you hear and see what is happening?

▶ Have a few share, and record the interesting words on sticky notes to put on the chart.

## Summarize and Apply

Summarize the learning and remind children to notice the author's choice of words when they read.

> What did you learn today about an author's choice of words? Use the chart to help you remember.

▶ Review the chart and write the principle at the top.

> As you read today, notice the interesting words the author chooses to make you see or hear or feel what something is like. Use a sticky note to mark a page with interesting words to share when we meet after independent work time.

## Share

Following independent work time, gather children together in the meeting area to talk about the author's choice of words in the book they read.

> Give a thumbs-up if you found some interesting words while reading today.

▶ Have a few children share.

## Extend the Lesson (Optional)

After assessing children's understanding, you might decide to extend the learning.

▶ Poets often use interesting words in their poems. Read some poetry with the class and talk about the poets' choice of words.

▶ **Drawing/Writing About Reading** Keep a list of interesting words children notice in books they read. Encourage them to use the list as a resource when they write stories and poems.

### Writers choose interesting words.

| Book | Interesting Words |
|---|---|
| Mud | squish  squck  sop |
| Puddles | We slog through wet grass... slup, slup, slup / Skip beneath the leaves... drip, drip, drip |
| Subway Ride | We zip through tunnels dark as night |

**Reading Minilesson Principle**
## Sometimes writers compare one thing to another.

### Analyzing the Writer's Craft

#### You Will Need

▸ familiar books with figurative language, such as the following:

- *One Tiny Turtle* by Nicola Davies, from Text Set: Nicola Davies

- *Puddles* by Jonathan London, from Text Set: Poetic Language

▸ chart paper and markers

▸ sticky notes

#### Academic Language / Important Vocabulary

▸ compare

▸ comparison

#### Continuum Connection

▸ Notice a writer's use of descriptive language, including invented words and other playful forms (p. 35)

▸ Notice a writer's choice of interesting words (p. 35)

### Goal

Understand the meaning of literary language authors use to make comparisons.

### Rationale

Authors sometimes use figurative language to compare an abstract concept with a more concrete object to make the former easier to visualize or understand. Supporting children in understanding that authors use literary language to compare things allows them to understand the meaning of the text more deeply and to enjoy the language and message of the text fully.

### Assess Learning

Observe children when they talk about how authors make comparisons in stories. Notice if there is evidence of new learning based on the goal of this minilesson.

▸ Can children recognize a comparison when they hear or read one?

▸ Are they able to explain what the comparison tells?

▸ Do children understand the words compare and comparison?

## Minilesson

To help children think about the minilesson principle, engage them in a short discussion of examples of figurative language (comparisons). Here is an example.

▸ Show the cover of *One Tiny Turtle*. Read the first paragraph on page 8.

> What do you notice about how Nicola Davies told you the size of the turtle? What does that help you understand about the turtle?

> A bottle top is very small, so the author is telling you that a baby turtle is very small, about as big as a bottle cap.

▸ Write and draw on the chart paper to show what the author compares.

▸ Read the first three lines on page 14 and the first two lines on page 21.

> The author has compared the size of the turtle to a bottle cap, a dinner plate, and a barrel. Why do you think the author did that?

▸ Read page 14 beginning on the fourth line.

> What do you notice the author did here? What is the author telling you about the turtle's shell?

▸ Write and draw on the chart what the author compares.

## Have a Try

Invite the children to apply the new thinking about when authors make comparisons with a partner.

▶ Show the cover of *Puddles*. Read the page that begins, "At the pond . . ." through the text on the following page.

> What do you notice? What does that help you understand?

▶ Invite a few pairs to share. Write and draw on the chart.

> The author compares the birds flapping to applause, or clapping. This comparison helps you know what the birds sound like.

## Summarize and Apply

Summarize the learning and remind children to notice when authors makes comparisons as they read.

> Why do authors compare one thing to another? Look at the chart to help you remember.

▶ Write the principle at the top of the chart.

> As you read today, notice if the author compares two things, or tells how two things are the same. Mark the page with a sticky note. You could also mark an example of an interesting word that the author uses.

## Share

Following independent work time, gather children together in the meeting area to talk about how an author makes comparisons.

> Give a thumbs-up if you found an example of comparison while reading.

▶ Choose a few children to share.

## Extend the Lesson (Optional)

After assessing children's understanding, you might decide to extend the learning.

▶ During interactive read-aloud or shared reading, encourage children to notice and talk about comparisons the author makes.

▶ **Drawing/Writing About Reading** Use shared or interactive writing to make up some comparisons that children might use in their own writing.

Sometimes writers compare one thing to another.

| Turtle's size | Looks like | |
| Turtle's shells | Feels like | |
| Birds flapping | Sounds like | |

RML 3

LA.U8.RML3

**Reading Minilesson Principle**
## Writers use descriptive language to show you what they mean.

## Analyzing the Writer's Craft

### You Will Need

▶ familiar books with literary language, such as the following:

  • *Puddles* by Jonathan London, from Text Set: Poetic Language

  • *The Relatives Came* by Cynthia Rylant, from Text Set: Family

  • *One Tiny Turtle* by Nicola Davies, from Text Set: Nicola Davies

▶ chart paper and markers

▶ sticky notes

### Academic Language / Important Vocabulary

▶ descriptive language

▶ author

### Continuum Connection

▶ Understand the meaning of some literary language (language of books as opposed to typical oral language) (p. 35)

### Goal

Infer the meaning of literary language.

### Rationale

Authors use literary language to describe ideas that are abstract or difficult to understand. Supporting children to notice and understand literary language allows them to infer what the author is trying to say and to understand the text more deeply.

### Assess Learning

Observe children when they talk about literary language in stories. Notice if there is evidence of new learning based on the goal of this minilesson.

▶ Are children noticing and marking places in books where they ask, "What is the author really trying to say?"

▶ Can children describe what the author is trying to say?

▶ Do they understand the term *descriptive language*?

## Minilesson

To help children think about the minilesson principle, show examples of descriptive language and discuss what the author really means. Here is an example.

▶ Read pages 1–3 of *Puddles*.

  What does the author really mean by "Cuddle between fright and glee and want it to stop and never stop"? Look at the illustrations and think about how you feel about thunderstorms to help you figure it out.

▶ Record responses on the chart paper. Then show the cover of *The Relatives Came*.

  Remember this book, *The Relatives Came*? Listen to the descriptive language Cynthia Rylant uses to show you this part of the story.

▶ Read the page that starts with "Finally, after a long time."

  Listen to this part: "then we crawled back into our beds that felt too big and too quiet. We fell asleep." What is she showing you about how the characters feel?

▶ Record responses on the chart.

  The author could have written, "We missed the relatives." But sometimes, authors use words in a way that makes a picture for the reader. This is called descriptive language. You have to think hard about descriptive language to know what the author is really trying to show you.

## Have a Try

Invite the children to think with a partner about what the author of *One Tiny Turtle* really means.

▶ Read the larger font on pages 26–28 from *One Tiny Turtle*.

Turn and talk to a partner about what Nicola Davies is showing in this part of the story.

▶ Have a few children share and record responses on the chart.

## Summarize and Apply

Summarize the learning and remind children to think about what the descriptive language means as they read.

▶ Review the chart.

What does the chart show about the language that authors sometimes use?

▶ Write the principle at the top of the chart.

As you read today, notice if you have to stop and think what the author's descriptive language means. Mark the page with a sticky note so that you can share the page when we meet after independent work time.

## Share

Following independent work time, gather children together in the meeting area to talk about what an author is trying to say in the book they read.

Give a thumbs-up if you found a place in a book where you had to think, "What does the author's descriptive language mean?"

▶ If no one found an example of literary language, ask if anyone found an interesting or made-up word or if any part of a book made a picture in their mind.

## Extend the Lesson (Optional)

After assessing children's understanding, you might decide to extend the learning.

▶ During interactive read-aloud, point out examples of descriptive language as you come upon them.

▶ **Drawing/Writing About Reading** Encourage children to draw and/or write about their ideas of what the author's descriptive language means.

Writers use descriptive language to show you what they mean.

| What the Author Says | What the Author Means |
|---|---|
| "Cuddle between fright and glee ..." | They are scared <u>and</u> excited. |
| "our beds that felt too big and too quiet." | I miss them already. |
| "grabbing paws miss only one turtle." | There were lots of baby turtles but only one lives to get to the sea. |

## Assessment

After you have taught the minilessons in this umbrella, observe children as they talk and write about their reading across instructional contexts: interactive read-aloud, independent reading and literacy work, guided reading, shared reading, and book club. Use *The Literacy Continuum* (Fountas and Pinnell 2017) to observe children's reading and writing behaviors across instructional contexts.

▶ What evidence do you have of new understandings related to poetic language?

- Do children notice an author's choice of interesting words?
- Can they infer the meaning of the literary or descriptive language they encounter in books?
- Do they understand the meaning of language used to make comparisons?
- Can they describe what the author really means when using descriptive or literary language?
- Do they use vocabulary such as *author, compare, interesting,* and *choice*?

▶ In what other ways, beyond the scope of this umbrella, are they talking about poetic language?

- Do children notice poetic language in independent reading or shared reading books?
- Do they notice and discuss poetic language in poems read together as a class?

Use your observations to determine the next umbrella you will teach. You may also consult Minilessons Across the Year (p. 51) for guidance.

## Link to Writing

After teaching the minilessons in this umbrella, help children link the new learning to their writing:

▶ Help children incorporate poetic language into their narrative writing. Support them in trying to use sound words or other playful forms of words to paint a picture in the reader's mind.

▶ Support children in writing poetry. Encourage them to use words that describe how something looks, feels, smells, or sounds.

▶ Teach children to experiment in their writing with interesting words they have heard in books read aloud.

## Minilessons in This Umbrella

**RML1**  Writers play with the way words look.

**RML2**  Writers play with where they place the words on a page.

**RML3**  Writers use punctuation in interesting ways.

**RML4**  Writers use speech and thought bubbles to show what characters are saying and thinking.

## Before Teaching Umbrella 9 Minilessons

Read and discuss books that feature a variety of notable print features, such as varied fonts, interesting placement of text, uses of punctuation, and speech and thought bubbles. Before teaching the minilesson on punctuation, make sure children have an understanding of a period, a question mark, and an exclamation point. Section Three: Strategies and Skills, Umbrella 3: Maintaining Fluency has minilessons on punctuation.

Use the following books from the *Fountas & Pinnell Classroom™ Interactive Read-Aloud Collection* text sets or choose books with interesting print from your library.

**Nonfiction: Questions and Answers**

*Best Foot Forward* by Ingo Arndt

*What Do You Do with a Tail Like This?* by Steve Jenkins and Robin Page

**Nicola Davies: Exploring the Animal World**

*Big Blue Whale*

**Mo Willems: Having Fun with Humor**

*I Am Invited to a Party!*

*Don't Let the Pigeon Drive the Bus!*

**Fiction and Nonfiction**

*Too Many Pears!* by Jackie French

**Exporing Nonfiction**

*Surprising Sharks by* Nicola Davies

**Humorous Stories**

*Imogene's Antlers* by David Small

*Dooby Dooby Moo* by Doreen Cronin

**Learning and Playing Together: School**

*A Fine, Fine School* by Sharon Creech

**Living and Working Together: Community**

*Blackout* by John Rocco

As you read aloud and enjoy these texts together, help children

- notice how writers play with words,

- notice when punctuation is used in an unusual or interesting manner, and

- notice and read words written in speech or thought bubbles.

**Questions: Nonfiction**

**Nicola Davies**

**Mo Willems**

**Fiction and Nonfiction**

**Nonfiction**

**Humorous Stories**

**School**

**Community**

## RML1
### LA.U9.RML1

**Reading Minilesson Principle**
## Writers play with the way words look.

### You Will Need

- three familiar books that contain a variety of print styles (differences in font, size, color, etc.), such as the following:
  - *Best Foot Forward* by Ingo Arndt, from Text Set: Questions: Nonfiction
  - *Big Blue Whale* by Nicola Davies, from Text Set: Nicola Davies
  - *I Am Invited to a Party!* by Mo Willems, from Text Set: Mo Willems
- chart paper and markers

### Academic Language / Important Vocabulary

- author
- word
- page

### Continuum Connection

- Notice how the placement, size, and color of the print can convey meaning (p. 36)

### Goal

Notice how the size and color of print can convey meaning.

### Rationale

When you guide children to notice when words in a book have a different color, size, or style from the surrounding text, they are more likely to understand the nuances of meaning conveyed through these design choices. They will gain more enjoyment from reading, better understand the book's content, and learn possibilities for their own writing.

### Assess Learning

Observe children when they talk about the print in books. Notice if there is evidence of new learning based on the goal of this minilesson.

- ▶ Do children notice when words on a page are printed in a different font, size, and/or color than the surrounding text?
- ▶ Do they understand the meaning conveyed by differences in print style?
- ▶ Can they use the words *author, word*, and *page* to talk about books?

## Minilesson

To help children think about the minilesson principle, engage them in a short discussion of different print style in books. Here is an example.

- ▶ Show page 8 of *Best Foot Forward* and read the two sentences at the top of the page.

  **What do you notice about the words *a tiger*?**

- ▶ If children need more guidance, ask how *a tiger* looks different from the other words on the page.

- ▶ Show several other pages and prompt children to talk about what they notice about the animal's name on each page.

  **Why do you think the author made the animals' names a different color and size from the other words on the page?**

- ▶ Record responses on the chart paper.
- ▶ Show the cover of *Big Blue Whale* and open to page 11. Point to the word *proouff*.

  **What do you notice about the word *proouff*? How do you think you should say this word when you read the book aloud? Why do you think the author made the letters get bigger and bigger?**

- ▶ Record responses on the chart.

## Have a Try

Invite the children to apply the new thinking with a partner.

▶ Read pages 24–25 of *I Am Invited to a Party!*

   Turn and talk to a partner about what you noticed about how the words look.

   Why do you think the author made the words *very fancy* look this way?

▶ Record responses on the chart.

## Summarize and Apply

Summarize the learning and remind children to notice the way words look as they read.

   What did you notice about some of the words in the books we talked about today? What are some reasons authors make words look different from the others? Look at the chart to help you remember.

▶ Write the principle at the top of the chart.

   When you read today, notice if any words look different from other words. If they do, think about why the author chose to do this.

## Share

Following independent work time, gather children together in the meeting area to talk about what they noticed about how the words looked in their book.

   Give a thumbs-up if the book you read had some words that looked different because the author played with the print.

▶ Ask children with a thumbs-up to show an example and explain why the author made the words look a certain way.

## Extend the Lesson (Optional)

After assessing children's understanding, you might decide to extend the learning.

▶ Continue to add to the chart as children encounter books with words styled uniquely.

▶ Show children how to use a computer to play with the way words look. Let them experiment with using different fonts, sizes, colors, and text effects in their writing. Remind them that the choices they make should add something for the reader.

▶ **Writing About Reading** Encourage children to play with the way words look when they write stories.

Writers play with the way words look.

| | | |
|---|---|---|
| | The name of each **animal** is big and in a different color. | The name of the animal is very important information. |
|  | The letters in the word proo**uff** get bigger and bigger. | It shows what the sound is like: starts quiet and gets louder. |
| | The words **very fancy** are written in a fancy way. | It shows what the word <u>fancy</u> means. |

Section 2: Literary Analysis

# RML2
## LA.U9.RML2

**Reading Minilesson Principle**
# Writers play with where they place the words on a page.

## Looking Closely at Print

### You Will Need

- three familiar books with varying placement of words on a page, such as the following:
  - *Too Many Pears!* by Jackie French, from Text Set: Fiction and Nonfiction
  - *What Do You Do with a Tail Like This?* by Steve Jenkins and Robin Page, from Text Set: Questions: Nonfiction
  - *Surprising Sharks* by Nicola Davies, from Text Set: Nonfiction
- chart paper and markers

### Academic Language / Important Vocabulary

- author
- word
- page

### Continuum Connection

- Notice how the placement, size, and color of the print can convey meaning (p. 35)
- Notice the placement of words on a page in relation to the illustrations (p. 35)

## Goal

Notice how the placement of the words on a page can convey meaning.

## Rationale

When you guide children to notice interesting ways words are placed on a page, they are more likely to notice nuances of meaning. They will gain more enjoyment from reading and better understand the book's content. They can also use these techniques and noticings to their writing.

## Assess Learning

Observe children when they talk about the print in books. Notice if there is evidence of new learning based on the goal of this minilesson.

- Do children notice words that are placed on a page in an interesting way?
- Can they infer why an author played with the placement of words on a page?
- Do they understand the meaning that is conveyed through the placement of the words on a page?
- Do they use vocabulary such as *author, word,* and *page*?

# Minilesson

To help children think about the minilesson principle, engage them in a short discussion of how authors play with placing words on a page in a book. Here is an example.

- Show and read pages 21–22 of *Too Many Pears!*

  What do you notice about how the words look on these pages?

  Why do you think the author placed the words on this page so they're shaped like a mountain?

- Record responses on the chart paper.
- Read pages 5–6 of *What Do You Do with a Tail Like This?* Point to the words above the elephant.

  What do you notice about these words? Why do you think the author placed the words on the page like this?

- Record responses on the chart. If time allows, repeat with the words beneath the mole, and the words above the skunk on page 13.

## Have a Try

Invite the children to apply the new thinking with a partner.

▶ Show and read pages 6–7 of *Surprising Sharks*.

Turn and talk to a partner about what you notice about the word *shark*. Why do you think the author placed the word *shark* this way?

▶ Ask a few to share. Record responses on the chart.

## Summarize and Apply

Summarize the learning and remind children to notice where authors place words on a page.

Look at the chart. What does it show about how authors decide to place words in their books? The way authors place the words on a page can help you understand the meaning.

▶ Write the principle at the top of the chart.

When you read today, notice if words are placed in an interesting way. If you find an example, bring your book to share.

## Share

Following independent work time, gather children together in the meeting area to talk about the author's placement of words.

Give a thumbs-up if the author of the book you read played with placing the words on a page.

▶ Ask a few with a thumbs-up to share. If no one had words placed in an interesting fashion, ask if anyone noticed anything else about the words in the book.

## Extend the Lesson (Optional)

After assessing children's understanding, you might decide to extend the learning.

▶ Show children examples of words placed in interesting ways on a page. Before reading, ask them to predict why the author placed the words on the page in a particular way. After reading, discuss whether the children's predictions were correct.

▶ **Writing About Reading** Encourage children to play with placing words on a page when they write stories.

Writers play with where they place the words on a page.

| Too Many Pears! by Jackie French | The author makes the words look like a mountain. | It helps you understand how tall the dish of pears is. |
| Big Blue Whale by Nicola Davies | The author makes the words look like what an animal can do with its body. | It helps you understand how different animals use their body parts. |
| Surprising Sharks by Nicola Davies | The author makes the shark's fin look like a triangle. | It helps you notice what a shark's fin is shaped like. |

**Section 2: Literary Analysis**

# RML3
## LA.U9.RML3

### Reading Minilesson Principle
## Writers use punctuation in interesting ways.

### Looking Closely at Print

**You Will Need**

▸ three familiar books with punctuation used in interesting ways (ellipses, multiple exclamation points, interrobangs, etc.), such as the following:

  • *Imogene's Antlers* by David Small, from Text Set: Humorous Stories

  • *Dooby Dooby Moo* by Doreen Cronin, from Text Set: Humorous Stories

  • *Don't Let the Pigeon Drive the Bus!* by Mo Willems, from Text Set: Mo Willems

▸ chart paper and markers

▸ sticky notes prepared for the chart

**Academic Language / Important Vocabulary**

▸ author

▸ dots

▸ sentence

▸ punctuation

▸ period

▸ exclamation point

▸ question mark

**Continuum Connection**

▸ Recognize and reflect some simple punctuation with the voice (e.g., period, question mark, exclamation mark) when reading in chorus or individually (p. 121)

## Goal

Notice how writers use punctuation in interesting ways to communicate meaning.

## Rationale

When you guide children to notice how authors use punctuation in interesting ways to communicate meaning, they better understand the meaning, which can affect expression. They might begin to use punctuation in interesting ways in their writing.

## Assess Learning

Observe children when they talk about how authors use punctuation in interesting ways. Notice if there is evidence of new learning based on the goal of this minilesson.

▸ Do children notice examples of punctuation being used in interesting ways?

▸ Can they infer why authors make particular choices for using punctuation?

▸ Do they understand terminology related to punctuation?

## Minilesson

To help children think about the minilesson principle, engage them in a short discussion of how authors play with punctuation in a book to convey meaning. Here is an example.

▸ Show the cover of *Imogene's Antlers* and read the title. Open to the second-to-last page of the book, and read the text.

> Look closely at this sentence. What do you notice?

▸ If children need more guidance ask: *What do you notice about the punctuation at the end of the sentence? Why do you think there are three dots instead of just one?*

> Authors use three dots to show the sentence isn't over. It means the sentence keeps going.

▸ Turn the page and read the text.

> Why do you think the author decided to use three dots instead of ending the sentence and starting a new one?

▸ Record responses on the chart paper.

▸ Read page 3 of *Dooby Dooby Moo*.

> Why do you think the author used two or three exclamation points?

> How do you think the author wants you to read that sentence?

▸ Record children's responses on the chart.

> Authors sometimes use more than one exclamation point when they want to show that something is extra exciting or surprising.

## Have a Try

Invite the children to talk with a partner about how Mo Willems uses punctuation.

▶ Open to page 20 of *Don't Let the Pigeon Drive the Bus!* Point to and read the box that says "What's the big deal?!"

   Turn and talk to a partner about why you think the author used the punctuation like this.

▶ Invite a few to share, and record responses on the chart.

## Summarize and Apply

Summarize the learning and remind children to notice the author's use of punctuation as they read.

   Why do authors use punctuation in their writing in interesting ways?

▶ Review the chart and write the principle at the top.

   When you read today, notice if the author uses punctuation in interesting ways. If so, think about why the author might have decided to do that.

**Writers use punctuation in interesting ways.**

| | ... | • The sentence will keep going. • Something surprising is about to happen. |
| | !!! | • The writer of the ad is very, very excited about the talent show. |
| | !? | • The pigeon is both excited and asking a question at the same time. |

## Share

Following independent work time, gather children together in the meeting area to talk about the use of interesting punctuation in the book.

   Give a thumbs-up if you read a book with interesting punctuation. How did the author use punctuation in an interesting way?

   How did it help you read the sentence?

## Extend the Lesson (Optional)

After assessing children's understanding, you might decide to extend the learning.

▶ Have children read aloud sentences with interesting punctuation. Compare how those sentences sound with the way traditionally punctuated sentences sound.

▶ Show children the same sentence with two different types of end punctuation, e.g., "I am going to school today." and "I am going to school today!!!" Discuss how the meaning changes.

▶ **Writing About Reading** When children write, encourage them to think about using punctuation in interesting ways to convey meaning.

## Looking Closely at Print

### You Will Need

- two familiar books with speech and thought bubbles, such as the following:
  - *A Fine, Fine School* by Sharon Creech, from Text Set: School
  - *Blackout* by John Rocco, from Text Set: Community
- chart paper and markers

### Academic Language / Important Vocabulary

- author
- character
- speech bubble
- thought bubble

### Continuum Connection

- Adjust the voice to recognize dialogue in the body of the text and in speech bubbles or unspoken thoughts in thought bubbles (p. 121)

## Goal

Notice when writers use speech and thought bubbles to show what characters are saying and thinking.

## Rationale

When you guide children to notice speech and thought bubbles, they better understand what characters are saying and thinking. These noticings will help them to better understand the characters' traits, motivations, and intentions.

## Assess Learning

Observe children when they talk about the print in books. Notice if there is evidence of new learning based on the goal of this minilesson.

- Do children notice speech and thought bubbles in books?
- Do they understand the purpose of speech bubbles and thought bubbles?
- Can they distinguish between speech and thought bubbles?
- Do they use vocabulary such as *author, character, speech bubble,* and *thought bubble*?

## Minilesson

To help children think about the minilesson principle, engage them in a short discussion of speech and thought bubbles. Here is an example.

- Show page 6 of *A Fine, Fine School*.

  What do you notice about the illustrations on these pages?

- Point to and read the text in the first speech bubble.

  Who is saying these words? How can you tell?

- Repeat with the second speech bubble.

  Authors use speech bubbles to show what a character is saying.

- Draw a speech bubble on the chart paper, using the chart as a model.
- Point to the thought bubble at the bottom of page 6 and read the text.

  What do you notice about this bubble? How is it different from the other bubbles on the page? Why do you think it looks different from the other bubbles?

  This is called a thought bubble because it shows what a character is thinking. Thought bubbles are shaped like a cloud.

- Draw a thought bubble on the chart, using the chart as a model.

## Have a Try

Invite the children to work with a partner to identify speech bubbles.

▶ Read aloud and show pages 3–4 of *Blackout*. Point to the speech bubbles.

> Turn and talk to a partner about whether these are speech bubbles or thought bubbles. How can you tell?

▶ Invite a few pairs to share their thinking.

## Summarize and Apply

Summarize the learning and remind children to read the speech or thought bubbles in books.

> Why do authors sometimes use speech or thought bubbles?

▶ Review the chart and write the principle at the top.

> When you read today, notice if there are any speech or thought bubbles in your book.
> Remember to read the words in the speech or thought bubbles so you will know what the characters are saying or thinking.

## Share

Following independent work time, gather children together in the meeting area to talk about thought or speech bubbles in their reading.

> Who read a book today that has speech or thought bubbles? What did you find out about the characters from the speech or thought bubbles?

## Extend the Lesson (Optional)

After assessing children's understanding, you might decide to extend the learning.

▶ Encourage children to include speech and thought bubbles in their writing.

▶ **Writing/Drawing About Reading** Read aloud a story that has dialogue, but no speech bubbles. Use shared or interactive writing to rewrite part of the story using speech bubbles. Discuss how using speech bubbles changes the story.

Writers use speech and thought bubbles to show what characters are saying and thinking.

This is what I am saying...

...and this is what I am thinking.

## Assessment

After you have taught the minilessons in this umbrella, observe children as they talk about print and write about their reading across instructional contexts: interactive read-aloud, independent reading and literacy work, guided reading, shared reading, and book club. Use *The Literacy Continuum* (Fountas and Pinnell 2017) to observe children's reading and writing behaviors across instructional contexts.

- ▶ What evidence do you have of new understandings related to looking closely at print?
  - Do children notice when certain words are styled or interestingly placed on the page?
  - Do children notice when writers use punctuation in interesting ways?
  - Can they discuss why authors make certain choices about the presentation of print?
  - Do children understand how to read the speech or thought bubbles to know what characters are saying and thinking?
  - Do they use vocabulary such as *author, character, speech bubble, thought bubble*, and *page*?
- ▶ In what other ways, beyond the scope of this umbrella, are the children talking about the words in books?
  - Are children noticing and talking about the ways authors play with language?

Use your observations to determine the next umbrella you will teach. You may also consult Minilessons Across the Year (p. 51) for guidance.

## Link to Writing

After teaching the minilessons in this umbrella, help children link the new learning to their writing:

- ▶ Encourage children to think about print when they write their texts. Suggest that they vary the size, color, or style of certain words or phrases.
- ▶ Remind them that they can place the words on the page in interesting ways.
- ▶ Help children experiment with using punctuation in interesting ways.
- ▶ When they are writing and illustrating stories with dialogue, propose that they place some of the dialogue in speech bubbles.

## Minilessons in This Umbrella

**RML1**   The author tells who the book is written for in the dedication.

**RML2**   The author gives information about the book in the author's note.

**RML3**   Authors thank the people who helped them with the book in the acknowledgments.

**RML4**   Some books have an author page that gives information about the person who wrote the book.

## Before Teaching Umbrella 10 Minilessons

Read and discuss fiction and nonfiction picture books with text resources (peritext): dedication, author's note, acknowledgments, and about the author page. Look for books with everyday life themes appropriate for children's cognitive development and that engage their intellectual curiosity and emotions. Use the following texts from the *Fountas & Pinnell Classroom™ Interactive Read-Aloud Collection* or choose texts with text resources from your library.

**Journeys Near and Far**

> *When This World Was New* by D. H. Figueredo

**Taking Care of Each Other: Family**

> *Papá and Me* by Arthur Dorros
>
> *Max and the Tag-Along Moon* by Floyd Cooper

**Mo Willems: Having Fun with Humor**

> *Knuffle Bunny* by Mo Willems
>
> *Knuffle Bunny Too* by Mo Willems

**Having Fun with Language: Rhyming Texts**

> *Sitting Down to Eat* by Bill Harley

**Celebrating Diversity**

> *Two Eggs, Please* by Sarah Weeks
>
> *To Be a Kid* by Maya Ajmera and John D. Ivanko

**Using Numbers: Books with Counting**

> *Moja Means One* by Muriel Feelings
>
> *Handa's Hen* by Eileen Browne

**Learning and Working Together: School**

> *Elizabeti's School* by Stephanie Stuve-Bodeen

**Bob Graham: Exploring Everyday Life**

> *The Silver Button* by Bob Graham

As you read aloud and enjoy these texts together, help children

- think and talk about the books with one another, and
- notice various text resources.

**Journeys**

**Family**

**Mo Willems**

**Rhyming Texts**

**Diversity**

**Using Numbers**

**School**

**Bob Graham**

**Section 2: Literary Analysis**

**Reading Minilesson Principle**
# The author tells who the book is written for in the dedication.

## Noticing Text Resources

### You Will Need

- three or four familiar books that have a dedication page, such as the following:
  - *When This World Was New* by D. H. Figueredo, from Text Set: Journeys
  - *Papá and Me* by Arthur Dorros, from Text Set: Family
  - *Knuffle Bunny: A Cautionary Tale* by Mo Willems, from Text Set: Mo Willems
- chart paper and markers
- a basket of books that have a dedication page

### Academic Language / Important Vocabulary

- dedication
- author

### Continuum Connection

- Notice some text resources outside the body (peritext): e.g., dedication, acknowledgments, author's note, endpapers (p. 36)
- Understand the purpose of some text resources: e.g., dedication, acknowledgments, author's note (p. 36)

## Goal

Understand the purpose of the dedication in a book.

## Rationale

The dedication in a book sometimes clues the reader into something about the story or the author. Revisiting the dedication after reading the story might provide deeper insight. Supporting children in thinking about the dedication helps them notice elements in the story they may not have noticed.

## Assess Learning

Observe children when they talk about the peritext of a book. Notice if there is evidence of new learning based on the goal of this minilesson.

- ▷ Do children notice when there is a dedication page?
- ▷ Are they able to talk about why the author wrote the dedication?
- ▷ Do they use the terms *dedication* and *author* correctly?

## Minilesson

To help children think about the minilesson principle, engage them in a short discussion of the purpose of an author's dedication in a book. Here is an example.

- ▷ Show the cover of *When This World Was New*.

    Remember this story? We are going to talk about one part of this book.

- ▷ Read the dedication.

    What do you think it means?

- ▷ Record responses on the chart paper, generalizing them, so the chart is a resource for evaluating other dedications.

    This part of the book is called the dedication.

- ▷ Show *Papá and Me*. Read the dedications.

    What are you thinking?

- ▷ Record responses on the chart.
- ▷ Show *Knuffle Bunny*.

    Mo Willems put his dedication on the very last page.

- ▷ Read the dedication.

    What do you think about this dedication?

- ▷ Record responses on the chart.

    The real Trixie is Mo Willems' daughter!

## Have a Try

Invite the children to talk with a partner about the dedication of a book.

▶ Give each pair a book that they know. Quickly read the dedication for partners.

> Talk about the dedication with your partner.

▶ Add responses to the chart.

## Summarize and Apply

Summarize the learning and remind children to look for a dedication in a book when they read.

> What can you learn from the author's dedication? Look at the chart if you need help remembering.

▶ Write the principle at the top of the chart.

> Choose a book from this basket. As you read today, notice if the author wrote a dedication. Bring the book to the meeting area with you when meet after independent work time.

▶ You may need to circulate and read the dedication for many of the children.

## Share

Following independent work time, gather children together in the meeting area to talk about what they learned in the dedication in the book they read.

> Give a thumbs-up if you found a dedication.

▶ Invite a few children to share the person the book was written for and whether it made them think differently about the book.

## Extend the Lesson (Optional)

After assessing children's understanding, you might decide to extend the learning.

▶ Be sure to read the dedication page in books you share with the class during interactive read-aloud or shared reading. Revisiting the dedication after reading the book may provide better understanding or appreciation of the book.

▶ When children complete a book in writers' workshop, encourage them to write a dedication page.

The author tells who the book is written for in the dedication.

| To my wife... who encouraged me to write this story | Thank someone |
|---|---|
| For the fathers and sons | Tell who the author was thinking about |
| To the real Trixie | Tell who the idea for the character came from |

Noticing Text Resources

## You Will Need

- three or four familiar books with an author's note, such as the following:
  - *Sitting Down to Eat* by Bill Harley, from Text Set: Rhyming Texts
  - *Two Eggs, Please* by Sarah Weeks, from Text Set: Diversity
  - *Moja Means One: Swahili Counting Book* by Muriel Feelings, from Text Set: Using Numbers
- chart paper and markers
- a basket of books with an author's note

## Academic Language / Important Vocabulary

- author's note
- introduction

## Continuum Connection

- Notice some text resources outside the body (peritext): e.g., dedication, acknowledgments, author's note, endpapers (pp. 36, 39)
- Understand the purpose of some text resources: e.g., dedication, acknowledgments, author's note (pp. 36, 39)

## Goal

Understand the purpose of the author's note in a book.

## Rationale

The author's note provides information for the reader. It might explain where the idea for the book came from, why the book is set in a particular place, or a message the author wants the reader to understand. Supporting children in reading and thinking about the author's note encourages them to find out all they can about a book, helping them understand the book more deeply.

## Assess Learning

Observe children when they talk about the peritext of a book. Notice if there is evidence of new learning based on the goal of this minilesson.

- Do children recognize and understand the purpose of the author's note in a book?
- Are they able to explain what they learned about the book from the author's note?
- Do they use vocabulary such as *author's note* and *introduction*?

## Minilesson

To help children think about the minilesson principle, engage them in a short discussion of the author's note in a book. Here is an example.

- Read aloud pages 1–3 of *Sitting Down to Eat*.

   At the end of this book, the author wrote a section titled About the Story.

- Read the about the story.

   What do you notice about this part of the book?

- Record responses on the chart paper. If responses are too specific, expand to the big idea. For example, "The author wrote the story with his son" could be expanded on the chart to, "Authors tell where ideas for books come from."

   Sarah Weeks also wrote an author's note at the beginning of *Two Eggs*.

- Read the note on the inside cover of *Two Eggs*.

   What do you notice about this author's note? How did it help you?

- Record responses on the chart.

## Have a Try

Invite the children to apply the new thinking with a partner.

▶ Begin reading the introduction of *Moja Means One*, through the sentence, "It is the language of about 45 million people in the eastern part of Africa." Then skip to the last sentence of the second paragraph and read through to the end of the introduction.

In this book, *Moja Means One*, the author wrote an author's note called an introduction.

Turn and talk to a partner about what you learned from this author's note.

▶ Have a few children share and record their responses.

## Summarize and Apply

Summarize the learning and remind children to look for an author's note in the book when they read.

What can you learn from an author's note or introduction in a book? You can use the chart.

▶ Write the principle at the top of the chart.

Choose a book from this basket. As you read, notice if the book has an author's note, an introduction, or information about the story. Bring the book with you after independent work time.

## Share

Following independent work time, gather children together in the meeting area to share what they learned from the author's notes in the book they read.

Today you learned that sometimes authors give extra information. Who found an author's note?

▶ Choose a few children to share.

## Extend the Lesson (Optional)

After assessing children's understanding, you might decide to extend the learning.

▶ Share an author's note when you encounter one during interactive read-aloud or shared reading.

▶ When children complete a book in writers' workshop, encourage them to write an author's note.

---

**The author gives information about the book in the author's note.**

- where idea came from

- similar stories

- best way to read a book

- song

- how it became a book

- reason for writing

- information about the author

## Noticing Text Resources

### You Will Need

- three or four familiar books with acknowledgments, such as the following:
  - *Handa's Hen* by Eileen Browne, from Text Set: Using Numbers
  - *Knuffle Bunny Too: A Case of Mistaken Identity* by Mo Willems, from Text Set: Mo Willems
  - *To Be a Kid* by Maya Ajmera and John D. Ivanko, from Text Set: Diversity
- chart paper and markers
- a basket of books that include acknowledgments

### Academic Language / Important Vocabulary

- acknowledgments
- author

### Continuum Connection

- Notice some text resources outside the body (peritext): e.g., dedication, acknowledgments, author's note, endpapers (p. 36)
- Understand the purpose of some text resources: e.g., dedication, acknowledgments, author's note (p. 36)

### Goal

Understand the purpose of acknowledgments in a book.

### Rationale

The acknowledgments in a book allow the author to thank people who helped with the process of writing and publishing the book. The help might have been editorial, technical, or research related. Encouraging children to read the acknowledgments helps them to understand that a published book requires the work of many people.

### Assess Learning

Observe children when they talk about the peritext of a book. Notice if there is evidence of new learning based on the goal of this minilesson.

- Do children recognize and understand the purpose of the acknowledgments in a book?
- Are they able to explain what they learned about the author and/or the book from the acknowledgments?
- Do children use vocabulary such as *acknowledgments* and *author*?

## Minilesson

To help children think about the minilesson principle, engage them in a short discussion of the author's acknowledgments in a book. Here is an example.

- Read the acknowledgments in *Handa's Hen*.

  What does this part tell you?

- Record responses on the chart paper.
- Read the acknowledgments in *Knuffle Bunny Too*.

  What do you think the word *acknowledgments* means?

- Record responses on the chart.

## Have a Try

Invite the children to talk about acknowledgments with a partner.

▶ Read the acknowledgments from *To Be a Kid*.

What do you notice the author is saying? Turn and talk to a partner.

▶ Invite a few pairs to share and record responses.

▶ Read the photographer acknowledgment.

What do you notice the photographer is saying? Turn and talk to a partner.

▶ Invite a few pairs to share and record responses.

## Summarize and Apply

Summarize the learning and remind children to look for the acknowledgments in a book when they read.

What are acknowledgments, and why do authors write them?

▶ Write the principle at the top of the chart.

Choose a book from this basket. As you read today, notice if the author wrote acknowledgments. Bring the book with you to share.

Authors thank the people who helped them with the book in the acknowledgments.

Thank you for...

...helping research or find information.

...taking the photos.

...thinking this book was a good idea.

...the money to help make this book.

Author

...help when writing this book.

## Share

Following independent work time, gather children together in the meeting area to share what they learned from the acknowledgments in the book they read.

Today you learned that authors thank people who helped them with the book in the acknowledgments. Who found an example?

▶ Choose a few children to share.

## Extend the Lesson (Optional)

After assessing children's understanding, you might decide to extend the learning.

▶ Point out the acknowledgments in books during interactive read-aloud and shared reading.

▶ When children write books, encourage them to include an acknowledgments page.

**Reading Minilesson Principle**
## Some books have an author page that gives information about the person who wrote the book.

### Noticing Text Resources

### Goal

Understand the purpose of a page that gives information about the author.

### Rationale

An author's brief biography, in an about the author section, might include information about where the author lives, the author's past experiences, what made the person decide to be an author, or background about the book. Knowing something about the author strengthens children's engagement with the book, especially when they can connect details of the author's life to the book or even their own lives.

### Assess Learning

Observe children when they talk about the peritext of a book. Notice if there is evidence of new learning based on the goal of this minilesson.

- Do children recognize when a book has information about the author?
- Do they notice connections between the author's life and the book?
- Do they use academic language, such as *author*?

## Minilesson

To help children think about the minilesson principle, engage them in a short discussion of the about the author's information in a book. Here is an example.

- Show *Elizabeti's School* and read aloud the part about the authors.

  What kind of information did you learn?

  What do you notice about the author's life and *Elizabeti's School*?

  The author lived for a while in Africa, which might be why she decided to have her story take place there.

- Record responses on the chart paper. Then read about the author of *Max and the Tag-Along Moon*.

  What kind of information did you learn?

  How does it help you understand a bit more about the book?

- Record responses on the chart.

## Have a Try

Invite the children to talk with a partner about an author page.

▶ Read and show the title page through page 7 of *The Silver Button*.

> Think about the story so far and the pictures. Now listen to what I read about the author.

▶ Read about the author on the jacket flap.

> Turn and talk to a partner. What kind of information did you learn from this section? What do you think about this information?

▶ Have a few children share. Record responses on the chart.

## Summarize and Apply

Summarize the learning and remind children to read about the author in the book when they read.

> Tell where you can look in a book to find information about an author.

▶ Write the principle at the top of the chart.

> Choose a book from this basket. As you read today, notice if the book tells something about the author. Bring the book with you to share when we come back together after independent work time.

## Share

Following independent work time, gather children together in the meeting area to talk about the about the author section in a book.

> Today you learned some books have a part that has information about the author. Who found an example?

▶ Choose a few children to share. Children can also share other parts of the book they notice, such as the dedication or acknowledgments.

## Extend the Lesson (Optional)

After assessing children's understanding, you might decide to extend the learning.

▶ Go to the official website of a favorite author to find out more information about the author.

▶ During writers' workshop, encourage children to include information about the author in their writing.

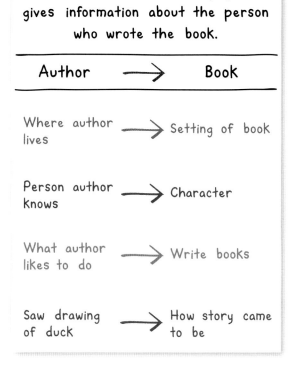

Some books have an author page that gives information about the person who wrote the book.

| Author | → | Book |
|---|---|---|
| Where author lives | → | Setting of book |
| Person author knows | → | Character |
| What author likes to do | → | Write books |
| Saw drawing of duck | → | How story came to be |

Section 2: Literary Analysis

## Assessment

After you have taught the minilessons in this umbrella, observe children as they talk and write about text resources in their reading across instructional contexts: interactive read-aloud, independent reading and literacy work, guided reading, shared reading, and book club. Use *The Literacy Continuum* (Fountas and Pinnell 2017) to observe children's reading and writing behaviors across instructional contexts.

▶ What evidence do you have of new understandings related to text resources?

- Do children understand the purpose of a dedication?

- Can they explain what an author's note is?

- Are they able to describe how the author's note helped them understand the book?

- Do children understand the purpose of the acknowledgments?

- Are they able to explain the relationship between an author's note and the content of the book?

- Can they describe how reading about the author helped them understand the book?

- Can children use vocabulary such as *dedication, author's note,* and *acknowledgments* when they talk about text resources?

▶ In what other ways, beyond the scope of this umbrella, are children talking about text resources?

- Do children express an interest in learning more about a particular author?

- Are they noticing other parts of a book, such as the table of contents, sidebars, and headings?

Use your observations to determine the next umbrella you will teach. You may also consult Minilessons Across the Year (p. 51) for guidance.

## Link to Writing

After teaching the minilessons in this umbrella, help children link the new learning to their writing:

▶ Help children incorporate the different text resources into their writing during writers' workshop. They can incorporate different text resources when writing personal narratives, informational pieces, or poetry. Teach children to write a dedication, acknowledgments, about the author, and, if appropriate, an author's note.

## Minilessons in This Umbrella

**RML1**  Nonfiction books are alike in many ways.

**RML2**  The definition of nonfiction is what is always true about it.

**RML3**  Nonfiction authors give information about a topic they know a lot about.

**RML4**  Nonfiction authors write about topics they care about.

**RML5**  Think about what you know about a topic before you read.

**RML6**  Think about what you learned about a topic after you read.

## Before Teaching Umbrella 11 Minilessons

Genre study (see p. 37) supports children in knowing what to expect when beginning to read a text of a particular genre. This umbrella uses an inquiry process to engage children in the study of nonfiction. The first step of this genre study is to collect a set of texts that are clear and varied examples of nonfiction. Use the following texts from the *Fountas & Pinnell Classroom™ Interactive Read-Aloud Collection* and *Independent Reading Collection* or choose nonfiction books from your library.

**Exploring Nonfiction**

*Water: Up, Down, and All Around* by Natalie M. Rosinsky

*Surprising Sharks* by Nicola Davies

**Nonfiction: Questions and Answers**

*Best Foot Forward* by Ingo Arndt

**Studying Fiction and Nonfiction**

*Ice Bear: In the Steps of the Polar Bear* by Nicola Davies

**Understanding the Natural World: Planting and Growing**

*Plant Packages* by Susan Blackaby

**Independent Reading Collection**

*Cats* by Cari Meister

*Born to Be a Butterfly* by Karen Wallace

*Bones* by Stephen Krensky

As you read aloud and enjoy these texts together, help children to

- notice characteristics of nonfiction books, and
- talk about the information they are learning from the texts.

**Nonfiction**

**Questions and Answers**

**Fiction and Nonfiction**

**Planting and Growing**

**Independent Reading Collection**

Section 2: Literary Analysis

**Reading Minilesson Principle**
# Nonfiction books are alike in many ways.

## Studying Nonfiction

### You Will Need

- familiar nonfiction books, such as books from text sets Exploring Fiction and Studying Fiction and Nonfiction
- chart paper and markers
- a basket of familiar nonfiction books

### Academic Language / Important Vocabulary

- nonfiction
- information
- fact
- topic

### Continuum Connection

- Connect texts by obvious categories: e.g., author, character, topic, genre, illustrator (p. 37)
- Understand that there are different types of texts and that you can notice different things about them (p. 37)
- Notice and understand when a book is nonfiction (true information) (p.37)

## Goal

Notice characteristics of nonfiction books.

## Rationale

Leading children through an inquiry process to discover commonalities of the nonfiction genre gives them a reason to look closely at the texts and think through what it is that makes them nonfiction. When children know what to expect from nonfiction books, they are better prepared to anticipate the characteristics and understand the information in the books.

## Assess Learning

Observe children when they talk about how nonfiction books are alike. Notice if there is evidence of new learning based on the goal of this minilesson.

- Do children notice ways that nonfiction books are alike?
- Are they able to talk about the characteristics of nonfiction books?
- Do they use the terms *nonfiction, information, fact,* and *topic* correctly?

## Minilesson

To help children think about the minilesson principle, engage them in an inquiry process to notice how all nonfiction books are alike. Here is an example.

- Briefly revisit a variety of familiar nonfiction books. As you show a few pages from each book, ask children to talk about each in a few words.

  How are all these nonfiction books alike?

- As children share, help them decide whether the characteristic is *always* or *often* a part of nonfiction books. Record responses on the chart paper.

- If children need assistance noticing different characteristics, consider offering the following prompts:

  What do you notice about how the authors of these nonfiction books tell the information?

  What do you notice about the illustrations or photographs?

- Show children pages with different text features, such as diagrams, labels, maps, etc.

  What other features do you notice in these nonfiction books that you don't often see in fiction books?

## Summarize and Apply

Summarize the learning and remind children to think about how nonfiction books are alike as they read.

> How are nonfiction books alike? Look at the chart if you need to.

▶ Review the chart, emphasizing which characteristics are *always* part of nonfiction books and which characteristics are *often*, but not always included.

> If you read from the nonfiction basket today, see if you notice ways nonfiction books are alike. Bring the book when we meet so you can share.

## Share

Following independent work time, gather children together in the meeting area to talk about what they notice about how nonfiction books are alike.

> Who read a nonfiction book today? If you did, raise your hand if you noticed something we had on the noticings chart.

▶ As needed, read through the noticings chart to prompt the conversation.

> Did anyone notice other ways nonfiction books are alike? Share what you noticed.

## Extend the Lesson (Optional)

After assessing children's understanding, you might decide to extend the learning.

▶ Continue to add to the noticings chart during interactive read-aloud and shared reading.

▶ Host nonfiction book clubs in which children select nonfiction books, read the books, and discuss. (Refer to the book clubs umbrella in Section Two: Literary Analysis.)

---

### Nonfiction
**Noticings:**

| Always | Often |
|---|---|
| What we noticed: | |
| • The author gives facts and information about a topic. | • The author includes other special features that give information. |
| • The author knows a lot about the topic. | |
| • There are pictures or photographs, and sometimes other features, which give information. | |

**Reading Minilesson Principle**
# The definition of nonfiction is what is always true about it.

## Studying Nonfiction

### You Will Need

- nonfiction noticings chart from RML1
- chart paper
- markers

### Academic Language / Important Vocabulary

- nonfiction
- definition
- special features
- facts
- information

### Continuum Connection

- Understand that there are different types of texts and that you can notice different things about them (p. 37)
- Notice and understand when a book is nonfiction (true information) (p. 37)

## Goal

Write a definition of nonfiction.

## Rationale

When you collaborate with children to define the nonfiction genre, you help them to think about the most important characteristics of the genre based on their knowledge at that time. Using an inquiry process will allow them to construct their understandings of the nonfiction genre so they will be able to identify nonfiction books as they encounter them independently and use their knowledge to anticipate their content and features.

## Assess Learning

Observe children as they develop a definition of nonfiction. Notice if there is evidence of new learning based on the goal of this minilesson.

- Are children able to describe characteristics of nonfiction books?
- Do they understand the working description of the nonfiction genre?
- Can they categorize nonfiction books as they read independently?
- Do children use vocabulary such as *nonfiction, facts,* and *information* correctly?

## Minilesson

To help children think about the minilesson principle, engage them in a developing a definition for the nonfiction genre. Here is an example.

> Today, we are going to think together about how nonfiction books are alike. Look at the nonfiction noticings chart and think how we can tell what is always true about nonfiction books. We are going to write a definition of nonfiction books.

- Show and review the nonfiction noticings chart from RML1.

> What things are always true about nonfiction books? We can use this information to tell how all nonfiction books are alike.

- Write the title *Nonfiction Books* on the chart paper, reading the words aloud as you write.

> Turn and talk with a partner about how you would describe nonfiction books to another reader.

- After time for discussion, ask a few volunteers to share their thinking. Create a the definition on the chart paper, using the children's suggestions.

## Summarize and Apply

Summarize the learning and remind children to think about the definition of nonfiction as they read.

> Read with me the definition we wrote for nonfiction books.

> A definition is always true about something, so what we wrote is always true about nonfiction books.

> During independent work time today, read at least one nonfiction book from this basket and think about if it matches our definition of nonfiction books. Bring it with you when we come back together.

## Share

Following independent work time, gather children together in the meeting area in a circle to talk about the definition of nonfiction books.

> Who would like to share the nonfiction book they read today? How does it match our definition of nonfiction on the chart?

## Extend the Lesson (Optional)

After assessing children's understanding, you might decide to extend the learning.

▶ Host nonfiction book clubs in which children select nonfiction books, and then read and discuss them in groups to gain further understanding of the characteristics of the genre. (Refer to the book clubs umbrella in Section Two: Literary Analysis.)

▶ Revisit the definition of nonfiction as children gain more knowledge about the genre. Revise the definition based on new noticings.

---

## Nonfiction Books...

Nonfiction books give information about real people, places, and things.

They often include special features that give more information.

---

# RML 3
## LA.U11.RML3

**Reading Minilesson Principle**
## Nonfiction authors give information about a topic they know a lot about.

## Studying Nonfiction

### You Will Need

- three or four familiar, simple expository texts such as the following:
  - *Water: Up, Down, and All Around* by Natalie M. Rosinsky, from Text Set: Nonfiction
  - *Surprising Sharks* by Nicola Davies, from Text Set: Nonfiction
  - *Best Foot Forward* by Ingo Arndt, from Text Set: Questions and Answers
- chart paper and markers

### Academic Language / Important Vocabulary

- nonfiction
- topic
- fact
- information
- author

### Continuum Connection

- Understand that a writer is presenting facts about a single topic (p. 38)

## Goal

Understand nonfiction authors have to know or find out a lot of information about a topic in order to write about it.

## Rationale

Children need to understand, first, that a nonfiction book is about a single topic, even if a book is divided into smaller subtopics. Then they will begin to understand that an author has to work hard to research and learn about the topic in order to write about it.

## Assess Learning

Observe children when they talk about nonfiction books. Notice if there is evidence of new learning based on the goal of this minilesson.

- ▶ Are children able to identify the topics of nonfiction books?
- ▶ Do they understand that nonfiction authors know a lot about the topic?
- ▶ Do they use vocabulary such as *nonfiction, topic, information, fact,* and *author*?

## Minilesson

To help children think about the minilesson principle, engage them in a discussion of how authors become experts on a topic. Here is an example.

> Show *Water: Up, Down, and All Around* and read the title.
>
> What is this book about? How can you tell?

▶ Record responses on the chart paper.

> Is the whole book about water? How do you suppose the author knew enough about water to write this book?
>
> Natalie Rosinsky probably had to do a lot of research on water before she could write about it. Where do you think she found her information?

▶ Show *Surprising Sharks* and read the title.

> What is this book about?

▶ Write responses on the chart.

> So, Nicola Davies had to know a lot about sharks to write this book.

▶ Read the about the author section on the final page. Explain that a zoologist is a scientist who studies animals.

> How do you think Nicola Davies learned so much about sharks?

## Have a Try

Invite the children to talk about the topic of *Best Foot Forward* with a partner.

▶ Read the title and show some pages of *Best Foot Forward*.

> Turn and talk to a partner about what you think the topic of this book is.

▶ Record responses on the chart.

> How do you think the author learned about all the different types of animal feet?

## Summarize and Apply

Summarize the learning and remind children to think about the topic of the book as they read.

> What did you learn today about how nonfiction authors write their books?

▶ Review the chart and write the principle at the top.

> If you read a nonfiction book during independent work time, think about the topic and how the author might have learned about it. Be ready to share the topic of your book when we come back together after independent work time.

## Share

Following independent work time, gather children together in the meeting area to talk about nonfiction books.

> Who wants to share your book and the topic the author knows a lot about?

▶ Invite a few children to share.

## Extend the Lesson (Optional)

After assessing children's understanding, you might decide to extend the learning.

▶ Use shared writing to make an ongoing list of topics children know about and topics they would like to learn about as a resource for writing ideas and book choices.

▶ **Drawing/Writing About Reading** Have children draw or write about a familiar nonfiction book in a reader's notebook, identifying the topic.

---

**Nonfiction authors give information about a topic they know a lot about.**

| Nonfiction Book | Author | Topic |
|---|---|---|
| Water Up, Down, and All Around | Natalie M. Rosinsky | Water |
| Surprising Sharks | Nicola Davies | Sharks |
| Best Foot Forward | Ingo Arndt | Animal Feet |

# RML 4
## LA.U11.RML4

**Reading Minilesson Principle**
# Nonfiction authors write about topics they care about.

## Studying Nonfiction

### You Will Need

- three or four familiar nonfiction texts with an about the author, such as the following:
  - *Surprising Sharks* by Nicola Davies, from Text Set: Nonfiction
  - *Best Foot Forward* by Ingo Arndt, from Text Set: Questions and Answers
  - *Ice Bear: In the Steps of the Polar Bear* by Nicola Davies, from Text Set: Fiction and Nonfiction
- chart paper and markers

### Academic Language / Important Vocabulary

- nonfiction
- topic
- author

### Continuum Connection

- Infer the writer's attitude toward a topic [how the writer "feels"] (p. 38)

### Goal

Understand that the author probably feels a certain way about the topic of the book.

### Rationale

When children think about the author's attitude toward a topic, they are building a foundation of critical thinking. Eventually, it will be important for them to realize that the way an author feels about a topic can influence what or how the author writes about the topic.

### Assess Learning

Observe children when they talk about nonfiction books. Notice if there is evidence of new learning based on the goal of this minilesson.

- Are children able to make and support inferences about an author's attitude toward the topic of a book?
- Can they acquire information about an author from the about the author section and discuss what they learned?
- Do they use vocabulary such as *nonfiction, topic,* and *author*?

## Minilesson

To help children think about the minilesson principle, engage them in a discussion of an author's attitude toward the topic of a nonfiction book. Here is an example.

- Show *Surprising Sharks*.

  What is this book about? Think about why someone would want to write about sharks. How do you think the author, Nicola Davies, feels about sharks? What makes you think that? Let's read about Nicola Davies and see if you're right.

- Read the information about the author on the last page.

  What did you learn about how Nicola Davies feels about sharks? What did you learn about why she wrote this book?

- Record responses on the chart paper.

- Show *Best Foot Forward*.

  What is this book about? How do you think the author, Ingo Arndt, feels about animals? Let's learn more about him.

- Read the about the author page.

  It says he "advocates for nature conservation." That means he wants to be sure plants and animals are cared for. How do you think Mr. Arndt feels about animals? Why do you think he wrote this book?

- Record responses on the chart.

## Have a Try

Invite the children to talk about Nicola Davies with a partner.

▸ Read the biography at the back of *Ice Bear: In the Steps of the Polar Bear*. Then, read the page titled About Polar Bears.

> Turn and talk with a partner about how you think the author, Nicola Davies, feels about polar bears and why she might have written this book.

▸ After discussion, ask volunteers to share ideas and record responses on the chart.

## Summarize and Apply

Summarize the learning and remind children to think about how the author feels about the topic of the book as they read.

> What did you learn today about nonfiction authors and their topics?

▸ Write the principle at the top of the chart.

> If you read a nonfiction book today, think about how the author feels about the topic. Be ready to share what you think and why when we meet after independent work time.

## Share

Following independent work time, gather children together in the meeting area to talk about how the author feels about the topic in a book.

> Who read a nonfiction book and would like to share how the author feels about the topic?

## Extend the Lesson (Optional)

After assessing children's understanding, you might decide to extend the learning.

▸ Explore authors' websites to learn more about why authors wrote books the children are familiar with and how the authors feel about the topics.

▸ **Drawing/Writing About Reading** When children are wondering what to write about for a nonfiction book, remind them to think of a topic they care about.

**Nonfiction authors write about topics they care about.**

- Nicola Davies loves sharks.
- She wants people to respect and protect sharks.

- Ingo Arndt likes taking photos of wildlife.
- He wants to help nature.

- Nicola Davies loves the Arctic.
- She wants people to know how to save polar bears.

**Section 2: Literary Analysis**

# RML5

## LA.U11.RML5

**Reading Minilesson Principle**
# Think about what you know about a topic before you read.

## Studying Nonfiction

### You Will Need

- two or three simple expository texts that children have not previously read, such as the following from *Independent Reading Collection*:
  - *Cats* by Cari Meister
  - *Born to Be a Butterfly* by Karen Wallace
  - *Bones* by Stephen Krensky
- chart paper and markers

### Academic Language / Important Vocabulary

- nonfiction
- topic
- fact
- information
- author

### Continuum Connection

- Use background knowledge of content to understand nonfiction topics (p. 37)

## Goal

Think about prior knowledge of a topic before reading nonfiction.

## Rationale

When children think about what they already know about a topic before they read a nonfiction book, they are better prepared to learn and understand new information. This allows children to begin to make connections between their prior knowledge and the new information.

## Assess Learning

Observe children as they prepare to read nonfiction books. Notice if there is evidence of new learning based on the goal of this minilesson.

- Can children identify the topic of a nonfiction book before reading it?
- Can they talk about what they already know about the topic before reading a nonfiction book?
- Can children explain why it is helpful to think about what they already know about the topic before reading?
- Do children understand vocabulary such as *topic, fact,* and *information*?

## Minilesson

To help children think about the minilesson principle, engage them in thinking about the topic of a nonfiction book before reading. Here is an example.

- Show the cover of a nonfiction book that children are not familiar with, such as *Cats*. Read the title and the author's name.

  What do you think the topic of this book is? What do you know about cats?

- Record responses on the chart paper.

  You already know a lot about cats, but you can learn even more if you read this book.

- Display another unfamiliar book, such as *Born to Be a Butterfly*, and read the title and the author's name.

  What do you think is the topic of this book? What do you know about butterflies?

- Record responses on the chart.

  You know a lot about butterflies. Thinking about what you know about a topic before you read a nonfiction book gets you ready for new information you might learn from reading the book.

## Have a Try

Invite the children to talk about the topic of *Bones* with a partner.

▶ Display an unfamiliar book, such as *Bones*. Read the title.

> What do you think is the topic of this book? Turn and talk to a partner about what you already know about bones. You can talk about different kinds of bones, what bones are for, what kinds of animals have bones, or anything else you know about bones.

▶ Record responses on the chart.

## Summarize and Apply

Summarize the learning and remind children to think about what they know about a topic before they read.

> Why is it helpful to think about what you already know about a topic before you begin to read?

▶ Write the principle at the top of the chart.

> Today, you are going to read a nonfiction book during independent reading. Before you read, share what you know about the topic with a partner.

## Share

Following independent work time, gather children together in the meeting area to talk about what they knew of the topic before they read a nonfiction book.

> Turn to a partner and say one thing that you already knew about the topic of your book and one thing that was new to you.

## Extend the Lesson (Optional)

After assessing children's understanding, you might decide to extend the learning.

▶ Before reading a new nonfiction book aloud, encourage children to talk about what they already know about the book's topic. Follow up the reading by asking about whether what they already knew matched what was in the book.

▶ Invite children to explore a topic online before an interactive read-aloud on the topic. Invite them to compare the information.

### Think about what you know about a topic before you read.

| Book | What I Already Know |
|------|---------------------|
|  | • Cats meow and purr.<br>• Cats make good pets.<br>• Cats are mammals. |
| Born to Be a Butterfly | • Caterpillars turn into butterflies.<br>• Butterflies have beautiful wings.<br>• One type of butterfly is a monarch butterfly. |
|  | • People have lots of bones.<br><br>• Many animals have bones. |

*Section 2: Literary Analysis*

# RML 6
### LA.U11.RML6

**Reading Minilesson Principle**
# Think about what you learned about a topic after you read.

## Studying Nonfiction

### You Will Need

- two or three familiar nonfiction books, such as the following:
  - *Surprising Sharks* by Nicola Davies, from Text Set: Nonfiction
  - *Water: Up, Down, and All Around* by Natalie M. Rosinsky, from Text Set: Nonfiction
  - *Plant Packages* by Susan Blackaby, from Text Set: Planting and Growing
- chart paper and markers

### Academic Language / Important Vocabulary

- nonfiction
- topic
- fact
- information

### Continuum Connection

- Gain new information from both pictures and print (p. 37)
- Use background knowledge of content to understand nonfiction topics (p. 37)

## Goal

Think about newly acquired knowledge after reading nonfiction.

## Rationale

When you teach children to think about what they learned about a topic after they read a nonfiction book, they begin to develop self-awareness about their reading, and are more likely to remember the newly acquired knowledge. This will help them to begin to make connections across content areas.

## Assess Learning

Observe children when they talk about nonfiction books. Notice if there is evidence of new learning based on the goal of this minilesson.

- Can children identify the topic of a nonfiction book?
- Can children talk about what they learned about the topic after reading the book?
- Do they use vocabulary such as *nonfiction, information, fact,* and *topic*?

## Minilesson

To help children think about the minilesson principle, engage them in thinking about the topic of a nonfiction book after reading. Here is an example.

- Display *Surprising Sharks*. Briefly review the book, reading all or parts of pages 8–15.

   Before you read this book, you thought about what you knew about sharks. Now that you have read the book, what new information did you learn?

- Record new learning on the chart paper.
- Display and briefly review *Water: Up, Down, and All Around*, rereading pages 4–9.

   What did you already know about water before you read this book?

   What new information did you learn?

- Record new learning on the chart.

   Taking time to think about what you know before you read and then what you learned after you read will help you remember the new information.

## Have a Try

Invite the children to talk about what they learned from *Plant Packages* with a partner.

▸ Show the cover of *Plant Packages* and reread pages 4–11.

> Listen as I reread some of this book, and think about what you learned about seeds. Turn and talk to a partner about something you learned from this book.

▸ Invite a few children to share, and record responses on the chart.

## Summarize and Apply

Summarize the learning and remind children to think about the topic of the book after they read.

> Why is it important to think about what you learned about a topic of a nonfiction book after you read?

▸ Write the principle at the top of the chart.

> Choose a nonfiction book to read during independent work time. After you finish reading, think about something you knew about the topic before you read and something you learned from reading the book. Be ready to share what you learned when we come back together.

## Share

Following independent work time, gather children together in the meeting area to talk about what they learned from reading a nonfiction book.

> Turn and talk to a partner about something you knew about the topic before you read and something you learned from reading the book.

## Extend the Lesson (Optional)

After assessing children's understanding, you might decide to extend the learning.

▸ Discuss what children know about the topic of a nonfiction book both before and after reading. Encourage them to compare what they knew before with what they know after: Do they know more about the topic? Did they learn that something they thought was true is not true?

▸ **Drawing/Writing About Reading** After reading a new nonfiction book, have children draw or write about what they learned from the book in a reader's notebook.

### Think about what you learned about a topic after you read.

| | |
|---|---|
|  | • The smallest kind of shark is the dwarf lantern shark.<br><br>• Sharks come in all shapes and sizes. |
|  | • Water covers more than 70% of Earth's surface.<br><br>• Heat turns water into water vapor. |
|  | • Everything that a seed needs to make a new plant is inside it.<br><br>• Some seeds have barbs and burrs. Some are shaped like wings. |

Section 2: Literary Analysis

## Assessment

After you have taught the minilessons in this umbrella, observe children as they talk and write about nonfiction reading across instructional contexts: interactive read-aloud, independent reading and literacy work, guided reading, shared reading, and book club. Use *The Literacy Continuum* (Fountas and Pinnell 2017) to observe children's reading and writing behaviors across instructional contexts.

▶ What evidence do you have of new understandings related to the characteristics of nonfiction?

- Can children describe the characteristics of nonfiction books?
- Can they identify the topic of a nonfiction book?
- Do they think about what they know about the topic of a book before reading it?
- Are they able to talk about what they learned about a topic after reading a book?
- Are they able to use vocabulary such as *topic* and *nonfiction*?

▶ In what other ways, beyond the scope of this umbrella, are children talking about nonfiction books?

- Do children notice the ways nonfiction books are organized?
- Do they notice and use text features, such as headings or a table of contents?
- Can they talk about illustrations and graphics in nonfiction books?

Use your observations to determine the next umbrella you will teach. You may also consult Minilessons Across the Year (p. 51) for guidance.

## Read and Revise

After completing the steps in the genre study process (see page XX), help children read and revise their definition of the genre based on their new understandings.

▶ **Before:** Nonfiction books give information about real people, places, and things. They often include special features that give more information.

▶ **After:** Nonfiction books give information about real people, places, and things. They often include special features, like photographs, maps, and labels, that give more information.

## Minilessons in This Umbrella

**RML1**   Sometimes nonfiction authors use questions and answers.

**RML2**   Sometimes nonfiction authors tell about something in the order it happens.

**RML3**   Sometimes nonfiction authors group information that goes together.

**RML4**   Sometimes nonfiction authors tell how to do something.

**RML5**   Sometimes nonfiction authors tell information like a story.

## Before Teaching Umbrella 12 Minilessons

Before teaching this umbrella, teach the minilessons in Umbrella 11: Studying Nonfiction. This umbrella expands on noticings observed during a nonfiction genre study. Read and discuss nonfiction books with the children with familiar, engaging topics in which the writer organized the information in a variety of ways. Use the following texts from the Fou*ntas & Pinnell Classroom*™ *Interactive Read-Aloud Collection* and *Shared Reading Collection* or choose engaging nonfiction books from your library.

**Nonfiction: Questions and Answers**

*What Do You Do with a Tail Like This?* by Steve Jenkins

*Best Foot Forward* by Ingo Arndt

*A Cool Summer Tail* by Carrie A. Pearson

**Nicola Davies Exploring the Animal World**

*Big Blue Whale* by Nicola Davies

**Understanding the Natural World: Planting and Growing**

*From Seed to Plant* by Gail Gibbons

*Plant Packages: A Book About Seeds* by Susan Blackaby

**Exploring Nonfiction**

*What If You Had Animal Teeth?* by Sandra Markle

**Exploring Fiction and Nonfiction**

*Milk: From Cow to Carton* by Aliki

**Shared Reading Collection**

*Boomer's Checkup* by Aaron Mack

*The Cactus Hotel* by Abbey Grace Moore

As you read aloud and enjoy these texts together, help children

- notice and discuss questions and answers in the text,
- understand chronological sequences,
- identify the main idea of each section of the text,
- notice when authors give directions or steps for how to do something, and
- notice when the text is structured like a story.

**Questions and Answers**

**Nicola Davies**

**Planting and Growing**

**Nonfiction**

*What If You Had Animal Teeth? by Sandra Markle*

**Fiction and Nonfiction**

**Shared Reading Collection**

Section 2: Literary Analysis

**Reading Minilesson Principle**
## Sometimes nonfiction authors use questions and answers.

### Noticing How Authors Organize Nonfiction

#### You Will Need

▸ three or four familiar nonfiction books using a question-and-answer format, such as the following from Text Set: Questions and Answers

- *What Do You Do with a Tail Like This?* by Steve Jenkins

- *Best Foot Forward* by Ingo Arndt

- *A Cool Summer Tail* by Carrie A. Pearson

▸ chart paper and markers

#### Academic Language / Important Vocabulary

▸ nonfiction

▸ information

▸ author

▸ organize

▸ question

▸ answer

#### Continuum Connection

▸ Notice when a writer uses a question-and-answer structure (p. 37)

▸ Use some academic language to talk about literary features: e.g., question and answer (p. 39)

### Goal

Identify the way an author organizes information using questions and answers in a nonfiction text.

### Rationale

When you teach children to notice how nonfiction books are organized, they will begin to notice that authors choose to present the information in a way that helps the reader understand the content and makes the topic interesting. They also learn ways to organize information in nonfiction writing and present it in a variety of interesting ways.

### Assess Learning

Observe children when they talk about nonfiction books. Notice if there is evidence of new learning based on the goal of this minilesson.

▸ Are children able to identify questions and answers in nonfiction books?

▸ Do they understand that sometimes nonfiction authors use questions and answers to organize information or to make the book interesting?

▸ Do they use vocabulary such as *nonfiction, information, author, organize, question*, and *answer*?

## Minilesson

To help children think about the minilesson principle, engage them in a short discussion of nonfiction books with a question-and-answer format. Here is an example.

▸ Show *What Do You Do with a Tail Like This?* Read the page that says "What do you do with a nose like this?"

> What kind of sentence is this? Look at the punctuation mark for a clue. This is a question. What do you think will be on the next page?

▸ Read the next page.

> On this page, the author answers the question from the last page.

▸ Record examples of questions and answers from the book on the chart paper.

▸ Show *Best Foot Forward*. Read the question on page 6 and the answer on page 8.

> What question does the author ask? What is the answer to the question?

▸ Record responses on the chart.

> What did you notice about how the writers organized the information in these two books? Sometimes authors use questions and answers to present information in nonfiction books. Why do you think they do this?

## Have a Try

Invite the children to talk with a partner about *A Cool Summer Tail.*

▶ Read aloud the first four pages of *A Cool Summer Tail.*

Turn and talk to a partner about what questions and answers you heard.

▶ Ask a few pairs to share. Record responses on the chart. Review the chart.

The author used questions from baby animals and answers from adult animals to teach you about staying cool. How is this book like the other two books you heard today?

## Summarize and Apply

Summarize the learning and remind children to notice when an author uses questions and answers.

What is one way you learned that nonfiction authors can organize information in books? Look at the chart to help you remember. Why might authors do this?

▶ Write the principle at the top of the chart.

If you read a nonfiction book today, notice whether the author uses questions and answers. If so, be ready to share examples when we come back together.

## Share

Following independent work time, gather children together in the meeting area to talk about nonfiction books.

Give a thumbs-up if you read a nonfiction book that has questions and answers.

What are some examples of questions and answers in your book?

## Extend the Lesson (Optional)

After assessing children's understanding, you might decide to extend the learning.

▶ During guided reading or interactive read-aloud, encourage children to notice questions and answers in nonfiction books.

▶ Use shared or interactive writing to write an informational book using a question-and-answer format.

**Sometimes nonfiction authors use questions and answers.**

| Title | Question | Answer |
|---|---|---|
| *What Do You Do With a Tail Like This?* | What do you do with a nose like this? | If you're a platypus, you use your nose to dig in the mud. |
| *Best Foot Forward* | Whose foot is this? | A tiger's |
| *A Cool Summer Tail* | How do humans stay cool in the summer, Mama? | They sweat through their skin when it's hot. |

Section 2: Literary Analysis

**Reading Minilesson Principle**

# Sometimes nonfiction authors tell about something in the order it happens.

### Noticing How Authors Organize Nonfiction

## You Will Need

- two or three familiar nonfiction texts that are organized chronologically, such as the following:
  - *Big Blue Whale* by Nicola Davies, from Text Set: Nicola Davies
  - *From Seed to Plant* by Gail Gibbons, from Text Set: Planting and Growing
- chart paper and markers

## Academic Language / Important Vocabulary

- nonfiction
- information
- author
- organize
- order

## Continuum Connection

- Identify the organization of a text: e.g., time order or established sequences such as number, time of day, days of the week, or seasons (p. 37)
- Understand when a writer is telling information in order (a sequence) (p. 37)

## Goal

Identify the way an author organizes information in the order it happens in a nonfiction book.

## Rationale

When children understand that some nonfiction books are organized chronologically, they are better able to find and comprehend the information. The learning will help them when writing nonfiction stories.

## Assess Learning

Observe children when they talk about nonfiction books. Notice if there is evidence of new learning based on the goal of this minilesson.

- Can children identify nonfiction books that tell about something in the order it happens (chronological order)?
- Are they able to identify and talk about what happens first, next, and last in a chronologically organized nonfiction book?
- Do they use vocabulary such as *nonfiction, information, author, organize,* and *order*?

## Minilesson

To help children think about the minilesson principle, engage them in a short discussion of nonfiction books that are organized chronologically. Here is an example.

- Show *Big Blue Whale*. Read pages 17–25. As you read, guide children to notice the chronological sequence of the book by asking questions such as the following:
  - *What does the blue whale do in the summer?*
  - *What does it do in the winter?*
  - *What does it do after that?*
- Record responses on the chart paper.

  The author of this book tells lots of interesting facts about the life of a blue whale. How do you think the author decided which facts to write first, which facts to write next, and which facts to write at the end?

  Nicola Davies tells about a whale's life in the order it happens, from first to last. When you tell about a book like this, you can use words like *first, next,* and *last.*

## Have a Try

Invite the children to talk about *From Seed to Plant* with a partner.

▶ Show *From Seed to Plant*. Read the first line of each of the following pages: *The beginning of a plant, When the sun shines, Up grows a shoot, The plant grows bigger,* and *Finally.*

> Turn and talk to a partner about what happens first, next, and last to the plant.

▶ Ask a few pairs to share. Record responses on the chart. Review the chart.

## Summarize and Apply

Summarize the learning and remind children to think about how a nonfiction book can be organized in the order it happens.

> What is another way you learned that nonfiction authors can organize their books? What is the order they can use? Look at the chart to help you remember.

▶ Write the principle at the top of the chart.

> If you read a nonfiction book today, notice whether the author is telling about something in the order it happens. If so, be ready to share what happens in your book when we come back together.

Sometimes nonfiction authors tell about something in the order it happens.

## Share

Following independent work time, gather children together in the meeting area to talk about a nonfiction book that tells something in the order it happens.

> Who read a nonfiction book that tells about something in the order it happens?

> What happened first, next, and last in your book?

## Extend the Lesson (Optional)

After assessing children's understanding, you might decide to extend the learning.

▶ During guided reading or interactive read-aloud, encourage children to notice how a nonfiction book is organized.

▶ Use interactive writing to create a timeline of events in a familiar chronological nonfiction book.

**Reading Minilesson Principle**
# Sometimes nonfiction authors group information that goes together.

## Noticing How Authors Organize Nonfiction

### You Will Need

- three or four familiar, simple expository texts that are organized by subtopic, such as the following:
  - *Plant Packages: A Book About Seeds* by Susan Blackaby, from Text Set: Planting and Growing
  - *What If You Had Animal Teeth?* by Sandra Markle, from Text Set: Nonfiction
- chart paper and markers

### Academic Language / Important Vocabulary

- nonfiction
- information
- topic
- group
- organize
- author

### Continuum Connection

- Notice that a nonfiction writer puts together information related to the same topic (category) (p. 37)

## Goal

Identify the way an author groups information that goes together in a nonfiction text.

## Rationale

When children understand the information in some nonfiction books is grouped by subtopics, they are better able to find and comprehend information and make connections between related ideas.

## Assess Learning

Observe children when they talk about nonfiction books. Notice if there is evidence of new learning based on the goal of this minilesson.

- Do children notice when information is grouped together in a nonfiction book?
- Can they identify examples of nonfiction books that are organized by subtopics?
- Do they use vocabulary such as *nonfiction, information, topic, group, organize,* and *author*?

## Minilesson

To help children think about the minilesson principle, engage them in a short discussion of nonfiction books that are organized into subtopics. Here is an example.

- Show *Plant Packages: A Book About Seeds.*

    What is this whole book about?

- Read pages 4–5.

    What information does the author put on these pages?

    The topic of the book is seeds, but here the author groups together information about a smaller part of the topic, different kinds of seeds.

- Read pages 8–11.

    What information does she put together on these pages?

    These pages are about the ways seeds travel.

    The author first writes facts about kinds of seeds and then she writes about the ways seeds travel. She groups together similar information or information that is connected.

- Start a graphic organizer, as shown on the sample chart, with children's responses. Then repeat with the part of the book about how to plant seeds.

## Have a Try

Invite the children to talk about *What If You Had Animal Teeth?* with a partner.

▶ Show *What If You Had Animal Teeth?* Read page 4.

Turn and talk to a partner about what information the author groups together on this page.

▶ Repeat with pages 14 and 24.

You noticed that the author groups together information about a different animal's teeth on each page.

## Summarize and Apply

Summarize the learning and remind children to think about how sometimes nonfiction authors group information together.

▶ Review the chart and write the principle at the top.

If you read a nonfiction book today, notice if the author groups information that goes together. If so, be ready to share an example when we come back together.

## Share

Following independent work time, gather children together in the meeting area to talk about nonfiction books.

Who read a nonfiction book in which the author put information into groups?

What were the groups of information in your book?

## Extend the Lesson (Optional)

After assessing children's understanding, you might decide to extend the learning.

▶ During guided reading or interactive read-aloud, encourage children to notice how a nonfiction book is organized.

▶ If appropriate for your children, teach a minilesson on headings (see Umbrella 14: Using Text Features to Gain Information).

▶ **Drawing/Writing About Reading** Use interactive writing to create a graphic organizer of the subtopics in another familiar nonfiction book.

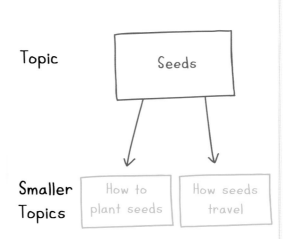

Sometimes nonfiction authors group information that goes together.

Topic — Seeds

Smaller Topics — How to plant seeds / How seeds travel

## Noticing How Authors Organize Nonfiction

### You Will Need

- two or three nonfiction books that contain steps or directions, such as the following:
  - *Milk: From Cow to Carton* by Aliki, from Text Set: Fiction and Nonfiction
  - *Plant Packages: A Book About Seeds* by Susan Blackaby, from Text Set: Planting and Growing
- chart paper and markers

### Academic Language / Important Vocabulary

- nonfiction
- author
- direction
- step
- information
- organize

### Continuum Connection

- Notice when a writer is describing a step-by-step procedure (p. 37)

### Goal

Understand that authors sometimes organize information as a sequence of steps or directions.

### Rationale

When children understand how information in a nonfiction book is organized, they know what to expect. When children realize information can presented in a sequence of steps or directions, they understand the information is in the order it happens.

### Assess Learning

Observe children when they talk about nonfiction books. Notice if there is evidence of new learning based on the goal of this minilesson.

- Do children notice when a nonfiction book contains information that is organized as directions or steps showing how to do something?
- Can children summarize what to do first, next, and last after reading directions in a nonfiction book?
- Do they use vocabulary such as *nonfiction, author, direction, step, information,* and *organize*?

## Minilesson

To help children think about the minilesson principle, engage them in a short discussion of nonfiction books using sequence of steps or directions. Here is an example.

- Show the cover of *Milk: From Cow to Carton*. Read pages 30–31.

  If you want to make butter, what do you need to do first? What should you do second? What should you do third? What should you do last?

- Write responses on the chart paper.

  What do you notice about how the author organized the information on these two pages?

  How do you think she decided what to write first, next, and last?

  The author gives directions or steps for making butter. Notice that I used numbers on the chart to show the order of the steps.

## Have a Try

Invite the children to talk about how an author organized information with a partner.

▶ Show the cover of *Plant Packages: A Book About Seeds*. Read pages 15–17.

> Turn and talk to a partner about what you noticed about how the author organized the information. How did the author let you know the order of the steps?

## Summarize and Apply

Summarize the learning and remind children to notice the organization of the book when they read.

> Talk about how authors show you how to do something.

▶ Write the principle on the top of the chart.

> Choose a nonfiction book to read today. If the author of your book gives directions for how to do something, read the directions and think about what you need to do first, next, and last.

## Share

Following independent work time, gather children together in the meeting area to talk about nonfiction books.

> Who read a nonfiction book with directions or steps? What did you learn to do?

> What do you do first, next, and last?

▶ If no one read a book with steps, ask about other organizations (e.g., questions and answers, chronological order).

## Extend the Lesson (Optional)

After assessing children's understanding, you might decide to extend the learning.

▶ After doing an activity with multiple steps (e.g., cooking, arts-and-crafts activity), use shared or interactive writing to summarize the steps.

▶ After reading aloud a nonfiction book containing steps or directions, write each step on a separate index card or sentence strip. Scramble the cards, and have children put them in the correct order.

---

Sometimes nonfiction authors tell how to do something.

Directions for Making Butter

1. Pour a pint of heavy cream into a bowl.

2. Beat it hard.

3. Keep beating it.

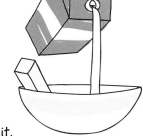

4. Pour out the whey.

---

# RML5
## LA.U12.RML5

### Reading Minilesson Principle
# Sometimes nonfiction authors tell information like a story.

**Noticing How Authors Organize Nonfiction**

## You Will Need

- two or three narrative nonfiction books, such as the following from *Shared Reading Collection*:
  - *Boomer's Checkup* by Aaron Mack
  - *The Cactus Hotel* by Abbey Grace Moore
- chart paper and markers

## Academic Language / Important Vocabulary

- nonfiction
- story
- author
- information
- events

## Continuum Connection

- Notice and understand the characteristics of some specific nonfiction genres: e.g., narrative nonfiction (p. 37)
- Understand that some nonfiction books are like a story (narrative structure) (p. 37)

## Goal

Understand that some nonfiction authors tell information in the form of a story.

## Rationale

Children need to know that sometimes a nonfiction book may sound like a story, but the author is giving information. They need to be taught to distinguish between fiction and nonfiction to prepare them for analyzing and understanding the content.

## Assess Learning

Observe children when they talk about nonfiction books. Notice if there is evidence of new learning based on the goal of this minilesson.

- ▷ Do children notice that some nonfiction books are structured like a story?
- ▷ Can they identify the information they learned from a narrative nonfiction book?
- ▷ Do they use vocabulary such as *nonfiction, story, author, information,* and *events*?

## Minilesson

To help children think about the minilesson principle, engage them in a short discussion of narrative nonfiction books. Here is an example.

- ▷ Show *Boomer's Checkup* and read the title.

    As you listen, think about whether this is a fiction story or a nonfiction book.

- ▷ Read the whole book aloud.

    Is this a fiction or nonfiction book? How can you figure that out?

    The author seems to be telling a story about taking a dog to the vet. Think about what you know about made-up stories. What do you know about made-up stories?

    A made-up story has characters and things that happen to them. Who are the people and animal in this book? What happens to the people and animal?

- ▷ Write responses on the chart paper.

    This is a nonfiction book because the author gives real information, but it is like a made-up story because it has people and an animal and the events happen in order. Sometimes nonfiction authors tell the information like a story.

## Have a Try

Invite the children to talk about *The Cactus Hotel* with a partner.

▶ Show *The Cactus Hotel*.

> I'm going to read a book called *The Cactus Hotel*. As I read, think about how you can tell if it's fiction or nonfiction.

▶ Read aloud enough of the book for the children to get a sense of the story.

> Turn and talk to a partner about what you noticed about how the author tells the information in this book. How is it like a story? How is it different?

▶ Ask a few pairs to share. Record responses on the chart.

## Summarize and Apply

Summarize the learning and remind children to think about how the author is telling information when they read a nonfiction book.

▶ Review the chart.

> What is one way nonfiction authors can tell information?

▶ Write the principle at the top of the chart.

> If you read a nonfiction book today, think about how the author organizes or tells the information. Bring your book to share when we meet.

## Share

Following independent work time, gather children together in the meeting area to talk about a nonfiction book that reads like a story.

> Give a thumbs-up if you read a nonfiction book that is told like a story. What information did you learn?

## Extend the Lesson (Optional)

After assessing children's understanding, you might decide to extend the learning.

▶ Use shared or interactive writing to have children write a narrative nonfiction text about a social studies or science topic they are learning.

▶ After reading a narrative nonfiction book, use shared or interactive writing to write a summary of the story.

**Sometimes nonfiction authors tell information like a story.**

| | Like a Story | Like Nonfiction |
|---|---|---|
| Boomer's Checkup | • It is a story about Calvin and his dad taking their dog, Boomer, to the vet for a checkup. | • The author tells information about vet checkups. |
| The Cactus Hotel | • It is a story about animals that live in a cactus. | • The author tells information about how cactuses are homes for animals. |

Section 2: Literary Analysis

## Assessment

After you have taught the minilessons in this umbrella, observe children as they talk and write about their nonfiction reading across instructional contexts: interactive read-aloud, independent reading and literacy work, guided reading, shared reading, and book club. Use *The Literacy Continuum* (Fountas and Pinnell 2017) to observe children's reading and writing behaviors across instructional contexts.

▶ What evidence do you have of new understandings related to organizational patterns in nonfiction?

- Do children notice and discuss questions and answers in nonfiction texts?
- Can children identify the chronological sequence of events in a nonfiction text?
- Do children talk about the main idea of each section in a nonfiction text?
- Do children notice when authors give directions or steps for how to do something?
- Do they notice when a nonfiction text is structured like a story?
- Do they understand how narrative nonfiction is different from fiction?
- Are they using vocabulary such as *nonfiction, information, organize,* and *topic*?

▶ In what other ways, beyond the scope of this umbrella, are children talking about nonfiction?

- Are children talking about illustrations and graphics in nonfiction books?
- Are children noticing text features, such as headings, tables of contents, and indexes?

Use your observations to determine the next umbrella you will teach. You may also consult Minilessons Across the Year (p. 51) for guidance.

## Link to Writing

After teaching the minilessons in this umbrella, help children link the new learning to their writing:

▶ Throughout the year, give children various opportunities to practice writing nonfiction texts that use each of the organizational patterns discussed in this umbrella. Whenever children are writing a nonfiction text, remind them of ways they can organize nonfiction and encourage them to choose the organizational pattern that makes the most sense for their topic.

## Minilessons in This Umbrella

**RML1**  Authors and illustrators use illustrations, photographs, and labels to give information about a topic.

**RML2**  Authors and illustrators use maps to give information.

**RML3**  Authors and illustrators use diagrams to give information.

## Before Teaching Umbrella 13 Minilessons

Read and discuss nonfiction books with children on familiar, engaging topics with a variety of graphics, including illustrations, photographs, maps, and diagrams. Technically illustrations include any images that accompany a text including photographs. At this grade level we are distinguishing photographs from other kinds of illustrations. Before teaching this umbrella, consider teaching Umbrella 11: Learning About Nonfiction, which engages children in an inquiry about the nonfiction genre. Use the following books from the *Fountas & Pinnell Classroom™ Interactive Read-Aloud Collection* text sets or choose nonfiction books with a variety of graphics features from your library.

**Exploring Nonfiction**

   *Tools* by Ann Morris

   *Surprising Sharks* by Nicola Davies

**Understanding the Natural World: Planting and Growing**

   *Plant Packages: A Book About Seeds* by Susan Blackaby

   *From Seed to Plant* by Gail Gibbons

**Living and Working Together: Community**

   *Be My Neighbor* by Maya Ajmera and John D. Ivanko

**Understanding the Natural World: Oceans**

   *Sea Turtles* by Gail Gibbons

**Nicola Davies: Exploring the Animal World**

   *Big Blue Whale* by Nicola Davies

As you read aloud and enjoy these text together, help children

- notice and discuss how the illustrations, photographs, and labels give information about the topic, and

- read labels on maps and diagrams to learn information.

**Nonfiction**

**Planting and Growing**

**Community**

**Oceans**

**Nicola Davies**

Section 2: Literary Analysis

**Reading Minilesson Principle**

# Authors and illustrators use illustrations, photographs, and labels to give information about a topic.

## Learning Information from Illustrations and Graphics

### You Will Need

- two or three familiar nonfiction books with illustrations or photographs, such as the following:

  - *Tools* by Ann Morris, from Text Set: Nonfiction

  - *Plant Packages* by Susan Blackaby, from Text Set: Planting and Growing

  - *Be My Neighbor* by Maya Ajmera and John D. Ivanko, from Text Set: Community

- chart paper with three columns prepared with headings (see next page)

- markers

- sticky notes in three different colors (three that say *Labels*; two that say *Photographs*; one that says *Illustrations*)

### Academic Language / Important Vocabulary

- nonfiction
- illustration
- photograph

### Continuum Connection

- Gain new understandings from illustrations (p. 39)

- Notice and search for information in a variety of graphics: e.g., drawing with label or caption, photograph with label or caption, diagram, map with legend (p. 39)

### Goal

Learn to look for information in illustrations, especially those with labels.

### Rationale

Children need to know that authors use the illustrations, photographs, and labels to give information. Sometimes the illustrations, photographs, and labels give the same information as the words, but other times they give additional information or show information in a new way.

### Assess Learning

Observe children when they talk about illustrations, photographs, and labels in nonfiction books they have read or heard. Notice if there is evidence of new learning based on the goal of this minilesson.

▶ Do children notice and talk about the illustrations, photographs, or labels in nonfiction books?

▶ Can they describe what they learned from the illustrations, photographs, or labels in a nonfiction book?

▶ Do they understand the terms *nonfiction, illustration,* and *photograph*?

## Minilesson

To help children think about the minilesson principle, engage them in a short discussion of illustrations, photographs, and labels in nonfiction books. Here is an example.

▶ Read aloud page 14 of *Tools* and show the photographs.

This is a nonfiction book called *Tools*. Remember that a nonfiction book gives information. Where on this page do you find information?

The words say "We cook with tools," and the photographs show people cooking with tools. The photographs help you learn more about how people cook with tools.

▶ Record responses on the chart paper and have a child place the correct sticky notes in the middle column. Then read and show pages 5–7 from *Plant Packages*.

Where on these pages do you find information?

What are these (labels) called?

Why do you think there are labels in this book?

▶ Record responses and have a child place the correct sticky notes on the chart.

The words tell how seeds come in all shapes and sizes, and the illustrations and labels show what different seeds look like. The illustrations and labels help you learn more about the shapes and sizes of different seeds.

## Have a Try

Invite the children to talk about the photographs in *Be My Neighbor* with a partner.

▶ Read and show page 7 from *Be My Neighbor*.

Turn and talk to a partner about the information you learned. What did the photographs teach you about homes in different places?

▶ Invite a few pairs to share. Record responses on the chart and have a child place the final sticky notes.

## Summarize and Apply

Summarize the learning and remind children to notice the illustrations, photographs, and labels as they read nonfiction books.

What can you learn from illustrations, photographs, and labels in a book? Use the chart to help you remember.

▶ Write the principle at the top of the chart.

Choose a nonfiction book to read today. Remember to look closely at the illustrations, photographs, and labels. Think about the information you learn, and be ready to share when we meet together after independent work time.

## Share

Following independent work time, gather children together in the meeting area to talk about the illustrations, photographs, and labels in their reading.

Turn and talk to a partner about what you learned from the illustrations, photographs, or labels in the nonfiction book you read.

## Extend the Lesson (Optional)

After assessing children's understanding, you might decide to extend the learning.

▶ Discuss the differences between illustrations and photographs and lead a discussion about why a nonfiction author might choose one over the other.

▶ Open a nonfiction book to a page and cover the print. Have children look at the illustration or photograph and infer what the words will tell.

▶ **Drawing/Writing About Reading** Read a page from a nonfiction text (without showing the illustrations or photographs) and have children draw a picture in a reader's notebook that shows what they learned.

Authors and illustrators use illustrations, photographs, and labels to give information about a topic.

| Book | Illustrations, Photographs, or Labels? | What did you learn? |
|---|---|---|
| | Photographs / Labels | People cook with tools. |
| Plant Packages | Illustrations / Labels | Seeds can look different. |
| Be My Neighbor | Photographs / Labels | Homes in different countries can look alike. |

**Reading Minilesson Principle**
# Authors and illustrators use maps to give information.

## Learning Information from Illustrations and Graphics

## Goal

Understand the purpose of a map and how to read the information on the map.

## Rationale

Teaching children how to use maps in nonfiction books helps them to visualize the locations of places discussed in the text. Being able to visualize the location will help them to better understand the content.

## Assess Learning

Observe children when they talk about maps in nonfiction books they have read. Notice if there is evidence of new learning based on the goal of this minilesson.

▸ Do children understand the purpose of maps?

▸ Can they explain what they learned from maps in books?

▸ Do they use vocabulary such as *author, nonfiction, information,* and *map*?

## Minilesson

To help children think about the minilesson principle, engage them in a short discussion of maps in nonfiction books. Here is an example.

▸ Remind children of the book *Tools* by showing the cover and briefly reviewing a few pages. Turn to page 32.

> What do you notice about the picture on this page? Who knows what this kind of picture is called?

▸ Read the sentence at the top of the page. Point to and read the names of the different countries labeled on the map.

> This picture is called a map. What does the map show you?

▸ Record responses on the chart paper.

▸ Show the cover of *Big Blue Whale*. Show pages 20–21.

> What do you notice about the image or picture on this page? Where are the children pointing? These children are pointing at a globe, which is a special kind of map that is round like Earth.

▸ Read the captions around the globe. When you read a place's name (e.g., North Pole), point to it on the globe.

> What does this map show you about whales?

▸ Record responses on the chart.

## Have a Try

Invite the children to talk about the map in *Be My Neighbor* with a partner.

▶ Show pages 1–2 of *Be My Neighbor*. Point to and read the labels on the photographs.

▶ Turn to the world map at the end of the book. Point to and read the names of Israel, Papua New Guinea, Oman, and Spain on the map.

> These are the names of countries. Turn and talk to a partner about what you notice about this map and what information it gives.

## Summarize and Apply

Summarize the learning and remind children to think about what they can learn from a map when they read.

> Why do you think authors put maps in nonfiction books? How do they help you?

▶ Write the principle and review the responses.

> Today during independent work time, read a nonfiction book from this basket with a partner. Think about what information you can learn from the maps.

## Share

Following independent work time, gather children together in the meeting area to talk about maps.

> Give a thumbs-up if you found a map in your book.

▶ Ask a few children to share the information they learned from the map.

## Extend the Lesson (Optional)

After assessing children's understanding, you might decide to extend the learning.

▶ Gather books with maps. Discuss with the children how the maps are similar and different.

▶ Either as a class or individually, have children create a nonfiction book about their community. Each page can focus on a different place and include a map.

▶ Read a selection of books that are about or take place around the world. After reading each book, write the title on a sticky note and help a volunteer place its location on a world map.

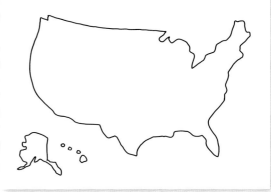

**Authors and illustrators use maps to give information.**

- Maps show where different places are.

- Maps show how far apart places are.

- Maps help you understand the places in the book.

# RML3
## LA.U13.RML3

Reading Minilesson Principle
# Authors and illustrators use diagrams to give information.

Learning Information from Illustrations and Graphics

## You Will Need

- two or three familiar nonfiction books that contain diagrams, such as the following:
  - *Surprising Sharks* by Nicola Davies, from Text Set: Nonfiction
  - *Sea Turtles* by Gail Gibbons, from Text Set: Oceans
  - *From Seed to Plant* by Gail Gibbons, from Text Set: Planting and Growing
- chart paper and markers

## Academic Language / Important Vocabulary

- diagram
- information

## Continuum Connection

- Notice and search for information in a variety of graphics: e.g., drawing with label or caption, photograph with label or caption, diagram, map with legend (p. 39)

## Goal

Understand a diagram's purpose and how to read it to get information.

## Rationale

Children need to know that diagrams show information in a way that is different from, but complementary to, the text. When children understand how to acquire information from diagrams in nonfiction books, they can understand better the parts of something and/or how those parts work together. They will be better able to understand the topic of the book and how facts or ideas are related to each other.

## Assess Learning

Observe children when they talk about diagrams in nonfiction books they have read. Notice if there is evidence of new learning based on the goal of this minilesson.

- ▶ Do children notice and understand the purpose of diagrams?
- ▶ Can children talk about what they learned from diagrams?
- ▶ Do they understand the words *diagram* and *information*?

## Minilesson

To help children think about the minilesson principle, engage them in a discussion of diagrams in nonfiction books. Here is an example.

- ▶ Show pages 14–15 of *Surprising Sharks*.

  What do you notice about these pages?

- ▶ Read the labels on the diagram, pointing to each one as you read it. Point to the line next to the word *tail*.

  Why do you think there's a line here? What does the line mean?

  How do the words and lines on the drawing help you learn?

- ▶ Record responses on the chart paper.

  This is a special kind of illustration called a diagram. A diagram is a drawing that shows the parts of something that the words tell about. Sometimes a diagram makes it easier to understand the topic of a nonfiction book.

- ▶ Show pages 28–29 of *Sea Turtles*.

  What do you notice about the illustrations on these pages?

- ▶ Read all the text on the pages, pointing to each element as you read it.

  Why do you think Gail Gibbons put diagrams of turtles on these pages? What did you learn from the diagrams?

- ▶ Record responses on the chart.

## Have a Try

Invite the children to talk about the diagram in *From Seed to Plant* with a partner.

> Show page 5 of *From Seed to Plant*. Read the sentence at the bottom of the page, and then point to and read each label on the diagram.

>> Why do you think the author decided to use a diagram on this page?

>> Turn and talk to a partner about what you learned from this diagram.

> Invite a few pairs to share. Record responses.

## Summarize and Apply

Summarize the learning and remind children to look for diagrams when they read.

>> What did you learn today about diagrams? Use the chart to help you remember.

> Write the principle at the top of the chart.

>> Choose a nonfiction book to read today. If the book you read has diagrams, look carefully at them and remember to read the labels. Think about how the diagrams help you learn more about the book's topic. Be ready to share your example when we come back together after independent work time.

## Share

Following independent work time, gather children in the meeting area to talk about diagrams.

>> Who read a nonfiction book that has diagrams? What did you learn from the diagrams?

> If no one found a diagram, ask who found other kinds of graphics (photograph, illustration, map).

## Extend the Lesson (Optional)

After assessing children's understanding, you might decide to extend the learning.

> Use shared or interactive writing to create a diagram of a familiar topic (e.g., parts of the human body).

> **Writing/Drawing About Reading** After reading aloud and discussing a book about an animal, have children make a diagram of that animal's body parts in a reader's notebook.

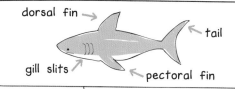

Authors and illustrators use diagrams to give information.

dorsal fin → | ← tail
gill slits → | ← pectoral fin

The diagram shows what a shark's body parts are called and what they look like.

Diagrams of a sea turtle and a turtle show how they are different.

The diagram of a flower shows what the different parts are called.

**Section 2: Literary Analysis**

## Assessment

After you have taught the minilessons in this umbrella, observe children as they talk and write about illustrations and graphics in their reading across instructional contexts: interactive read-aloud, independent reading and literacy work, guided reading, shared reading, and book club. Use *The Literacy Continuum* (Fountas and Pinnell 2017) to observe children's reading and writing behaviors across instructional contexts.

- What evidence do you have of new understandings related to learning information from illustrations and graphics?
  - Do children talk about what they learned from illustrations, photographs, and other graphics in nonfiction books?
  - Do children read and understand labels?
  - Do they know how to read and talk about maps and diagrams?
  - Are they using language like *illustration, photograph, map,* and *diagram*?
- In what other ways, beyond the scope of this umbrella, are children talking about nonfiction?
  - Are children noticing the different ways nonfiction texts are organized?
  - Are they noticing text features, such as headings, tables of contents, and sidebars?

Use your observations to determine the next umbrella you will teach. You may also consult Minilessons Across the Year (p. 51) for guidance.

## Link to Writing

After teaching the minilessons in this umbrella, help children link the new learning to their writing:

- Give children numerous opportunities to write nonfiction books throughout the school year. Let them decide whether they want to use illustrations, photographs, maps, and/or diagrams in their books, and help them find or create relevant graphics. Remind them to use images that help the reader learn more information about the topic, and encourage them to add labels when appropriate.

## Minilessons in This Umbrella

**RML1**  The author uses headings to tell you what the part is about.

**RML2**  The table of contents lists the important topics in a nonfiction book.

**RML3**  Authors and illustrators use sidebars to give information about a topic.

## Before Teaching Umbrella 14 Minilessons

Before teaching the minilessons in this umbrella, we recommend that you teach the minilessons in Umbrella 11: Studying Nonfiction, which engage children in an inquiry about the nonfiction genre. The minilessons in this umbrella expand on noticings that emerge from a genre study of nonfiction. You may also want to teach the minilessons in Umbrella 12: Noticing How Authors Organize Nonfiction prior to starting this umbrella.

To prepare for this umbrella, expose children to nonfiction books with familiar, engaging topics that include a variety of text and organizational features, such as headings, tables of contents, and sidebars. Use the following books from the *Fountas & Pinnell Classroom™ Interactive Read-Aloud Collection* text sets and *Shared Reading Collection* or choose books from your library that have examples of nonfiction text features.

**Living and Working Together: Community**

*Be My Neighbor* by Maya Ajmera and John D. Ivanko

**Exploring Nonfiction**

*Water: Up, Down, and All Around* by Natalie M. Rosinsky

*Surprising Sharks* by Nicola Davies

*What If You Had Animal Teeth?* by Sandra Markle

**Understanding the Natural World: Planting and Growing**

*Plant Packages* by Susan Blackaby

**Nonfiction: Questions and Answers**

*Best Foot Forward* by Ingo Arndt

**Shared Reading Collection**

*How Animals Eat* by Mary Ebeltoft Reid

As you read aloud and enjoy these texts together, help children

• notice headings and discuss the main idea of each page or section,

• notice and use the table of contents and index, if applicable, and

• notice and discuss information that is provided in sidebars.

**Community**

**Nonfiction**

What If You Had Animal Teeth? by Sandra Markle

**Planting and Growing**

**Questions and Answers**

**Shared Reading Collection**

**Section 2: Literary Analysis**

**Reading Minilesson Principle**
# The author uses headings to tell you what the part is about.

## Using Text Features to Gain Information

- two or three nonfiction books with headings, such as the following:
  - *Be My Neighbor* by Maya Ajmera and John D. Ivanko, from Text Set: Community
  - *Water: Up, Down, and All Around* by Natalie M. Rosinsky, from Text Set: Nonfiction
  - *Plant Packages* by Susan Blackaby, from Text Set: Planting and Growing
- chart paper and markers
- sticky notes

## Academic Language / Important Vocabulary

- nonfiction
- heading
- author

## Continuum Connection

- Notice and use organizational tools: e.g., table of contents, heading, sidebar (p. 39)
- Understand the purpose of some organizational tools: e.g., table of contents, heading, sidebar (p. 39)

## Goal

Understand the purpose of headings as an organizational tool.

## Rationale

When children understand why an author uses headings in a nonfiction book, they begin to internalize the concept of text structure or organization. Children who have learned that nonfiction writers group together similar information (see Umbrella 12: Noticing How Authors Organize Nonfiction) will more readily understand the use and purpose of headings.

## Assess Learning

Observe children when they talk about nonfiction books. Notice if there is evidence of new learning based on the goal of this minilesson.

- ▶ Can children identify headings and explain their purpose?
- ▶ Can they describe the physical differences between headings and body text (font size, color, etc.)?
- ▶ Can they use headings to predict what a page or section will be about?
- ▶ Do they use the terms *nonfiction, heading,* and *author*?

## Minilesson

To help children think about the minilesson principle, engage them in a short discussion of headings in nonfiction books. Here is an example.

- ▶ Point to the heading on pages 17–18 of *Be My Neighbor*.

  What do you notice about these words? How do they look different from the other print on the page?

- ▶ Read the heading.

  What do you think this page will be about?

- ▶ Read the rest of the text on the page.

  The big text at the top of a page is called a heading. What did the heading tell you? Headings help you know what the part of the book is about.

- ▶ Open to page 4 of *Water: Up, Down, and All Around*.

  Who can point to the heading at the top of this page?

- ▶ Read the heading.

  What do you think this part of the book will be about? The heading on this page tells you that you are going to read about where raindrops come from.

## Have a Try

Invite the children to talk about a heading in *Plant Packages* with a partner.

▸ Point to and read the heading on page 8 of *Plant Packages*.

  Turn and talk to a partner about what you think this section of the book will be about.

▸ Read pages 8–11.

  Now turn and talk to a partner about the information you will find in this part of the book. Give a thumbs-up if you were right about the information in this part.

## Summarize and Apply

Summarize the learning and remind children to think about headings when they read.

▸ Make a chart to summarize what children have learned about headings.

  Why do authors use headings? How can you recognize a heading?

  During independent work time today, you will read a nonfiction book. Notice whether your book has headings. If you read a book with headings, mark the page with a sticky note so you can share the page.

## Share

Following independent work time, gather children together in the meeting area to talk about the headings in the book they read.

  Give a thumbs-up if you read a nonfiction book with headings. What did the headings tell you?

## Extend the Lesson (Optional)

After assessing children's understanding, you might decide to extend the learning.

▸ When children write nonfiction texts, encourage them to include headings.

▸ Read aloud a nonfiction book that does not have headings. If possible, use a big book or shared reading text, so it is large enough for all children to see. Discuss with children what the heading for a particular page or section could be. Write the new heading on a sticky note, and invite a volunteer to stick it on the top of the page.

---

**The author uses headings to tell you what the part is about.**

- Headings help you know what each part of the book is about.

- Headings can help you find information in a book.

- Headings are bigger than the other words on the page.

- Headings are sometimes a different color from the other words.

Kinds of Dogs

**Reading Minilesson Principle**

## The table of contents lists the important topics in a nonfiction book.

### Using Text Features to Gain Information

### Goal

Understand the purpose of the table of contents as an organizational tool.

### Rationale

Teaching children to use a table of contents helps them learn what topics will be covered in a book and find where the information is located. A table of contents also helps them notice and think about the organization of the book.

### Assess Learning

Observe children when they talk about nonfiction books. Notice if there is evidence of new learning based on the goal of this minilesson.

- Do children know how to use a table of contents?
- Can they explain the purpose of a table of contents?
- Do they use vocabulary such as *information, table of contents,* and *topic*?

## Minilesson

To help children think about the minilesson principle, engage them in a short discussion of the table of contents in nonfiction books. Here is an example.

- Show *Water: Up, Down, and All Around* and read the title. Open to the table of contents. Read the table of contents, pointing to each element as you read it.

  What do you notice about this page?

- Reread the first line and point to the number 4.

  What do you think the number 4 means?

- Turn to page 4 and read the heading.

  What do you notice?

- Repeat this with another entry if necessary to confirm children's understanding of how the table of contents relates to the rest of the book.

  How does a table of contents help you?

- Record responses on the chart paper.

## Have a Try

Invite the children to talk about the table of contents in *Plant Packages* with a partner.

▶ Show *Plant Packages* and read the title. Turn to the table of contents and read it aloud.

Turn and talk to a partner about what the table of contents tells you about this book.

What page would you go to if you wanted to learn how seeds travel?

▶ Repeat with a few other entries.

## Summarize and Apply

Summarize the learning and remind children to notice and use the table of contents when they read a nonfiction book.

How does a table of contents help you when you read a nonfiction book? Look at the chart to help you remember.

▶ Write the principle at the top of the chart.

Choose a nonfiction book to read today. If your book has a table of contents, use it to find out what you will read about and where things are in the book. Be ready to share your book when we meet after independent work time.

## Share

Following independent work time, gather children together in the meeting area to talk about nonfiction books.

Give a thumbs-up if you read a nonfiction book that has a table of contents.

Tell how you used the table of contents.

## Extend the Lesson (Optional)

After assessing children's understanding, you might decide to extend the learning.

▶ Use interactive or shared writing to create a table of contents for a nonfiction book that does not already have one.

---

**The table of contents lists the important topics in a nonfiction book.**

- A table of contents tells you what you are going to read about.

- A table of contents helps you know where things are.

> **Table of Contents**
>
> Where Do Raindrops Come From? .. 4
>
> The Water Cycle ................ 6
>
> Where Does Water Go? .......... 15

**Section 2: Literary Analysis**

# RML 3

### LA.U14.RML3

### Reading Minilesson Principle
## Authors and illustrators use sidebars to give information about a topic.

## Using Text Features to Gain Information

### You Will Need

- two or three nonfiction books with sidebars, such as the following:
  - *Best Foot Forward* by Ingo Arndt, from Text Set: Questions and Answers
  - *How Animals Eat* by Mary Ebeltoft Reid, from *Shared Reading Collection*
  - *What If You Had Animal Teeth?* by Sandra Markle, from Text Set: Nonfiction
- chart paper and markers
- sticky notes

### Academic Language / Important Vocabulary

- nonfiction
- information
- author
- sidebar
- topic

### Continuum Connection

- Notice and use organizational tools: e.g., table of contents, heading, sidebar (p. 39)
- Understand the purpose of some organizational tools: e.g., table of contents, heading, sidebar (p. 39)

### Goal

Notice when nonfiction authors include extra information to help the reader understand the topic.

### Rationale

When children know to look for and think about the additional information provided in sidebars, they gain a deeper understanding of the book's topic. This understanding can encourage further reading about the topic.

### Assess Learning

Observe children when they talk about nonfiction books they have read. Notice if there is evidence of new learning based on the goal of this minilesson.

- ▸ Do children notice sidebars in nonfiction books?
- ▸ Do they understand why authors sometimes include sidebars?
- ▸ Do they discuss the extra information they learn from sidebars?
- ▸ Do they use vocabulary such as *nonfiction, information, author, sidebar,* and *topic*?

## Minilesson

To help children think about the minilesson principle, engage them in a short discussion of sidebars in nonfiction books. Here is an example.

- ▸ Read and point to the sidebar on page 8 of *Best Foot Forward*.

  What do you notice about these words? How are they different from the other print on the page?

  Why do you think the author put these words in a box?

  Sometimes authors of nonfiction include more information about the topic in a box off to the side. This is called a sidebar.

- ▸ Read pages 4–5 of *How Animals Eat*, pointing to the words as you read them.

  Look at the words on page 4 and the words on page 5. What do you notice? Where does the author give you more information about orangutans?

- ▸ Record responses on the chart paper.

  The author of this book put extra facts about animals in the sidebars. When you read a nonfiction book, remember to read all parts of the page, so you don't miss anything.

## Have a Try

Invite the children to talk about a sidebar in *What If You Had Animal Teeth?* with a partner.

> As you listen to me read, think about how the author of this book provides more information.

▶ Read and show page 4 of *What If You Had Animal Teeth?*

> Turn and talk to a partner about how the author provides more facts about beavers on this page. The author tells extra information about a beaver's front teeth in the sidebar.

## Summarize and Apply

Summarize the learning and remind the children to notice the sidebars as they read nonfiction books.

> How does reading the sidebars help you as a reader?

▶ Review the chart and write the principle at the top.

> Choose a nonfiction book to read today, and remember to read every part of every page. If your book has sidebars, mark a page with a sticky note so you can share your book when we come back together.

## Share

Following independent work time, gather children together in the meeting area to talk about nonfiction books.

> Give a thumbs-up if you read a nonfiction book with sidebars. What did you learn from the sidebars?

> What else did you notice in your book?

## Extend the Lesson (Optional)

After assessing children's understanding, you might decide to extend the learning.

▶ Use shared or interactive writing to create a nonfiction text with sidebars.

▶ When children write nonfiction texts, encourage them to include extra information about the topic in sidebars.

▶ After reading aloud a nonfiction book with sidebars, use shared or interactive writing to make a list of the information included in a sidebar.

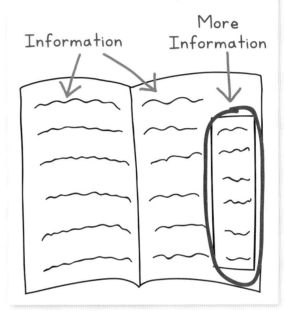

Authors and illustrators use sidebars to give information about a topic.

Information    More Information

## Assessment

After you have taught the minilessons in this umbrella, observe children as they talk and write about their reading across instructional contexts: interactive read-aloud, independent reading and literacy work, guided reading, shared reading, and book club. Use *The Literacy Continuum* (Fountas and Pinnell 2017) to observe children's reading and writing behaviors across instructional contexts.

▶ What evidence do you have of new understandings related to using text features to gain information?

- Do children read headings?
- Can they explain how the headings relate to the content on the page or section?
- Are children able to use a table of contents and an index to find information?
- Do children read and discuss the information in sidebars?
- Are they using language like *information, topic, headings, table of contents,* and *sidebar*?

▶ In what other ways, beyond the scope of this umbrella, are children talking about nonfiction?

- Are children noticing the ways authors choose to organize nonfiction (question and answer, sequence, etc.)?
- Are they talking about illustrations and graphics in nonfiction books?

Use your observations to determine the next umbrella you will teach. You may also consult Minilessons Across the Year (p. 51) for guidance.

## Link to Writing

After teaching the minilessons in this umbrella, help children link the new learning to their writing:

▶ When children write nonfiction books, remind them to use headings to separate information about different subtopics. Suggest they use sidebars to include extra facts about the topic. Encourage them to include a table of contents to help readers find information.

## Minilessons in This Umbrella

**RML1**  A fantasy is a story that could never happen in real life.

**RML2**  Realistic fiction is a story that is made up by the author but could happen in real life.

**RML3**  The writer can make a made-up character seem real or not real.

**RML4**  A fiction book can be realistic fiction or fantasy.

## Before Teaching Umbrella 15 Minilessons

Read and discuss a variety of fiction books with the children that are easily identifiable as realistic fiction or fantasy. Use the following books from the *Fountas & Pinnell Classroom™ Interactive Read-Aloud Collection* text sets or choose realistic fiction and fantasy books from your library.

**Celebrating Diversity**

*Two Eggs, Please* by Sarah Weeks

**Journeys Near and Far**

*When This World Was New* by D. H. Figueredo

*Isla* by Arthur Dorros

*Dear Juno* by Soyung Pak

*Bailey Goes Camping* by Kevin Henkes

**Using Your Imagination**

*Can I Bring Woolly to the Library, Ms. Reeder?* by Lois G. Grambling

*The Gruffalo* by Julia Donaldson

*Emma Kate* by Patricia Polacco

**Bob Graham: Exploring Everyday Life**

*"Let's Get a PUP!" Said Kate* by Bob Graham

*How to Heal a Broken Wing* by Bob Graham

As you read aloud and enjoy these texts together, help children

- notice and discuss events that could not happen in real life,
- notice and discuss events that could happen in real life, and
- discuss whether particular characters seem like real people or animals.

**Diversity**

**Journeys**

**Imagination**

**Bob Graham**

Section 2: Literary Analysis

**Reading Minilesson Principle**
# A fantasy is a story that could never happen in real life.

## Understanding Realistic Fiction vs. Fantasy

### You Will Need

- three or four familiar fantasy books, such as the following:
  - *Two Eggs, Please* by Sarah Weeks, from Text Set: Diversity
  - *Isla* by Arthur Dorros, from Text Set: Journeys
  - *Can I Bring Woolly to the Library, Ms. Reeder?* by Lois G. Grambling, from Text Set: Imagination
- chart paper and markers

### Academic Language / Important Vocabulary

- fantasy
- fiction
- character
- story
- real

### Continuum Connection

- Understand when a story could happen in real life (realistic fiction) and when it could not happen in real life (traditional literature, animal fantasy) (p. 34)

## Goal

Understand when a story could not happen in real life.

## Rationale

When children understand that some stories cannot happen in real life, they are better able to understand and talk about characters and events in fantasy stories. This lays the foundation for them to learn how to identify realistic fiction stories.

## Assess Learning

Observe children when they talk about fiction stories. Notice if there is evidence of new learning based on the goal of this minilesson.

- Do children understand that a fantasy story could not happen in real life?
- Are they able to identify specific parts of a fantasy story that could not happen in real life?
- Do they use vocabulary such as *fantasy, fiction, character, story,* and *real*?

## Minilesson

To help children think about the minilesson principle, engage them is a short discussion of what a fantasy is. Here is an example.

- Show *Two Eggs, Please*. Read the first five pages.

  What do you notice about the characters in this story? Are the animals the same or different from animals in real life? How are they different?

- Record responses on the chart paper.

  This story could not happen in real life because animals can't really order eggs. They also don't wear clothes. This is a special kind of fiction called fantasy. Fantasy stories cannot happen in real life. Sometimes that makes them really fun to read. What do you think?

- Show *Isla*. Read the page that begins, "We fly over forests." Then, read the page that reads, "We fly to the busy old city."

  Can people fly in real life? Could this story happen in real life?

- Record responses on the chart.

  This story about two people flying is a fantasy because people can't really fly. The writer is using her imagination to show how much her grandmother loves the island and how the girl imagines it.

## Have a Try

Invite the children to discuss if *Can I Bring Woolly to the Library, Ms. Reeder?* is a fantasy stories with a partner.

▶ Read the double-page spread from *Can I Bring Woolly to the Library, Ms. Reeder?* that begins, "If I brought Woolly to the library."

> Turn and talk to a partner about if this story could happen in real life and how you know.
>
> What are you thinking about fantasy stories?

▶ Record responses on the chart.

## Summarize and Apply

Summarize the learning and remind children to think if a story is a fantasy as they read.

> What did you learn today about stories that are fantasy? Look at the chart to remember.

▶ Write the principle at the top of the chart.

> When you read today, notice if your book is a fantasy. If it is a fantasy, be ready to share your book when we meet after independent work time.

## Share

Following independent work time, gather children together in the meeting area to talk about whether the story they read is a fantasy.

> Turn and talk to a partner about the book you read. If it is a fantasy, explain how you know it is a fantasy.

## Extend the Lesson (Optional)

After assessing children's understanding, you might decide to extend the learning.

▶ Use interactive writing to create a list of familiar books that are fantasies.

▶ **Drawing/Writing About Reading** Have children draw or write about a familiar fantasy story in a reader's notebook. Ask children to identify specific things in their drawing or writing that could not happen in real life.

### A fantasy is a story that could never happen in real life.

| Book | Why It's a Fantasy (It can't happen in real life.) |
|---|---|
| | Animals talk, wear clothes, and order eggs at a restaurant. |
| | People fly. |
| | A woolly mammoth goes to the library and writes his name. |

**Section 2: Literary Analysis**

**Reading Minilesson Principle**
# Realistic fiction is a story that is made up by the author but could happen in real life.

## Understanding Realistic Fiction vs. Fantasy

### You Will Need

- three or four familiar realistic fiction books, such as the following:
  - *When This World Was New* by D.H. Figueredo and *Dear Juno* by Soyung Pak, from Text Set: Journeys
  - *"Let's Get a PUP!" Said Kate* by Bob Graham, from Text Set: Bob Graham
- chart paper and markers

### Academic Language / Important Vocabulary

- realistic fiction
- character
- real

### Continuum Connection

- Understand when a story could happen in real life (realistic fiction) and when it could not happen in real life (traditional literature, animal fantasy) (p. 34)

## Goal

Understand when a story could happen in real life.

## Rationale

When children understand that some stories could happen in real life, they are better able to understand, talk about, and make authentic personal connections with characters and events in realistic fiction stories. This understanding of realistic fiction will help them to distinguish between fiction and nonfiction.

## Assess Learning

Observe children when they talk about stories they have read. Notice if there is evidence of new learning based on the goal of this minilesson.

- ▶ Do children understand that realistic fiction stories could happen in real life?
- ▶ Are they able to identify parts of a realistic fiction story and talk about how they could happen in real life?
- ▶ Do they use vocabulary such as *realistic fiction*, *character*, and *real*?

## Minilesson

To help children think about the minilesson principle, engage them in a short discussion about realistic fiction. Here is an example.

- ▶ Show *When This World Was New*. Read the page that begins, "He helped me into a pair of boots."

  What is the boy doing on this page?

  In real life, could a boy's father help him put on boots and a coat?

- ▶ Record responses on the chart paper.

  *When This World Was New* is a story that could happen in real life. This is a special kind of fiction called realistic fiction. The word *realistic* means "could really happen."

- ▶ Show *Dear Juno*. Read the page that begins, "At school, Juno showed."

  What is happening on this page?

  In real life, could a boy go to school and show his class his grandmother's picture? Could he write a letter?

- ▶ Record responses on the chart.

  This story is realistic fiction because everything in this story could happen in real life. A boy really could go to school and write a letter to his grandmother.

## Have a Try

Invite the children to talk about *"Let's Get a PUP!" Said Kate* with a partner.

▶ Read the pages from *"Let's Get a PUP!" Said Kate* that begin with "At home, Dave was everything" and end with "they dressed and left immediately."

> Turn and talk to a partner about this story. Could it happen in real life?

▶ Invite a few pairs to share. Record responses on the chart.

> What are you thinking about realistic fiction stories?

## Summarize and Apply

Summarize the learning and remind children to think about whether the story is a realistic fiction as they read.

> What did you learn today about realistic fiction? Use the chart to help you remember.

> When you are reading today, notice if your book is realistic fiction. If it is, be ready to share your book when we meet after independent work time.

## Share

Following independent work time, gather children together in the meeting area to talk about if the story they read is realistic fiction.

> Turn and talk to a partner about the book you read. Tell if it is realistic fiction. If it is, tell your partner what happens in the story that could happen in real life. If it is not, tell why.

## Extend the Lesson (Optional)

After assessing children's understanding, you might decide to extend the learning.

▶ Gather some fiction books that children have read and enjoyed. Have them help you categorize them into piles of realistic fiction and fantasy.

▶ Use interactive writing to create a list of familiar, realistic fiction books.

▶ **Drawing/Writing About Reading** Have children draw or write about a familiar, realistic fiction book in a reader's notebook. Ask children to identify the part of the story in their drawing or writing that could happen in real life.

**Realistic fiction is a story that is made up by the author but could happen in real life.**

| Book | Why It's Realistic Fiction (It could happen in real life.) |
|---|---|
| When This World Was New | A boy wears boots and a coat and goes to school. |
| dear juno | A boy goes to school and writes a letter to his grandmother. |
| Let's Get a PUP! | A puppy makes a mess, cries in a box, and licks people's faces. |

**Section 2: Literary Analysis**

# The writer can make a made-up character seem real or not real.

## Understanding Realistic Fiction vs. Fantasy

### You Will Need

- three or four familiar fiction books, some with real characters, some without, such as the following from Text Set: Journeys:
  - *Bailey Goes Camping* by Kevin Henkes
  - *When This World Was New* by D.H. Figueredo
  - *Dear Juno* by Soyung Pak

### Academic Language / Important Vocabulary

- character
- fiction
- real

### Continuum Connection

- Understand the difference between realistic characters and those that appear in fantasy (p. 35)

## Goal

Understand the difference between realistic characters and those that appear in fantasy.

## Rationale

When children understand the difference between realistic characters and those in fantasy, they are better able to understand, talk about, and make authentic personal connections with fictional characters. This will support their understanding of fiction and nonfiction.

## Assess Learning

Observe children when they talk about characters in stories they have read. Notice if there is evidence of new learning based on the goal of this minilesson.

- Are children able to explain their observations about characters?
- Are they able to discuss if a character seems real or not and justify their opinions?
- Do they use vocabulary such as *character*, *fiction*, and *real*?

## Minilesson

To help children think about the minilesson principle, engage them in a short discussion as to what makes a character seem real or not real. Here is an example.

- Divide the chart paper down the middle. Label one side *Real* and the other side *Not Real*.
- Read the first three pages of *Bailey Goes Camping*.

  Who are the characters in this story? Are they real or not real?

  Bruce, Betty, and Bailey are bunnies. How does the writer make them seem not real?

  On which side of the chart should I put the bunnies?

- Record responses on the chart.

  You noticed that the characters in this story don't seem real because they are bunnies that wear clothes and go camping.

- Read the first four pages of *When This World Was New*. Ask questions similar to those above to guide children in determining whether the characters seem real or not real. Record responses on the chart.

## Have a Try

Invite the children to talk about Juno in *Dear Juno* with a partner.

▶ Read the two pages from *Dear Juno* beginning with "After school, Juno ran to his backyard" and ending with "he placed everything in an envelope."

> Turn and talk to a partner about why Juno seems real.

> Where should I write about Juno on the chart?

▶ Record responses on the chart.

## Summarize and Apply

Summarize the learning and remind children to think about how the writer makes the made-up character seem real or not real as they read.

> How do you know if characters in stories seem real or not real?

▶ Write the principle at the top of the chart.

> If you read a fiction book today, think about whether the characters seem real or not. Be ready to talk about the characters when we come back together.

## Share

Following independent work time, gather children together in the meeting area to talk about whether the made-up character in the story they read seems real or not real.

> Turn and talk to a partner about the book you read. If you read a fiction book, tell if the characters seem real or not and why you think that.

## Extend the Lesson (Optional)

After assessing children's understanding, you might decide to extend the learning.

▶ Continue to add to the chart as children read and listen to other fiction books.

▶ Use interactive writing to create lists of characters that seem real or not real in familiar fiction books.

▶ **Drawing/Writing about Reading** Have children draw or write about a character in a familiar fiction book in a reader's notebook. Ask children to show or tell what makes the character seem real or not real.

---

**The writer can make a made-up character seem real or not real.**

| Real | Not Real |
|------|----------|
|  |  |
| • Real boys can move to another country and fly in planes. | • Bunnies can't wear clothes, talk, or go camping. |
| • Real boys can write letters and draw pictures. | |

**Reading Minilesson Principle**
# A fiction book can be realistic fiction or fantasy.

## Understanding Realistic Fiction vs. Fantasy

### You Will Need

- three or four familiar, realistic fiction and fantasy books, such as the following:
  - *The Gruffalo* by Julia Donaldson and *Emma Kate* by Patricia Polacco, from Text Set: Imagination
  - *How to Heal a Broken Wing* by Bob Graham, from Text Set: Bob Graham
- chart paper and markers

### Academic Language / Important Vocabulary

- realistic fiction
- fantasy
- story
- character

### Continuum Connection

- Understand that fiction stories are imagined (p. 34)
- Understand when a story could happen in real life (realistic fiction) and when it could not happen in real life (traditional literature, animal fantasy) (p. 34)

## Goal

Identify whether a story is realistic fiction or fantasy.

## Rationale

When children understand the difference between realistic fiction and fantasy, they are better prepared for the thinking they will need to do as they read and will, therefore, better understand the text. This will allow them to know what to expect in the story.

## Assess Learning

Observe children when they talk about fiction books. Notice if there is evidence of new learning based on the goal of this minilesson.

- Are children able to identify the characters and major events in a story?
- Are they able to distinguish between what could be real and what could not be real in a fiction story? Can they explain how they know?
- Do they use vocabulary such as *realistic fiction*, *fantasy*, *story*, and *character*?

## Minilesson

To help children think about the minilesson principle, engage them in a short discussion of the differences between realistic fiction and fantasy. Here is an example.

- Divide the chart paper down the middle. Label one side *Realistic Fiction* and the other side *Fantasy*.
- Show *The Gruffalo*.

  As I read, think whether this story could happen in real life or not.

- Read the first three pages of text.

  Are the animals like animals in real life?

  Is this book realistic fiction or fantasy? Where should I write about this book on the chart?

  What makes this a fantasy story?

- Record responses on the chart paper.

  You know this story is a fantasy because animals can't talk, and there's no such thing as a gruffalo.

- Show *How to Heal a Broken Wing*.

  As I read, think about whether this book is realistic fiction or fantasy.

- Begin reading on the page from *How to Heal a Broken Wing* that begins "A loose feather can't" and end on the page that says, "a bird may fly again."

> Where shall I write about this book on the chart? What makes you think that?

▶ Record responses.

## Have a Try

Invite the children to talk about whether *Emma Kate* is realistic fiction or fantasy with a partner.

▶ Read the last two pages from *Emma Kate* with text.

> Turn and tell a partner if you think this is realistic fiction or fantasy. Tell what you think and why.

▶ Invite a few pairs to share with the class. Record responses on the chart.

## Summarize and Apply

Summarize the learning and remind children to think about whether the story is a realistic fiction or fantasy as they read.

> How do you know if a book is realistic fiction or fantasy? Look at the chart for help.

▶ Write the principle at the top of the chart.

> If you read a fiction book today, think about whether it is realistic fiction or fantasy and be ready to tell how you know which one it is. Bring your book when we meet.

## Share

Following independent work time, gather children together in the meeting area to talk about whether the story they read is a realistic fiction or fantasy.

> Who would like to tell if the story you read is realistic fiction or fantasy and why?

## Extend the Lesson (Optional)

After assessing children's understanding, you might decide to extend the learning.

▶ Some children may notice that parts of fantasy stories sometimes appear to be real. Discuss how if parts of a story cannot happen in real life, then the whole story is fantasy.

▶ **Drawing/Writing About Reading** Use interactive writing to write about a familiar fiction book. Include whether the story is realistic fiction or fantasy and how children know.

### A fiction book can be realistic fiction or fantasy.

| Realistic Fiction | Fantasy |
|---|---|
|  |  |
| • A boy and his family can help a bird with a broken wing. | • A mouse talks. The gruffalo is not a real animal.<br><br>• An elephant talks, sleeps in a bed, and has an imaginary friend, and that can't happen in real life. |

**Section 2: Literary Analysis**

## Assessment

After you have taught the minilessons in this umbrella, observe children as they talk and write about their reading of realistic fiction and fantasy across instructional contexts: interactive read-aloud, independent reading and literacy work, guided reading, shared reading, and book club. Use *The Literacy Continuum* (Fountas and Pinnell 2017) to observe children's reading and writing behaviors across instructional contexts.

▶ What evidence do you have of new understandings related to distinguishing realistic fiction and fantasy?

- Can children identify a story as being realistic fiction or fantasy?
- Do children discuss what makes characters seem real or not?
- Do they use academic vocabulary related to realistic fiction and fantasy, such as *real, character, realistic fiction,* and *fantasy*?

▶ In what other ways, beyond the scope of this umbrella, are children talking about realistic fiction and fantasy?

- Do children talk about what they find funny in fiction texts?
- Have they begun to notice and discuss playful language in fiction?

Use your observations to determine the next umbrella you will teach. You may also consult Minilessons Across the Year (p. 51) for guidance.

## Link to Writing

After teaching the minilessons in this umbrella, help children link the new learning to their writing:

▶ When children write their own fiction stories, talk with them about whether the story will be realistic fiction or fantasy. Review the charts from this umbrella so that children have a good idea about what writers do to make their stories seem real or not real.

## Minilessons in This Umbrella

| RML1 | Folktales are alike in many ways. |
|---|---|
| RML2 | The definition of a folktale is what is always true about it. |
| RML3 | Folktales are old stories that have been told for many years. |
| RML4 | Folktales have good and bad characters. |
| RML5 | Folktales have a lesson at the end. |
| RML6 | In folktales, characters use cleverness or trickery to solve the problem. |
| RML7 | Good characters are usually rewarded. Bad characters are not. |
| RML8 | The storyteller repeats words and sentences in folktales. |
| RML9 | Versions of the same folktale are alike and different in some ways. |

**Folktales**

## Before Teaching Umbrella 16 Minilessons

Genre study supports children in knowing what to expect when reading a text in a genre. They develop understanding of the genre's distinguishing characteristics and tools to navigate a variety of texts (see pp. 36–38). Before beginning a genre study of folktales, children must read and enjoy multiple examples.

For this genre study, collect a variety of folktales, including modern rewritings. Use the following text sets from the *Fountas & Pinnell Classroom™ Interactive Read-Aloud Collection* or choose folktales from your library:

**Folktales: Versions**

### Sharing Cultures: Folktales

*The Tale of Rabbit and Coyote* by Tony Johnston

*Mrs. Chicken and the Hungry Crocodile* by Won-Ldy Paye and Margaret H. Lippert

*Once a Mouse* by Marcia Brown

*The Princess and the Pea* by Rachel Isadora

### Folktales: Exploring Different Versions

*The Gingerbread Man* by Eric A. Kimmel

*The Gingerbread Boy* by Richard Egielski

*The Little Red Hen: An Old Fable* by Heather Forest

*The Little Red Hen* by Lucinda McQueen

*Goldilocks and the Three Bears* by Jan Brett

*The Three Snow Bears* by Jan Brett

As you read aloud and enjoy these texts together, help children to

- notice similar types of characters and story outcomes, and
- notice language patterns (e.g., repeating phrases or words).

## Studying Folktales

### You Will Need

- a basket of familiar folktales
- prepared chart paper with the headings *Folktales* and *Noticings*, and sections for *Always* and *Often*
- markers
- sticky notes

### Academic Language / Important Vocabulary

- folktale
- alike
- always
- often
- characters
- lesson

### Continuum Connection

- Connect texts by obvious categories: e.g., author, character, topic, genre, illustrator (p. 34)
- Understand that there are different types of texts and that you can notice different things about them (p. 34)
- Understand that the same types of characters may appear over and over again in traditional literature: e.g., sly, brave, silly, wise, greedy clever (p. 35)

### Goal

Notice and understand the characteristics of the folktale genre.

### Rationale

When children develop understandings through an inquiry about the folktale genre, they form a deeper understanding of the text and genre as they notice the recurring motifs in traditional literature. As they examine these imagined stories, they learn about cultures other than our own and begin to understand universal truths that can be applied to their lives.

### Assess Learning

Observe children when they talk about folktales. Notice if there is evidence of new learning based on the goal of this minilesson.

- Can children describe how folktales are alike?
- Do they understand that some characteristics *always* occur in folktales, and some characteristics *often* occur?
- Do they understand *folktale, alike, always, often, characters*, and *lesson*?

## Minilesson

To help children think about the minilesson principle, engage them in a short discussion about folktales, based on their observations made after reading a variety of them. Here is an example.

- Place children into small groups. Provide each group with several examples from the basket of familiar folktales. Prompt children to look at the covers and illustrations. Allow time for discussion.

  Turn and talk with your group about the ways the folktales are alike. What did you notice about the ways the folktales are alike, or the same?

- As children share, help them decide whether the characteristic is *always* or *often* a part of folktales by asking other groups if the books they revisited had the same characteristics. Record responses on the chart paper.

- Select several folktales to revisit in more detail as a whole group.

  What other things do you notice about these folktales?

- As children talk about the characteristics of folktales and how they are alike, consider providing one or more of the following prompts:

  How do you know this story has been told over many years?

  What do you notice about the characters? What are they like?

  What lesson do the characters learn?

What do you notice about the way the characters behave? Are they good or bad?

Do you learn a lesson from these stories? What is it?

## Summarize and Apply

Summarize the learning and remind children to think about how folktales are alike as they read.

▶ Review the chart.

When you read today, choose a folktale. As you read, think about what we wrote on the chart and place a sticky note on a page if you notice one of those things in your book. Be ready to share the book when we meet after independent work time.

## Share

Following independent work time, gather children together in the meeting area in groups of three to talk about how folktales are alike.

Share the title of the folktale you read. Show the pages with sticky notes and talk about what you noticed.

▶ After each person in the group has shared, summarize the ways the folktales are alike.

## Extend the Lesson (Optional)

After assessing children's understanding, you might decide to extend the learning.

▶ Look for the characteristics on the chart when new folktales are read. Continue to add to the chart as children notice other similarities.

▶ Teach specific minilessons on characteristics the children notice (see other minilessons in this umbrella).

# Folktales

## Noticings:

| Always | Often |
|---|---|
| • The story has been around for a long time. | • The characters are animals that act like people. |
| • The characters are good or bad. | • The characters use cleverness or trickery to solve the problem. |
| • There is a lesson in the end. | • The bad characters are punished and the good characters are rewarded. |
| | • Some of the words and sentences repeat. |

# RML2

**LA.U16.RML2**

**Reading Minilesson Principle**
## The definition of a folktale is what is always true about it.

## Studying Folktales

### You Will Need

- chart from RML1
- chart paper and markers
- a familiar folktale, such as *Goldilocks and the Three Bears* by Jan Brett, from Text Set: Folktales: Versions
- a basket of folktales

### Academic Language / Important Vocabulary

- folktale
- definition

### Continuum Connection

- Notice and understand the characteristics of some specific fiction genres: e.g., realistic fiction, folktale, fairy tale, fable, animal fantasy (p. 34)

## Goal

Create a working definition of the folktale genre.

## Rationale

Writing a genre definition is one part of a genre study. When you work with children to construct a concise definition of a genre, summarizing the essential features, you help them name the important characteristics of that genre based on their knowledge at that time. Over time with more reading of folktales, children can revise the definition. The inquiry process allows them to form their understandings so they will know what to expect when they read a book of a particular genre.

## Assess Learning

Observe children when they talk about folktales. Notice if there is evidence of new learning based on the goal of this minilesson.

- Do they understand that the definition of a folktale is always true?
- Do they use vocabulary such as *folktale* and *definition*?

## Minilesson

To help children think about the minilesson principle, engage them in a collaborative development of a definition of folktales. Here is an example.

- Review the folktales chart (from RML1) with the children.

    Let's think about what you have noticed about folktales. Let's write a definition of a folktale. The definition will tell what a folktale is always like.

- Write the words *Folktales are* on the chart paper, reading them as you write.

    Turn and talk with a partner about how you could finish this sentence in a few words. Use the noticings chart to help you.

- After time for talking, ask volunteers to provide suggestions for ways to finish the sentence. Combine children's ideas to create a definition as a whole class. Write the definition on the chart.

## Have a Try

Invite the children to discuss with a partner whether *Goldilocks and The Three Bears* is a folktale.

▶ Review the definition.

> Think about *Goldilocks and the Three Bears* and the definition we wrote for folktales. Turn and talk with a partner about whether *Goldilocks and the Three Bears* matches the definition of a folktale.
>
> Is *Goldilocks and the Three Bears* a folktale? Why do you think so?

▶ Have children turn and talk. Allow time for discussion.

## Summarize and Apply

Summarize the learning and remind children to think about the folktale definition as they read.

> What does a definition of folktales tell us?

▶ Reread the definition.

> Choose a folktale from this basket when you read today. Think about the definition of folktales and if the book you read follows this definition. Bring the book when we meet after independent work time so you can share.

## Share

Following independent work time, gather children together in the meeting area in groups of three to talk about the definition of folktales.

▶ Review the definition chart.

> Show the folktale that you read today to your group and talk about how it matches the definition.

## Extend the Lesson (Optional)

After assessing children's understanding, you might decide to extend the learning.

▶ Revisit and revise the definition of a folktale as children gain new understandings (see p. 302).

▶ Have children help organize a folktale bin or section of the classroom library.

▶ Have children role-play favorite folktales in small groups. After the performance, ask others to talk about how the folktale matches the definition.

# Folktales

Folktales are made-up stories that have been told and retold for a long time.

The characters are either good or bad, and everyone learns a lesson in the end.

# RML 3
### LA.U16.RML3

**Reading Minilesson Principle**
## Folktales are old stories that have been told for many years.

## Studying Folktales

### You Will Need

- three familiar folktales, such as the following:
  - *The Princess and the Pea* by Rachel Isadora, from Text Set: Folktales
  - *The Little Red Hen* by Lucinda McQueen, from Text Set: Folktales: Versions
  - *The Little Red Hen: An Old Fable* by Heather Forest, from Text Set: Folktales: Versions
- a basket of folktales, including different versions of the same folktale
- chart paper and markers

### Academic Language / Important Vocabulary

- folktale
- retold

### Continuum Connection

- Notice and understand the characteristics of some specific fiction genres: e.g., realistic fiction, folktale, fairy tale, fable, animal fantasy (p. 34)
- Notice and remember literary language patterns that are characteristic of traditional literature: e.g., *once upon a time, long ago and far away, happily ever after* (p. 35)

### Goal

Understand that folktales are old stories that have been retold over many years.

### Rationale

When you guide children to recognize that traditional literature has been around for many years, they begin to develop an understanding that folktales tell universal truths. They then can apply lessons learned to their lives.

### Assess Learning

Observe children when they talk about folktales they have read or heard. Notice if there is evidence of new learning based on the goal of this minilesson.

- Do children notice clues showing that a folktale has been around for many years?
- Do children understand that folktales can be retold by the author?
- Can children recognize that there are different versions of the same folktale?
- Do they use the terms *folktale* and *retold* correctly?

## Minilesson

To help children think about the minilesson principle, engage them in a short discussion of how long folktales have been around. Here is an example.

- Prepare a chart with *Folktales are old stories that have been told for many years* at the top. Show the cover of *The Princess and the Pea*.

  My grandma heard this story when she was little. That is a clue this story has been told for many years.

- Sketch *The Princess and the Pea* and record this clue on the chart. Continue recording clues throughout the lesson.

  Listen for another clue that this story has been told for many years.

- Read page 1.

  What did you notice? When you hear *once upon a time*, this is a clue that the story has been told for many years. Sometimes, folktales begin with *once upon a time*. Let's look at the cover for other clues.

- Point and read *Retold by*.

  *Retold* means that the author is telling a story again or in a new way. How does *retold* tell you that the story has been told for many years?

- Show the cover of *The Little Red Hen: An Old Fable*, reading aloud as necessary the words *retold by* and *old fable*.

Look at the cover of this folktale and see if you notice clues that this story has been told for many years. What do you notice? Record responses on the chart.

## Have a Try

Invite the children to talk with a partner about *The Little Red Hen*.

▶ Show the cover and read the title and the first page of *The Little Red Hen*.

> Turn and talk with a partner about the clues that help you know this story has been around for a long time.

▶ Point out that this book is a different version of the same story as Heather Forest's book and it begins with *once upon a time*.

## Summarize and Apply

Summarize the learning and remind children that folktales have been around for a long time as they read.

> How can you tell if a folktale has been around for a very long time? Look at the chart to help you remember.

▶ Write the principle at the top of the chart.

> When you read today, choose a folktale from the basket. As you read, think about how the story has been told for many years and notice any clues that help you know this. Bring the book when we meet so you can share.

## Share

Following independent work time, gather children in groups of three to talk about folktales.

> Share the title of the folktale you read. Talk about what you noticed.

## Extend the Lesson (Optional)

After assessing children's understanding, you might decide to extend the learning.

▶ Use the library or look online to locate old versions of familiar folktales. Read the old version and a new version. Have children talk about how the folktale has changed.

▶ Have children retell a familiar folktale in their own words. Have them say *Retold by* _____ before they tell the story to reinforce that the story has been around for a long time.

---

**Folktales are old stories that have been told for many years.**

### Clues

| The Princess and the Pea | The Little Red Hen |
|---|---|
| • Grandma read it when she was little. | • There are different versions. |
| • It starts with "Once upon a time." | • It starts with "Once upon a time." |
| • It says "retold" by the author. | • It says "retold" by the author. |

## Studying Folktales

### You Will Need

- three familiar folktales, such as the following:
  - *The Gingerbread Boy* by Richard Egielski, from Text Set: Folktales: Versions
  - *The Little Red Hen: An Old Fable* by Heather Forest, from Text Set: Folktales: Versions
  - *Mrs. Chicken and the Hungry Crocodile* by Won-Ldy Paye and Margaret H. Lippert, from Text Set: Folktales

- chart paper and markers

- sticky notes with sketches of the gingerbread boy, old man, old lady, fox, red hen, cat, dog, mouse, white hen and chicks, and crocodile

- a basket of folktales

### Academic Language / Important Vocabulary

- folktale
- character
- behave
- sneaky
- hardworking
- lazy
- clever

### Continuum Connection

- Understand that the same types of characters may appear over and over again in traditional literature: e.g., sly, brave, silly, wise, greedy, clever (p. 35)

## Goal

Understand that folktale characters are usually either good or bad.

## Rationale

When you help children understand the common character traits found in traditional literature, they establish a personal connection with the characters and gain a better understanding of characters' feelings and emotions. These character traits are easy to recognize because they are either good or bad, so they can begin to differentiate between characters.

## Assess Learning

Observe children when they talk about characters in folktales they have read or heard. Notice if there is evidence of new learning based on the goal of this minilesson.

- Can children identify the good and bad characters in a folktale?
- Can they explain what makes a character good or bad?
- Do children use vocabulary such as *folktale*, *character*, and *behave*?

## Minilesson

To help children think about the minilesson principle, engage them in a short discussion of distinguishing good and bad characters in folktales. Here is an example.

- Revisit pages 1–4 of *The Gingerbread Boy*.

  Think about how the gingerbread boy behaves. Does the boy behave in a good or a bad way when he runs off?

- Help children see that the boy is naughty when he runs off, which gets him into trouble. Have a volunteer add the sticky note of the gingerbread boy to the chart under *Bad*.

  Now think about the fox. The fox pretends to be nice, but he is really sneaky. In which column does the fox go? What about the old man and the old woman?

- Have children add the sticky notes to the chart.

  In folktales like *The Gingerbread Boy*, characters behave in either good or bad ways.

  Now think about the characters in the folktale *The Little Red Hen: An Old Fable*. Which character behaves in a good way and which characters do not?

  The hen is hardworking, but the dog, cat, and mouse are lazy, aren't they?

- Have children add the sticky notes to the chart.

## Have a Try

Invite the children to talk with a partner about the characters in *Mrs. Chicken and the Hungry Crocodile*.

▷ Show *Mrs. Chicken and the Hungry Crocodile*.

> Turn and talk with a partner about what the crocodile really wants to do with the baby chicks and how Mrs. Chicken saves her babies. Who is the good character and who is bad?

▷ Have children add sticky notes to the chart.

## Summarize and Apply

Summarize the learning and remind children to think about whether the characters are good or bad in a folktale as they read.

▷ Write the principle at the top of the chart.

> How do you know if a folktale is a good character or bad character?

> When you read today, choose a folktale from the basket. As you read, think about how the characters act and if they behave in a good or bad way. Be ready to share the book when we come back together.

## Share

Following independent work time, gather children in groups of three to talk about the characters in folktales.

> Share the title of the folktale you read. Talk about the characters in the folktale and how they behave. Are they good characters or bad characters?

## Extend the Lesson (Optional)

After assessing children's understanding, you might decide to extend the learning.

▷ Have children draw and cut out the main characters in favorite folktales and retell the story, adding the characters to the correct side of the chart.

▷ Assist the children in learning vocabulary words to describe the actions of characters in folktales (e.g., *sly, brave, silly, wise, greedy, kind, tricky*).

**Reading Minilesson Principle**
## Folktales have a lesson at the end.

### You Will Need

- three familiar folktales, such as the following:
  - *The Gingerbread Man* by Eric A. Kimmel, from Text Set: Folktales: Versions
  - *The Princess and the Pea* by Rachel Isadora, from Text Set: Folktales
  - *Once a Mouse* by Marcia Brown, from Text Set: Folktales
- chart paper and markers
- sentence strips (optional)
- a basket of folktales

### Academic Language / Important Vocabulary

- folktale
- lesson

### Continuum Connection

- Infer the "lesson" in traditional literature (p. 34)
- Understand that the "lesson" in fantasy or traditional literature can be applied to their own lives (p. 34)
- Notice when a character changes or learns a lesson (p. 34)

### Goal

Infer the lesson of folktales.

### Rationale

When you teach children to identify the lesson learned in traditional literature, they begin to follow story events and anticipate outcomes. This will help them to apply the lessons learned to their lives.

### Assess Learning

Observe children when they talk about folktales they have read or heard. Notice if there is evidence of new learning based on the goal of this minilesson.

- ▶ Do children understand that folktales teach a lesson?
- ▶ Are they able to talk about the lesson learned in a folktale?
- ▶ Do children use vocabulary such as *folktale* and *lesson*?

## Minilesson

To help children think about the minilesson principle, engage them in a short discussion of identifying the lesson in a folktale. Here is an example.

- ▶ Show the cover of *The Gingerbread Man*.

  Do you remember what happened to the gingerbread man? What could he have done differently so that he could have escaped from the fox?

  Do you think he might have been eaten anyway, no matter what?

- ▶ Review the pages that show him running away from the house and talking to a person he couldn't really trust—the fox.

  What lesson did you learn from this folktale?

- ▶ Using children's suggestions and prompting as needed, write the lesson on the chart paper or on a sentence strip and attach it to the chart. Draw a quick sketch of the gingerbread man next to the lesson.

- ▶ Repeat the activity with *The Princess and the Pea*, assisting children to understand the lesson of the folktale. Add the lesson to the chart or on a sentence strip and attach it to the chart.

## Have a Try

Invite the children to with a partner about the lesson in *Once a Mouse*.

▶ Show *Once a Mouse*.

Turn and talk with a partner about the lesson you learn from reading this folktale.

▶ As needed, point out pages that guide children to understand the lesson. Write the lesson on the chart or a sentence strip and add to the chart.

## Summarize and Apply

Summarize the learning and remind children to think about the lesson at the end of the folktale.

▶ Write the principle at the top of the chart.

How can you use the lessons in folktales?

When you read today, choose a folktale from this basket. Think about the lesson you learn from reading the story. Bring the book when we come back together so you can share.

## Share

Following independent work time, gather children together in the meeting area in a circle to talk about lessons in folktales.

If you learned a lesson from the folktale you read today, give a thumbs-up.

▶ Ask two or three of the children to share the lesson they learned.

Were any of the lessons similar to the ones on the chart?

## Extend the Lesson (Optional)

After assessing children's understanding, you might decide to extend the learning.

▶ As you read additional folktales, add the lesson learned to the chart. Have children talk about the lessons learned and notice similar lessons.

▶ Have children talk about ways the lessons learned in folktales can be applied to their lives.

---

**Folktales have a lesson at the end.**

 Do not run away or talk to strangers.

 Do not judge others before you know them.

 Be grateful to others who help you.

**Reading Minilesson Principle**

# In folktales, characters use cleverness or trickery to solve a problem.

## Studying Folktales

### You Will Need

- three familiar folktales, such as the following:
  - *The Tale of Rabbit and Coyote* by Tony Johnston, from Text Set: Folktales
  - *Mrs. Chicken and the Hungry Crocodile* by Won-Ldy Paye and Margaret H. Lippert, from Text Set: Folktales
  - *The Gingerbread Boy* by Rochard Egielski, from Text Set: Folktales: Versions
- chart paper and markers
- six sticky notes: three that say *cleverness*, three that say *trickery*
- a basket of folktales with characters that use cleverness or trickery

### Academic Language / Important Vocabulary

- folktale
- problem
- cleverness
- tricky
- trickery

### Continuum Connection

- Notice recurring themes or motifs in traditional literature and fantasy: e.g., struggle between good and evil, magic, fantastic or magical objects, wishes, trickery, transformations [p. 34]
- Infer characters' intentions, feelings, and motivations using text and pictures [p. 35]
- Understand that the same types of characters may appear over and over again in traditional literature: e.g., sly brave, silly, wise, greedy, clever [p. 35]

## Goal

Notice that folktales characters often use cleverness or trickery to solve a problem.

## Rationale

When children think about character traits and motivations, they develop an understanding of the character's decisions and how they interact with other characters in the story. This deepens their understanding of the text, encourages them to make predictions, and requires them to think carefully about how others behave.

## Assess Learning

Observe children when they talk about folktales they have read or heard. Notice if there is evidence of new learning based on the goal of this minilesson.

- Do children recognize when characters use cleverness and trickery to solve problems in folktales?
- Do children use vocabulary such as *folktale*, *problem*, *cleverness*, *tricky*, and *trickery*?

## Minilesson

To help children think about the minilesson principle, engage them in a short discussion as to how characters solve problems in folktales. Here is an example.

- Show the cover of *The Tale of Rabbit and Coyote*.

  Think about what Rabbit did so he would not be eaten by the man and the coyote. How did Rabbit save himself?

  Rabbit was clever and tricky. He tricked the man and the coyote.

- Sketch Rabbit on the chart paper. Ask a child to place one *cleverness* and one *trickery* sticky note next to the sketch of the rabbit.

  Rabbit solved his problems with cleverness and trickery.

- Show the cover of *Mrs. Chicken and the Hungry Crocodile*.

  Think about Mrs. Chicken and how she saved her family from the crocodile. What did Mrs. Chicken do?

  In what ways is Mrs. Chicken like Rabbit?

- Sketch Mrs. Chicken. Ask a volunteer to place another pair of sticky notes next to Mrs. Chicken.

## Have a Try

Invite the children to talk about the problem in *The Gingerbread Boy* with a partner.

> Turn and talk to a partner about how the fox solved the problem of catching the gingerbread boy.

▶ As children talk, sketch the gingerbread boy on the chart.

> How did the fox solve his problem?

▶ Have a child place the remaining sticky notes to the sketch of the gingerbread boy.

## Summarize and Apply

Summarize the learning and remind children to notice whether the character uses cleverness or trickery to solve the problem in the folktale they read.

> Look at the chart. What do these characters have in common? How do they solve problems?

▶ Write the principle at the top of the chart.

> When you read today, choose a folktale from the basket. If you find a character that uses cleverness and trickery, mark the page with a sticky note and bring the book when we meet after independent work time.

## Share

Following independent work time, gather children together in a circle to talk about characters in folktales.

> Give a thumbs-up if you read a folktale with a character that is clever and uses trickery.

▶ Have children share what they noticed. Sketch any of the characters and have a child add a new pair of sticky notes next to the characters.

## Extend the Lesson (Optional)

After assessing children's understanding, you might decide to extend the learning.

▶ Have children role-play clever characters from favorite folktales. Afterward, have them talk about how the character is clever and uses trickery to solve a problem.

▶ **Drawing/Writing About Reading** Have children write in a reader's notebook about folktale characters using cleverness or trickery to solve a problem.

In folktales, characters use cleverness or trickery to solve a problem.

cleverness    trickery

cleverness    trickery

cleverness    trickery

**Reading Minilesson Principle**
# Good characters are usually rewarded. Bad characters are not.

## Studying Folktales

### You Will Need

- three familiar folktales, such as the following:
  - *The Princess and the Pea* by Rachel Isadora from Text Set: Folktales
  - *Once a Mouse* by Marcia Brown, from Text Set: Folktales
  - *The Little Red Hen* by Lucinda McQueen from Text Set: Folktales: Versions
- chart paper and markers
- sticky notes with sketches of the princess, mouse, red hen, cat, and dog
- a basket of folktales

### Academic Language / Important Vocabulary

- folktale
- character
- reward

### Continuum Connection

- Notice story outcomes that are typical of traditional literature: e.g., cleverness overcomes power, good defeats evil (p. 34)

## Goal

Notice that in folktales the good characters are rewarded, and the bad characters are not.

## Rationale

When you help children learn about the consequences of a character's actions, they understand more about the common characteristics of folktales, develop a stronger comprehension of the text, and begin to connect lessons learned by a character to their lives.

## Assess Learning

Observe children when they talk about characters in folktales they have read or heard. Notice if there is evidence of new learning based on the goal of this minilesson.

- Do children notice that in folktales good characters are usually rewarded, and bad characters are not?
- Do they understand why a character is rewarded or not rewarded?
- Do children use vocabulary such as *folktale*, *character*, and *reward*?

## Minilesson

To help children think about the minilesson principle, engage them in a short discussion of distinguishing characters being rewarded in a folktale. Here is an example.

> Do you remember that folktales have good and bad characters? Today let's think about what happens to those characters.

- Show the cover of *The Princess and the Pea*.

> Think about the princess and how she behaved in a good, honest way. What did she get for being honest about being a true princess?

> The princess was rewarded for being true and honest. In which column on the chart should I put the princess?

- Show the cover of *Once a Mouse*.

> Now think about the mouse and how he behaved when he turned into a tiger. What happened to the animal when he was not thankful for what the hermit did for him? The tiger (mouse) was not rewarded because he was ungrateful. In which column should I put the mouse?

> Why do you think the authors of folktales reward good characters and not bad characters?

## Have a Try

Invite the children to talk with a partner about *The Little Red Hen*.

▶ Show the cover of *The Little Red Hen*.

Turn and talk with a partner about what happens to the dog, cat, and goose because of the way they behave toward the hen.

▶ After time for discussion, ask volunteers to place the sticky notes in the correct column on the chart.

## Summarize and Apply

Summarize the learning and remind the children to notice what happens to good characters and bad characters in folktales as they read.

What kind of character is rewarded at the end of a folktale? Look at the chart to help you remember.

What kind of character is not rewarded?

▶ Write the principle at the top of the chart.

Today, choose a folktale from the basket to read and notice what happens to the characters at the end of the folktale. Bring the book when we meet so you can share.

## Share

Following independent work time, gather children together in groups of four to talk about characters in folktales.

Share with your group a character in the folktale you read who is rewarded and one that is not rewarded. Tell why.

## Extend the Lesson (Optional)

After assessing children's understanding, you might decide to extend the learning.

▶ As you read additional folktales with good characters that are rewarded or bad characters that are not, have children place the character in the correct column on the chart.

▶ **Drawing/Writing About Reading** Have children write about what happens to a folktale character in a reader's notebook.

Good characters are usually rewarded. Bad characters are not.

| Book | Good—Rewarded | Bad—Not Rewarded |
|---|---|---|

**Reading Minilesson Principle**
# The storyteller repeats words and sentences in folktales.

## Studying Folktales

### You Will Need

▸ two or three familiar folktales, such as the following from Text Set: Folktales: Versions:
  • *The Little Red Hen: An Old Fable* by Heather Forest
  • *Goldilocks and the Three Bears* by Jan Brett
▸ chart paper and markers
▸ two speech bubbles cut out of construction paper: one says *Not I!* and the other says *Somebody has been ...*
▸ tape or glue stick
▸ a basket of folktales

### Academic Language / Important Vocabulary

▸ folktale
▸ repeat

### Continuum Connection

▸ Join in on repeated words, phrases, and sentences after hearing them several times [p. 34]
▸ Notice when a book has repeating episodes or language patterns [p. 35]

## Goal

Notice repeating words or phrases in folktales.

## Rationale

When children hear a group of folktales, they begin to understand that folktales are stories that were told orally for many years. They begin to recognize that many folktales have repeating language that can be easily remembered and repeated by the listeners.

## Assess Learning

Observe children when they talk about folktales they have read or heard. Notice if there is evidence of new learning based on the goal of this minilesson.

▸ Do children notice that folktales sometimes have repeating words or phrases?
▸ Are they able to join in on repeated words or phrases in folktales?
▸ Do they use vocabulary such as *folktale* and *repeat*?

## Minilesson

To help children think about the minilesson principle, engage them in a short discussion of repeating words and phrases in folktales. Here is an example.

▸ Read aloud pages 9–10, emphasizing *Not I*.

> Listen to these words from *The Little Red Hen: An Old Fable*. What do you notice?

> The animals keep saying, "Not I!"

▸ Ask a child to attach the *Not I* speech bubble to the chart near the book cover.
▸ Read aloud page 15 of *Goldilocks and the Three Bears*. As you read, emphasize the words *Somebody has been*. Ask a child to add the *Somebody has been ...* speech bubble to the chart.

> What can you say about some of the words in these two folktales?

## Have a Try

Invite the children to apply the new thinking about the language in folktales.

▸ Reread pages 9–10 and 15 again and have children join in with you on the repeated words and phrases.

> Why do you think authors repeated words in their folktales?

> Folktales were told aloud for many years, and people had to remember them. They were not written down like they are today. The repeating words made them easier to remember. Do you think they also make the story better? How?

## Summarize and Apply

Summarize the learning and remind children to look for repeated words and phrases in folktales as they read.

▸ Review the chart and write the principle at the top.

> Why do storytellers repeat words and sentences in folktales?

> Today when you read, choose a folktale from the basket. If you find words that repeat, place a sticky note on the page. You can write the word on the sticky note if you like. Bring the book when we meet after independent work time.

## Share

Following independent work time, gather children in a circle to talk about repeating words and phrases in folktales.

> Give a thumbs-up if you read a folktale that has words or phrases that repeat.

▸ Read (or ask the child to read) the repeated words, and then have the class join in.

## Extend the Lesson (Optional)

After assessing children's understanding, you might decide to extend the learning.

▸ Encourage children to role-play favorite folktales, with others joining in on repeating words or phrases.

▸ As you read more folktales, invent hand gestures with the children to use as they repeat words or phrases.

The storyteller repeats words and sentences in folktales.

Not I!

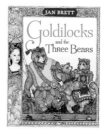

Someone has been ...

Section 2: Literary Analysis

# RML9

LA.U16.RML9

**Reading Minilesson Principle**
## Versions of the same folktale are alike and different in some ways.

## Studying Folktales

### You Will Need

- two sets of the same familiar folktale in different versions, such as these from Text Set: Folktales: Versions:
  - *The Little Red Hen* by Lucinda McQueen
  - *The Little Red Hen: An Old Fable* by Heather Forest
  - *Goldilocks and the Three Bears* by Jan Brett
  - *The Three Snow Bears* by Jan Brett
- chart paper and markers
- a basket with folktales organized into sets of versions of the same folktale

### Academic Language / Important Vocabulary

- folktale
- version

### Continuum Connection

- Connect texts by obvious categories: e.g., author, character, topic, genre, illustrator (p. 34)

### Goal

Versions of the same folktale can be alike in some ways and different in other ways.

### Rationale

When children analyze the ways multiple versions of the same folktale are similar and different, they begin to understand that these stories have been retold for many years and learn about diversity as they hear a story told in different ways and from multiple perspectives. They can begin to connect the stories to diverse places and cultures.

### Assess Learning

Observe children when they talk about folktales they have read or heard. Notice if there is evidence of new learning based on the goal of this minilesson.

- Do children notice when they read a different version of a folktale they know?
- Are children able to talk about what is alike and what is different in the versions?
- Do they use vocabulary such as *folktale* and *version*?

## Minilesson

To help children think about the minilesson principle, engage them in a short discussion of identifying similarities and differences in versions of the same folktale. Here is an example.

- Show the covers of *The Little Red Hen* and *The Little Red Hen: An Old Fable*.

  These two books are different versions of the same folktale. Let's look for clues about how they are the same and how they are different.

- On the chart paper, draw a Venn diagram with the folktale title at the top.
- Read the information on the covers.

  What do you notice?

- As children respond, add a sketch of each cover in the Venn diagram, along with the authors' names.

  What characters do you notice?

- As children respond, add *hen*, *dog*, and *cat* to the similar section of the Venn diagram and add the *mouse* and the *goose* to the different sections.
- Revisit pages 21–22 of *The Little Red Hen* and pages 17–20 of *The Little Red Hen: An Old Fable*.

  What do you notice?

▶ As children respond, add to the Venn diagram. Review the things that are the same and different from the two versions.

## Have a Try

Invite the children to talk about the chart with a partner.

> Turn and talk with a partner about the chart we just made. Is there anything else that is the same or different about the two versions of the story about the little red hen?

## Summarize and Apply

Summarize the learning and remind children to notice different versions of the same folktale.

▶ Review the chart and write the principle at the top.

> Why do you think versions of the same folktale are alike in some ways and different in some ways?

> Today when you read, choose a folktale from the basket and think if you have ever listened to a different version of the folktale.

## Share

Following independent work time, gather children together in the meeting area to talk about folktales.

> Hold your book in front of you with the cover facing out. Find another person who has a different version of the book you read. Sit with that person.

> Turn and talk about what is alike and different in your versions of the folktale.

## Extend the Lesson (Optional)

After assessing children's understanding, you might decide to extend the learning.

▶ Ask the librarian to give book talks for different versions of the same folktales.

▶ Use a Venn diagram for comparing two or more versions of the same folktale.

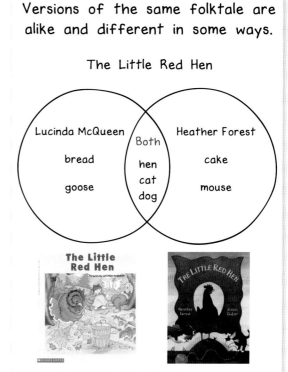

Versions of the same folktale are alike and different in some ways.

The Little Red Hen

Lucinda McQueen — bread — goose

Both — hen — cat — dog

Heather Forest — cake — mouse

The Little Red Hen

## Assessment

After you have taught the minilessons in this umbrella, observe children talking and writing about their reading across instructional contexts: interactive read-aloud, independent reading and literacy work, guided reading, shared reading, and book club. Use *The Literacy Continuum* (Fountas and Pinnell 2017) to observe children's reading and writing behaviors across instructional contexts.

 ▶ What evidence do you have of new understandings related to the characteristics of folktales?

  • Can children note characteristics of folktales, including that they have been told for many years, there are good and bad characters, and there is a lesson at the end?

  • Do they recognize recurring types of characters and their outcomes?

  • Can they recognize repetition in folktales?

  • Can they compare versions of the same folktale?

  • Do children use terms such as *lesson, problem, character, cleverness,* and *tricky* when discussing folktales?

 ▶ In what other ways, beyond the scope of this umbrella, are children talking about folktales and fiction?

  • Are children talking about problem and solution?

  • Do they notice that fictional characters are not real?

Use your observations to determine the next umbrella you will teach. You may also consult Minilessons Across the Year (p. 51) for guidance.

## Read and Revise

After completing the steps in the genre study process, help children to read and revise their definition of the genre based on their new understandings.

 ▶ **Before:** Folktales are made-up stories that have been told and retold for a long time. The characters are either good or bad, and everyone learns a lesson in the end.

 ▶ **After:** Folktales are made-up stories that have been told and retold for many years. The characters are either good or bad, and everyone learns a lesson in the end. There can be different versions of the same story.

## Minilessons in This Umbrella

**RML1**   The illustrations and the words show where a story happens.

**RML2**   The place is important to the story.

## Before Teaching Umbrella 17 Minilessons

Read and discuss books with children that take place in different locations. Include books with places that are an important part of the story. Use the following books from the *Fountas & Pinnell Classroom™ Interactive Read-Aloud Collection* text sets or choose books from your library in which the setting is important.

**Using Numbers: Books with Counting**

*Over on a Mountain: Somewhere in the World* by Marianne Berkes

*Moja Means One: Swahili Counting Book* by Muriel Feelings

**Bob Graham: Exploring Everyday Life**

*How to Heal a Broken Wing* by Bob Graham

**Journeys Near and Far**

*Bailey Goes Camping* by Kevin Henkes

*Down the Road* by Alice Schertle

As you read aloud and enjoy these texts together, help your children

• notice where a story takes place based on evidence in the book, and

• think about how the location is important to the story.

**Using Numbers**

**Bob Graham**

**Journeys**

**Reading Minilesson Principle**

# The Illustrations and the words show where a story happens.

## Thinking About Where Stories Take Place

### You Will Need

- three or four familiar books with easily identified settings, such as the following:
  - *Over on a Mountain: Somewhere in the World* by Marianne Berkes, from Text Set: Using Numbers
  - *How to Heal a Broken Wing* by Bob Graham, from Text Set: Bob Graham
  - *Moja Means One: Swahili Counting Book* by Muriel Feelings, from Text Set: Using Numbers
- chart paper and markers
- sticky notes

### Academic Language / Important Vocabulary

- author
- illustrator
- happen
- place

### Continuum Connection

- Recall important details about setting after a story is read (p. 34)

## Goal

Help children infer where a story takes place from the pictures and words.

## Rationale

When children notice details in the words and illustrations that show location, they learn the author made a deliberate choice about where the story takes place because the setting has to make sense with the story. They also will begin to learn how to analyze the author's and illustrator's craft and to notice whether there is a relationship between the setting and the story's problem or characters.

## Assess Learning

Observe children when they talk about where stories take place. Notice if there is evidence of new learning based on the goal of this minilesson.

- Are children able to identify where a story happens using the words and illustrations?
- Do they use vocabulary such as *author*, *illustrator*, *happen*, and *place*?

## Minilesson

To help children think about the minilesson principle, engage them in a short discussion about setting. Here is an example.

- Show page 1 of *Over on a Mountain: Somewhere in the World*. Read the first sentence.

  Where does this part of the story happen?

  How do the author and the illustrator use their words and illustrations to tell you where the llamas live?

- Record responses on the chart paper. Then, choose several other pages and look for clues that tell where the story takes place.

- Show pages 1–2 of *How to Heal a Broken Wing*.

  Now think about the book *How to Heal a Broken Wing*. What do you see in this illustration that tells you where this story takes place?

- Record responses on the chart.

- Read pages 1–2.

  The author's words tell you this is a city, but you already knew that because you looked at the illustration.

## Have a Try

Invite the children to talk about setting with a partner.

▶ Show and read the page with the number 5 of *Moja Means One: Swahili Counting Book*.

 How does this illustration help you know where the story takes place? Turn and talk with a partner.

▶ Record responses on the chart.

 The author's words give you more details about where the story takes place.

▶ Display and read the page with the number 7.

 Turn and talk to a partner about where this part of the story happens.

▶ Record responses on the chart.

## Summarize and Apply

Summarize the learning and remind children to think about where the story happens as they read.

 How can you tell where a story happens?

▶ Review the chart and write the principle at the top.

 When you read today, think about where the story happens. Put sticky notes on pages with words or illustrations that show where the story happens.

## Share

Following independent work time, gather children together in the meeting area to talk about setting.

 Turn and talk with a partner about where the story you read happens. Use your book to show a partner the words and illustrations that helped you know where the story happens.

## Extend the Lesson (Optional)

After assessing children's understanding, you might decide to extend the learning.

▶ During interactive read-aloud and shared reading, ask children to share what they notice about the setting. (Use the word *setting* only if your children are ready for it.)

**The illustrations and the words show where a story happens.**

| Title | Where the Story Happens |
|---|---|
|  | It happened in the mountains. |
| 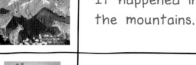 | It happened in the city. |
| 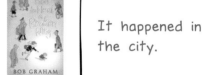 | It happened in the grassy savannah. It happened under the water. |

Section 2: Literary Analysis

# RML2
## LA.U17.RML2

**Reading Minilesson Principle**
## The place is important to the story.

## Thinking About Where Stories Take Place

### Goal

Understand the setting of the story and infer why it is important.

### Rationale

As children explore the importance setting has on the plot and characters of a story, they learn that where a story happens is an integral part of the story. When children analyze the significance of where a story takes place, they broaden their understanding of the author's and illustrator's craft and the story itself.

### Assess Learning

Observe children when they talk about why the setting is important in stories. Notice if there is evidence of new learning based on the goal of this minilesson.

▶ Are children able to identify the place, or setting?

▶ Are they able to describe why the location of a story is important to the story?

## Minilesson

To help children think about the minilesson principle, engage them in a short discussion of the importance of setting to a story. Here is an example.

▶ Show the cover of *Bailey Goes Camping*.

> Remember Bailey stays home while his older brother and sister go camping. Where does Bailey go camping?

▶ Record responses on the chart paper.

> Why is it important to the story that Bailey has a camping adventure at home instead of out in the woods? Why do you think the author, Kevin Henkes, decided to have this story take place at home?

> Now think about *Over on a Mountain: Somewhere in the World*. What kinds of places did you read about in this story?

▶ Revisit illustrations as needed to prompt the conversation. Record responses on the chart.

> I notice a lot of maps. I wonder why the illustrator decided to include so many maps in this story.

▶ Show a page with a map.

> Why is it important that you know where these different places are?

## Have a Try

Invite the children to talk about setting with a partner.

▶ Show and reread pages 1–2 of *Down the Road*.

> Where does this story take place? Turn and talk with a partner about why it is important to know where this story happens.

▶ Ask several volunteers to share. Record responses on the chart and review the chart.

## Summarize and Apply

Summarize the learning and remind children to think about where the story takes place and why that is important to the story as they read.

▶ Review the chart and write the principle at the top.

> Today you noticed that where a story takes place is important in helping you understand the story.

> When you read today, think about where the story takes place and why that might be important to the story. Bring the book when we meet after independent work time so you can share what you found.

## Share

Following independent work time, gather children together in the meeting area to talk about the importance of the setting to a story.

> Turn and talk to a partner about where the book you read takes place and why that is important to the story.

## Extend the Lesson (Optional)

After assessing children's understanding, you might decide to extend the learning.

▶ Continue to notice and think about the importance of setting in stories during interactive read-aloud and shared reading.

▶ Choose stories that have a similar plot but take place in different locations so children can compare, e.g., counting stories that take place in different locations.

▶ **Drawing/Writing About Reading** Use interactive writing to record places children read about and why those places are important to the story.

### The place is important to the story.

| Title | Where the Story Happens | Why the Place Is Important |
|---|---|---|
| *Bailey Goes Camping* — Kevin Henkes | Bailey's house | Bailey learns that he can have fun camping at home. |
| *Over on a Mountain* | Mountains around the world | Different animals live on different mountains. |
| *Down the Road* | Hetty's house and the dusty road | The story is mostly about when Hetty goes down the dusty road. |

## Assessment

After you have taught the minilessons in this umbrella, observe children talking and writing about settings in their reading across instructional contexts: interactive read-aloud, independent reading and literacy work, guided reading, shared reading, and book club. Use *The Literacy Continuum* (Fountas and Pinnell 2017) to observe children's reading and writing behaviors across instructional contexts.

▶ What evidence do you have of new understandings related to where a story takes place?

- Can children identify where a story happens?

- In what ways do children use background knowledge to help them understand where a story takes place?

- Can they infer why the location where a story takes place is important to the story?

- Do they recognize that stories take place in different locations?

- Do they use vocabulary related to setting, such as *place*?

▶ In what other ways, beyond the scope of this umbrella, are the children talking about stories?

- Are children noticing details in the illustrations?

- Do they talk about the characters in stories?

Use your observations to determine the next umbrella you will teach. You may also consult Minilessons Across the Year (p. 51) for guidance.

## Link to Writing

After teaching the minilessons in this umbrella, help children link the new learning to their writing or drawing about reading:

▶ Encourage children to use words and pictures to show the setting of the stories when they write.

## Minilessons in This Umbrella

**RML1**  A story has a problem that gets solved.

**RML2**  Stories start with a problem and end with a solution.

**RML3**  Think about how the story will end.

**RML4**  When you tell about a story, tell who, where, and what happened.

## Before Teaching Umbrella 18 Minilessons

Read and discuss a variety of high-quality fiction picture books that have a simple problem and solution and events that are easily followed by children. However, RML3 relies on using a book that children have not yet read so that they can make authentic predictions. The minilessons in this umbrella use books from the following text sets from the *Fountas & Pinnell Classroom™ Interactive Read-Aloud Collection* as examples. However, you will want to select fiction books based on the experiences and interests of your children.

**The Importance of Friendship**

*Leon and Bob* by Simon James

**Mo Willems: Having Fun with Humor**

*I Am Invited to a Party!* by Mo Willems

*Knuffle Bunny: A Cautionary Tale* by Mo Willems

**Kevin Henkes: Exploring Characters**

*Chrysanthemum* by Kevin Henkes

**The Importance of Kindness**

*Pet Show* by Ezra Jack Keats

*Wilfred Gordon McDonald Partridge* by Mem Fox

**Standing Up for Yourself**

*King of the Playground* by Phyllis Reynolds Naylor

As you read aloud and enjoy these texts together, help children

- think about the problem in the story and how it gets solved,
- notice the structure of stories, including events that lead to the problem being solved,
- think about how the story might end, and
- summarize a story, including the problem, events, and solution.

**Friendship**

**Mo Willems**

**Kevin Henkes**

**Kindness**

**Standing Up**

**Section 2: Literary Analysis**

**Reading Minilesson Principle**
## A story has a problem that gets solved.

### Understanding Simple Plot: Problem and Solution

#### You Will Need

- three or four familiar fiction books with a simple problem and solution, such as the following:
  - *Leon and Bob* by Simon James, from Text Set: Friendship
  - *I Am Invited to a Party!* by Mo Willems, from Text Set: Mo Willems
  - *Chrysanthemum* by Kevin Henkes, from Text Set: Kevin Henkes
- chart paper and markers
- sticky notes

#### Academic Language / Important Vocabulary

- problem
- solution

#### Continuum Connection

- Notice and understand a simple plot with a problem and solution. (p. 35)
- Use some academic language to talk about literary features: e.g., beginning, ending, problem, character, solution, main character (p. 35)

### Goal

Notice and understand a simple plot with a problem and solution.

### Rationale

Children will be able to explore the problem and solution in a story as they begin to recognize the structure of a fiction story. When children identify and talk about the problem and solution in simple narratives, they can predict what might happen next in the story, follow the important events, and think about the lives of the characters more deeply.

### Assess Learning

Observe children when they talk about a problem and solution in a story. Notice if there is evidence of new learning based on the goal of this minilesson.

- ▶ Can children identify the problem and the solution in a story?
- ▶ Do they use academic language, such as *problem* and *solution*?

## Minilesson

To help children think about the minilesson principle, engage them in a short discussion of identifying the problem and solution in a story. Here is an example.

- ▶ Show and read page 4 of *Leon and Bob*.

  This is Leon eating breakfast with his make-believe friend, Bob. Turn and talk with a partner why you think Leon has an imaginary friend. Think about the problem Leon has.

  What is his problem?

- ▶ Record responses on the chart paper.
- ▶ Show and read the last pages of the story.

  Here is Leon playing with his new friend, Bob. How is Leon's problem solved?

- ▶ Introduce the word *solution* if needed. Record responses on the chart.
- ▶ Show the cover of *I Am Invited to a Party!*

  Think about the problem Piggie has in *I Am Invited to a Party!*

- ▶ Read pages 8–9.

  What is Piggie's problem?

- ▶ Record responses on the chart.

  Do you remember how Gerald helps Piggie solve her problem?

## Have a Try

Invite the children to talk with a partner about Chrysanthemum's problem.

- Revisit page 7 in *Chrysanthemum* and pages 26–30, if necessary.

  Turn and talk with a partner about Chrysanthemum's problem and how it was solved.

  Who helped solve it?

- After time for discussion, ask children to share as you record responses on the chart.

## Summarize and Apply

Summarize the learning and remind children to notice the character's problem and solution as they read.

  What did you learn today about problems in stories? Look at the chart to help you remember.

- Write the principle at the top of the chart.

  When you read today, think about the problem and how it gets solved. Sometimes the character solves it, but sometimes the character gets help. Put a sticky note on pages that show the problem and solution. Bring the book when we meet later so you can share.

## Share

Following independent work time, gather children in the meeting area to talk about the problem and solution in their reading.

  Turn and talk to a partner about the problem and solution in the story you read. Who solved the problem?

## Extend the Lesson (Optional)

After assessing children's understanding, you might decide to extend the learning.

- Encourage children to role-play characters from stories. Have them include the problem and solution.

- Before starting to read aloud a book during interactive read-aloud, tell children to give a thumbs-up when they hear the problem and then the solution.

- **Drawing/Writing About Reading** Have children write and draw in a reader's notebook about the problem and solution in a story that they read or listen to.

### A story has a problem that gets solved.

| | Problem | Solution |
|---|---|---|
|  Leon and Bob | Leon is lonely. He does not have a real friend. | Leon meets the boy next door named Bob. |
| I Am Invited to a Party! | Piggie has never been to a party. She does not know what to wear. | Gerald helps Piggie think about what to wear. |
| Chrysanthemum | Children make fun of Chrysanthemum's name. She feels sad. | The music teacher has a long name, too. |

**Reading Minilesson Principle**
# Stories start with a problem and end with a solution.

## Understanding Simple Plot: Problem and Solution

### You Will Need

- three or four familiar fiction books with a problem, events, and a solution, such as the following:
  - *Knuffle Bunny: A Cautionary Tale* by Mo Willems, from Text Set: Mo Willems
  - *Wilfred Gordon McDonald Partridge* by Mem Fox, from Text Set: Kindness
- chart paper and markers
- sticky notes

### Academic Language / Important Vocabulary

- problem
- event
- solution

### Continuum Connection

- Follow a plot with multiple events (p. 35)
- Notice and understand when a problem is solved (p. 35)

## Goal

Understand the structure of a story with a problem that is solved.

## Rationale

When children think about the way stories are structured, they can anticipate how a story goes and read with more confidence and ability. They can begin to think analytically about the story's problem and predict ways it might be solved. They can notice characters' attempts to solve the problem and events in the story and think critically about the solution.

## Assess Learning

Observe children when they talk about stories they have read or heard. Notice if there is evidence of new learning based on the goal of this minilesson.

- Are children able to talk about the problem, events, and solution in a story?
- Do they show understanding of the order of events?
- Do they use academic language, such as *problem*, *event*, and *solution*?

## Minilesson

To help children think about the minilesson principle, engage them in a short discussion of a problem, events, and solution in a story. Here is an example.

- Review the problem, the main events, and the solution in *Knuffle Bunny*. Start by showing page 12.

  Think about the problem Trixie has in *Knuffle Bunny*. What is Trixie's problem?

- Record responses on the chart paper.

  Before Trixie finds a solution to her problem, other things happen in the story, don't they? The things that happen in a story are called *events*.

- Continue by showing page 13 and then pages 21–22.

  What event happens next?

- Record responses.

- Show page 30, when Trixie's dad looked harder and found Knuffle Bunny.

  What is the solution to Trixie's problem?

- Record responses.

  You told the problem, events, and solution in *Knuffle Bunny*. Where do you usually learn the problem in a story? Where do you usually find the solution?

## Have a Try

Invite the children to talk with a partner about the problem in *Wilfred Gordon McDonald Partridge*.

▶ Read aloud the pages of *Wilfred Gordon McDonald Partridge* on which the problem, a couple of important events, and the solution appear.

▶ Have children turn and talk with a partner briefly at each stopping point.

> Did this story start with the problem and end with the solution, like *Knuffle Bunny*?

## Summarize and Apply

Summarize the learning and remind children to notice the problem, events, and the solution as they read.

▶ Review the chart and talk about how a story usually goes—it starts with a problem and ends with a solution, with events in between.

> When you read today, think about the problem and how it gets solved. Put a sticky note on pages that show the problem and solution. Bring the book when we come back together so you can share.

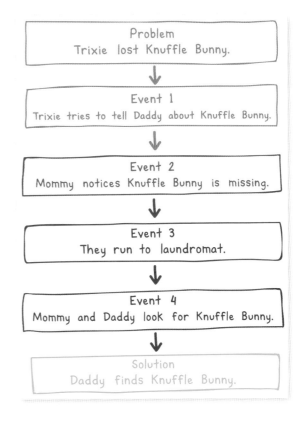

## Share

Following independent work time, gather children in the meeting area to talk about the problem and solution in their reading.

> Turn and talk to a partner about where you noticed the problem and where you noticed the solution. Did the story start with a problem and end with a solution?

## Extend the Lesson (Optional)

After assessing children's understanding, you might decide to extend the learning.

▶ Ask children to identify the problem, events, and solution in other books you read as a class or in books read independently.

▶ **Drawing/Writing About Reading** Support children in using a reader's notebook to include the problem, events, and solution in books they read through words and/or drawings.

# RML3
## LA.U18.RML3

### Reading Minilesson Principle
# Think about how the story will end.

## Understanding Simple Plot: Problem and Solution

### You Will Need

- an unfamiliar fiction book that lends to making authentic predictions, such as *King of the Playground* by Phyllis Reynolds Naylor, from Text Set: Standing Up
- chart paper and markers

### Academic Language / Important Vocabulary

- character
- problem
- solution
- predict
- ending

### Continuum Connection

- Predict story outcomes (p. 35)

## Goal

Predict how a story will end.

## Rationale

When children predict how a story might end, they engage with the story as they think throughout the reading. By using evidence from the text to support their thinking, they begin to think analytically about the text and make connections between background knowledge and story information to make sense of the story.

## Assess Learning

Observe children when they talk about stories they have read or heard. Notice if there is evidence of new learning based on the goal of this minilesson.

- ▶ Can children predict how a story might end?
- ▶ Do they talk about whether the story had a good ending?
- ▶ Do they base their predictions on text evidence and/or background knowledge?
- ▶ Do they use academic language, such as *character*, *problem*, *predict*, *ending*, and *solution*?

## Minilesson

To help children think about the minilesson principle, engage them in a short discussion of predicting how a story might end. Here is an example.

- ▶ Show the cover of a book that is unfamiliar to the children, such as *King of the Playground*.

    Today we are going to read a story you have not heard before. What is going on in the illustration?

    It looks like one boy is not being nice to another boy on the playground. Let's read and see if that is what the story is about.

- ▶ Show and read page 1.

    I wonder if Kevin is going to the playground. I wonder if that is why he doesn't feel brave and lucky.

- ▶ Show and read pages 2–3.

    What problem is Kevin having at the playground?

- ▶ Record responses on the chart paper. Guide children to make logical predictions about how the story will end.

    Based on what you know, how do you think this story might end? Why do you think that?

Let's finish the story and learn if any of these things happen at the end.

❱ Read the rest of the story.

## Have a Try

Invite the children to talk about their predictions with a partner.

> Turn and talk with a partner about how you thought *King of the Playground* would end and why you thought that. Tell whether you thought the ending was good.

❱ After discussion, ask a few to share. Record new responses on the chart. Note that some children had different predictions, and that's okay as long as everyone has a reason for the prediction.

## Summarize and Apply

Summarize the learning and remind children to think about how the story will end while they read.

> How do you predict how a story might end? How did you make your prediction?

❱ Write the principle at the top of the chart.

> If you read a book for the first time today, predict how the story might end. Bring the book when we come back together so you can share.

## Share

Following independent work time, gather children together to talk about their reading.

> If you read a book for the first time today, tell how you thought the book would end and why you thought that. Tell whether you thought your book had a good ending.

## Extend the Lesson (Optional)

After assessing children's understanding, you might decide to extend the learning.

❱ During interactive read-aloud, have the children think about how the story might end. Prompt them to talk about the text evidence and/or background knowledge they based their predictions on. Also explain that readers sometimes change their predictions as they read more of the story.

❱ **Drawing/Writing About Reading** During interactive read-aloud, stop at a pivotal moment in the story and have the children draw a quick sketch of what they think will happen next. Continue with the story to confirm their predictions.

**Think about how the story will end.**

### King of the Playground

| Problem | Sammy is being a bully to Kevin at the playground. |
|---|---|
| Predictions | More kids could come and tell Sammy to leave.<br>Kevin could teach Sammy to be nice.<br>Sammy's mom could come and tell him to stop. |
| Ending | Kevin stands up for himself, and they become friends. |

**Reading Minilesson Principle**
# When you tell about a story, tell who, where, and what happened.

## Understanding Simple Plot: Problem and Solution

- two or three familiar fiction books with a problem, events, and solution, such as the following:
  - *Pet Show* by Ezra Jack Keats, from Text Set: Kindness
  - *Knuffle Bunny: A Cautionary Tale* by Mo Willems, from Text Set: Mo Willems
- chart paper and markers

**Academic Language / Important Vocabulary**

- character
- problem
- event
- solution

**Continuum Connection**

- Include the problem and its resolution in telling what happened in a text [p. 35]

## Goal

Tell who, where, and what happened in a story with a problem and solution.

## Rationale

As children explore the structure of fiction stories, they will consider what happens to the characters (who) at the beginning, middle, and ending. Understanding the structure enables them to summarize and talk about what they have read. When children include the setting, problem, events, and solution as they retell a story, they demonstrate comprehension of the main ideas, recognize the structure, and begin to apply these ideas as they talk about books and write stories.

## Assess Learning

Observe children when they tell what happened in a story. Notice if there is evidence of new learning based on the goal of this minilesson.

- ▶ Do children talk about the characters, places, problem, events, and solution in a story?
- ▶ Do they tell the events in the order they happened?
- ▶ Do children use academic language, such as *character, problem, event,* and *solution*?

# Minilesson

To help children think about the minilesson principle, demonstrate how to tell the important parts of a story. Here is an example.

- ▶ Summarize a familiar fiction book, such as *Pet Show*.

    Notice what I tell you about a story you know. Archie wanted to enter his cat in a pet show, but he couldn't find his cat. His friends went to the pet show, but Archie stayed home. At the last minute, Archie went with a jar that looked empty. Archie said it had a germ named Al in it. A woman came up to the judges with a cat that looked familiar. The woman won a blue ribbon for the cat with the longest whiskers. Archie won a blue ribbon for the quietest pet. The woman said to Archie the cat was his. Archie took the cat, but he wouldn't take the blue ribbon. He said it looked good on the woman.

- ▶ Write the title on the prepared chart paper.

    What things did you notice I included when I talked about the story?

- ▶ Record responses on the chart. Reread the chart when it is complete.

## Have a Try

Invite the children to tell a partner about *Knufle Bunny*.

▶ Show the cover of *Knuffle Bunny: A Cautionary Tale*.

Turn and talk with a partner about the characters, place, problem, events, and solution.

▶ After time for discussion, ask volunteers to tell about the story to the group. Emphasize each story element as they do. Record responses on the chart.

## Summarize and Apply

Summarize the learning and remind children to think about who, where, and what happened as they read.

When you talk about a story, what can you talk about? How should you tell about the events?

▶ Write the principle at the top of the chart.

When you read today, think about how you might talk about this story. Bring your book when we come back together so you can talk about it.

## Share

Following independent work time, gather children in the meeting area in groups of three to talk about who, where, and what happened in their reading.

Show the book you read and tell about the story. Include the character, place, problem, events, and solution. Remember to tell what happened in order.

## Extend the Lesson (Optional)

After assessing children's understanding, you might decide to extend the learning.

▶ Using finger puppets, have children act out a story. Encourage them to include the problem, events, and solution.

▶ **Drawing/Writing About Reading** Use shared writing to write a simple summary of a story the class has read during interactive read-aloud. Follow the outline on the chart.

| When you tell about a story, tell who, where, and what happened. | | |
|---|---|---|
| Who | Archie the woman cat | Trixie her daddy her mommy |
| Where | pet show | laundromat |
| What happened | Archie lost his cat. He found it at the pet show. | Trixie lost Knuffle Bunny. Her Daddy helped her find it. |
| | | |

Section 2: Literary Analysis

## Assessment

After you have taught the minilessons in this umbrella, observe children talking and writing about their reading across instructional contexts: interactive read-aloud, independent reading and literacy work, guided reading, shared reading, and book club. Use *The Literacy Continuum* (Fountas and Pinnell 2017) to observe children's reading and writing behaviors across instructional contexts.

▶ What evidence do you have of new understandings related to the plot?

- Can children identify the problem and solution in a simple narrative?
- Do children talk about how a story might end?
- Are children able to summarize a story by telling about the characters, place, problem, events, and solution?
- Do they use the academic terms *character*, *problem*, *event*, and *solution* appropriately when discussing plot?

▶ In what other ways, beyond the scope of this umbrella, are the children talking about character, place, problem, events, and solution?

- Have children noticed how characters in folktales solved their problems?
- Do children think about how the illustrations go with the story?
- Do they notice that sometimes characters learn a lesson in a story?

Use your observations to determine the next umbrella you will teach. You may also consult Minilessons Across the Year (p. 51) for guidance.

## Link to Writing

After teaching the minilessons in this umbrella, help children link the new learning to their writing or drawing about reading:

▶ Encourage children to write stories that include characters, place, problems, events, and solutions when they write independently.

## Minilessons in This Umbrella

**RML1**  Stories have important characters.

**RML2**  The characters' faces and bodies show how they feel.

**RML3**  What the characters say and do shows how they are feeling.

**RML4**  What the characters say and do shows how they feel about other characters.

**RML5**  Sometimes you feel the same way as a character in a story.

## Before Teaching Umbrella 19 Minilessons

Read and discuss books with characters whose feelings can be observed through words and illustrations. Use books from the following text sets from the *Fountas & Pinnell Classroom™ Interactive Read-Aloud Collection* or choose similar books from your library.

**Taking Care of Each Other: Family**

> *When I Am Old with You* by Angela Johnson
>
> *A Birthday Basket for Tia* by Pat Mora

**Kevin Henkes: Exploring Characters**

> *Sheila Rae, the Brave* by Kevin Henkes
>
> *Julius, the Baby of the World* by Kevin Henkes

**Learning and Playing Together: School**

> *Elizabeti's School* by Stephanie Stuve-Bodeen
>
> *Jamaica's Blue Marker* by Juanita Havill
>
> *A Fine, Fine School* by Sharon Creech

As you read aloud and enjoy these texts together, help your children

- notice the important characters in stories,
- notice how the characters' faces and bodies show how they feel,
- notice what characters say and do to understand how they feel,
- notice what characters say and do to understand how they feel about the other characters in the story, and
- notice how characters feel and think about if they have ever felt the same way.

**Family**

**Kevin Henkes**

**School**

**Section 2: Literary Analysis**

**Understanding Characters and Their Feelings**

### You Will Need

- three or four familiar books with clear main characters, such as the following:
  - *When I Am Old with You* by Angela Johnson, from Text Set: Family
  - *Elizabeti's School* by Stephanie Stuve-Bodeen and *Jamaica's Blue Marker* by Juanita Havill, from Text Set: School
- chart paper and markers

### Academic Language / Important Vocabulary

- character
- important

### Continuum Connection

- Give reasons (either text-based or from personal experience) to support thinking (p. 34)

## Goal

Identify important characters in simple narratives.

## Rationale

When children begin to recognize that characters are a key element of fiction, they will be able to determine which people or animals the story is mostly about. When children learn to identify and think about the important characters in a story, they begin to appreciate the meaning of the text and can discuss it with others.

## Assess Learning

Observe children when they talk about stories they have read or heard. Notice if there is evidence of new learning based on the goal of this minilesson.

- ▌ Are children able to identify the important characters in stories?
- ▌ Can children differentiate between important characters and supporting characters?
- ▌ How do they talk about the important characters from books they read independently?
- ▌ Do they use the term *character* in conversation about fiction books?

## Minilesson

To help children think about the minilesson principle, engage them in a short discussion of identifying the important characters in a story. Here is an example.

- ▌ Show the cover of *When I Am Old with You*.

  Who is this story mostly about?

- ▌ Write the principle at the top of the chart paper and record children's responses.

  The grandaddy and the grandson are the characters in this story. How do you know the grandaddy and the grandson are the most important characters?

  Now let's think about the important characters in another story you know.

- ▌ Show a few pages from *Elizabeti's School*.

  There are many characters in this story, but who is the story mostly about?

- ▌ Record responses on the chart.

  How do you know Elizabeti is the most important character in this story?

  Can the title of a book help you know who the important characters are in a story?

## Have a Try

Invite the children to talk about characters with a partner.

▶ Show the cover of *Jamaica's Blue Marker*.

> Turn and talk to a partner about who the most important characters are in this story and why you think that.

▶ Record responses on the chart.

## Summarize and Apply

Summarize the learning and remind children to think about the important characters as they read.

▶ Review the chart and write the principle at the top.

> How can you tell who the important characters are in a story?

> When you read a story today, think about the important characters. Bring the book when we come back together so you can share the names of the important characters in the story and tell how you know they are important.

## Share

Following independent work time, gather children together in the meeting area to talk about the important characters in their story.

> Turn and talk with a partner about the important characters in the story you read. Tell your partner which character is important and how you know that.

## Extend the Lesson (Optional)

After assessing children's understanding, you might decide to extend the learning.

▶ Add to the minilesson chart as you read more stories. Be sure to have children explain how they know which are the main characters.

▶ Encourage children to use simple costumes and props to role-play an important character from a book they are reading.

▶ When children are writing stories, remind them to think about which character is the most important and how they can let their readers know that.

### Stories have important characters.

| This book ... | is mostly about ... |
|---|---|
| *When I Am Old with You* | Grandaddy Grandson |
| *Elizabeti's School* | Elizabeti |
| *Jamaica's Blue Marker* | Jamaica Russell |

**Reading Minilesson Principle**
# The characters' faces and bodies show how they feel.

## Understanding Characters and Their Feelings

### You Will Need

- three or four familiar books with main characters, such as the following:
  - *A Birthday Basket for Tia* by Pat Mora, from Text Set: Family
  - *A Fine, Fine School* by Sharon Creech, from Text Set: School
  - *Sheila Rae, the Brave*, from Text Set: Kevin Henkes
- chart paper and markers
- five sticky notes, each with a face that shows an expression: happy, sad, angry, brave, scared

### Academic Language / Important Vocabulary

- character
- feelings
- illustration

### Continuum Connection

- Infer characters' intentions, feelings, and motivations using text and pictures (p. 35)

## Goal

Infer characters' feelings using the illustrations.

## Rationale

As children begin to understand that picture book illustrations are fundamental in connecting with the text to communicate ideas, they begin to understand the story. When children can infer characters' emotions from the illustrations, it supports their development of empathy.

## Assess Learning

Observe children when they talk about stories they have read or heard. Notice if there is evidence of new learning based on the goal of this minilesson.

- ▶ Are children able to infer what the characters are feeling by looking at the illustrations?
- ▶ How do they talk about the characters' feelings?
- ▶ Do they use vocabulary such as *character*, *feelings*, and *illustration*?

# Minilesson

To help children think about the minilesson principle, engage them in a short discussion of how the illustrations show how the characters are feeling. Here is an example.

- ▶ Show the cover of *A Birthday Basket for Tia*.

  Do you remember the characters Cecilia and Tia in *A Birthday Basket for Tia*?

  Look closely at their faces on the cover. How do you think they are feeling?

- ▶ Have a child place the sticky note with the happy face on the chart paper.

  What do you notice in the illustration that shows you they feel happy?

  They look happy when they are smiling and hugging, don't they?

- ▶ Record responses on the chart. Then show page 16 of *A Fine, Fine School*.

  The children on this page have to go to school on weekends and all summer. Notice the illustration. How do you think the children feel about that?

- ▶ Have children place the sad and angry sticky notes on the chart.

  Let's look at the children's faces and bodies. What part of their faces and bodies shows you how they are feeling?

- ▶ Record responses on the chart.

## Have a Try

Invite the children to talk with a partner about the characters in *Sheila Rae, the Brave*.

▶ Show page 7 of *Sheila Rae, the Brave*.

What is happening in the story here? Think about how the important characters, Louise and Sheila Rae, are feeling. Turn and talk to a partner about how this illustration shows you how they are feeling.

▶ Record responses on the chart.

## Summarize and Apply

Summarize the learning and remind the children to think about how illustrations show how the characters are feeling.

How can you use illustrations to tell the characters' feelings? Look at the chart to help you remember.

▶ Write the principle at the top of the chart.

When you read today, look at the illustrations to find out how the characters feel. Bring your book when we come back together so you can share an illustration that shows how a character feels.

## Share

Following independent work time, gather children together in the meeting area in groups of three to talk about how illustrations show the characters' feelings.

Did you notice illustrations in your book that show the characters' feelings? Share your illustrations and talk about how they show the characters' feelings.

## Extend the Lesson (Optional)

After assessing children's understanding, you might decide to extend the learning.

▶ Have children study how illustrators draw faces and bodies to show the characters' feelings.

▶ Engage children in dramatic play using facial and body expressions to convey meaning while other children infer their feelings.

▶ Remind children to draw how their characters feel when they write and illustrate stories.

### The characters' faces and bodies show how they feel.

| Title | Character | How Character Feels | How You Know |
|---|---|---|---|
| *Cecilia* | Cecilia Tia | happy | Cecilia and Tia smile and hug. |
| *A FINE, FINE SCHOOL* | Tillie and the other children | sad | They have grumpy faces. |
| | | angry | They show their teeth and pull their hair. |
| *SHEILA RAE, THE BRAVE* | Sheila Rae Louise | brave | Sheila is smiles and holds her head high. |
| | | scared | Louise's eyes are covered. |

# RML3
## LA.U19.RML3

**Reading Minilesson Principle**
# What the characters say and do shows how they are feeling.

## Understanding Characters and Their Feelings

### You Will Need

- three or four familiar books with main characters whose feelings are easily identified, such as the following:
  - *A Birthday Basket for Tia* by Pat Mora, from Text Set: Family
  - *A Fine, Fine School* by Sharon Creech, from Text Set: School
  - *Julius, the Baby of the World,* from Text Set: Kevin Henkes
- chart paper and markers
- sticky notes

### Academic Language / Important Vocabulary

- character
- feelings

### Continuum Connection

- Infer character's intentions, feelings, and motivations using text and pictures (p. 35)

## Goal

Infer characters' feelings as revealed through their dialogue and behavior.

## Rationale

When children evaluate a character's words (dialogue) and actions (behavior) to infer feelings, they deepen their understanding of the text as well as expand their empathy skills.

## Assess Learning

Observe children when they talk about characters in stories they have read or heard. Notice if there is evidence of new learning based on the goal of this minilesson.

- ◗ Are children able to infer characters' feelings from the dialogue and behavior?
- ◗ Can they identify words and illustrations that show characters' feelings?
- ◗ Do they use vocabulary such as *character* and *feelings*?

# Minilesson

To help children think about the minilesson principle, engage them in a short discussion of how they know the characters' feelings from what they say and do in a story. Here is an example.

- ◗ Show the cover of *A Birthday Basket for Tia.*

    Think about Cecilia. How does she feel about Tia? How do you know?

- ◗ Record responses on the chart paper.

    Where in the book can you look to find out how Cecilia feels about Tia?

- ◗ Revisit a few sections of the story with children, as needed, to prompt the conversation.

- ◗ Record responses on the chart paper.

    Now think about another story you know.

- ◗ Show the cover and then read the last page of *A Fine, Fine School.*

    How are the children feeling on the last page of the story?

- ◗ Record responses on the chart.

    What tells or shows you how they feel?

- ◗ If necessary, guide children to conclude that they can find out how characters feel by noticing what the characters say and do.

## Have a Try

Invite the children to act out Lilly's feelings in *Julius, Baby of the World* with a partner.

▶ Reread pages 6–7 of *Julius, the Baby of the World*.

How does Lilly feel about her baby brother in this part of the story? With a partner, take turns pretending to be Lilly and do and say things to show how Lilly is feeling.

▶ After the role-play, invite a few pairs to share the words and actions they used. Record responses on the chart.

## Summarize and Apply

Summarize the learning and remind children to notice what the characters say and do as they read.

How can you tell how a character is feeling? Look at the chart to help you remember.

▶ Write the principle at the top of the chart.

When you read today, notice what a character says or does to know how that character is feeling. Use a sticky note to mark a few examples.

## Share

Following independent work time, gather children in groups of three to talk about characters' feelings.

Tell how the character in your book was feeling. Tell the words or show the pictures that help you know how the character was feeling.

## Extend the Lesson (Optional)

After assessing children's understanding, you might decide to extend the learning.

▶ Continue to add to the chart as you read stories with characters that show how they feel in their words and actions.

▶ Have children act out scenes from books and encourage them to focus on how the characters are feeling in their words and behavior.

▶ Remind children to write about and draw how their characters feel when they write and illustrate stories.

### What the characters say and do shows how they are feeling.

| Title | Character | How Character Feels | How You Know |
|---|---|---|---|
| | Cecilia | She loves Tia. | She collects special gifts for her. |
| A FINE, FINE SCHOOL | Tillie Children | They feel happy. | They carried the principal around and smiled. |
| JULIUS THE BABY OF THE WORLD | Lilly | She is angry. | Lilly says, "And I hate Julius." |

# RML 4
## LA.U19.RML4

**Reading Minilesson Principle**
# What the characters say and do shows how they feel about other characters.

## Understanding Characters and Their Feelings

### You Will Need

- three or four familiar books with main characters, such as the following:
  - *A Birthday Basket for Tia* by Pat Mora and *When I Am Old with You* by Angela Johnson, from Text Set: Family
  - *Julius, the Baby of the World*, from Text Set: Kevin Henkes
- chart paper and markers
- sticky notes

### Academic Language / Important Vocabulary

- character
- feel
- illustration

### Continuum Connection

- Infer characters' intentions, feelings, and motivations using text and pictures (p. 35)

### Goal

Infer how characters feel about other characters as revealed through their dialogue and behavior.

### Rationale

When children notice the words and behavior of characters, they can begin to infer how the characters feel about each other. This allows the children to deepen their understanding of the characters and the story, as well as develop empathy.

### Assess Learning

Observe children when they talk about characters in stories they have read or heard. Notice if there is evidence of new learning based on the goal of this minilesson.

- Are children able to infer how characters feel about other characters from what they say and do?
- Can they identify the words and illustrations that tell how a character feels about another character?
- Do they use vocabulary such as *character*, *feeling*, and *illustration*?

## Minilesson

To help children think about the minilesson principle, engage them in a short discussion of how they know how characters feel about other characters from what they say and do. Here is an example.

- Show and read the section on the page that shows the mixing bowl.

    How can you tell how Tia feels about Cecilia?

- Record responses on the chart paper, guiding children to notice what Tia says and does.
- Show and read the last page of *When I Am Old with You*.

    How does this page let you know how the boy feels about his grandaddy?

- Record responses on the chart.
- Lead children to infer that what characters say and do lets you know how they feel about other characters in the story.

## Have a Try

Invite the children to talk with a partner about *Julius, the Baby of the World*.

▶ Show *Julius, the Baby of the World*.

How does Lilly feel about her brother? What is she doing and saying?

▶ Read the back cover.

Turn and talk with a partner about what Lilly is doing and how the words show her feelings.

▶ After discussion, ask a few volunteers to share. Record responses on the chart.

## Summarize and Apply

Summarize the learning and remind children to think about how characters feel about other characters as they read.

How does the author let you know how one character feels about another character? Look at the chart to help you answer.

▶ Write the principle at the top of the chart

When you read today, notice what characters say and do. Think how that shows their feelings about each other. Use a sticky note to mark examples.

## Share

Following independent work time, gather children together in groups of three to talk about how characters in the story felt about the other characters.

Tell how the characters in your book feel about each other. Tell the words or show the picture that lets you know.

## Extend the Lesson (Optional)

After assessing children's understanding, you might decide to extend the learning.

▶ During interactive read-aloud and shared reading, talk about what characters say and do in stories to show their feelings about each other.

▶ Have children act out scenes from books with a focus on words and body language to show the characters' feelings about each other.

▶ **Drawing/Writing About Reading** Have children draw characters from stories in a reader's notebook. Encourage them to tell and show what the characters say and do to show their feelings about other characters.

**What the characters say and do shows how they feel about other characters.**

| Title | How Character Feels About Others | How You Know |
|---|---|---|
| | Tia cares about Cecilia. | Says: "Cecilia, you are a very good cook." Does: Tia puts her arm around Cecilia. |
| | The boy loves his grandaddy. | Says: "Grandaddy, I will sit in a big rocking chair beside you." Does: The grandson and grandaddy hug and smile. |
| | Lilly doesn't like her baby brother yet. | Says: Lilly says, "And, I hate Julius." Does: She makes a mean, scary face. |

Section 2: Literary Analysis

**Reading Minilesson Principle**
# Sometimes you feel the same way as a character in a story.

## Understanding Characters and Their Feelings

### You Will Need

▸ three or four familiar books with main characters, such as the following:

- *Jamaica's Blue Marker* by Juanita Havill and *Elizabeti's School* by Stephanie Stuve-Bodeen, from Text Set: School

- *When I Am Old with You* by Angela Johnson, from Text Set: Family

▸ chart paper and markers

▸ sticky notes

### Academic Language / Important Vocabulary

▸ character

▸ feel

### Continuum Connection

▸ Learn from vicarious experiences with characters in stories (p. 35)

## Goal

Relate characters' feelings to their lives.

## Rationale

As children begin to explore the intentions, feelings, and motivations of characters, they will begin to make connections to their own lives. When children relate their experiences to those of characters in stories, they develop a deeper understanding of the characters' feelings and motivations, which supports comprehension and strengthens personal connections to the characters. They begin to learn that reading fiction can give you insights into yourself.

## Assess Learning

Observe children when they talk about characters in stories they have read or heard. Notice if there is evidence of new learning based on the goal of this minilesson.

▸ Are children able to infer what the characters are feeling?

▸ Can they relate texts to their lives by connecting to a time when they felt similarly as one of the characters?

▸ Do they use vocabulary such as *character* and *feel*?

## Minilesson

To help children think about the minilesson principle, engage them in a short discussion of how they have felt like a character feels. Here is an example.

▸ Show and reread page 10 of *Jamaica's Blue Marker* that begins with "When she looked at the ugly blue squiggles."

How does Jamaica feel?

▸ Record responses on the chart paper.

Put your thumb up if you have ever felt like Jamaica does here. That means you understand how Jamaica feels.

▸ On sticky notes, write the names of a few of the children who raised their thumb. Place on the chart. Then show and reread pages 1–2 of *Elizabeti's School*.

How does Elizabeti feel about going to her new school?

▸ Record responses on the chart.

Have you ever felt like Elizabeti feels here?

▸ Add sticky notes with the names of a few children who have felt the same way as Elizabeti.

## Have a Try

Invite the children to talk with a partner about the boy in *When I Am Old with You*.

▶ Show the cover of *When I Am Old with You*.

Remember how this boy thinks about doing special things with his grandaddy? Turn and talk with a partner about how the boy feels. Talk about a time when you felt like the boy, enjoying time with a family member or a special friend.

▶ After discussion, ask a few volunteers to share. Record responses on the chart.

## Summarize and Apply

Summarize the learning and remind children to think about whether they have felt like a character is feeling as they read.

Look at the chart to remember how you can really understand the characters in a story.

▶ Write the principle at the top of the chart.

When you read today, notice how a character is feeling. Think about if you have ever felt like that before. Bring the book when we come back together so you can share.

## Share

Following independent work time, gather children together in the meeting area to talk about when they have felt like a character felt in a story.

How does a character feel in the story you read? Was there a time when you felt the same?

## Extend the Lesson (Optional)

After assessing children's understanding, you might decide to extend the learning.

▶ Continue to have children think about times they felt the same as characters in books.

▶ Choose different characters from books and have children think of a time when they felt the same way as the character. Role-play the time.

▶ Drawing/Writing About Reading Encourage children to write and draw in a reader's notebook about a time they felt like a character in a story they have read or listened to.

Sometimes you feel the same way as a character in a story.

| | | | |
|---|---|---|---|
| *Jamaica's Blue Marker* | Jamaica | angry | Kiara, Jack |
| *Elizabeti's School* | Elizabeti | nervous | Abdul, Emma |
| *When I Am Old with You* | Grandson Grandaddy | happy | Ben, Carlos, Olivia |

## Assessment

After you have taught the minilessons in this umbrella, observe children as they talk and write about characters and their feelings while reading across instructional contexts: interactive read-aloud, independent reading and literacy work, guided reading, shared reading, and book club. Use *The Literacy Continuum* (Fountas and Pinnell 2017) to observe children's reading and writing behaviors across instructional contexts.

▶ What evidence do you have of new understandings related to characters?

- Can children identify the most important character(s) in a story?
- Are children using the illustrations to understand how a character feels?
- Can they infer characters' feelings through words and actions?
- Are they able to infer how characters feel about other characters based on text and illustrations?
- In what ways do children relate characters' feelings to their own lives?
- Do they use the terms *character, feel, feelings,* and *illustrations* when talking about characters?

▶ In what other ways, beyond the scope of this umbrella, are the children talking about characters?

- Do children identify with characters' feelings and problems?
- Do children notice that sometimes a character changes at the end of a story?
- Do they make predictions about what a character will do next?

Use your observations to determine the next umbrella you will teach. You may also consult Minilessons Across the Year (p. 51) for guidance.

## Link to Writing

After teaching the minilessons in this umbrella, help children link the new learning to their writing or drawing about reading:

▶ Encourage children to use feeling words, dialogue, and detailed facial illustrations to convey emotions in their writing or drawing.

## Minilessons in This Umbrella

**RML1**    The words and pictures show what a character looks like on the outside.

**RML2**    The words and pictures show what a character is like on the inside.

**RML3**    Think about why a character says or does something.

**RML4**    Use what you know about a character to predict what the character will do next.

**RML5**    Think about whether you would like to be friends with a character.

## Before Teaching Umbrella 20 Minilessons

Before teaching these minilessons, make sure that children are reading fiction books for independent reading (or have fiction books in their book bags or boxes). Together, read and discuss a variety of high-quality fiction picture books that have characters with traits that are observable through words, illustrations, and story events. Use the following texts from the *Fountas & Pinnell Classroom™ Interactive Read-Aloud Collection* or choose books from your library that include characters with observable traits.

**Mo Willems: Having Fun with Humor**

*Elephants Cannot Dance!*
   by Mo Willems

*Don't Let the Pigeon Drive the Bus!*
   by Mo Willems

**Kevin Henkes: Exploring Characters**

*Chrysanthemum* by Kevin Henkes

*Julius, the Baby of the World*
   by Kevin Henkes

*Sheila Rae, the Brave*
   by Kevin Henkes

**The Importance of Friendship**

*Wallace's Lists* by Barbara Bottner
   and Gerald Kruglik

**Learning and Playing Together: School**

*David's Drawings*
   by Cathryn Falwell

**Bob Graham: Exploring Everyday Life**

*"Let's Get a Pup!" Said Kate*
   by Bob Graham

**Standing Up for Yourself**

*Amazing Grace* by Mary Hoffman

As you read aloud and enjoy these texts together, help children

- notice what a character is like on the outside based on the words and the illustrations,

- notice what a character is like on the inside based on the words and the illustrations,

- think about why characters behave the way they do,

- use what they know about the character to predict what the character might do next, and

- consider if they would want to be friends with a character.

**Mo Willems**

**Kevin Henkes**

**Friendship**

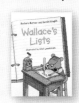

**School**

**Bob Graham**

**Standing Up**

Section 2: Literary Analysis

# RML1
### LA.U20.RML1

**Reading Minilesson Principle**
## The words and pictures show what a character looks like on the outside.

## Knowing Characters Inside and Out

### You Will Need

- three or four familiar fiction books with clearly identified character traits, such as the following:
  - *Elephants Cannot Dance!* by Mo Willems, from Text Set: Mo Willems
  - *Chrysanthemum* and *Julius, the Baby of the World* by Kevin Henkes, from Text Set: Kevin Henkes
- chart paper and markers

### Academic Language / Important Vocabulary

- character
- author
- illustrator

### Continuum Connection

- Use evidence from the text to support statements about the text (p. 34)
- Recall important details about characters after a story is read (p. 35)

## Goal

Notice the physical characteristics of characters from the pictures and words in a story.

## Rationale

When children think about physical character traits, they begin to think about the way the author and illustrator portray characters and how this influences the reader's understanding of the character.

## Assess Learning

Observe children when they talk about the physical characteristics of characters in books they have read or heard. Notice if there is evidence of new learning based on the goal of this minilesson.

- ▶ Are children able to describe what a character looks like (is like on the outside)?
- ▶ Can children explain how they know what a character is like on the outside from both the words and the pictures?
- ▶ Do they use academic language such as *character*, *author*, and *illustrator*?

## Minilesson

To help children think about the minilesson principle, engage them in a short discussion of characters' physical characteristics. Here is an example.

- ▶ Show the cover of *Elephants Cannot Dance!*

  Here is Piggie on the cover.

- ▶ On the chart paper, sketch Piggie.

  What does Piggie look like on the outside?

- ▶ Record responses on the chart.

- ▶ Show the cover of *Chrysanthemum*.

  Now think about what the author tells you about what Chrysanthemum looks like on the outside as I read from this page.

- ▶ Read the part of page 6 that describes what Chrysanthemum wears.

  How does the author describe Chrysanthemum?

- ▶ Record responses on the chart.

- ▶ Show the illustration.

  What do you notice about how the illustrator draws Chrysanthemum?

  How do you think the illustrator knew what to draw?

- ▶ Record responses and add a sketch of Chrysanthemum.

## Have a Try

Invite the children to talk about how Julius is described in *Julius, the Baby of the World* with a partner.

▶ Read the description of Julius on page 4 from *Julius, the Baby of the World* and show the illustration.

Turn and talk about how the author and illustrator describe Julius. With your partner, pretend you are Julius' parents and you are holding Julius.

▶ Ask a few volunteers to share about Julius and record responses on the chart.

## Summarize and Apply

Summarize the learning and remind children to think about what characters are like on the outside.

How can you tell what characters are like on the outside? Look at the chart to help you remember.

▶ Write the principle at the top of the chart.

When you read today, think about what a character looks like on the outside. Notice both the words and the pictures.

## Share

Following independent work time, gather children in the meeting area to talk about what a character is like on the outside.

Turn and talk about what you noticed about the outside of a character from the story you read. Show the pages with the pictures and words about the character.

## Extend the Lesson (Optional)

After assessing children's understanding, you might decide to extend the learning.

▶ Have children create characters from favorite books using construction paper and craft supplies. When finished, have them glue the characters to the chart, and read the story to the class. Ask children to suggest words and pictures from the story showing what the characters are like on the outside.

▶ **Drawing/Writing About Reading** After independent reading, have children write in a reader's notebook what a character is like on the outside. Remind them to use the author's words and the illustrator's pictures.

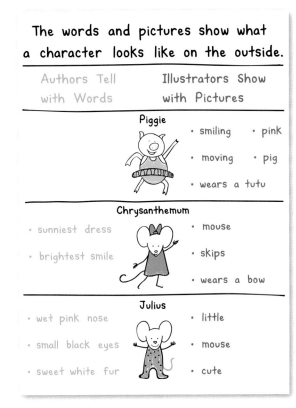

The words and pictures show what a character looks like on the outside.

| Authors Tell with Words | Illustrators Show with Pictures |
|---|---|
| **Piggie** | |
| | • smiling  • pink |
| | • moving  • pig |
| | • wears a tutu |
| **Chrysanthemum** | |
| • sunniest dress | • mouse |
| • brightest smile | • skips |
| | • wears a bow |
| **Julius** | |
| • wet pink nose | • little |
| • small black eyes | • mouse |
| • sweet white fur | • cute |

## RML 2
**LA.U20.RML2**

# The words and pictures show what a character is like on the inside.

## Knowing Characters Inside and Out

### You Will Need

- three or four familiar fiction books with clearly identified character traits, such as the following:
  - *Chrysanthemum* and *Sheila Rae, the Brave* by Kevin Henkes, from Text Set: Kevin Henkes
  - *David's Drawings* by Cathryn Falwell, from Text Set: School
- chart paper and markers
- sticky notes

### Academic Language / Important Vocabulary

- character
- author
- illustrator

### Continuum Connection

- Infer a character's traits from story events (p. 35)
- Infer characters' intentions, feelings, and motivations using text (p. 35)

## Goal

Notice character traits from the author's words and illustrator's pictures.

## Rationale

When children think about character traits, they think about the way the author and illustrator portray characters. This helps the children make a personal connection with the characters, providing a deeper understanding of a character's feelings and motivations.

## Assess Learning

Observe children when they talk about a character's feelings and motivations in books they have read or heard. Notice if there is evidence of new learning.

- Are children able to describe what a character feels or thinks (is like on the inside)?
- Can children explain how they know what a character is like on the inside from the words and the pictures?
- Do they use academic language such as *character*, *author*, and *illustrator*?

## Minilesson

To help children think about the minilesson principle, engage them in a short discussion of characters' feelings and motivations. Here is an example.

- Show the cover of *Chrysanthemum*. Read the first sentence on page 8.

  What does Victoria say? What kind of person would talk that way?

  The author shows what Victoria is like by what she says. You can't see inside Victoria to know what she is like, so the author tells you what she says and does. That's how you learn what Victoria is like on the inside.

- Record responses on the chart paper. Show the illustration of Victoria.

  How does the illustrator show you what Victoria is like on the inside?

  How do you think the illustrator knew what to draw?

- Record responses on the chart. Show the cover of *Sheila Rae, the Brave*.

  What does the author tell you about Sheila Rae in the title?

- Record responses on the chart.

  Listen as I read and think about what the author tells you about what Sheila Rae is like on the inside.

- Read the first page. Discuss with children how the author tells what Sheila Rae is like on the inside. Record responses on the chart.

▸ Discuss how the illustrator shows what Sheila Rae is like on the inside. Record responses on the chart.

## Have a Try

Invite the children to talk with a partner about how they can tell what a character is like on the inside.

▸ Show the dedication page and then page 6 from *David's Drawings*.

> Turn and talk about what the illustrator shows you about David on the inside.

▸ After time for discussion, ask children to share ideas and record responses on the chart.

## Summarize and Apply

Summarize the learning and remind children to think about what characters are like on the inside as they read.

> How can you tell what characters are like on the inside? Look at the chart.

▸ Write the principle at the top of the chart.

> When you read today, notice what a character is like on the inside by paying attention to the author's words and the illustrator's pictures. Write the character's name on a sticky note and draw a picture of the character. Bring the book and sticky note when we come back together after independent work time so you can share.

## Share

Following independent work time, gather children in the meeting area to share.

▸ Prepare a blank chart, modeled after the chart you made during the minilesson. Invite a few children to add their sticky notes to the chart and describe how they knew what the character was like on the inside. Help them write a few words about the character.

## Extend the Lesson (Optional)

After assessing children's understanding, you might decide to extend the learning.

▸ Have children dress up as favorite characters and act out the characters' inside traits.

▸ **Drawing/Writing About Reading** Have children draw and write about what a character from a book they are reading independently is like on the inside.

---

### The words and pictures show what a character is like on the inside.

| Authors Tell with Words | Illustrators Show with Pictures |
|---|---|
| Mean <br> • says mean things | Victoria  <br> • angry eyes <br> • covering mouth |
| Brave <br> • wasn't afraid of anything | Sheila Rae  <br> • kisses spiders |
| Shy | David  <br> Creative <br> • draws lots of pictures <br> Happy on his own <br> • walks alone <br> • sits alone |

# RML3
## LA.U20.RML3

**Reading Minilesson Principle**
# Think about why a character says or does something.

## Knowing Characters Inside and Out

### You Will Need

- three or four familiar fiction books with clearly identified character traits, such as the following:
  - *Don't Let the Pigeon Drive the Bus!* by Mo Willems, from Text Set: Mo Willems
  - *Julius, the Baby of the World* and *Sheila Rae, the Brave* by Kevin Henkes, from Text Set: Kevin Henkes
- chart paper and markers

### Academic Language / Important Vocabulary

- character

### Continuum Connection

- Use evidence from the text to support statements about the text (p. 34)
- Infer characters' intentions, feelings, and motivations using text and pictures (p. 35)

### Goal

Infer a character's motivations and intentions using a story's words and pictures.

### Rationale

When children are encouraged to think about why a character says or does something, they begin to think about the motivations of the character. This helps them understand important concepts in the story and develop empathy for the characters.

### Assess Learning

Observe children when they talk about what a character says or does in a story they have read or heard. Notice if there is evidence of new learning based on the goal of this minilesson.

> ▶ Are children able to tell why characters do and say things in a story?
> ▶ Can children think and talk about characters' motivations, supporting their thinking with text evidence?
> ▶ Do they use the academic term *character*?

## Minilesson

To help children think about the minilesson principle, engage them in a short discussion of what characters say or do in stories. Here is an example.

> ▶ Show the cover of *Don't Let the Pigeon Drive the Bus!*
>> What does the pigeon keep doing throughout this story?
>> Why do you think he says and does all those things?
>
> ▶ Show the end pages and talk about why children think the pigeon keeps asking to drive.
>> What does that tell you about the pigeon? What is he thinking about and feeling?
>
> ▶ Record responses on the chart paper.
>> Think about Lilly in *Julius, the Baby of the World* as you listen to this page.
>
> ▶ Read the first two sentences from page 5.
>> Why do you think Lilly asks if she can talk like a normal person after Julius leaves?
>> Why do you think Lilly shouted when she asked that question?
>> How do you think Lilly was feeling? What does that tell you about her?
>
> ▶ Record responses on the chart.

## Have a Try

Invite the children to share their thoughts about Sheila Rae with a partner.

> Now think about Sheila Rae in *Sheila Rae, the Brave*. Remember when she was lost and very scared?

▶ Read and show page 17.

> Turn and talk with a partner about why you think Sheila tells herself that she is brave and fearless.

▶ After time for discussion, record responses on the chart.

## Summarize and Apply

Summarize the learning and remind children to think about why a character says or does something as they read.

> How can you learn more about what a character is like? Look at the chart to remember.

▶ Write the principle at the top of the chart.

> When you read today, think about a character in the book and why the character does or says something. Bring your book when we meet after independent work time.

## Share

Following independent work time, gather children in the meeting area in groups of three or four to talk about why the character says or does something in the book they read.

> Talk about the book you read today and why a character said or did something in the story. Show your classmates an illustration of the character doing or saying something.

## Extend the Lesson (Optional)

After assessing children's understanding, you might decide to extend the learning.

▶ During interactive read-aloud, occasionally pause to ask why a character does or says something. Make sure children are able to use evidence from the text to support their statement.

▶ **Drawing/Writing About Reading** Encourage children to draw and write in a reader's notebook about why a character does or says things in a story.

---

**Think about why a character says or does something.**

| What Character Does or Says | | Why |
|---|---|---|
| Begs, yells <br> • tricks and tantrums | Pigeon  | He dreams of driving the bus. |
| Asks if she can can be loud when Julius leaves <br> • shouts | Lilly  | She doesn't want to be quiet. <br> • jealous <br> • angry that she has to be quiet |
| Says she is brave and fearless | Sheila Rae  | She is scared and lost. |

**Reading Minilesson Principle**
## Use what you know about a character to predict what the character will do next.

### Knowing Characters Inside and Out

#### You Will Need

- several fiction books that lend themselves to making predictions about characters that children have not yet read or heard, such as the following:
  - *"Let's Get a Pup!" Said Kate* by Bob Graham, from Text Set: Bob Graham
  - *Amazing Grace* by Mary Hoffman, from Text Set: Standing Up
- chart paper and markers

#### Academic Language / Important Vocabulary

- character
- next

#### Continuum Connection

- Give reasons (either text-based or from personal experience) to support thinking (p. 34)
- Use evidence from the text to support predictions (I think ... because ...) (p. 34)

### Goal

Predict what the character will do next based on the character's motivations and traits.

### Rationale

When children predict what a character might do next, using evidence from the story, they begin to think critically about the text, which improves comprehension. Constantly making predictions will engage children with the story and will help them build a personal connection with the character.

### Assess Learning

Observe children when they predict what a character will do next. Notice if there is evidence of new learning based on the goal of this minilesson.

- Can children predict what a character might do next in a story?
- Do they support their predictions with evidence from the text and illustrations?

## Minilesson

To help children think about the minilesson principle, engage them in predicting what a character will do next. Here is an example.

- Show the cover of *"Let's Get a Pup!" Said Kate*.

  When you listen, think about what might happen next to Kate. Think about how the characters act and feel.

- Show and read the front end paper.

  Kate liked having Tiger sleep on her bed. She feels lonely now that Tiger is gone. Think about what Kate might do next. What would you do?

- Record responses on the chart paper. Ask for details to support their thinking. Show the copyright and title page.

  Let's see what happens next. Kate is really in a hurry to get to her parents' room. What might happen next?

- Record responses on the chart. Show and read pages 1–2.

  Notice Kate's body. How is she feeling?

  How does knowing how she feels help you think about what might happen next?

- Continue reading, pausing to talk about character details and asking for predictions. Add ideas to the chart. Read the back endpaper.

  Did one of the ideas you talked about happen to Kate? It's okay if you are not correct when you think about what could happen next. Sometimes the author surprises you.

## Have a Try

Invite the children to practice making a prediction with a partner.

▶ Show the cover of *Amazing Grace*. Read pages 1–2.

　Turn and talk about what Grace might do next and why you think that.

▶ Read through page 14.

　Grace has a problem. She wants to be Peter Pan, but the children are telling her she can't. Turn and talk about what might happen next. Tell what you know about Grace that makes you think that.

▶ Repeat with a few more pages if necessary.

## Summarize and Apply

Summarize the learning and remind children to always think about what a character might do next.

　Look at the chart. What did you learn today about what to think about when you read?

▶ Write the principle at the top of the chart.

　If you read a fiction book today, think about what might happen next to the character.

## Share

Following independent work time, gather children in the meeting area to talk about their prediction of what the character would do next.

　If you read a book for the first time today, talk about what you thought might happen next to the character. Why did you think that?

## Extend the Lesson (Optional)

After assessing children's understanding, you might decide to extend the learning.

▶ During interactive read-aloud, pause to ask what might happen next to a character. Encourage children to talk about what they know about the character to support their predictions.

Use what you know about a character to predict what the character will do next.

| What will the character do next? | What's the reason? |
|---|---|
| Kate might get a cat. | She likes a cat to sleep on her bed. |
| Kate might want a dog. | She is playing with a dog on the cover. |
| Kate might get a stuffed animal. | She feels lonely at night. |
| Kate might ask her parents for a new cat. | She is very excited about something. |
| Kate might want a dog. | It is summer, and she is lonely. |
| Kate might ask a friend to come over and play. | She has a lot of energy and bounces on the bed. |

# RML5
**LA.U20.RML5**

**Reading Minilesson Principle**
# Think about whether you would like to be friends with a character.

## Knowing Characters Inside and Out

### You Will Need

- three or four familiar fiction books with clearly identified character traits, such as the following:
  - *Wallace's Lists* by Barbara Bottner and Gerald Kruglik, from Text Set: Friendship
  - *Elephants Cannot Dance!* by Mo Willems, from Text Set: Mo Willems
  - *David's Drawings* by Cathryn Falwell, from Text Set: School
- chart paper and markers

### Academic Language / Important Vocabulary

- character
- opinion

### Continuum Connection

- Give reasons (either text-based or from personal experience) to support thinking (p. 34)
- Express opinions about characters and their behavior: e.g., funny, bad, silly, nice, friendly (p. 35)

## Goal

Express opinions about characters based on their traits and motivations using evidence from the text.

## Rationale

When you teach children to consider whether they could be friends with a character, you help them learn to express opinions about characters. This requires children to think carefully about how a character behaves, which deepens comprehension and their connections to the character.

## Assess Learning

Observe children when they talk about a character they could be friends with in a story they have read or heard. Notice if there is evidence of new learning based on the goal of this minilesson.

- Are children able to explain why they could be friends with a character and use text evidence to support their thinking?
- Do they use vocabulary such as *character* and *opinion*?

## Minilesson

To help children think about the minilesson principle, engage them in a short discussion of characters they would want as a friend, which is a way of helping children learn to express an opinion about a character. Here is an example.

- Show the cover of *Wallace's Lists*.

  What do you think about Wallace? Would you like to be friends with him?

  What things about Wallace would make him a good friend or not a good friend?

- Record responses on the chart paper.

  When you tell what you think about Wallace, you are telling your opinion.

- Revisit a few pages that show Piggie and Gerald dancing together in *Elephants Cannot Dance!*

  Who would like to be friends with Piggie?

  What is it about Piggie that makes her a good friend or not a good friend?

- Record responses on the chart.

## Have a Try

Invite the children to talk with a partner about whether they would be friends with David from *David's Drawings*.

▸ Show a few pages of David in *David's Drawings*.

> Think about David. What could I draw for him?

▸ Draw a quick sketch of David.

> Turn and talk about whether you would like to be friends with David and why you think that. If you would like to be friends with David, take a sticky note and put it under Yes. If not, put a sticky note under No.

▸ After discussion, ask children to share and explain their opinions.

## Summarize and Apply

Summarize the learning and remind children to think about whether they would like to be friends with a character.

> What's a way to think about what a character is like? Look at the chart to help you.

▸ Write the principle at the top of the chart.

> When you read today, think about whether you would or would not like to be friends with a character in the story and why. You will share your opinions when we meet after independent work time.

## Share

Following independent work time, gather children in the meeting area to talk about whether they would like to be friends with a character in their book.

> Turn and talk about the character from the book you read. Tell if you want to be friends with the character and why. Show the part of the story that made you decide if you want to be friends.

## Extend the Lesson (Optional)

After assessing children's understanding, you might decide to extend the learning.

▸ **Drawing/Writing About Reading** Have children write about characters they come across during independent reading and whether they would like to be friends with the character. Encourage them to give evidence from the story to support their opinions.

---

**Think about whether you would like to be friends with a character.**

| Yes | Wallace | No |
|---|---|---|
| Brave<br>Shares<br>Helps his friend | | Worries too much about his lids<br>Doesn't like adventures |
| Yes | Piggie | No |
| She is fun.<br>She is nice to Gerald when he is sad.<br>She wears fun clothes. | | |
| Yes | David | No |

## Assessment

After you have taught the minilessons in this umbrella, observe children as they talk and write about their reading across instructional contexts: interactive read-aloud, independent reading and literacy work, guided reading, shared reading, and book club. Use *The Literacy Continuum* (Fountas and Pinnell 2017) to observe children's reading and writing behaviors across instructional contexts.

▶ What evidence do you have of new understandings related to character traits?

- Do children notice how the author uses words and the illustrator uses pictures to show character traits?
- Can children determine what a character is like on the outside and the inside based on the words and pictures?
- Do children form opinions about characters?
- Can children talk about why characters behave the way they do?
- Can they predict what a character might do next based on text evidence?
- Can they support their statements with evidence from the text?
- Do children use academic language, such as *character, author, illustrator,* and *opinion,* when talking about characters?

▶ In what other ways, beyond the scope of this umbrella, are the children talking about characters?

- Do children notice that some characters change at the end of a story?
- Are they writing about characters in a reader's notebook?

Use your observations to determine the next umbrella you will teach. You may also consult Minilessons Across the Year (p. 51) for guidance.

## Link to Writing

After teaching the minilessons in this umbrella, help children link the new learning to their writing:

▶ Encourage children to include details in their stories (in both words and pictures) to show the reader more about what the characters are like.

## Minilessons in This Umbrella

**RML1**  Sometimes a character changes from the beginning to the end of a story.

**RML2**  Sometimes a character learns a lesson in a story.

**RML3**  Sometimes characters from different books learn the same lesson.

## Before Teaching Umbrella 21 Minilessons

Read and discuss a variety of high-quality fiction picture books with characters who change and learn lessons that are observable through words, illustrations, and story events. Use the following books from the *Fountas & Pinnell Classroom™ Interactive Read-Aloud Collection* text sets or choose books from your library that have characters who change from beginning to end.

### Standing Up for Yourself

*Stand Tall, Molly Lou Melon* by Patty Lovell

*Bootsie Barker Bites* by Barbara Bottner

*Amazing Grace* by Mary Hoffman

*King of the Playground* by Phyllis Reynolds Naylor

### Celebrating Diversity

*The Name Jar* by Yangsook Choi

*My Name Is Yoon* by Helen Recorvits

### Kevin Henkes: Exploring Characters

*Julius, the Baby of the World* by Kevin Henkes

As you read aloud and enjoy these texts together, help children

- notice when characters change,
- think about when a character learns a lesson and relate it to their lives, and
- notice that different books often teach the same lesson.

**Standing Up**

**Diversity**

**Kevin Henkes**

**Section 2: Literary Analysis**

**Reading Minilesson Principle**
## Sometimes a character changes from the beginning to the end of a story.

### Understanding That Characters Can Change

#### You Will Need

- three or four familiar fiction books with characters that change from the beginning to the end, such as the following:
  - *King of the Playground* by Phyllis Reynolds Naylor, from Text Set: Standing Up
  - *Julius, the Baby of the World* by Kevin Henkes, from Text Set: Kevin Henkes
- chart paper and markers

#### Academic Language / Important Vocabulary

- character
- change

#### Continuum Connection

- Notice when a character changes or learns a lesson (p. 34)

### Goal

Notice when a character changes from the beginning to the end of a story.

### Rationale

When children evaluate how and why a character changes from the beginning to the end of a story, they explore character development and make personal connections to the characters. This connection deepens their understanding of character's feelings and motivations.

### Assess Learning

Observe children when they talk about how characters change in stories. Notice if there is evidence of new learning based on the goal of this minilesson.

- ▶ Do children notice when a character changes from the beginning to the end of the story?
- ▶ Can children explain why a character changes?
- ▶ Do they use vocabulary such as *character* and *change*?

## Minilesson

To help children think about the minilesson principle, engage them in a short discussion of how characters can change from the beginning to the end of a story. Here is an example.

- ▶ Revisit page 3 of *King of the Playground*.

  **What do you remember about how Sammy treated Kevin?**

- ▶ Write the title and a sketch of Sammy, and columns for Beginning, Why, and End on the chart paper. Record responses on the chart paper.

- ▶ Revisit the last few pages.

  **How did Sammy act at the end?**

  **How did Sammy act at the end compared with how he acted at the beginning of the story?**

  **Why do you think Sammy changed the way he acted with Kevin?**

- ▶ Record responses on the chart.

## Have a Try

Invite the children to talk with a partner about how Lilly changes in *Julius, the Baby of the World*.

▶ Open *Julius, the Baby of the World* flat to show the front and back covers at the same time.

> The front cover shows how Lilly felt at the beginning of the story, and the back cover shows how she felt at the end. Turn and talk with a partner about how Lilly changed.

▶ After discussion, ask children to share ideas and record responses on the chart.

▶ Read the last five pages.

> Turn and talk with a partner about why Lilly changes.

▶ Ask volunteers to share and record responses.

## Summarize and Apply

Summarize the learning and remind children to think about how characters change.

> What did you learn today about characters? Look at the chart to help you.

▶ Write the principle at the top of the chart.

> There is usually a reason why the characters change. This is important to think about.

> When you read today, notice if a character changes from the beginning to the end of the story. Think about why the character changes. You will share later.

## Share

Following independent work time, gather children together in the meeting area to talk about a character that changed in the story they read.

> Turn and talk about the story you read and how a character changed from the beginning to the end. Be sure to talk about why the character changed.

## Extend the Lesson (Optional)

After assessing children's understanding, you might decide to extend the learning.

▶ Have children create two versions of a character and glue them back-to-back on a craft stick. On one side, have them draw the character at the beginning of the story and on the other side, the character at the end. In pairs, have them tell about the character using the craft stick to explain how and why the character changed.

**Sometimes a character changes from the beginning to the end of a story.**

| Beginning | Why | End |
|---|---|---|
| Sammy said he would do mean things to Kevin. | King of the playground Kevin stood up to Sammy. | Sammy played with Kevin. |
| Lilly is mean to Julius. | Julius, the Baby of the World Cousin Garland was mean to Julius. | Lilly loves Julius. |

**Section 2: Literary Analysis**

# RML 2

## LA.U21.RML2

**Reading Minilesson Principle**
## Sometimes a character learns a lesson in a story.

**Understanding That Characters Can Change**

## You Will Need

- three or four familiar fiction books with characters that learn a lesson, such as the following:
  - *The Name Jar* by Yangsook Choi, from Text Set: Diversity
  - *King of the Playground* by Phyllis Reynolds Naylor and *Amazing Grace* by Mary Hoffman, from Text Set: Standing Up
- chart paper and markers
- sticky notes

## Academic Language / Important Vocabulary

- character
- lesson

## Continuum Connection

- Notice when a fiction writer is "teaching a lesson" (p. 34)
- Notice when a character changes or learns a lesson (p. 35)
- Learn from vicarious experiences with characters in stories (p. 35)

## Goal

Notice when a character learns a lesson and relate the lesson to their lives.

## Rationale

When children connect the lessons learned by characters to their own lives, they begin to empathize with the characters. This empathy will contribute to stronger comprehension of the text and a better connection to the characters.

## Assess Learning

Observe children when they talk about lessons characters learn in stories they have read or heard. Notice if there is evidence of new learning based on the goal of this minilesson.

- Are children able to talk about the lesson a character learns?
- Can children apply a lesson from a story to their lives?
- Do they use vocabulary such as *character* and *lesson*?

# Minilesson

To help children think about the minilesson principle, engage the children in a short discussion of how to identify lessons characters learn. Here is an example.

> Sometimes the character in a story learns a lesson. Do you remember Unhei in *The Name Jar*? What lesson does Unhei learn about her name?

- On the chart paper, write the title, a sketch of Unhei, and the lesson she learns.

  > How does knowing about the lesson Unhei learns help you in your life?

- Write a few of children's ideas on sticky notes and add them to the chart.

  > Think about the lesson that Kevin learns in *King of the Playground*.

  > What lesson does Kevin learn about standing up to a bully?

- Record responses on the chart.

  > What can you learn from Kevin?

- Write a few of children's ideas on sticky notes and add to the chart.

## Have a Try

Invite the children to talk with a partner about the lesson Grace learns in *Amazing Grace*.

▶ Reread page 21–24 of *Amazing Grace*.

  What lesson does Grace learn?

▶ Record responses on the chart.

  Turn and talk with a partner about what you can learn from the lesson Grace learns. Write your idea on a sticky note and put it on the chart.

▶ Talk about the responses added to the chart.

## Summarize and Apply

Summarize the learning and remind children to think about the lesson a character learns as they read.

  What happens to a character, sometimes, at the end of a story? Look at the chart to help you remember.

▶ Write the principle at the top of the chart.

  When you read today, think about the lesson the character learns. Think about if you have ever learned a lesson like that or if the lesson will help you in your life. You will share that when we come together after independent work time.

## Share

Following independent work time, gather children together in the meeting area to talk about a character that learned a lesson in the story they read.

  Raise your hand if you read a book with a character that learned a lesson. Talk about the lesson.

▶ After a child shares, ask others to talk about if they have learned a similar lesson, or how the lesson will help them in their lives.

## Extend the Lesson (Optional)

After assessing children's understanding, you might decide to extend the learning.

▶ Encourage children to write about a time they learned a lesson like a character from a story. This can be a topic for independent writing.

▶ **Drawing/Writing About Reading** Have children write in a reader's notebook the lesson a character learns.

**Sometimes a character learns a lesson in a story.**

| | The character learns... | I can learn to... |
|---|---|---|
| Unhei in The Name Jar | To love her name | Love my name (Ava) / Be happy with myself (Jacob) |
| Kevin in King of the Playground | To stand up against bullies | Defend myself (Evan) / Say no to bullies (Hasan) |
| Grace in Amazing Grace | To believe in herself | Try things even if I look different (Nisha) / Believe in myself (Yasmine) |

Section 2: Literary Analysis

**Reading Minilesson Principle**
# Sometimes characters from different books learn the same lesson.

**Understanding That Characters Can Change**

## You Will Need

- a variety of familiar fiction books in which characters learn a lesson, such as the following:
  - *My Name Is Yoon* by Helen Recorvits, from Text Set: Diversity
  - *Bootsie Barker Bites* by Barbara Bottner, from Text Set: Standing Up
  - *Stand Tall, Molly Lou Melon* by Patty Lovell, from Text Set: Standing Up
- chart from RML2
- three prepared 4" x 6" sticky notes with the character name and book title
- sentence strip with the minilesson principle

## Academic Language / Important Vocabulary

- character
- lesson

### Continuum Connection

- Connect texts by obvious categories: e.g., author, character, topic, genre, illustrator (p. 34)
- Notice when a fiction writer is "teaching a lesson" (p. 34)

## Goal

Connect characters across texts and understand that, often, different books teach the same lesson.

## Rationale

When children notice a lesson learned across different texts, they begin to recognize common themes authors write about. This recognition allows children to predict what will happen next and gain insight into an author's craft.

## Assess Learning

Observe children when they talk about the same lesson characters learn in more than one story they have read or heard. Notice if there is evidence of new learning based on the goal of this minilesson.

- Are children able to talk about a common lesson learned in different texts?
- Do they use vocabulary such as *character* and *lesson*?

## Minilesson

To help children think about the minilesson principle, engage them in a short discussion of identifying lessons characters learn. Here is an example.

- Review the chart from RML2. Then show the cover of *My Name Is Yoon*.

  What lesson does Yoon learn?

  She learned to love her name. Do you remember another character that learned the same lesson?

- Have a child attach the note to where it belongs: in the first column on the chart, next to or below *Unhei*.

  Yoon learns a lesson like Unhei because they both learn to love their names.

- Show *Bootsie Barker Bites*.

  What lesson does the girl learn in *Bootsie Barker Bites*?

  Is that lesson like the lesson another character learns?

  The girl learns to stand up for herself, the way Kevin did in *King of the Playground*.

- Have a child attach the note to where it belongs on the chart: next to or below *Kevin*.

## Have a Try

Invite the children to identify the lesson that Molly Lou learns in *Stand Tall, Molly Lou Melon* and find a similar lesson on the chart.

▶ Read the last page of *Stand Tall, Molly Lou Melon*.

Turn and talk to a partner about what lesson Molly Lou learns and then look at the chart to see if another character learns the same lesson.

▶ After time for discussion, ask a child to place the sticky note on the chart.

## Summarize and Apply

Summarize the learning and remind children to think about the lesson a character learns as they read.

What did you notice today about the lessons that characters learn? Look at the chart to remember.

▶ Add the principle for this minilesson to the top of the chart.

When you read today, notice if a character learns a lesson. Then think about whether you know of another character that learns the same lesson. Bring the book when we meet after independent work time so you can share.

## Share

Following independent work time, gather children together in the meeting area in pairs or small groups to talk about characters that learned the same lesson.

Turn and talk about the lesson learned by the character you read about. Is that lesson the same as the lesson learned by other characters you know?

## Extend the Lesson (Optional)

After assessing children's understanding, you might decide to extend the learning.

▶ Add characters to the chart as the children find additional examples in books they listen to or read independently. Create new categories of lessons learned as children discover them.

▶ Have children organize book baskets by lessons learned. Add labels to the baskets.

### Sometimes characters from different books learn the same lesson.

| | The character learns... | I can learn to... |
|---|---|---|
| Unhei in The Name Jar / Yoon in My Name is Yoon | To love her name | Love my name (Ava) / Be happy with me (Jacob) |
| Kevin in King of the Playground / The little girl in Bootsie Barker Bites | To stand up against bullies | Defend myself (Evan) / Say no to bullies (Hasan) |
| Grace in Amazing Grace / Molly Lou in Stand Tall, Molly Lou Melon | To believe in herself | Try things even if I look different (Nisha) / Believe in myself (Yasmine) |

## Assessment

After you have taught the minilessons in this umbrella, observe children as they talk and write about their reading across instructional contexts: interactive read-aloud, independent reading and literacy work, guided reading, shared reading, and book club. Use *The Literacy Continuum* (Fountas and Pinnell 2017) to observe children's reading and writing behaviors across instructional contexts.

▶ What evidence do you have of new understandings related to character change?

- Can children talk about how and why characters change in a given story?

- Are they able to tell when a character learns a lesson?

- Can they talk about how characters from different texts sometimes learn similar lessons?

- Do children use vocabulary such as *character, change,* and *lesson* when talking about characters?

▶ In what other ways, beyond the scope of this umbrella, are the children talking about characters?

- Do children notice how the illustrations convey information about the characters?

Use your observations to determine the next umbrella you will teach. You may also consult Minilessons Across the Year (p. 51) for guidance.

## Link to Writing

After teaching the minilessons in this umbrella, help children link the new learning to their writing:

▶ Use interactive writing to help the children add to the class chart of the lessons learned by characters in different books.

## Minilessons in This Umbrella

**RML1**   Writers use rhyming words in their books.

**RML2**   Writers make rhythm with the way their words sound.

**RML3**   Writers use sound words to help you understand and enjoy the story.

**RML4**   Writers use made-up words or nonsense words to make a story funny or interesting.

**RML5**   Writers repeat a word or a few words to make stories funny or interesting.

**RML6**   Writers use words that all start with the same sound.

## Before Teaching Umbrella 22 Minilessons

Read and discuss books with words that have rhyme, repetition, and rhythm. Use the following books from the *Fountas & Pinnell Classroom™ Interactive Read-Aloud Collection* text sets or choose books from your library that have rhyme, repetition, and the other characteristics addressed in these minilessons.

**Having Fun with Language: Rhyming Texts**

*Mrs. McNosh Hangs Up Her Wash* by Sarah Weeks

*The Day the Goose Got Loose* by Reeve Lindbergh

*One of Each* by Mary Ann Hoberman

**Mo Willems: Having Fun with Humor**

*Elephants Cannot Dance!* by Mo Willems

**Humorous Stories**

*Dooby Dooby Moo* by Doreen Cronin

*That's Good! That's Bad!* by Margery Cuyler

**Nicola Davies: Exploring the Animal World**

*Just Ducks!* by Nicola Davies

As you read aloud and enjoy these texts together, help children

* notice when an author uses rhyming words or uses words to make a rhythm,
* think about how an author uses sound words in a story,
* think about how authors play with words to make a story interesting,
* notice when an author repeats words, and
* notice when an author uses alliteration in a story.

**Rhyming Texts**

**Mo Willems**

**Humorous Stories**

**Nicola Davies**

**Section 2: Literary Analysis**

# RML1

## LA.U22.RML1

**Reading Minilesson Principle**
## Writers use rhyming words in their books.

**Analyzing the Way Writers Play with Language**

### You Will Need

- two or three familiar texts with rhyming words, such as the following from Text Set: Rhyming Texts:
  - *Mrs. McNosh Hangs Up Her Wash* by Sarah Weeks
  - *The Day the Goose Got Loose* by Reeve Lindbergh
- chart paper and markers
- sticky notes
- basket of books with rhyming text

### Academic Language / Important Vocabulary

- rhyme
- author

### Continuum Connection

- Notice a writer's use of playful or poetic language and sound devices: e.g., nonsense words, rhythm, rhyme, repetition, refrain, onomatopoeia (p. 35)

### Goal

Notice how and when authors use rhyme.

### Rationale

Children enjoy the rhymes they hear in songs, poems, and stories. When children notice how and when authors use rhyme in stories, they will focus on both the meaning and rhyme to think about what word will come next in the story, as well as find increased enjoyment in language and books.

### Assess Learning

Observe children when they talk about rhyming words in books they have read or heard. Notice if there is evidence of new learning based on the goal of this minilesson.

- Are children able to identify rhyming words?
- Can they use vocabulary such as *rhyme* and *author*?

## Minilesson

To help children think about the minilesson principle, engage them in a short discussion of rhyming words in stories. Here is an example.

- Show *Mrs. McNosh Hangs Up Her Wash*. Read page 4, emphasizing the rhyming words.

  Which words rhyme?

- Record the rhyming words on the chart paper.

  Now listen to the next page. I am going to leave one word out. See if you can figure out what the word is by looking at the illustration and listening for the rhyme.

- Read page 5, stopping before the word *news*.

  What do you think the word might be that rhymes with *shoes*?

- Record the rhyming words on the chart.

  Why do you think an author, like Sarah Weeks, uses rhyming words in her book?

### Have a Try

Invite the children to talk about rhyming words with a partner.

- Show pages 3–4 from *The Day the Goose Got Loose*.

Think about how the author uses rhyme in this story. Turn and talk with a partner about the rhyming words. How do they make the story more fun to read?

▶ After time for discussion, invite children to share the rhymes as you record the responses.

## Summarize and Apply

Summarize the learning and remind children to notice rhyming words as they read.

What did you learn about the kinds of words authors sometimes use in their books?

▶ Write the principle at the top of the chart.

The books in this basket have rhyming words. Select a book from this basket to read today. Put a sticky note on a page that has rhyming words so that you can share when we meet after independent work time.

## Share

Following independent work time, gather children together in the meeting area to talk about rhyming words.

Give a thumbs-up if you found words that rhyme in your book.

▶ Invite children to share with the class. Add the rhyming words to the chart. Review the chart.

## Extend the Lesson (Optional)

After assessing children's understanding, you might decide to extend the learning.

▶ During shared reading, notice and use highlighter tape to mark words that rhyme. Point out that some have the same spelling at the end (e.g., *sad* and *mad*) and some are different (e.g., *shoes* and *news*).

▶ At an ABC center, invite children to sort rhyming words. Include some rhymes that are spelled differently at the end. Ask children to record words that rhyme in the same column.

▶ **Drawing/Writing About Reading** Encourage children to notice when authors use rhyme. They then can write and draw pictures of the rhyming words in a reader's notebook.

### Writers use rhyming words in their books.

| Book with Rhyming Words | Rhymes |
|---|---|
| *Mrs. McNosh Hangs Up Her Wash* | shirts skirts shoes news |
| *the day the goose got loose* — REEVE LINDBERGH STEVEN KELLOGG | goose loose mad had sad |

**Analyzing the Way Writers Play with Language**

## You Will Need

- three or four familiar texts with rhythmic language, such as the following:
  - *The Day the Goose Got Loose* by Reeve Lindbergh, from Text Set: Rhyming Texts
  - *Just Ducks!* by Nicola Davies, from Text Set: Nicola Davies
  - *Elephants Cannot Dance!* by Mo Willems, from Text Set: Mo Willems
- chart paper and markers
- basket of books using rhythm

## Academic Language / Important Vocabulary

- author
- rhythm

## Continuum Connection

- Notice a writer's use of playful or poetic language and sound devices: e.g., nonsense words, rhythm, rhyme, repetition, refrain, onomatopoeia (p. 35)

## Goal

Notice how authors create rhythm with their words.

## Rationale

Children enjoy the rhythms they hear in music, nature, and language. They often invent rhythms while humming and tapping. When children notice how authors use rhythm in stories, they will be inspired to find enjoyment in language and books, and begin to experiment with rhythm in their writing.

## Assess Learning

Observe children when they talk about rhythm in the books they have read or heard. Notice if there is evidence of new learning based on the goal of this minilesson.

- ▶ Are children able to identify when and how the author creates rhythm with words?
- ▶ Do they use vocabulary such as *author* and *rhythm*?

## Minilesson

To help children think about the minilesson principle, engage them in a short discussion and demonstration of rhythm in stories. Here is an example.

- ▶ Show the cover of *The Day the Goose Got Loose*. Read pages 17–18 with rhythm, clapping to the beat.

  What do you notice about how these words sound?

  You can tap along to these words, can't you? These words have a rhythm. What does the rhythm make you think of in this story?

- ▶ Record responses on the chart paper.
- ▶ Reread the text, inviting children to join in on the clapping.
- ▶ Show page 7 of *Just Ducks!*

  Listen as I read this page of *Just Ducks!* and think about how the words sound.

- ▶ Read the page with rhythm, moving your hand in a wave motion as you say "flows through the town."

  What does the rhythm of these words make you think about?

- ▶ Record responses on the chart. Read this page several more times, having children join in on the words and hand motion.

## Have a Try

Invite the children to listen for the rhythm in *Elephants Cannot Dance!*

▸ Show and read pages 34–37 from *Elephants Cannot Dance!*, adding rhythm to your voice.

> Turn and talk to a partner about what you noticed about the rhythm and what these words made you feel like doing.

▸ Invite a few pairs to share their noticings and add the responses to the chart.

## Summarize and Apply

Summarize the learning and remind children to notice when there is rhythm in the book they read.

> What did you learn today about how writers can make words sound?

▸ Write the principle at the top of the chart.

> When you read today, notice if the author creates a rhythm with the words. Select a book from this basket to read today. Bring the book when we come back after independent work time so you can share any rhythms that you find.

## Share

Following independent work time, gather children together in the meeting area to talk about their reading.

> Give a thumbs-up if you found rhythm in your book.

▸ Invite children to share examples and add these to the chart. Review the chart.

## Extend the Lesson (Optional)

After assessing children's understanding, you might decide to extend the learning.

▸ Encourage children to notice different rhythms in books and poems you read. Continue to add to the chart.

▸ Gather jump ropes and go to the gym or playground to explore the rhythm of jump rope chants in books. After reciting and jumping, stop to reflect on the rhythms children notice in the chants.

▸ Invite children to tap out rhythms to lines of books or favorite poems. Children can use their hands, feet, or simple instruments to make different beats to accompany a text.

| Writers make rhythm with the way their words sound. ||
| Book | Feeling |
| --- | --- |
| | The words make us feel like a goose hopping around a farmyard. |
| | The words make us feel like a duck might feel floating down the river. |
| | The words make us feel like trying to dance like Elephant. |

# RML3

**LA.U22.RML3**

### Reading Minilesson Principle
# Writers use sound words to help you understand and enjoy the story.

## Analyzing the Way Writers Play with Language

### You Will Need

- three or four familiar texts with onomatopoetic words, such as the following:
  - *Just Ducks!* by Nicola Davies, from Text Set: Nicola Davies
  - *One of Each* by Mary Ann Hoberman, from Text Set: Rhyming Texts
  - *That's Good! That's Bad!* by Margery Cuyler, from Text Set: Humorous Stories
- chart paper and markers
- basket of books with onomatopoeia
- sticky notes

### Academic Language / Important Vocabulary

- author
- sound words

### Continuum Connection

- Notice a writer's use of playful or poetic language and sound devices: e.g., nonsense words, rhythm, rhyme, repetition, refrain, onomatopoeia (p. 35)

## Goal

Notice how authors use onomatopoetic words.

## Rationale

Children recognize sound words at a very young age, noticing and imitating sounds they hear both in nature and in urban environments. When children read and discuss books in which authors use sound words, they will begin to recognize how sounds can be written in stories to make readers "hear" what is happening. They also will begin to incorporate sound words into their writing.

## Assess Learning

Observe children when they talk about sound words in books they have read or heard. Notice if there is evidence of new learning based on the goal of this minilesson.

- Can children identify sound words in stories?
- Are they able to talk about what the sound word represents?
- Do they use vocabulary such as *author* and *sound words*?

## Minilesson

To help children think about the minilesson principle, engage them in a demonstration and a short discussion of sound words in stories. Here is an example.

- Read page 6 of *Just Ducks!*

  How does the author let you know how the duck sounds?

- Record responses on the chart paper.

  The word *quack* sounds like the way ducks actually talk, doesn't it?

- Show the cover of *One of Each*.

  The author of *One of Each*, Mary Ann Hoberman, also uses sound words in this story. Listen for the sound words as I read part of the story.

- Read the first line on page 6.

  What sound words do you notice? What do they make you "hear"?

- Record responses on the chart.

  Why do you think an author might choose to use sound words in a book?

## Have a Try

Invite the children to work with a partner to identify sound words in *That's Good! That's Bad!*

▶ Show and read page 4 from *That's Good! That's Bad!*

Turn and talk to a partner about the sound words that the author, Margery Cuyler, uses on this page and what the words sound like.

▶ Record their noticings on the chart.

## Summarize and Apply

Summarize the learning and remind children to notice how authors use sound words when they read.

What kind of words do authors use to make you "hear" a story so that you can understand and enjoy it? Look at the chart to help you remember.

▶ Write the principle at the top of the chart.

If you read a book from this basket today, put a sticky note on a page that has sound words. Bring the book when we come back together after independent work time so you can share those sound words.

## Share

Following independent work time, gather children together in the meeting area to talk about sound words in the books they read.

Give a thumbs-up if you found a sound word in the book you read.

▶ Invite children to share examples and add them to the chart. Read the sound words together.

## Extend the Lesson (Optional)

After assessing children's understanding, you might decide to extend the learning.

▶ When reading other books, invite children to notice if they recognize a sound word, and talk about how it adds to the story. If there are no sound words, invite children to think of some that would be appropriate for the story.

▶ Make a sound word mural by creating a scene of a farm, city, or another environment you are studying, and invite children to make animals or objects with construction paper. Then, add sound words in speech bubbles to the mural.

Writers use sound words to help you understand and enjoy the story.

| Book | Sound Word | What the Sound Word Means |
|---|---|---|
| Just Ducks! | quack-quack | This word sounds like ducks talking. |
| One of Each | tick-tock | This word sounds like a clock. |
| That's Good! That's Bad! | pop! glug! glug! | These words sound like a giraffe drinking water. |

**Section 2: Literary Analysis**

# RML4
## LA.U22.RML4

### Reading Minilesson Principle
## Writers use made-up words or nonsense words to make a story funny or interesting.

## Analyzing the Way Writers Play with Language

### You Will Need

- two or three familiar texts with playful language, such as the following:
  - *Dooby Dooby Moo* by Doreen Cronin, from Text Set: Humorous Stories
  - *That's Good! That's Bad!* by Margery Cuyler, from Text Set: Humorous Stories
- chart paper and markers
- sticky notes
- basket of books with playful language

### Academic Language / Important Vocabulary

- author
- nonsense

### Continuum Connection

- Notice a writer's use of playful or poetic language and sound devices: e.g., nonsense words, rhythm, rhyme, repetition, refrain, onomatopoeia (p. 35)

### Goal

Notice how authors play with made-up or nonsense words to make a text interesting or funny.

### Rationale

When children begin to recognize how authors play with words in their stories, they become more comfortable with language and learn to use words more flexibly. Because children naturally enjoy playing with sounds and words, they will enjoy a story with made-up or nonsense words and become more engaged. They then will begin to play with words in their stories.

### Assess Learning

Observe children when they talk about made-up words or nonsense words in books they have read or heard. Notice if there is evidence of new learning based on the goal of this minilesson.

- Are children able to identify when an author makes up words or uses nonsense language?
- Can they describe how playful language makes a story funny or interesting?
- Do they understand the word *nonsense*?

## Minilesson

To help children think about the minilesson principle, engage them in a short discussion of how authors use made-up words or nonsense words in stories. Here is an example.

- Show page 9 from *Dooby Dooby Moo*. Read the page, singing the animal words to the tune of "Twinkle, Twinkle, Little Star."

  What do you notice about the words I read to you?

  How do the words make the book more fun to read?

- Record responses on the chart paper. Read page 12 as if a duck is snoring.

  Why are these words fun to read?

- Record responses on the chart.

- Continue reading more pages from the book if children need further examples.

## Have a Try

Invite the children to talk with a partner about the language in *That's Good! That's Bad!*

> Margery Cuyler likes to play with words. Listen as I read this page and think about why the words are funny or interesting.

❱ Read page 18, emphasizing *up, up, up* and *WHOOSH!*

> Turn and talk to a partner about what the language the author uses does to the story.

❱ Record responses on the chart.

## Summarize and Apply

Summarize the learning and remind children to notice made-up or nonsense words when they read.

> What did you learn today about how authors can make a story funny or interesting to read? You noticed that when an author makes up words or uses them in silly ways, you enjoy reading the story.

❱ Write the principle at the top of the chart.

> If you read a book from this basket, put a sticky note on a page where the author uses playful language, like made-up words or nonsense words. Bring your book when we meet after independent work time.

## Share

Following independent work time, gather children together and have them talk about made-up or nonsense words they found in their reading.

> Give a thumbs-up if you found some made-up or nonsense words in your book.

❱ Invite children to share examples and add these to the chart. If you have taught the previous minilessons in this umbrella, ask children to also note examples of rhyming words, rhythm, or sound words.

## Extend the Lesson (Optional)

After assessing children's understanding, you might decide to extend the learning.

❱ Invite children to use a video recorder to record reading a page or two of text with playful language. Encourage them to have a conversation about how the author uses playful language to make the story more interesting or fun to read.

---

**Writers use made-up words or nonsense words to make a story funny or interesting.**

| Book | Playful Language | Why the Words Are Fun |
|------|------------------|------------------------|
| *Dooby Dooby Moo* | Dooby Dooby Dooby Moo | It is fun to hear the animals sing a song we know. |
| | Whacka, whacka quaaaack | A snoring duck is funny. |
| *That's Good! That's Bad!* | . . . up, up, up onto its shoulders, WHOOSH! | The words show the elephant lifting the boy very high and very fast. |

# RML5
## LA.U22.RML5

**Reading Minilesson Principle**
# Writers repeat a word or a few words to make stories funny or interesting.

## You Will Need

- two or three familiar texts with repeating phrases or words, such as the following:
  - *Mrs. McNosh Hangs Up Her Wash* by Sarah Weeks, from Text Set: Rhyming Texts
  - *Elephants Cannot Dance!* by Mo Willems, from Text Set: Mo Willems
  - *One of Each* by Mary Ann Hoberman, from Text Set: Rhyming Texts
- chart paper and markers
- sticky notes
- basket of books with repetition

## Academic Language / Important Vocabulary

- author
- repeat

## Continuum Connection

- Notice a writer's use of playful or poetic language and sound devices: e.g., nonsense words, rhythm, rhyme, repetition, refrain, onomatopoeia (p. 35)

## Goal

Notice how authors repeat words or phrases to make a text interesting or funny.

## Rationale

Children have heard many songs, poems, and stories in which a word or phrase repeats. While providing interest and pattern to a story, these repeating words and phrases also act as invitations for children to join in on the reading, increasing oral fluency. Noticing and discussing when and why authors do this will add to their enjoyment and appreciation of stories. It may inspire young writers to use repetition in their stories.

## Assess Learning

Observe children when they talk about repeating words or phrases in books they have read or heard. Notice if there is evidence of new learning based on the goal of this minilesson.

- Are children able to identify words and phrases that repeat in books?
- How do they show understanding of the reasons why authors choose to repeat words?
- Do they understand the words *author* and *repeat*?

## Minilesson

To help children think about the minilesson principle, engage them in a demonstration and short discussion of how authors use repeating words in phrases. Here is an example.

- Show page 4 of *Mrs. McNosh Hangs Up Her Wash*. Teach the children the words and have them join in with you to recite the rhyme.

   What do you notice about the words?

   What words does Sarah Weeks use more than once, or repeat? Why do you think she repeats the words *she hangs up*?

- Record responses on the chart paper.

- Show pages 44–45 of *Elephants Cannot Dance!* Have children join in as you read Elephant's words when he repeats *tried*.

   What word does Mo Willems have Elephant say over and over?

   Why do you think he does that?

- Record responses on the chart.

   Mo Willems wants you to know how Elephant is feeling, so he repeats the word *tried*, doesn't he?

## Have a Try

Invite the children to talk with a partner about an author's use of repetition.

▶ Show and read pages 2–3 of *One of Each*.

Turn and talk about the words Mary Ann Hoberman repeats and why you think she does that.

▶ Record responses on the chart.

## Summarize and Apply

Summarize the learning and remind children to look for repeated words when they read.

What did you learn today about how writers make their books fun and interesting to read? Look at the chart to help you remember.

▶ Write the principle at the top of the chart.

If you read a book from this basket today, put a sticky on a page where the author repeated some words. Think about why the author chose to do that so you can share with us after independent work time.

| Writers repeat a word or a few words to make stories funny or interesting. | | |
|---|---|---|
| Book | Repeating Language | Message |
| *Mrs. McNosh Hangs Up Her Wash* | She hangs up | Mrs. McNosh has a lot of laundry. |
| *Elephants Cannot Dance!* | I have tried! And tried! And tried! | Elephant is trying hard to dance like Piggie, but it is too hard for him. |
| *That's Good! That's Bad!* | One little | Oliver's house is little, and he has only one of each small thing. |

## Share

Following independent work time, gather children together in the meeting area to talk about repeating words they found in their reading.

Give a thumbs-up if you found repeated words in your book.

▶ Invite children to share the pages they marked. Also invite them to share other ways that they have learned authors use playful language to make their books fun and interesting to read.

## Extend the Lesson (Optional)

After assessing children's understanding, you might decide to extend the learning.

▶ While reading big books and poems, notice repeated words and phrases. Mark the repetitions with highlighter tape and invite children to join in.

▶ **Drawing/Writing About Reading** Encourage children to notice when authors use repetition in the books they are reading. They then can write the repeating word or phrase and draw pictures of the scene in a reader's notebook.

**Reading Minilesson Principle**
## Writers use words that all start with the same sound.

### Analyzing the Way Writers Play with Language

#### You Will Need

- three or four familiar texts with alliteration, such as the following:
  - *Just Ducks!* by Nicola Davies, from Text Set: Nicola Davies
  - *One of Each* by Mary Ann Hoberman, from Text Set: Rhyming Texts
  - *That's Good! That's Bad!* by Margery Cuyler, from Text Set: Humorous Stories
- chart paper and markers
- basket of books with alliteration

#### Academic Language / Important Vocabulary

- author
- repeats
- sound

#### Continuum Connection

- Notice a writer's use of playful or poetic language and sound devices: e.g., nonsense words, rhythm, rhyme, repetition, refrain, onomatopoeia (p. 35)

### Goal

Notice how authors use alliteration in a text.

### Rationale

At this age, children are beginning to recognize the sounds at the beginning of words. When children notice alliteration, they will understand and appreciate the sounds of language and may begin to experiment with using alliteration in stories they write independently.

### Assess Learning

Observe children when they talk about alliteration in books they have read or heard. Notice if there is evidence of new learning based on the goal of this minilesson.

- ▶ Are children able to identify an author's use of alliteration?
- ▶ Are they able to explain the effect of alliteration?
- ▶ Can they explain why an author might choose to include alliteration?
- ▶ Are children using language such as *author, repeats,* and *sound*?

## Minilesson

To help children think about the minilesson principle, engage them in a short discussion of identifying alliteration. Here is an example.

- ▶ Show page 21 of *Just Ducks!* Read the page, and then have the children join in with you as you read it again.

  What do you notice about some of the words?

  In the first line on this page, Nicola Davies starts some words with the same sound. She repeats the same first sound for two of the words. Why do you think she decided to use the words *roost in the reeds* instead of *sleep in the grass* to talk about what the ducks are doing?

- ▶ Record responses on the chart paper.
- ▶ Show the last pages of *One of Each*. Read the last two lines, and then invite the children to join in as you read together.

  Which words start with the same sound?

- ▶ Record responses on the chart.

  Why do you think Mary Ann Hoberman decided to use words that all start with the letter *p*?

- ▶ Record responses on the chart.

## Have a Try

Invite the children to work with a partner to notice alliteration in *That's Good! That's Bad!*

▶ Show page 12 of *That's Good! That's Bad!* Read the page several times, pointing to the words, and providing an opportunity for all children to learn and say the words.

▶ Turn and talk about the words that start with the same sound. Why do you think the author decided to use these words?

## Summarize and Apply

Summarize the learning and remind children to notice examples of alliteration when they read.

> What did you learn today about how authors can make their books fun and interesting to read? Use the chart to help you remember.

▶ Write the principle at the top of the chart.

> If you read a book from this basket today, put a sticky note on a page where there are several words that begin with the same sound. Bring the book when we meet after independent work time.

## Share

Following independent work time, gather children together in the meeting area in a circle to talk about examples of alliteration they found in their reading.

> Give a thumbs-up if you found an example of words together that begin with the same sound.

▶ Invite children to share examples and add these to the chart. Also invite them to share examples of other ways authors use playful language to make their books fun and interesting to read.

## Extend the Lesson (Optional)

After assessing children's understanding, you might decide to extend the learning.

▶ Make a class ABC alliteration book. For each page, invite children to suggest words that begin with the same letter (e.g., *a busy bee on a ball*). These can be silly and playful, and children can add illustrations to match the words.

---

**Writers use words that all start with the same sound.**

| Book | Words that Start the Same | Thoughts |
|------|---------------------------|----------|
| *Just Ducks!* | roost in the reeds | It's an interesting way to say ducks are sleeping in the grass. The words begin with the letter r. |
| *One of Each* | pieces of plum, peach, and pear | This is fun to say. The fruits all start with the letter p. |
| *That's Good! That's Bad!* | scary snake | The beginning sound sounds like a snake. They both begin with the letter s. |

## Assessment

After you have taught the minilessons in this umbrella, observe children talking and writing about their reading across instructional contexts: interactive read-aloud, independent reading and literacy work, guided reading, shared reading, and book club. Use *The Literacy Continuum* (Fountas and Pinnell 2017) to observe children's reading and writing behaviors across instructional contexts.

▶ What evidence do you have of new understandings related to language play?

- Can children recognize rhymes in stories?
- Are they able to identify when and how an author uses rhythm?
- Do they notice and identify sound words in books?
- Can they express ways in which authors play with words to make a story more fun or interesting to read?
- Do they notice when an author uses repetition?
- Are they able to recognize when an author uses alliteration?
- Do children use vocabulary such as *rhyme, rhythm, nonsense, repeat,* and *sound* to talk about the way writers play with language?

▶ In what other ways, beyond the scope of this umbrella, are the children talking about how authors play with language?

- Do children comment on author's craft (e.g., interesting word choice, descriptive language, comparisons)?
- Are they noticing other places, besides fiction books, in which authors play with language (e.g., folktales, poetry)?

Use your observations to determine the next umbrella you will teach. You may also consult Minilessons Across the Year (p. 51) for guidance.

## Link to Writing

After teaching the minilessons in this umbrella, help children link the new learning to their writing or drawing about reading:

▶ Encourage children to incorporate a variety of playful language in their writing, using the books they have studied as examples.

## Minilessons in This Umbrella

**RML1**  Illustrations show important information about the story.

**RML2**  Illustrators show movement and sound in the pictures to help you understand the story.

**RML3**  Illustrators choose colors to create a feeling.

**RML4**  Illustrators change the colors to change the feeling.

**RML5**  Illustrators show time passing in the pictures to help you understand the story.

## Before Teaching Umbrella 23 Minilessons

Read and discuss fiction picture books with strong illustrative support. Choose books with topics and ideas that are familiar and engaging to children, and closely mirror children's experiences. Use the following books from the *Fountas & Pinnell Classroom™ Interactive Read-Aloud Collection* text sets or choose fiction books with strong illustrative support from your classroom library.

**Bob Graham: Exploring Everyday Life**

*The Silver Button*

*April and Esme: Tooth Fairies*

*"Let's Get a Pup!" Said Kate*

*How to Heal a Broken Wing*

**Journeys Near and Far**

*Isla* by Arthur Dorros

*Dear Juno* by Soyung Pak

**Understanding the Natural World: Planting and Growing**

*The Dandelion Seed* by Joseph Anthony

As you read aloud and enjoy these texts together, help children

- notice how the illustrations support an understanding of the story,

- notice the details illustrators put into the illustrations,

- notice how illustrators use color to show feelings, and

- discuss the passage of time in books and how illustrators show it.

**Bob Graham**

**Journeys**

**Planting and Growing**

**Section 2: Literary Analysis**

# RML1
### LA.U23.RML1

**Reading Minilesson Principle**
## Illustrations show important information about the story.

**Looking Closely at Illustrations**

### You Will Need

- three or four books with illustrations with a lot of story detail, such as the following from Text Set: Bob Graham:
  - *"Let's Get a Pup!" Said Kate*
  - *April and Esme: Tooth Fairies*
  - *How to Heal a Broken Wing*
- chart paper and markers

### Academic Language / Important Vocabulary

- illustrator
- illustrations
- characters

### Continuum Connection

- Understand that an illustrator created the pictures in the book (p. 36)
- Gain new information from both pictures and print (p. 34)

### Goal

Gain new information from the illustrations in fiction texts.

### Rationale

When you encourage children to notice details in illustrations, they can develop a deeper understanding of the story and the illustrator's craft. The words and pictures in fiction books together communicate meaning.

### Assess Learning

Observe children when they talk about illustrations in books they have read or heard. Notice if there is evidence of new learning based on the goal of this minilesson.

- ▶ Are children able to identify an illustration that provides important details about the story?
- ▶ Are children able to describe how the illustration helped them to understand details in the story?
- ▶ Do they use vocabulary such as *illustrator*, *illustrations*, and *characters*?

## Minilesson

To help children think about the minilesson principle, engage them in a short discussion of how illustrations support the story. Here is an example.

- ▶ Show the cover of *"Let's Get a Pup!" Said Kate*. Turn to the page that begins, "At home, Dave was everything."

    As I read, pay careful attention to the illustrations.

- ▶ Read the page aloud and show the illustration.

    Talk about what Bob Graham did with the illustrations to help you understand more about Dave, the pup.

- ▶ Guide children to understand that the illustrations show what the character did, the character's actions. Write this on the chart paper. If necessary, include a sketch of Dave to support children.

    Now let's take a look at *April and Esme: Tooth Fairies*.

- ▶ Display the page that begins, "Yes!"

    April and Esme are about to leave for their first tooth collection. How does the illustration help you understand how the mom and dad feel?

- ▶ Guide children to understand that this time the illustration shows characters' feelings. Record this on the chart. If necessary, include a sketch of a family.

    Why do you think the illustrator drew the illustration this way?

## Have a Try

Invite the children to talk with a partner about the kind of information shown in an illustration from *How to Heal a Broken Wing*.

▶ Show the page in *How to Heal a Broken Wing* that reads, "But a broken wing can sometimes heal."

> Turn and talk with your partner about how the illustrations help you know what Will and his family do to help the bird.

▶ Invite a few children to share. Record responses on the chart. If necessary, include a sketch of a boy thinking to support children.

## Summarize and Apply

Summarize the learning and remind children to look at the illustrations as they read.

> How do the illustrations help you understand a story? Look at the chart to help you remember.

▶ Write the principle at the top of the chart.

> If you are reading a story with illustrations, notice the important details they show. Be ready to share an example when we meet after independent work time.

**Illustrations show important information about the story.**

| Title | Illustration Shows |
|---|---|
| Let's Get a Pup! BOB GRAHAM | Characters' actions |
| April and Esme Tooth Fairy Bob Graham | Characters' feelings through actions |
| How to Heal a Broken Wing BOB GRAHAM | How to do something / Characters' thoughts |

## Share

Following independent work time, gather children together in the meeting area to talk about the illustrations in the book they read.

> Who would like to share an illustration from your book and tell some important details that it shows?

## Extend the Lesson (Optional)

After assessing children's understanding, you might decide to extend the learning.

▶ Encourage children to continue to look for examples of illustrations that give important details about the story. Add these to the chart.

▶ Encourage children to think about how their illustrations can add details to the stories they write.

▶ **Drawing/Writing About Reading** Remind children to think about the details they will put in the illustrations they draw to accompany stories they write.

### Reading Minilesson Principle
## Illustrators show movement and sound in the pictures to help you understand the story.

## Looking Closely at Illustrations

### You Will Need

- three or four books whose illustrations show sound, such as the following:
  - *"Let's Get a Pup!" Said Kate* and *The Silver Button* by Bob Graham, from Text Set: Bob Graham
  - *Isla* by Arthur Dorros, from Text Set: Journeys
- chart paper and markers

### Academic Language / Important Vocabulary

- illustrations
- illustrator

### Continuum Connection

- Understand that an illustrator created the pictures in the book (p. 36)
- Notice how an illustrator shows the illusion of sound and motion in pictures (p. 36)

## Goal

Notice how an illustrator creates the illusion of sound and motion in illustrations.

## Rationale

When you teach children to notice the ways illustrators create the illusion of motion and sound in a story through illustrations, they will get more enjoyment out of the story and can think more deeply about the story and the illustrator's craft.

## Assess Learning

Observe children when they talk about the illustrations in the books they have read or heard. Notice if there is evidence of new learning based on the goal of this minilesson.

- ▶ Are children able to identify illustrations that show movement and sound?
- ▶ Can they describe the movement or sound the illustration suggests?
- ▶ Are children able to connect how the illustrations helped them to understand more about the story?
- ▶ Do they use the academic terms *illustrations* and *illustrator* correctly?

## Minilesson

To help children think about the minilesson principle, engage them in a short discussion of a story's illustrations. Here is an example.

- ▶ Show the front cover and then page 4 of *"Let's Get a Pup!" Said Kate.*

  Take a look at this page. How does the illustrator show the car is moving?

- ▶ Record responses on the chart paper.

  Illustrators also try to show sound.

- ▶ Show page 12 of *Isla.*

  There is so much happening on Abuela's and the girl's adventure! What kind of sound might Elisa Kleven, the illustrator, want you to imagine when looking at this page?

  You can almost hear the water spraying from the fountain.

## Have a Try

Invite the children to talk with a partner about the sounds indicated by the author of *The Silver Button*.

▶ Show the page of *The Silver Button* where the baby is born.

Turn and talk about the sounds you imagine on this page.

▶ Invite a few children to share. Record responses on the chart.

## Summarize and Apply

Summarize the learning and remind children to think about the illustrations as they read.

What did you learn today about what illustrators can show in their illustrations? Look at the chart to help you remember.

▶ Write the principle at the top of the chart.

If you are reading a book with illustrations, notice if the illustrator shows movement or sound.

Illustrators show movement and sound in the pictures to help you understand the story.

## Share

Following independent work time, gather children together in the meeting area to talk about the illustrations in the book they read.

Who would like to share an illustration that shows movement or sound?

What other details do you notice in the illustrations in your book?

## Extend the Lesson (Optional)

After assessing children's understanding, you might decide to extend the learning.

▶ Encourage children to continue to look for examples of movement and sound in illustrations. Add these to the chart.

▶ Provide opportunities for children to write about a personal experience. They can add illustrations that show movement or sound.

▶ **Drawing/Writing About Reading** When children draw a picture in a reader's notebook about a book they have read, encourage them to show movement or sound.

Section 2: Literary Analysis

**Reading Minilesson Principle**
## Illustrators choose colors to create a feeling.

### Looking Closely at Illustrations

#### You Will Need

- two or three books that use color to show mood, such as the following from Text Set: Bob Graham:
  - *"Let's Get a Pup!" Said Kate*
  - *How to Heal a Broken Wing*
- chart paper and markers
- sticky notes

#### Academic Language / Important Vocabulary

- characters
- illustrator
- feelings

#### Continuum Connection

- Understand that an illustrator created the pictures in the book (p. 36)
- Notice how the tone of a book is created by the illustrator's choice of colors (p. 36)

### Goal

Notice how the tone of a book is created by the illustrator's choice of colors.

### Rationale

Understanding the tone (how the writer feels about the story) or mood (the atmosphere or how the story makes the reader feel) of specific parts of the story is important in comprehending the deeper meaning of the story. Supporting children in noticing an illustrator's use of color allows them to understand the underlying feeling of a part of or the whole story.

### Assess Learning

Observe children when they talk about illustrations in the books they have read or heard. Notice if there is evidence of new learning based on the goal of this minilesson.

- Are children able to identify an illustration that used a color or several colors to create a feeling?
- Are children able to describe the feeling the color creates?
- Do they use vocabulary such as *characters*, *illustrator*, and *feelings*?

## Minilesson

To help children think about the minilesson principle, engage them in a short discussion of a story's illustrations. Here is an example.

- Read the page in *"Let's Get a Pup!" Said Kate* where the family walks away from Rosy.

  What do you notice about the color that Bob Graham used behind Rosy and the family?

- Record responses on the chart paper.

  How do you think the family feels here?

- Record responses on the chart.

  Now let's take a look at *How to Heal a Broken Wing*.

- Show the page that begins, "Will opened his hands."

  What do you notice about the colors Bob Graham used here? What kind of feelings do those colors show?

- Record responses on the chart.

## Have a Try

Invite the children to talk with a partner about the colors in *How to Heal a Broken Wing*.

▸ Show the two-page spread of *How to Heal a Broken Wing* with Will in the center of the page in yellow.

Turn and talk to a partner about what you notice about the colors Bob Graham chose to use on these pages. What feelings does he show with these colors?

▸ Invite a few children to share. Record responses on the chart. Review the chart.

## Summarize and Apply

Summarize the learning and remind children to think about the illustrations as they read.

What kinds of feelings can illustrators create using color?

▸ Write the principle at the top of the chart.

If you are reading a story with illustrations, notice how the colors show feelings or make you feel a certain way. If you find an example, mark the page with a sticky note and bring the book to share in group meeting.

## Share

Following independent work time, gather children together in the meeting area to talk about the illustrations in the book they read.

Today you learned that the illustrator sometimes uses color to show feelings in a story. Who would like to share an illustration from your book and tell how the illustration made you feel?

## Extend the Lesson (Optional)

After assessing children's understanding, you might decide to extend the learning.

▸ Encourage children to continue to look for examples of colors in illustrations that show feelings or tone. Add to the chart.

▸ **Drawing/Writing About Reading** Invite children to think about the colors they use in the illustrations that accompany their writing.

Illustrators choose colors to create a feeling.

| Title | Color | Feeling |
|-------|-------|---------|
| Let's Get a PUP! BOB GRAHAM | | sadness |
| How to Heal a Broken Wing BOB GRAHAM | | hope, joy, kindness |

# RML 4
## LA.U23.RML4

**Reading Minilesson Principle**
# Illustrators change the colors to change the feeling.

**Looking Closely at Illustrations**

## You Will Need

- two or three books that use colors to show the feelings of a story, such as the following:
  - *How to Heal a Broken Wing* by Bob Graham, from Text Set: Bob Graham
  - *The Dandelion Seed* by Joseph Anthony, from Text Set: Planting and Growing
- chart paper and markers
- sticky notes

## Academic Language / Important Vocabulary

- characters
- illustrator
- feelings

## Continuum Connection

- Understand that an illustrator created the pictures in the book (p. 36)
- Notice how the tone of a book changes when the illustrator shifts the color (p. 36)

## Goal

Notice how the feelings in a book change when the illustrator shifts the colors.

## Rationale

When the children notice how colors shift in illustrations, it helps them understand how the feelings in a story also change. Supporting children to notice color changes helps them to gain an awareness of the different feelings in a story. They will also learn to attend to the illustrator's craft in communicating the meaning of a story.

## Assess Learning

Observe children when they discuss illustrations in the books they have read or heard. Notice if there is evidence of new learning based on the goal of this minilesson.

- ▶ Are children able to identify illustrations that show a change in color, representing a change in the feeling (mood or tone) of the story?
- ▶ Are they able to describe the feelings the color change creates?
- ▶ Do children use vocabulary such as *characters, illustrator,* and *feelings* to talk about the use of color in books?

## Minilesson

To help children think about the minilesson principle, engage them in a short discussion of the illustrations in a story. Here is an example.

- ▶ Begin reading the page in *How to Heal a Broken Wing* that begins "No one looked down" and end on the two-page spread of Will picking up the bird.

  How does Bob Graham change the color in the illustrations? How does the feeling of the story change?

- ▶ Record responses on the chart paper.

  Now let's take a look at *The Dandelion Seed*.

- ▶ Show and read the page that says "Then the seed left the garden."

  Look carefully at the colors the illustrator used. Think about how the illustrator changed the feeling of the story with the colors.

- ▶ Show just the illustrations from "Then the seed left" to "more lonely."

  What do you notice here about how the illustrator changed the colors to change the feeling of the story?

## Have a Try

Invite the children to think about the colors in *How to Heal a Broken Wing*.

▶ Show the page in *How to Heal a Broken Wing* where Will first comes out of the subway and then the page near the end where Will comes out of the subway again.

> Turn and talk about what you notice about the change in color between these two illustrations.

▶ Invite a few children to share. Record responses on the chart.

## Summarize and Apply

Summarize the learning and remind children to think about the illustrations as they read.

> How can the illustrator show how the feeling in the story changes? Look at the chart to help you.

▶ Write the principle at the top of the chart.

> If you are reading a story with illustrations, notice if the illustrator changed the colors to change the feeling of the story. Think about how that helps you understand the feeling of the story is changing. If you find an example, mark the page with a sticky note and bring the book to share when we come together.

## Share

Following independent work time, gather children together in the meeting area to talk about the illustrations in the book they read.

> Who would like to share an example of an illustrator who changed color to show a different feeling in the story? What feelings do the colors show?

> What else did you notice about the illustrations in the book you read?

## Extend the Lesson (Optional)

After assessing children's understanding, you might decide to extend the learning.

▶ Encourage children to study the illustrations in the books they read and think about the decisions that the illustrator made when drawing the pictures.

▶ Provide opportunities for children to write about a personal experience. They can add illustrations utilizing color to demonstrate a change of feelings.

Illustrators change the colors to change the feeling.

**Section 2: Literary Analysis**

# RML5
## LA.U23.RML5

## Looking Closely at Illustrations

### You Will Need

- two or three books that show the passing of time, such as the following:
  - *How to Heal a Broken Wing* by Bob Graham, from Text Set: Bob Graham
  - *Dear Juno* by Soyung Pak, from Text Set: Journeys
- chart paper and markers
- sticky notes

### Academic Language / Important Vocabulary

- illustrations
- characters
- illustrator

### Continuum Connection

- Understand that an illustrator created the pictures in the book (p. 36)
- Notice how an illustrator shows the passage of time through illustrations (use of light, weather) (p. 36)

## Goal

Notice how an illustrator shows the passage of time through illustrations.

## Rationale

An illustrator often uses illustrations to show the passage of time to help the reader understand the story happens over a certain time period. The illustrations support a better understanding of the story.

## Assess Learning

Observe children when they discuss illustrations in the books they have read or heard. Notice if there is evidence of new learning based on the goal of this minilesson.

- Are children able to identify illustrations that demonstrate the passage of time in a story?
- Are children able to articulate how the illustration indicates the passage of time?
- Do they use vocabulary such as *illustrator*, *characters*, and *illustrations*?

## Minilesson

To help children think about the minilesson principle, engage them in a short discussion of the illustrations in a story. Here is an example.

- Show several pages of *How to Heal a Broken Wing*.

  How does Bob Graham show that time is passing? Talk about some details.

  Why does Bob Graham show in the pictures that time is passing?

- Record responses on the chart paper. Include a sketch of the moon and a calendar.

### Have a Try

Invite the children to talk with a partner about how the illustrator shows time passing in *Dear Juno*.

- Show the page in *Dear Juno* where Juno is sitting on the front porch with his letter. Then, turn to the page where Juno is climbing a tree to pull off a leaf. Finally, turn to the page where Juno is wearing a hat, scarf, and mittens.

  Turn and talk with your partner about how the illustrator shows that time passed as Juno wrote and received letters.

- After they turn and talk, invite a few children to share. Record responses on the chart. Review the chart.

## Summarize and Apply

Summarize the learning and remind children to think about the illustrations as they read.

> How can an illustrator show time passing in an illustration? Look at the chart to help you remember.

▶ Write the principle at the top of the chart.

> If you read a book with illustrations, notice how the illustrator shows time passing in the pictures. If you find an example, mark the page with a sticky note and bring the book to share when we come together.

## Share

Following independent work time, gather children together in the meeting area to talk about the illustrations in the book they read.

> Who would you like to like to share illustrations that show time passing?

## Extend the Lesson (Optional)

After assessing children's understanding, you might decide to extend the learning.

▶ Create a basket of interactive read-aloud texts that demonstrate the minilesson principle.

▶ Have children look for examples of time passage in illustrations as they read books independently, during interactive read-aloud, and shared reading. Add examples to the chart.

▶ **Drawing/Writing About Reading** Invite children to draw and write in a reader's notebook about a book they read and how the illustrations show the passage of time.

Illustrators show time passing in the pictures to help you understand the story.

| Title | Time |
| --- | --- |
| How to Heal a Broken Wing — BOB GRAHAM | April<br>S M T W T F S<br>　　　　　1　2<br>3　4　5　6　7　8　9<br>10 11 12 13 14 15 16<br>17 18 19 20 21 23 23<br>24 25 26 28 29 29 30 |
| dear juno — by Soyung Pak, illustrated by Susan Kathleen Hartung | |

Section 2: Literary Analysis

## Assessment

After you have taught the minilessons in this umbrella, observe children as they talk and write about their reading across instructional contexts: interactive read-aloud, independent reading and literacy work, guided reading, shared reading, and book club. Use *The Literacy Continuum* (Fountas and Pinnell 2017) to observe children's reading and writing behaviors across instructional contexts.

▶ What evidence do you have of new understandings related to how illustrations support the reader in understanding more about the story?

- Do children notice when the illustrator creates the illusion of sound or motion within the illustrations?

- Can children identify examples of how illustrators use colors to create or change a certain feeling in the book?

- Have they found examples of how an illustrator uses pictures to show the passage of time?

- Do they use vocabulary such as *illustrator, characters,* and *feelings* when talking about illustrations?

▶ In what other ways, beyond the scope of this umbrella, are children talking about illustrations?

- Do they notice when illustrators include multiple scenes on a page to show different actions?

- Can children identify examples of different ways illustrators utilize backgrounds to provide important information to the reader?

- Are children aware that authors and illustrators make decisions about the placement of words and illustrations on the page that impact meaning?

Use your observations to determine the next umbrella you will teach. You may also consult Minilessons Across the Year (p. 51) for guidance.

## Link to Writing

After teaching the minilessons in this umbrella, help children link the new learning to their writing:

▶ Help children use what they have learned about the details illustrators put into their illustrations when they illustrate their stories. Encourage children to think about their color choices as a way to impact the feeling within their stories. Support children in finding places in their stories where they can indicate sound or movement in the illustration.

# Section 3 | Strategies and Skills

The strategies and skills minilessons are designed to bring a few important strategic actions to temporary, conscious attention so that children can apply them in their independent reading. By the time children participate in these minilessons, they should have engaged these strategic actions successfully in shared or guided reading as they build in-the-head literacy processing systems. These lessons reinforce the effective reading behaviors.

# 3 Strategies and Skills

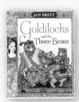

## Minilessons in This Umbrella

**RML1**   Look at the picture and think what would make sense.

**RML2**   Read the sentence again and get your mouth ready for the first sound.

**RML3**   Read the sentence again and think about what would make sense, sound right, and look right.

## Before Teaching Umbrella 1 Minilessons

Read and discuss shared reading texts that offer large print (big books), so the children understand the books and can participate in the reading. Use the selected texts from the *Fountas and Pinnell Classroom™ Shared Reading Collection* listed below, or choose big books from your library to support the concepts developed in this umbrella. Alternatively you could use a poem written in large print on chart paper for some of the lessons. If you have a document camera available you could use it to project a small book. Another helpful resource for supporting the teaching in these minilessons is *Fountas & Pinnell Prompting Guide, Part 1, for Oral Reading and Early Writing* (Fountas and Pinnell 2012).

### Shared Reading Collection

*Goldilocks and the Three Bears* by David Edwin

*In My Bag* by Amy Frank

*The Elephant* by Cordelia S. Finn

As you read aloud and enjoy these texts together, help children

- discuss what the book is about,

- notice details in the illustrations to support meaning,

- introduce language structures and support children in confirming what they read sounds right,

- demonstrate how to check if a word looks right, sounds right, and makes sense, and

- demonstrate how to reread and check if the word makes sense, sounds right, and looks right.

**Reading Minilesson Principle**
## Look at the picture and think what would make sense.

### Monitoring, Searching, and Self-Correcting

**You Will Need**

- an enlarged text, such as *In My Bag* by Amy Frank, from *Shared Reading Collection*
- sticky notes
- chart paper and markers

**Academic Language / Important Vocabulary**

- makes sense
- illustration

**Continuum Connection**

- With teacher support, use features of print with enlarged texts to search for and use visual information: e.g., letters, words, "first" and "last" word, period (p. 116)
- Make connections between the body of the text and the illustrations (p. 117)

### Goal

Use illustrations (meaning) to solve words while reading text.

### Rationale

When you teach children to search for and use information from the illustrations to help them read a word they don't know, they learn how to problem solve as they construct meaning from print. Eventually, they will integrate meaning, language, and print to achieve fluent reading.

### Assess Learning

Observe children as they use illustrations to gain meaning and notice if there is evidence of new learning based on the goal of this minilesson.

- Do children use illustrations to help them understand a word they do not know?
- Do they understand the terms *makes sense* and *illustration*?

## Minilesson

Provide an interactive lesson that helps children think about how to search for and use illustrations to understand unfamiliar words. Use enlarged text, such as a big book, so that all children can see the print clearly. Here is an example.

- Use *In My Bag* or another enlarged text. With a sticky note, cover the word *rock* in the sentence "I saw a big rock" on page 2. Show the page and read up to the sticky note. Then pause.

  What could this word be?

  Why do you think so?

  The girl is looking at a rock in the illustration, so the word could be *rock*. *Rock* would make sense.

- Remove the sticky note and confirm that the word is *rock*.
- Cover the word *bag* in the sentence "I put it in my bag" on page 3 and repeat the process.

  What could this word be?

  Why do you think so? Do you think the illustration could help you?

  The illustration shows the girl putting the rock into her bag, so it makes sense that the word could be *bag*.

- Remove the sticky note and confirm that the word is *bag*.
- Repeat the activity, covering the word flat in the sentence "I saw a flat rock" on page 10.

## Have a Try

Invite children to figure out a word with a partner.

▶ Cover the word *turtle* in the sentence *It was not a turtle!* on page 16. Read up to the covered word and pause.

> Turn and talk about what word would make sense in this sentence. Talk about the illustration and how that can help you think about what the word is.

▶ After time for discussion, ask children to share their thinking. Then, remove the sticky note so they can confirm their predictions.

## Summarize and Apply

Summarize the learning and remind children use illustrations to identify words they don't know.

> What is something you can do when you see a word you don't know?

> Let's make a chart to remember what you learned today.

▶ With children's help, make a simple chart as a reminder of the principle. Then write the principle at the top of the chart.

> When you read today, if you see a word you don't know, look at the illustration and think about what makes sense. Bring the book when we meet so you can share.

## Share

Following independent work time, gather children in groups of three.

> Did you see any words you did not know and then use an illustration to help you think about what makes sense? Show the word and the illustration to your group.

## Extend the Lesson (Optional)

After assessing children's understanding, you might decide to extend the learning.

▶ During guided reading and in reading conferences, reinforce the strategy by reminding children to look at the illustration and think about what word would make sense when they see a word they do not know. Use supporting language, such as *Can the illustration help you understand this part of the story?*

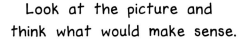

Section 3: Strategies and Skills

# RML2
### SAS.U1.RML2

**Reading Minilesson Principle**
## Read the sentence again and get your mouth ready for the first sound.

Monitoring, Searching, and Self-Correcting

### You Will Need

▶ an enlarged text, such as *The Elephant* by Cordelia S. Finn, from *Shared Reading Collection*

▶ sticky notes

▶ chart paper and markers

### Academic Language / Important Vocabulary

▶ make sense

▶ predict

▶ sound

▶ letter

▶ word

### Continuum Connection

▶ Begin to notice and connect features and parts of words, e.g., phonograms, first letter, word endings (p. 116)

## Goal

Use visual information (first letter) and meaning to predict a word.

## Rationale

When you teach children to search for and use visual information (first letter) to read a word, you support them in initiating problem-solving actions as readers. Ultimately, they will search for and use meaning, language, and print in an integrated way to achieve fluent reading.

## Assess Learning

Observe children when they predict a word and notice if there is evidence of new learning based on the goal of this minilesson.

▶ Do children reread the sentence, make the first sound of the unknown word, and think about what would make sense?

▶ Do they understand the terms *make sense*, *predict*, *sound*, *letter*, and *word*?

## Minilesson

To help children think about the minilesson principle, provide an interactive lesson using the first letter of an unknown word to predict what the word will be. Use enlarged text, such as a big book, so that all children can see the print clearly. Here is an example.

▶ Use *The Elephant* or another enlarged text. With a sticky note, cover only the letters *ead* of the word *head* on page 2, so that just the *h* shows. Begin reading and pause before the covered word.

> "The elephant has a big _____." I am going to read the sentence again and get my mouth ready for the first sound of the covered word. "The elephant has a big" /h/. Look at the illustration. What does it have that starts with /h/?

▶ Remove the sticky note and confirm that the word is *head*.

> *Head* begins with /h/.

> Let's do this again for another covered word.

▶ With a sticky note, cover the letters *ong* from the word *long* on page 6. Begin reading and pause before the covered word *long*.

> "The elephant has a /l/ trunk." Look at the illustration. What word describes the trunk and begins with /l/?

▶ Reveal the word.

> *Long* begins with /l/.

Repeat the process for the sentence "The elephant has a big body" on page 12 by covering the letters *ody* in the word *body*.

## Have a Try

Invite children to figure out a word with a partner.

Cover all but the first letter of the word *family* in the sentence *The elephant has a big family* on page 16. Read up to the covered word.

> Look at the first letter and get your mouth ready for the first sound. Turn and talk about what the covered word could be. Talk about if it makes sense.

After time for discussion, ask children to share their thinking. Then remove the sticky note so they can confirm their predictions.

## Summarize and Apply

Summarize the learning and remind children to get their mouths ready for the first sound when they come to a word they don't know.

> What is something you can do when you see a word you don't know?
>
> Let's make a chart to help you remember what you learned today.

With children's help, make a simple chart as a reminder of the principle. Then write the principle at the top of the chart.

> When you read today, if you see a word you don't know, read the sentence again and get your mouth ready for the first sound. Think about what makes sense. Bring the book when we meet so you can share.

## Share

Following independent work time, gather children in groups of three.

> Did you see any words you did not know and then get your mouth ready for the first sound? Show the word to your group and tell what you did.

## Extend the Lesson (Optional)

After assessing children's understanding, you might decide to extend the learning.

During guided reading and in reading conferences, reinforce the strategy by using supporting language, such as *Read that again and get your mouth ready for the first sound.*

Read the sentence again and get your mouth ready for the first sound.

The elephant has a big h

# RML3
### SAS.U1.RML3

**Reading Minilesson Principle**
# Read the sentence again and think about what would make sense, sound right, and look right.

## Monitoring, Searching, and Self-Correcting

### You Will Need

- one or two familiar shared reading books or poems, such as: *Goldilocks and the Three Bears* by David Edwin, from *Shared Reading Collection*
- sticky notes
- chart paper and markers

### Academic Language / Important Vocabulary

- makes sense
- looks right
- sounds right
- reread

### Continuum Connection

- Reread to search for and use information from language structure or meaning (pp. 436, 442, 448, 454, 460, 466)
- Use multiple sources of information (visual information in print, meaning/pictures, language structure) to monitor and self-correct (pp. 442, 448, 454, 460, 466)

## Goal

Reread and search for and use information from meaning, syntax, and visual information.

## Rationale

Readers use meaning, language, and print simultaneously in a smooth process. Teaching children to think about how sources of information fit together helps them improve efficiency, fluency, and flexibility when reading unknown words. The goal is for the teacher to engage in the strategic actions to problem solve.

## Assess Learning

Observe children by having them read aloud to you during guided and shared reading. Notice if there is evidence of new learning based on the goal of this minilesson.

- Do children problem solve by using multiple sources of information when they encounter an unknown word?
- Do they reread and then search for additional sources of information when they encounter an unknown word?
- Do they understand the terms *makes sense, looks right, sounds right,* and *reread*?

## Minilesson

To help children think about the minilesson principle, use the suggested text, or choose a poem or familiar big book. Here is an example.

- Cover the word *forest* on page 4 of *Goldilocks and the Three Bears* with a sticky note. Show the book, read the title, and then read page 3, pausing at the word *forest*.

  What could this word be? Why do you think that? Let's check to see if you are right. What letter(s) do you expect to see at the beginning of [insert predicted word]?

- If the children predict something other than the correct word, encourage them to talk about what else would make sense, sound right, and look right. Remove the sticky note.

  Are you right? Read the sentence with me, and check to make sure it makes sense, sounds right, and looks right.

- Read the sentence together.

  Does *forest* make sense, sound right, and look right?

- Repeat the process, with the word *answered* on page 11. Encourage the children to think about what would make sense and sound right.

## Have a Try

Invite the children to work with a partner to word solve.

▶ Repeat with the word *plopped* on page 12. Read the page, pausing at *plopped*.

> Turn and talk about what would sound right and make sense in this sentence.

▶ Invite a few children to share, then reread the sentence together.

## Summarize and Apply

Summarize the learning and remind children to think about monitoring their reading.

> If you come to a word you don't know, what can you do?

▶ Make a simple chart to help children remember what they learned in this lesson.

> When you read today, if there is a word you don't know, reread the sentence and think about what would make sense, sound right, and look right.

Think about what would make sense, sound right, and look right.

## Share

Following independent work time, gather children together in the meeting area to talk about how they monitored their reading.

> Who found a word you didn't know and reread the sentence to think about what would make sense, sound right, and look right?

▶ Invite a few children to share and show the page.

## Extend the Lesson (Optional)

After assessing children's understanding, you might decide to extend the learning through guided reading or independent reading. From the *Prompting Guide, Part 1* (Fountas and Pinnell 2012), use teaching, prompting, and reinforcing language, such as the following:

▶ *Do you know a word that would make sense, sound right, and look right?*

▶ *Try again and think about what would make sense, sound right, and look right.*

▶ *That made sense and sounded right, but did it look right?*

▶ *It makes sense, sounds right, and looks right.*

## Assessment

After you have taught the minilessons in this umbrella, observe children talking and writing about their reading across instructional contexts: interactive read-aloud, independent reading and literacy work, guided reading, shared reading, and book club. Use *The Literacy Continuum* (Fountas and Pinnell 2017) to observe children's reading and writing behaviors across instructional contexts.

▶ What evidence do you have of new understandings related to monitoring, searching and self-correcting?

- Do children check the picture and think about the story to decide what would make sense?

- Do children stop after an error and make multiple attempts until accurate?

- Do they reread to search for additional sources of information?

- Can children reread the sentence and get their mouth ready for the first sound(s)?

- Do they understand the terms *make sense, sound right, look right*, and *illustration*?

▶ In what other ways, beyond the scope of this umbrella, are children integrating in-the-head strategies and skills when they read?

- Are children using language patterns close to oral language to search for and use information?

- Do they break apart words to read them?

- Do children look for a part of a word that can help?

Use your observations to determine the next umbrella you will teach. You may also consult Minilessons Across the Year (p. 51) for guidance.

## Link to Writing

After teaching the minilessons in this umbrella, help children link the new learning to their writing or drawing about reading:

▶ When engaged in interactive writing and shared writing, support children in monitoring what is being written to ensure it makes sense, sounds right, and looks right. Support them in rereading to confirm and check all sources of information.

▶ Support children when they write independently to monitor themselves. Encourage children to reread to make sure that what they have written makes sense, sounds right, and looks right.

## Minilessons in This Umbrella

**RML1**   Use your finger to help you learn how to take apart new words.

**RML2**   Look for a part of the word that can help.

**RML3**   Use the information from the sentence or the book to understand the meaning of a word.

**RML4**   When you come to a word you don't know, you can work it out.

## Before Teaching Umbrella 2 Minilessons

Most of the teaching for word analysis strategies you do with your class will be done in shared reading and guided reading. But, sometimes, it's helpful to have a reminder of ways to problem solve unfamiliar words. In shared reading, read and discuss big books, so the children understand the books and can participate in the processing of the text. Use the selected texts from the *Fountas & Pinnell Classroom™ Shared Reading Collection* listed below, or choose big books from your library, to support the concepts developed in this umbrella. Alternatively, use large print charts (Shared Poetry Chart) or a text projected with a document camera so children can read the print. Read and discuss big books with opportunities for word solving multisyllabic words. Choose books with opportunities for discussing how to determine the meaning of a word through context and the support of illustrations. A helpful resource for supporting the teaching of these minilessons is *Fountas & Pinnell Prompting Guide, Part 1, for Oral Reading and Early Writing* (Fountas & Pinnell 2012).

### Shared Reading Collection

*Lots of Snow* by Joan Silver

*Inventions and Nature* by Nancy Geldermann

*The Cactus Hotel* by Abbey Grace Moore

*Captain Brock, Firefighter* by Andrea Delbanco

*Scrunch, the Caterpillar* by Stephen Krensky

As you read aloud and enjoy these texts together, help children

- look for parts of unknown words to help break them apart while reading,

- demonstrate how to break multisyllabic words apart with a finger, and

- discuss how to figure out what words mean by using context, or looking at the illustrations.

**Shared Reading**

Section 3: Strategies and Skills

## Solving Words

### You Will Need

- one or two familiar shared reading big books with multisyllabic words, such as *Lots of Snow* by Joan Silver from *Shared Reading Collection*
- card strip
- chart paper and markers
- copy of page 11 of *Lots of Snow* for each pair of children

### Academic Language / Important Vocabulary

- word
- word part
- take apart

### Continuum Connection

- When reading texts individually and with others, notice and connect features and parts of words: e.g., phonograms, first letter, word endings (p. 120)
- Use known word parts (some are words) to solve unknown larger words: e.g., *in/into, can/canvas; us, crust* (p. 369)

### Goal

Use a finger to help take apart two or three syllable words.

### Rationale

As readers begin to encounter multisyllabic words, they need to be taught a variety of ways to break these words apart efficiently without losing meaning. When children learn how to break words into syllables, they become better at solving words.

### Assess Learning

Observe children by having them read aloud to you during guided and shared reading. Notice if there is evidence of new learning based on the goal of this minilesson.

- Do children demonstrate a variety of ways take apart words?
- Do children use known word parts, prefixes, and suffixes to solve words?
- Do they understand the terms *word, word part,* and *take apart*?

## Minilesson

To help children think about the minilesson principle, engage them in a demonstration of taking apart new words. Here is an example.

- Hold up *Lots of Snow*. Read the title and then begin reading on page 5. Stop before the word *shouted*.

  Watch what I do to help me read this word.

- Move a card strip slowly across *shouted* to reveal each word part until you can read the whole word. Finish reading the sentence and then reread it.

  Listen as I take apart this word: /sh/, /out/, /ed/, shouted.

  What did you notice I did when I got to the word *shouted*?

  You can use your finger to take new words apart. You can say the first part and then the next part(s). Then you think about what makes sense. They are looking for their boots and Ben *shouted* to Rosa and Daisy. That makes sense.

- Repeat with the word *another* (an/oth/er) on page 7.

  Who can come up and break this word into parts?

  What did you do to help you read the word?

  Using your finger to break the word into parts helps when you don't know what the word is.

## Have a Try

Invite the children to practice breaking words apart with a partner.

▶ Repeat with the word *without* on page 11, stopping at *without*. Give pairs a copy of page 11.

> With your partner, work together to use your fingers to break this word into parts.

▶ Ask a few children to tell how they broke the word into parts and how it helped them. Reread the sentence.

> Ben, Rosa, and Daisy want to go sledding, but they need their sled to do that! *Without* makes sense and sounds right.

## Summarize and Apply

Summarize the learning and remind children to think about breaking apart new words.

> How can use your finger to take apart new words?

▶ Review the chart and write the principle at the top.

> If you get to a new word when you read today, use your finger to break it into parts.

## Share

Following independent work time, gather children together in the meeting area to talk about their reading.

> Who used a finger to help break apart a new word?

▶ Choose a few children to share with the class.

## Extend the Lesson (Optional)

After assessing children's understanding, you might decide to extend the learning by continuing to support them in guided or independent reading. From *Prompting Guide, Part 1* (Fountas and Pinnell 2012), use teaching, prompting, and reinforcing language, such as the following:

▶ *You can use your finger to break the word.*

▶ *Where can you break the word apart?*

▶ *Look at the first part.*

▶ *Say the first part. Say more. Now say the ending.*

Use your finger to help you learn how to take apart new words.

sh     sh

out    shout

ed    shouted

Section 3: Strategies and Skills

**Reading Minilesson Principle**

## Look for a part of the word that can help.

**Solving Words**

### You Will Need

- one or two familiar shared reading books or poems, such as *Scrunch, the Caterpillar* by Stephen Krensky from *Shared Reading Collection*
- sticky notes
- chart paper and markers

### Academic Language / Important Vocabulary

- word
- word part

### Continuum Connection

- Use known word parts (some are words) to solve unknown larger words: e.g., *in/into, can/canvas; us, crust* (p. 369)

### Goal

Search for and use familiar parts of a word to help read the word.

### Rationale

When you teach children to notice parts of a word they know, you increase their efficiency in problem solving unknown words while reading the continuous text. This allows them to improve fluency and focus on the meaning of the text.

### Assess Learning

Observe children by having them read aloud to you during guided and shared reading. Notice if there is evidence of new learning based on the goal of this minilesson.

- Do children use known word parts to read words?
- Do they use syllables to read a word?
- Do they use the terms *word* and *word part*?

## Minilesson

To help children think about the minilesson principle, choose a text that allows opportunities for using word parts. Here is an example.

- Cover the word *things* on page 6 of *Scrunch, the Caterpillar* with a sticky note. Show the book, read the title, and then read page 6, pausing at the word *things*. Remove the sticky note.

  Does anyone see a part in this word that would help you to read it?

- Have a child come up and show the parts that helped him.

  *Things* starts like the word *the* and the end of the word has /ings/. So the word is *things*. Let's read the sentence together and see if it sounds right and makes sense.

- Repeat with the word *maybe* on page 7.

  Look for a word part you know. Look for a part that can help you read the word.

- Repeat this process with the word *spin* on page 10.

  You can look for a part or parts of words you know and then think about what would make sense to help you to read the word.

## Have a Try

Invite the children to work with a partner to find a word part to solve a word.

▶ Repeat with the word *inside* on page 12. Read the page, pausing at *inside*. Remove the sticky note.

Turn and talk about a word part that can help you read this word.

▶ After turn and talk, ask a few children to describe what they did to read the word. Reread the sentence together.

## Summarize and Apply

Summarize the learning and remind children to think about using word parts.

What can help you when you come to a word that you don't know?

▶ Review the chart and write the principle at the top.

When you read, if you come to a word you are not sure of, look for a word part, and think about what would make sense.

Look for a part of the word that can help.

in-side
The word is inside!

## Share

Following independent work time, gather children together in the meeting area to talk about their reading.

Who found a word you didn't know and found a word part or parts that helped you read the word?

▶ Invite a few children to share and have them share the page from their books.

## Extend the Lesson (Optional)

After assessing children's understanding, you might decide to extend the learning through guided reading or independent reading. From *Prompting Guide, Part 1* (Fountas and Pinnell 2012), use teaching, prompting, and reinforcing language, such as the following:

▶ *You can say the first part.*

▶ *You can look for a part that might help.*

▶ *Say the first part. Now say more.*

▶ *Is that like another word you know?*

▶ *You looked for a part you know.*

**Reading Minilesson Principle**

# Use the information from the sentence or the book to understand the meaning of a word.

## You Will Need

- three or four familiar shared reading big books with vocabulary that can be supported through context and illustrations, such as the following from *Shared Reading Collection*:
  - *Inventions and Nature* by Nancy Geldermann
  - *The Cactus Hotel* by Abbey Grace Moore
  - *Captain Brock, Firefighter* by Andrea Delbanco
- chart paper and markers

## Academic Language / Important Vocabulary

- illustration
- information
- sentence

## Continuum Connection

- Use contextual information to understand the meaning of new words (p. 121)

## Goal

Use context and a book's illustrations to understand the meaning of a word.

## Rationale

Children learn how to derive the meaning of words within the connected text when you teach them how to search illustrations or use sentence and story context. This supports them to independently understand what they read.

## Assess Learning

Observe children by having them read aloud to you during guided and shared reading. Notice if there is evidence of new learning based on the goal of this minilesson.

- ▶ Can children use sentence context to determine the meaning of words?
- ▶ Do children use illustrations to determine the meaning of words?
- ▶ Do they understand the terms *illustration, information,* and *sentence*?

# Minilesson

To help children think about the minilesson principle, engage them in a discussion of using sentence context and illustrations to determine the meaning of unknown words. Here is an example.

- ▶ Show *Inventions and Nature*. Read pages 7 and 8.

  What do you think the word *hover* means? Why do you think that? The word *hover* means *to stay in one place in the air*. What on these two pages helped you to understand the meaning of the word *hover*?

  In the illustrations, both the helicopter and the bird are flying in one place. Each sentence says "It hovers in one place, moves forward and backward, and lands in tight spots." You can use information from the sentence and the illustrations to help you think about what the word means.

- ▶ Repeat using pages 8 and 9 from *The Cactus Hotel*.

  What do you think the word *burrow* means?

  Why do you think that?

  A burrow is a hole or tunnel dug by a small animal. You can see in the illustration that the scorpion's secret home is a hole under the cactus. The sentence tells you the scorpion's home is a hole. You can use the information from both the sentence and the illustration to help you think about what the word *burrow* means.

## Have a Try

Invite the children to practice using context with a partner.

❯ Show *Captain Brock, Firefighter*. Read page 9.

> Turn and talk about what you think the word *gear* means, and why you think that.

❯ Ask a few children to share.

> *Gear* means *equipment someone wears*. The photographs show the equipment and the sentences help you understand the meaning of the word *gear*.

## Summarize and Apply

Summarize the learning and remind children to think about what to do if they don't know the meaning of a word.

> How can sentences and illustrations help you understand the meaning of a word?

❯ Make a chart with the children to remind them how to use information from the book to learn what a word means.

> When you read today, if you come to a word you don't understand, use the information from the book, sentences, and illustrations to think about what the word means.

## Share

Following independent work time, gather children together in the meeting area to talk about their reading.

> Who came to a word you didn't understand when reading today? What did you do?

❯ Choose a few children to share.

## Extend the Lesson (Optional)

After assessing children's understanding, you might decide to extend the learning.

❯ Support children in determining the meaning of new words during guided reading and interactive read-aloud.

❯ During independent reading, have children mark with sticky notes words they are unsure of, and discuss how they can determine what the words mean.

❯ **Drawing/Writing About Reading** Ask children to use a reader's notebook to explain what new words mean, and what in the text or illustrations supports their thinking.

---

### If you don't know what a word means:

Look at the illustrations.

"It hovers in one place."

Read information in the sentence.

Think about the information in the book.

**Reading Minilesson Principle**

# When you come to a word you don't know, you can work it out.

## Solving Words

### You Will Need

- chart paper and markers

### Academic Language / Important Vocabulary

- illustration
- information
- sentence
- word part
- take apart

### Continuum Connection

- Use contextual information to understand the meaning of new words (p. 121)
- Use known word parts (some are words) to solve unknown larger words: e.g., *in/into, can/canvas; us, crust* (p. 369)

## Goal

Generate a list of ways to solve words.

## Rationale

To read the continuous text, students need to learn multiple actions for solving words. Generating a list of word-solving actions provides children with options to use when reading independently.

## Assess Learning

Observe children by having them read aloud to you during guided and shared reading. Notice if there is evidence of new learning based on the goal of this minilesson.

- Do children use a variety of actions to take words apart?
- Do children use their finger to take words apart?
- Do they use the meaning of the sentence to solve words?
- Do they use known parts to solve words?
- Do they understand the terms *illustration, information, sentence, word part,* and *take apart*?

## Minilesson

To help children think about the minilesson principle, engage them in creating a list of activities to use to solve words. Here is an example.

> We have been talking about different things you can do when you come to a word you don't know. Let's write these activities on a chart so you can remember what to try when you get to an unknown word. When you come to a word you don't know, what are some ways you can solve it? Turn and talk to your partner.

- After the partners share, ask for volunteers to share. Record responses on the chart paper. Add the minilesson principle to the top of the chart.

## Have a Try

Invite children to talk with a partner about something they have done to solve a word.

> Turn and talk with your partner about a time you solved a word you didn't know. What did you do?

## Summarize and Apply

Summarize the learning and remind children to think about what to do when they don't know a word.

> What can you do when you find words you don't know?

▶ Review the chart.

> When you read today, if you find a word that you don't know, try one of these ways to help you read the word.

## Share

Following independent work time, gather children together in the meeting area to talk about their reading.

> Who came to a word you didn't understand when reading today? What did you do? Was it something on the chart, or should we add to the chart?

## Extend the Lesson (Optional)

After assessing children's understanding, you might decide to extend the learning.

▶ During guided and independent reading time, remind students of the strategies they can use to solve words they don't know.

▶ Use the following prompts for teaching, prompting, and reinforcing from *Prompting Guide, Part 1* (Fountas and Pinnell 2012), to support students as they read.

- *Say the first part. Now say more.*
- *Use your finger to break the word.*
- *Think about what would make sense, sound right, and look right.*

▶ **Drawing/Writing About Reading** Support children in using analogies in going from a known word to a new word when writing.

---

**When you come to a word you don't know, you can work it out.**

- Look for a part you know.

- Look for a part that can help.

- Use your finger to break apart the word.

- Look at the illustration and think about what the word might mean.

- Think about the information in the sentence.

---

*Section 3: Strategies and Skills*

## Assessment

After you have taught the minilessons in this umbrella, observe children talking and writing about their reading across instructional contexts: interactive read-aloud, independent reading and literacy work, guided reading, shared reading, and book club. Use *The Literacy Continuum* (Fountas and Pinnell 2017) to observe children's reading and writing behaviors across instructional contexts.

▶ What evidence do you have of new understandings related to solving words?

- Do children use a variety of ways to take apart words?

- Are they able to use a finger to take words apart?

- Do children use known parts to solve words?

- Do children use sentence context to determine the meaning of words?

- Do they understand the terms *illustration, word part, information, sentence,* and *take apart*?

▶ In what other ways, beyond the scope of this umbrella, are they talking about solving words?

- When reading do children use prefixes and suffixes to take words apart?

- Do children use inflectional endings to take words apart?

- Do children make multiple attempts that are visually similar while trying to solve an unknown word?

- Are they independent in their ability to problem solve unknown words, while holding onto the meaning of what they are reading?

Use your observations to determine the next umbrella you will teach. You may also consult Minilessons Across the Year (p. 51) for guidance.

## Link to Writing

After teaching the minilessons in this umbrella, help children link the new learning to their writing or drawing about reading:

▶ When engaging in interactive, shared, and independent writing, reference classroom resources, such as an alphabet chart, consonant cluster chart, word wall, and name chart, to make connections between known words and new words.

▶ When engaging in shared writing, demonstrate how slow articulation of unknown words in writing relates to solving unknown words in reading.

Section 3: Strategies and Skills

## Minilessons in This Umbrella

**Shared Reading**

| RML1 | Make your voice go down and come to a full stop when you see a period. |
| RML2 | Make your voice go up when you see a question mark. |
| RML3 | Read the sentence with strong feeling when you see an exclamation point. |
| RML4 | Read the word with strong feeling when you see bold or dark print. |
| RML5 | Make your voice a little louder when you see a word in capital letters. |
| RML6 | Put your words together so it sounds like talking. |
| RML7 | Make your reading sound interesting. |
| RML8 | Make your reading sound smooth. |
| RML9 | Read the talk the way the character said it. |

## Before Teaching Umbrella 3 Minilessons

Read and discuss books that allow children to see print and have a variety of punctuation marks and print features. The primary focus is to support children's comprehension and enjoyment of books. For this umbrella, use texts, such as the following from the *Fountas & Pinnell Classroom™ Shared Reading Collection* or *Interactive Read-Aloud Collection*, or select books based on your children's interests, books that have fostered high engagement.

**Shared Reading Collection**

*Going on a Bear Hunt* retold by Margie Sigman

*Chicken Licken* retold by Owen Peterson

*Scram!* by Julie Reich

*Lots of Snow* by Joan Silver

*The Elephant* by Cordelia S. Finn

*The Three Little Pigs* retold by Helen Scully

*Up, Up, and Away* by Helen Scully

**Interactive Read-Aloud Collection**

**Mo Willems: Having Fun with Humor**

*Don't Let the Pigeon Drive the Bus!* by Mo Willems

**Mo Willems**

**Exploring Fiction and Nonfiction**

*Ice Bear* by Nicola Davies

**Fiction and Nonfiction**

As you read aloud and enjoy these texts together, help children

• understand how the tone of voice reflects meaning and punctuation,

• emphasize boldface or capitalized print to reflect meaning,

• use phrasing, pausing, stress, and intonation to read fluently, and

• think about dialogue and read it to sound like the characters are speaking.

**Reading Minilesson Principle**
## Make your voice go down and come to a full stop when you see a period.

---

Maintaining Fluency

### You Will Need

- pointer
- familiar large print book with simple sentences, such as *Going on a Bear Hunt* retold by Margie Sigman, from *Shared Reading Collection*
- chart paper and markers

### Academic Language / Important Vocabulary

- period
- sentence
- voice
- down
- full stop

### Continuum Connection

- Recognize and reflect some simple punctuation with the voice (e.g., period, question mark, exclamation mark) when reading in chorus or individually (p. 121)

---

### Goal

Learn how a reader's voice changes when reading aloud a sentence ending with a period.

### Rationale

Children need to recognize periods to understand how a reader's voice changes when a period is seen at the end of a sentence. When readers identify periods and then modulate their voices, they develop an understanding of the structure of language. They will include periods to show a full stop as they write independently.

### Assess Learning

Observe children when they read sentences ending with periods. Notice if there is evidence of new learning based on the goal of this minilesson.

- ▶ Are children able to pay attention to periods in a sentence?
- ▶ Are they able to change their voice when seeing a period?
- ▶ Do they notice how a voice goes down and comes to a full stop at a period?
- ▶ Are they able to talk about what a voice should sound like when they see a period?
- ▶ Do they use the terms *period*, *sentence*, and *voice* correctly?

## Minilesson

To help children think about the minilesson principle, engage them in a short demonstration and practice of reading sentences ending with periods. Here is an example.

- ▶ Cover sentences without periods on pages 2 and 8 of *Going on a Bear Hunt*.
- ▶ Show page 2.

  Who can come up and use the pointer to show the periods on this page from *Going on a Bear Hunt?* Now listen to how my voice changes as I come to each period.

- ▶ Read the sentences, emphasizing your voice going down and coming to a full stop after each period.

  Turn and talk about what you noticed that I did.

- ▶ After time for discussion, ask volunteers to share. Write the principle on the chart paper. Under the principle, write a sentence from the page, omitting the period, reading aloud as you do.

  Who can come up and add the period at the end of this sentence and read it?

---

▶ Repeat with the other two sentences on the page.

> Now let's read these sentences together.

▶ Have the children join in rereading and emphasizing their voices going down and coming to a full stop.

## Have a Try

Invite the children practice reading sentences that end with a period.

▶ Show page 8 of *Going on a Bear Hunt*. Read each sentence, asking children to repeat each one after you.

> Turn and quietly read this page to a partner. Make your voice go down and come to a full stop after each period.

## Summarize and Apply

Summarize the learning and remind children to make their voice go down and come to a full stop when they see a period.

> With a partner, read one or more pages from your book. Make your voice go down and come to a full stop after each period in a sentence.

## Share

Following independent work time, gather children together in the meeting area to make their voices go down and come to a full stop when they see a period.

> With a partner, read one or more pages from your book. Make your voice go down and come to a full stop after each period in a sentence.

## Extend the Lesson (Optional)

After assessing children's understanding, you might decide to extend the learning.

▶ As you read other books, show the page and have children search for periods.

▶ Play the *Forgotten Period* game. Write periods on several small sticky notes. After reading a story that has a page with multiple sentences ending in periods, write the words on chart paper, leaving off the periods. Read the page as a long run-on sentence and ask children to talk about what is missing. Have children come up and add the forgotten periods, with assistance, and then reread the sentences together as a class. Talk about how the periods help readers understand the story and why they are important.

---

Make your voice go down and come to a full stop when you see a period.

We're going on a bear hunt●

We're looking for a big one●

We're not afraid●

# RML2

**SAS.U3.RML2**

**Reading Minilesson Principle**
## Make your voice go up when you see a question mark.

**Maintaining Fluency**

## You Will Need

- highlighting tape or pointer
- familiar large-print books with question marks, such as these *Shared Reading Collection* books:
  - *Going on a Bear Hunt* retold by Margie Sigman
  - *Chicken Licken* retold by Owen Peterson
- chart paper and markers

## Academic Language / Important Vocabulary

- question
- question mark
- punctuation
- sentence
- voice
- up

## Continuum Connection

- Recognize and reflect some simple punctuation with the voice (e.g., period, question mark, exclamation mark) when reading in chorus or individually (p. 121)

## Goal

Learn how a reader's voice changes when reading aloud a sentence ending with a question mark.

## Rationale

Children need to recognize periods to understand how a reader's voice changes when a question mark is seen at the end of a sentence. When readers identify question marks and then modulate their voices, they develop an understanding of the structure of language. They will include question marks as they write independently.

## Assess Learning

Observe children when they read sentences ending with a question mark. Notice if there is evidence of new learning based on the goal of this minilesson.

- Are children able to change their voice when seeing a question mark?
- Do they notice how a reader's voice goes up at a question mark?
- Do they use the terms *question, question mark, sentence,* and *punctuation*?

## Minilesson

To help children think about the minilesson principle, engage them in a short demonstration and practice of reading sentences ending with question marks. Here is an example.

- Cover exclamation points on pages 6 and 10 of *Going on a Bear Hunt*. Show page 2.

  What do you notice at the end of the sentences on this page?

- Ask a volunteer to come up and use highlighting tape or a pointer to show the periods and question mark.

  As I read this page aloud, notice my voice as I read the sentences with periods and the question mark

- Read the sentences slowly, emphasizing how your voice changes depending on the punctuation.

  What did you notice about my voice as I read the last sentence with the question mark?

  Can you read the question with me as I write it?

- Reread the question with the class and write it on the chart, omitting the question mark.

  What do I need to add to the end, so you know to read this sentence like a question?

▶ Have a volunteer write the question mark at the end, and then reread it as a class. Repeat with pages 6 and 10.

## Have a Try

Invite the children to practice reading questions.

▶ Show *Chicken Licken*. As you reread the story, pause as you turn each page for children to identify question marks and then join in reading the sentences or repeat them after you.

## Summarize and Apply

Summarize the learning and remind children to make their voice go up when they see a question mark.

> What do you do when you see a question mark at the end of a sentence?

▶ Review the chart and write the principle at the top.

> When you read today, look for question marks in the sentences. Whisper read to practice making your voice go up when you read a question. If you find any question marks, bring the book when we meet so you can share.

## Share

Following independent work time, gather children together in the meeting area to share how to make their voices go up when they see a question mark.

> Did anyone find a question mark in your book today?

▶ Ask volunteers to show the pages and read the sentences ending in a question mark.

## Extend the Lesson (Optional)

After assessing children's understanding, you might decide to extend the learning.

▶ Play *Going on a Question Mark Hunt* using the chant from *Going on a Bear Hunt* to search for question marks in books. An alternative is to cut out card stock and write the question *What am I?* on each. Hide questions near objects and have children hunt for them, and then read and answer the questions so they can practice voice inflection. For example, hide a question near the pencil sharpener. The child who finds it would say, "What am I? I am a pencil sharpener."

▶ Talk about why authors use question marks in stories and why they are important.

Make your voice go up when you see a question mark.

Which way do we go?

Which way do we go?

Which way do we go?

# RML 3
### SAS.U3.RML3

**Reading Minilesson Principle**
## Read the sentence with strong feeling when you see an exclamation point.

## Maintaining Fluency

### You Will Need

- highlighting tape or pointer
- familiar large-print books with exclamation points, such as these *Shared Reading Collection* books:
  - *Going on a Bear Hunt* retold by Margie Sigman
  - *Scram!* by Julie Reich
- chart paper and markers

### Academic Language / Important Vocabulary

- exclamation point
- sentence
- strong feeling

### Continuum Connection

- Recognize and reflect some simple punctuation with the voice (e.g., period, question mark, exclamation mark) when reading in chorus or individually (p. 121)

## Goal

Learn how to read sentences aloud with exclamation points to reflect the meaning of the story.

## Rationale

Children need to recognize exclamation points to understand how a reader's voice changes when an exclamation point is noticed at the end of a sentence. When readers identify exclamation points and then modulate their voices, they develop an understanding of the structure of language and use them in writing.

## Assess Learning

Observe children when they read sentences with exclamation points. Notice if there is evidence of new learning based on the goal of this minilesson.

- ▶ Do children pay attention to exclamation points in sentences?
- ▶ Are they able to change their voice when seeing an exclamation point?
- ▶ Do they notice how a voice changes at an exclamation point?
- ▶ Do they use the terms *exclamation point, sentence,* and *strong feeling*?

## Minilesson

To help children think about the minilesson principle, engage them in a short demonstration and practice of reading sentences with exclamation points. Here is an example.

- ▶ Show page 4 of *Going on a Bear Hunt*.

  What do you notice at the end of the sentences on this page?

- ▶ Ask a volunteer to come up and use highlighting tape or a pointer to show the periods and exclamation points.

  As I read this page aloud, notice my voice when I read the sentences.

- ▶ Read the sentences slowly, emphasizing how your voice changes depending on the punctuation.

  What did you notice about my voice?

- ▶ Write the principle on the chart paper.

  Read the sentences with exclamation points with me.

- ▶ Reread the sentences and write each on the chart, omitting exclamation points.

  What do you need to add to the end of the sentence, so you know to read these sentences with strong feeling?

▶ Have a volunteer write the exclamation points at the end, and then reread the sentences as a class. Repeat activity with pages 6, 8, and 10.

## Have a Try

Invite the children to talk with a partner about exclamation points.

▶ Show page 8 of *Scram!*

> Remember when the family tried to move the cow off the road? Turn and talk to a partner about how you should read the word *shoo*! Why do you think the author added the exclamation point?

## Summarize and Apply

Summarize the learning and remind children to read with strong feelings when they see an exclamation point.

> How do you read the sentence when you see an exclamation point at the end of a sentence?

▶ Review the chart.

> When you read today, look for exclamation points in the sentences. Whisper read to practice reading with strong feeling. If you find any exclamation points, bring the book when we meet so you can share.

Read the sentence with strong feeling when you see an exclamation point.

Look !

We have to go through it !

We made it !

Look !

We have to go through it !

We made it !

## Share

Following independent work time, gather children together in the meeting area in a circle to share how to read with strong feelings when they see an exclamation point.

> Did anyone find an exclamation point in your book today?

▶ Ask volunteers to show the pages and read the sentences with exclamation points, assisting as needed.

## Extend the Lesson (Optional)

After assessing children's understanding, you might decide to extend the learning.

▶ As you read other books with exclamation points, have children join in and talk about how exclamation points affect the meaning of sentences.

▶ Talk about why authors choose to use exclamation points and how the meanings of sentences can change when an exclamation point is added or removed.

## RML4
**SAS.U3.RML4**

**Reading Minilesson Principle**
# Read the sentence with strong feeling when you see bold or dark print.

### Maintaining Fluency

**You Will Need**

▸ familiar large-print book with words in bold print, such as these *Shared Reading Collection* books:
  • *Lots of Snow* by Joan Silver
  • *The Elephant* by Cordelia S. Finn
▸ chart paper prepared with *The elephant has big* written multiple times
▸ thin and thick black markers

**Academic Language / Important Vocabulary**

▸ bold letters
▸ dark print
▸ strong feeling

**Continuum Connection**

▸ Recognize and reflect variations in print with the voice (e.g., italics, bold type, special treatments, font size) when reading in chorus or individually (p. 121)

### Goal

Learn how a reader's voice changes when reading aloud to make words written in bold letters sound important.

### Rationale

Children begin to explore how authors use bold letters to show a reader that those words should be read differently to emphasize their importance. When children learn to identify how a voice changes while reading words in bold print, they deepen their understanding of the text as well as the author's craft. They will apply this skill when writing independently.

### Assess Learning

Observe children when they read sentences with words in bold print. Notice if there is evidence of new learning based on the goal of this minilesson.

▸ Can children make their voices change when reading aloud a word in bold print?
▸ Do they use the terms *bold letters, dark print,* and *strong feeling*?

## Minilesson

To help children think about the minilesson principle, engage them in a short demonstration and practice of reading sentences with words printed in bold. Here is an example.

▸ Show page 4 from *Lots of Snow*.

   Listen as I read a few pages. Notice how the words look.

▸ Read page 4, and then show page 5.

   What do you notice about how the words look on this page? They are darker. Listen to my voice when I read the words in bold print.

▸ Read page 5 with feeling.

   Turn and talk about why you think the author wants you to read these words with strong feeling.

▸ After time for discussion, have the children share. Write the principle on the chart paper.

▸ Show page 2 of *The Elephant*.

   How did the author write the words on this page? Who can come up and trace the word that is in bold print?

▸ Give the child the thick black marker. After the child traces the word on the chart, add a quick sketch of an elephant's head after the sentence.

   Let's reread this sentence, changing our voices for the word in bold print.

▶ Reread together.

> Why did the author make some words in bold print?

▶ Repeat with additional pages in the story.

## Have a Try

Invite the children to practice reading bold words with a partner.

> Take turns reading the sentences from the chart with a partner. Make your voice sound just a little stronger and louder when you see the bold words.

## Summarize and Apply

Summarize the learning and remind children to read with strong feelings when they see bold or dark print.

> What do you do when you see a word in bold or dark print in a sentence?

▶ Review the chart.

> When you read today, notice any words in bold or dark print. Whisper read to practice reading the words a little stronger and louder. Bring the book when we meet so you can share.

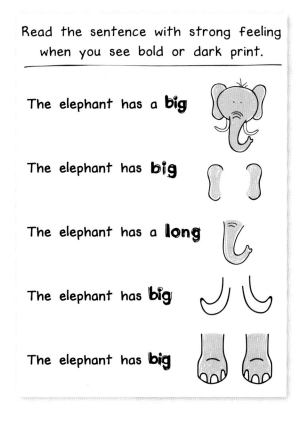

## Share

Following independent work time, gather children together in the meeting area in a circle to share how to read with strong feelings when they see bold or dark print.

> Did anyone find words in bold print in your book today?

▶ Ask volunteers to show the pages and read the words in bold print, assisting as needed.

## Extend the Lesson (Optional)

After assessing children's understanding, you might decide to extend the learning.

▶ From time to time when you encounter bold words while reading with children, read the words how they would sound with and without bold print, and then talk about why the author chose to make the words bold. Discuss how it changes the meaning if the words are read with strong feeling or without strong feeling.

**Reading Minilesson Principle**

# Make your voice a little louder when you see a word in capital letters.

## Maintaining Fluency

### You Will Need

- familiar books with words in all capital letters, such as these *Interactive Read-Aloud Collection* books:
  - *Don't Let the Pigeon Drive the Bus!* by Mo Willems, from Text Set: Mo Willems
  - *Ice Bear* by Nicola Davies, from Text Set: Fiction and Nonfiction
- chart paper and markers
- document camera (optional)

### Academic Language / Important Vocabulary

- capital letters
- voice
- important
- louder

### Continuum Connection

- Recognize and reflect variations in print with the voice (e.g., italics, bold type, special treatments, font size) when reading in chorus or individually (p. 121)

## Goal

Learn how a reader's voice changes when reading aloud to make words written in capital letters sound important.

## Rationale

Children begin to explore how authors use capitalization to show that some words should be read differently to emphasize their importance. When readers identify how a voice changes when reading capitalized words, they deepen their understanding of the text as well as the author's craft. They will begin to apply this skill when writing independently.

## Assess Learning

Observe children when they read sentences with words in all capital letters. Notice if there is evidence of new learning based on the goal of this minilesson.

- Do children notice how a voice changes when reading aloud a word in all capital letters?
- Can they change their voices when reading aloud a word in all capital letters?
- Do they use the terms *capital letters*, *voice*, *important*, and *louder*?

## Minilesson

To help children think about the minilesson principle, engage them in a short demonstration and practice of reading sentences with words in all capital letters. Here is an example.

- Show the cover of *Don't Let the Pigeon Drive the Bus!*

  Remember this funny story when you were told to watch the bus to make sure the pigeon doesn't drive?

- Show and read page 20. (Project the pages, if possible.)

  The pigeon does everything he can think of to get you to let him drive the bus, doesn't he?

- Show and read pages 21–22.

  What do you notice about how Mo Willems wrote these words?

- Write the principle on the chart paper. Under the principle, write the words from pages 21–22 and have the children join in to read with feeling.

  Turn and talk about why you think Mo Willems uses capital letters here.

- Add responses to the chart.

- Show page 11 of *Ice Bear*.

Do you remember this book that gives facts about polar bears?

▶ Point to the words *POLAR BEAR*.

Why do you think the Nicola Davies uses capital letters for the words *POLAR BEAR*?

▶ Add the words and children's ideas to the chart.

## Summarize and Apply

Summarize the learning and remind children to make their voice a little louder when they see words in all capital letters.

What do you do when you see a word in all capital letters?

▶ Review the chart.

When you read today, notice any words in all capital letters. Whisper read to practice reading them a little louder. Bring the book when we meet so you can share.

## Share

Following independent work time, gather children together in the meeting area in a circle to share how to make their voices a little louder when they see words in all capital letters.

Did anyone find words in all capital letters in your book today?

▶ Ask volunteers to show the pages and read the words in capital letters, assisting as needed.

## Extend the Lesson (Optional)

After assessing children's understanding, you might decide to extend the learning.

▶ When you read words in all capital letters, stop and ask children to notice how the reader's voice should change. Have children talk about the author's choice to use all capital letters and how it affects the meaning of the words

Make your voice a little louder when you see a word in capital letters.

### LET ME DRIVE THE BUS!

The pigeon feels it is very important to drive.

He is shouting in a loud voice.

### POLAR BEAR

Polar bears are important in this book.

The author wants to remind us that these are important animals.

**Reading Minilesson Principle**
## Put your words together so it sounds like talking.

Maintaining Fluency

### You Will Need

- familiar large-print book with easily read sentences, such as *Chicken Licken* retold by Owen Peterson, from *Shared Reading Collection*
- chart paper and markers

### Academic Language / Important Vocabulary

- words
- together

### Continuum Connection

- Use phrasing, pausing, word stress with intonation when reading in unison (p. 121)

### Goal

Read with phrasing when reading aloud.

### Rationale

Sentences are phrases strung together. When children parse sentences into meaningful phrases, their reading will sound like talking. This reflects the author's meaning and enhances children's understanding of the text.

### Assess Learning

Observe children when they read aloud. Notice if there is evidence of new learning based on the goal of this minilesson.

- Can children read words together in phrases?
- Do they sound like they are talking when they read dialogue?
- Are they able to monitor their oral reading for phrasing?
- Do they use the terms *words* and *together*?

## Minilesson

To help children think about the minilesson principle, engage them in a short demonstration and discussion of reading with appropriate phrasing. Here is an example.

- Show the cover of *Chicken Licken*.

  Listen to how I read the words on this page.

- Read page 4, pointing under each word, using a staccato voice.

  What did you notice about how I read the words on this page? I read each word separately. Listen as I read the same page again.

- Reread page 4 in a normal, expressive voice, pointing to each line.

  What did you notice about the way I read the words this time? I put my words together so that it sounds like talking.

  Listen to how I read the words on this page.

- Read page 7.

  What did you notice about how I read the words on this page? When you read, put your words together, so it sounds like you are talking. Your words almost touch each other when you say them.

- Write the sentence on the chart paper with a sketch. Add the minilesson principle to the chart.

## Have a Try

Invite the children to practice making the words sound like talking.

> Let's read a few pages of *Chicken Licken* together. I will read it first and then you try. Make sure you put your words together so it sounds like you are talking.

> ▶ Point to each line as you read, and then ask children to repeat the lines.

## Summarize and Apply

Summarize the learning and remind children to put their words together, so it sounds like talking as they read.

> What do you do to make your reading sound like you are talking?

> ▶ Review the chart.

> When you read your books today, whisper read to practice your reading. Make sure you put your words together so that it sounds like you are talking.

## Share

Following independent work time, gather children together in the meeting area to share reading aloud.

> Who practiced sounding like you were talking while reading? Turn and read one page to a partner.

## Extend the Lesson (Optional)

After assessing children's understanding, you might decide to extend the learning.

▶ Cut up familiar poems into phrases and place strips in a pocket chart for children to practice reading fluently.

▶ During guided reading, use prompts, such as these from *Prompting Guide, Part I* (Fountas and Pinnell 2012):

* *Read it like this (model phrase units). You need to listen to how your reading sounds. Listen to how I put my words together (model phrase units).*

* *Put your words together, so it sounds like talking. Try that again and put your words together even more. Are you listening to how your reading sounds?*

* *You made it sound like talking.*

* *You made your words almost touch each other.*

## Maintaining Fluency

### You Will Need

- familiar large-print book with interesting words, such as *The Three Little Pigs* retold by Helen Scully, from *Shared Reading* Collection
- chart paper and markers

### Academic Language / Important Vocabulary

- stress
- punctuation
- interesting

### Continuum Connection

- Use phrasing, pausing, word stress with intonation when reading in unison (p. 121)

## Goal

Read aloud with appropriate stress and intonation.

## Rationale

Making children aware of the rising and falling tones of their voices and teaching them how to use tone, pitch, and volume to reflect the meaning of the text will make their reading sound more interesting and enhance understanding. When children gain awareness of word stress, they increase comprehension.

## Assess Learning

Observe children when they read aloud. Notice if there is evidence of new learning based on the goal of this minilesson.

- Do children pay attention to punctuation?
- Do they sound like the characters in the story?
- Are they able to stress appropriate words to convey meaning?
- Do they understand the terms *stress, punctuation,* and *interesting*?

## Minilesson

To help children think about the minilesson principle, engage them in a short demonstration and discussion of reading with stress and intonation. Here is an example.

- Show *The Three Little Pigs*.

  Listen and think about how my voice is helping show the characters' feelings.

- Read page 8, making your voice sound like the characters, placing stress on the words *in, no,* and *not*.

  What did you notice about my voice? I made my reading sound interesting. My voice sounded like the characters were talking and I used a stronger voice when I read some of the words to make them sound important. I made my voice show excitement when I saw the exclamation mark.

  Listen to how I read the words on this page.

- Read page 9.

  What did I do with my voice to make my reading sound interesting?

- Make a chart to remind children to make their reading sound interesting. Add the minilesson principle to the top of the chart.

  When you read, make your reading sound interesting and think about what words you may want to read with more stress to make them sound important.

## Have a Try

Invite the children to practice making their reading sound interesting.

> Let's read the next few pages together. Make your voice sound like stories you have listened to me read.

▶ Have children repeat after you, or join in as you read together.

## Summarize and Apply

Summarize the learning and remind children to make their words sound interesting as they read aloud.

> How do you make your reading sound interesting?

> When you read your books today, whisper read to practice reading. Make sure to make the words sound interesting.

## Share

Following independent work time, gather children together in the meeting area to share their reading aloud.

> When you read today, did you make your reading sound interesting? Turn and read one page to a partner.

## Extend the Lesson (Optional)

After assessing children's understanding, you might decide to extend the learning.

▶ Use readers' theater to support children in their abilities to use their voices to express intonation and word stress.

▶ During guided reading, use prompts such as these from *Prompting Guide, Part I* (Fountas and Pinnell 2012):

- *Try that again and make that word sound important.*
- *Listen to how this sounds.*
- *Make your voice sound like the character is talking.*
- *Make your voice show that you understand what the author means.*
- *Make your voice go down when you see a period.*
- *How would _____ ask the question?*

Make your reading sound interesting.

I make my reading sound interesting!

## Maintaining Fluency

### You Will Need

- familiar large-print book with interesting words and easily read sentences, such as *Chicken Licken* retold by Owen Peterson, from *Shared Reading Collection*
- chart paper and markers

### Academic Language / Important Vocabulary

- smooth
- phrasing
- pausing
- stress
- interesting words

### Continuum Connection

- With group support, read orally with integration of all dimensions of fluency: e.g., pausing, phrasing, word stress, intonation, and rate (p. 121)

### Goal

Learn how to integrate phrasing, pausing, stress, and intonation to demonstrate fluent reading.

### Rationale

Teaching children to integrate all dimensions of fluency including appropriate rate, phrasing, pausing, stress, and intonation will help their oral reading sound smooth. They will be encouraged to use expressions in a way that demonstrates an understanding of the text and the author's craft.

### Assess Learning

Observe children when they read aloud. Notice if there is evidence of new learning based on the goal of this minilesson.

- ▶ Are children able to make their oral reading sound smooth?
- ▶ Are they monitoring how their oral reading sounds?
- ▶ Are they reading the text like they are telling a story?
- ▶ Do they understand the terms *smooth, phrasing, pausing, stress,* and *interesting words*?

## Minilesson

To help children think about the minilesson principle, engage them in a short demonstration and discussion of reading aloud smoothly. Here is an example.

- ▶ Show the cover of *Chicken Licken*.

  Remember how Chicken Licken thinks the sky is falling and wants to tell the king? Listen carefully to how my voice sounds as I read this page.

- ▶ Read pages 2–4 with appropriate rate, expression, pausing, and stress on words.

  What did you notice about my voice as I read? I made my voice sound like *Chicken Licken*. I made my voice get a little louder when I saw the exclamation points, and I made my voice go down and come to a full stop when I saw the periods. I stressed some words and put my words together like I was talking. This made my reading sound smooth and interesting.

  Listen to how I read the words on these pages.

- ▶ Read pages 5–7.

  What did you notice about how I read the words on these pages?

## Have a Try

Invite the children to practice their reading.

> Let's read the next few pages together. I will read it first, and then you will read together. Make sure your reading sounds smooth.

▶ Continue reading the next few pages, asking children to repeat after you.

## Summarize and Apply

Summarize the learning and remind children to make their reading sound smooth when reading aloud.

> How can you make your reading sound smooth?

▶ Make a chart to remind children how they can make their reading sound smooth. Add the principle to the top.

> When you read today, listen to how your reading sounds when you whisper read. Look at the chart to remember what to do to make your reading sound smooth.

## Share

Following independent work time, gather children together in the meeting area to share how to make their reading sound smooth when reading aloud.

> Turn and read one page to a partner. Read the page like you are telling a story.

## Extend the Lesson (Optional)

After assessing children's understanding, you might decide to extend the learning.

▶ Use readers' theater to provide practice for children to integrate the dimensions of fluency to convey meaning.

▶ During guided reading, use prompts, such as these from *Prompting Guide, Part 1* (Fountas and Pinnell 2012):

- *Listen to how I read this. Can you read it the same way?*
- *How do you think your reading sounds?*

Make your reading sound smooth.

Make your reading sound interesting.

Stress important words.

Read the punctuation.

Read like you are talking.

# RML 9
## SAS.U3.RML9

**Reading Minilesson Principle**
# Read the talk the way the character said it.

## Maintaining Fluency

### You Will Need

- card stock, cut into pieces to be used to cover portions of the story

- familiar large-print books with dialogue, such as these *Shared Reading Collection* books:
  - *Lots of Snow* by Joan Silver
  - *Up, Up, and Away* by Helen Scully

- chart paper and markers

### Academic Language / Important Vocabulary

- talk
- speak

### Continuum Connection

- Adjust the voice to recognize dialogue in the body of the text and in speech bubbles or unspoken thoughts in thought bubbles (p. 121)

## Goal

Read dialogue aloud to reflect the characters' feelings and meaning of the story.

## Rationale

When children understand that dialogue should be read to show the feelings of the characters, they develop insights into characters' motivations and begin to make connections between characters and their own lives.

## Assess Learning

Observe children when they read aloud. Notice if there is evidence of new learning based on the goal of this minilesson.

- Do children understand that dialogue should be read the way the characters would say it?

- Are they beginning to recognize the different ways authors describe how a character is speaking?

- Do they use the terms *talk* and *speak* correctly?

## Minilesson

To help children think about the minilesson principle, engage them in a short demonstration and discussion of reading dialogue aloud. Here is an example.

- Show page 2 from *Lots of Snow*, covering all but the first sentence with card stock.

  Remember this story about the kids who want to play in the snow? The characters do a lot of talking in the story. Let's reread some parts and think about how they say things.

- Read the first sentence with feeling.

  How does Rosa feel about the snow? Why do you think the author wrote that Rosa cried when she said the words?

- Make sure children understand that *cried* is used here to show that Rosa speaks in an excited voice, using the illustration to assist.

  Let's write the word *cried* to remember it later as a way a character can speak.

- Add *cried* to the chart paper in a speech bubble. Write the minilesson principle on the chart.

- Uncover the next sentence and repeat the activity, and then repeat with other pages with dialogue. As you do, add *said*, *shouted*, and *asked* to the chart, each in a different-color speech bubble.

How do the words sound differently when a character says words than when a character cries, shouts, or asks?

## Have a Try

Invite the children to practice reading the dialogue with a partner.

▶ Show page 9 from *Up, Up, and Away*.

> Here, the words are in a speech bubble, and the girl is saying, "I feel like a bird." Use the chart we made to practice saying the words in different ways with your partner.

## Summarize and Apply

Summarize the learning and remind children to read the talking in a book the way the character said it.

> Why should you read the way the character says it?

> When you read today, see if you find any characters talking. Practice reading the words the way the character says them while you whisper read.

## Share

Following independent work time, gather children together in the meeting area in a circle to share how to read aloud the talking in the book the way the character said it.

> Did anyone notice characters talking in your book today?

▶ Ask volunteers to show the pages and read the words in capital letters, assisting as needed.

## Extend the Lesson (Optional)

After assessing children's understanding, you might decide to extend the learning.

▶ Write simple dialogue on large speech bubbles. Have children say the dialogue in different ways to show how the speaker is feeling.

▶ As you read books with new words to describe how a character is speaking or feeling (e.g., whispered, laughed), add to the chart and talk about how that word affects the way the character speaks.

### Read the talk the way the character said it.

cried

said

shouted

asked

## Assessment

After you have taught the minilessons in this umbrella, observe children talking and writing about their reading across instructional contexts: interactive read-aloud, independent reading and literacy work, guided reading, shared reading, and book club. Use *The Literacy Continuum* (Fountas and Pinnell 2017) to observe children's reading and writing behaviors across instructional contexts.

▶ What evidence do you have of new understandings related to maintaining fluency?

- Can children identify periods, question marks, and exclamation points?
- Do they reflect the punctuation in their voices when they read aloud?
- Can children read words in bold print or capital letters and make them sound important?
- How do they talk about changes in a reader's voice depending on the type of punctuation, bold words, or capital letters in a story?
- Are children attempting to make their reading sound smooth and interesting?
- Are they beginning to use phrasing by putting their words together?
- Do children notice dialogue and begin to read it the way the character said it?
- Do they understand the terms *period, question mark, exclamation point, voice, capital letters, bold, stress,* and *pausing*?

▶ In what other ways, beyond the scope of this umbrella, are children talking about fluency?

- Do children talk about why an author decided to use a particular type of punctuation to match the meaning of the words in other books?
- Are children able to identify why an author chooses special types of print, such as bold words or capital letters, in other books?

Use your observations to determine the next umbrella you will teach. You may also consult Minilessons Across the Year (p. 51) for guidance.

## Link to Writing

After teaching the minilessons in this umbrella, help children link the new learning to their writing or drawing about reading:

▶ Encourage children to write or dictate sentences to correspond to their drawings, using periods, question marks, exclamation points, bold letters, or capital letters to match the intent of the sentence. As they read their writing back to you, encourage them to read with fluency and feeling.

Throughout the year, children will respond to what they read in a reader's notebook. These lessons help children use this important tool for independent literacy learning. At the beginning of the year, first graders will create mostly drawings in response to texts, but as the year progresses, they will increasingly use writing, too. All opportunities for drawing and writing about reading support the children in thinking about texts and articulating their understandings.

# 4 Writing About Reading

## Minilessons in This Umbrella

**RML1**    Collect your thinking in a reader's notebook.

**RML2**    Draw and write about yourself and the things you love.

**RML3**    Draw and write about your family.

**RML4**    Draw and write about your friends.

**RML5**    Draw and write about the things you like to do at home.

**RML6**    Draw and write about the things you like to do at school.

**RML7**    Draw and write about the places you like to go.

## Before Teaching Umbrella 1 Minilessons

The minilessons in this umbrella are examples of how to teach children to use the All About Me section of *Reader's Notebook: Primary* (Fountas and Pinnell 2014), but any reader's notebook can be used (see p. 46 for more information). The goal is for children to have a consistent place to collect their thinking, which can serve as a foundation for choosing books. Before teaching these minilessons, it would be helpful to do the following:

▶ Introduce the children to independent reading and how to select books from the classroom library (see Section One for minilessons on using the classroom library).

▶ Provide opportunities for children to hear and discuss books through interactive read-aloud. The All About Me section of *Reader's Notebook: Primary* is a place for children to draw and write about themselves, their families, and friends and to share about themselves as authors. Experiences with books will support them in thinking about their lives.

Use the following books from the *Fountas & Pinnell Classroom™ Interactive Read-Aloud Collection* text sets or choose similar books from your library:

**Learning and Playing Together: School**

*Elizabeti's School* by Stephanie Stuve-Bodeen

*A Fine, Fine School* by Sharon Creech

**The Importance of Friendship**

*Wallace's Lists* by Barbara Bottner and Gerald Kruglik

**Taking Care of Each Other: Family**

*A Birthday Basket for Tía* by Pat Mora

*The Relatives Came* by Cynthia Rylant

*Papá and Me* by Arthur Dorros

As you read aloud and enjoy these texts together, help children think about themselves and draw and write about books.

**School**

**Friendship**

**Family**

**Reader's Notebook**

**Reading Minilesson Principle**
# Collect your thinking in your reader's notebook.

### Introducing a Reader's Notebook

## You Will Need

- a reader's notebook for each child
- *Reader's Notebook: Primary* or chart paper resembling the cover of *Reader's Notebook: Primary*

## Academic Language / Important Vocabulary

- notebook
- cover

## Goal

Understand a reader's notebook is a special place to collect their thinking about themselves and books.

## Rationale

Children need to learn how to respond to reading in different modalities for a variety of purposes and audiences. A reader's notebook is a place for them to explain more about themselves as authors, keep records of their reading experiences, and share their thinking about books through drawing and writing.

## Assess Learning

Observe children when they use a reader's notebook. Notice if there is evidence of new learning based on the goal of this minilesson.

- Are children able to talk about their drawings on the front cover, exhibiting an understanding that the reader's notebook is unique to them?
- Do children show that they understand the purpose of a reader's notebook?

## Minilesson

To help children think about the minilesson principle, engage them in an exploration of a reader's notebook. Here is an example.

- Give each child a reader's notebook.

  Look through the reader's notebook. When you are finished, close the notebook.

- Provide one or two minutes for children to look at the notebooks.

  Turn and talk with your partner about what you notice about the reader's notebook.

- If the children are using a plain notebook, you will want to talk about what will go in it. You might have them place colored sticky notes as tabs to mark the three sections.

- Show the cover of *Reader's Notebook: Primary* or the prepared chart paper of the cover.

  The reader's notebook has three sections for you to collect your thinking. Open the front of the notebook to the orange tab that says All About Me. What do you think you will draw and write about in this section?

  Now turn to the blue tab that says Books I Read. What do you think you will draw and write about here?

  Find the green tab in the last section at the back of the book that says Letters and Words. How do you think you will use this section?

## Have a Try

Invite the children to talk with a partner about what they will draw on the cover of a reader's notebook.

> Think about what you would like to draw on the front cover. Turn and talk with a partner about what you plan to draw.

▶ After time for discussion, ask a few volunteers to share.

## Summarize and Apply

Summarize the learning and remind children to think about how they will use a reader's notebook.

> What can you do in a reader's notebook?

> During independent work time today, illustrate the front cover of your reader's notebook. First, write your name, school, and grade on the cover.

▶ Model the drawing and writing on the chart paper.

> Once you have written your name and illustrated the front cover, it will be your special notebook. Be ready to share your drawing when we meet after independent work time.

## Share

Following independent work time, gather children together in the meeting area in groups of three to share their drawings.

> Show the drawing you made on the cover of your reader's notebook and talk about your drawing.

## Extend the Lesson (Optional)

After assessing children's understanding, you might decide to extend the learning.

▶ Have children add to the front cover over time and integrate the use of a reader's notebook to collect their thinking about books from other instructional contexts, including interactive read-aloud and guided reading.

▶ Make color copies of the cover illustrations and display them on a bulletin board titled *We Love to Write and Draw About Reading*.

Section 4: Writing About Reading

**Reading Minilesson Principle**
# Draw and write about yourself and the things you love.

## Introducing a Reader's Notebook

### You Will Need

- a text about self-identity, such as *A Fine, Fine School* by Sharon Creech, from Text Set: School
- *Reader's Notebook: Primary* or chart paper resembling the Me page from *Reader's Notebook: Primary*
- markers
- a reader's notebook for each child

### Academic Language / Important Vocabulary

- reader's notebook

### Continuum Connection

- Draw or write about everyday actions noticed in a text: playing, making things, eating, getting dressed, bathing, cooking, shopping (p. 176)

## Goal

Personalize a reader's notebook by drawing and writing about themselves.

## Rationale

When children draw and write about themselves in a reader's notebook, they communicate what makes them unique and special. As children share about themselves with classmates, they become a community of readers and writers with shared interests who learn to select books independently and recommend books to others.

## Assess Learning

Observe children when they use a reader's notebook. Notice if there is evidence of new learning based on the goal of this minilesson.

- ▶ Do the children draw and write about themselves and what they love?
- ▶ Do they show their thinking about themselves in their drawing and writing?
- ▶ Do children use the term *reader's notebook* in conversation?

## Minilesson

To help children think about the minilesson principle, engage them in a short discussion of using a reader's notebook to tell about themselves. Here is an example.

> Remember how you learned about the fun things Tillie loved to do on the weekends in *A Fine, Fine School*? Think about the ways the author and illustrator used words and pictures to show you what Tillie loved to do.

▶ Revisit page 6 of *A Fine, Fine School*.

> What do you notice? Now, think about the things you love to do. Turn and talk about those things.

▶ Show the Me page from *Reader's Notebook: Primary* or the prepared chart paper.

> In a reader's notebook, you have a place to draw and write about the things you love to do on the Me page. Help me think about the Me page of my notebook. What could I draw and write on this page?

▶ Use children's responses as you model drawing and writing about yourself and the things you love to do on the page.

## Have a Try

Invite the children to talk with a partner about what they will draw on the Me page.

> Open your reader's notebook to the orange tab that says All About Me and find the Me page. On this page, you can draw and write about yourself. Think about the ideas you talked about. Turn and talk to a partner about what you are going to draw.

▶ After time for discussion, ask a few children to share what they are going to draw and write on the Me page.

## Summarize and Apply

Summarize the learning and remind children to use a reader's notebook to tell about themselves.

> How can you use a reader's notebook page to show your thinking about yourself? Think about what you told your partner you are going to put on your Me page.

> During independent work time, draw a picture to tell about yourself on your Me page. You can write about yourself on the lines under the drawing. Use only one page today to tell about yourself.

▶ Review your Me page. If children are using an alternative reader's notebook, show them where to label a page *Me*.

## Share

Following independent work time, gather children together in the meeting area to share their drawing and writing.

> Turn and talk to a partner about the Me page in your notebook. Listen to your partner and answer questions about your drawing and writing.

▶ After time for discussion, invite one or two pairs to share with the whole group.

## Extend the Lesson (Optional)

After assessing children's understanding, you might decide to extend the learning over several days.

▶ Assist children, as needed, with adding to the writing section of the Me page.

▶ Have children work together to paint an All About Us class mural, using ideas from their notebooks.

Section 4: Writing About Reading

## Introducing a Reader's Notebook

### You Will Need

- a book about family members, such as *Papá and Me* by Arthur Dorros, from Text Set: Family
- *Reader's Notebook: Primary* or chart paper resembling the My Family page from *Reader's Notebook: Primary*
- markers
- a reader's notebook for each child

### Academic Language / Important Vocabulary

- reader's notebook

### Continuum Connection

- Draw or write about everyday actions noticed in a text: playing, making things, eating, getting dressed, bathing, cooking, shopping (p. 176)

### Goal

Personalize a reader's notebook by drawing and writing about their families.

### Rationale

When young children draw and write about their families, they think about the special people in their lives. This will help them to make connections to characters in stories with families.

### Assess Learning

Observe children when they use a reader's notebook. Notice if there is evidence of new learning based on the goal of this minilesson.

- Are children able to draw and write about their families and what they love doing together?
- Do they use the term *reader's notebook* in conversation?

## Minilesson

To help children think about the minilesson principle, engage them in a short discussion of using a reader's notebook to draw and write about families. Here is an example.

> You learned of the special things the boy does with his father when you read *Papá and Me*. Listen as I reread a few pages and think about how the author and illustrator showed you some of the things the boy does with his dad.

- Revisit pages 3–6.

> What do you notice? What are some special things you like to do with people in your family?

- Show the My Family page from *Reader's Notebook: Primary* with information about your family or the prepared chart paper with information about your family.

> You can tell about your family and all the things you like to do together in a reader's notebook. Here is what I wrote and drew on the page in a reader's notebook.

- Read the words and describe the drawing.

> Turn and talk to a partner about what you notice.

- After time for discussion, ask volunteers to share their thinking.

## Have a Try

Invite the children to talk with a partner about what they will draw and write.

> Think about the My Family page in the reader's notebook. Turn and talk to a partner about who is in your family and what you love to do together.

▶ After time for discussion, ask a few children to share what they are going to draw and write on the My Family page.

## Summarize and Apply

Summarize the learning and remind children to use a reader's notebook to tell about their family.

> How can you use a reader's notebook page to show your thinking about your family? Today, during independent work time, draw a picture of your family and the things you like to do together. You can also write something about your family on the lines. Think about what you talked about with your partner. Draw and write only on the My Family page in your notebook. Bring your notebook when we meet so you can share.

▶ If children are using a plain reader's notebook, show them where to label a page *My Family*.

## Share

Following independent work time, gather children together in the meeting area in groups of three to share a reader's notebook.

> Show your My Family page and talk about the things you like to do with your family. Remember to listen to each other and answer questions about your drawing and writing.

## Extend the Lesson (Optional)

After assessing children's understanding, you might decide to extend the learning over several days.

▶ Provide follow-up minilessons to teach how to add details to their drawings.

▶ Use what children have written in a reader's notebook to help them choose books to read that will interest them.

My Family

I have a daughter named Liza. We like to kayak on the river by our house.

## Introducing a Reader's Notebook

### You Will Need

- a book about friendship that shows friends doing activities together, such as: *Wallace's Lists* by Barbara Bottner and Gerald Kruglik, from Text Set: Friendship
- *Reader's Notebook: Primary* or chart paper resembling the My Friends page from *Reader's Notebook: Primary*
- markers
- a reader's notebook for each child

### Academic Language / Important Vocabulary

- reader's notebook

### Continuum Connection

- Draw or write about everyday actions noticed in a text: playing, making things, eating, getting dressed, bathing, cooking, shopping (p. 176)

## Goal

Draw and write about themselves and friends in a reader's notebook.

## Rationale

Young children read many books about friendship and talk about how to care for others. When they draw and write about their friends, they make deeper connections to the characters and themes in the books they listen to and read.

## Assess Learning

Observe children when they use a reader's notebook. Notice if there is evidence of new learning based on the goal of this minilesson.

- ▶ Are children able to draw and write something about their friends?
- ▶ Can they explain what they like to do with their friends?
- ▶ Do they use the term *reader's notebook* in conversation?

## Minilesson

To help children think about the minilesson principle, engage them in a short discussion of using a reader's notebook to draw and write about their friends. Here is an example.

> In *Wallace's Lists* you learned about some things Wallace and his friend Albert enjoyed doing together.

- ▶ Revisit pages 21–25.

> What are some fun adventures Wallace and Albert had together? Turn and talk to a partner about some fun adventures you like to have or fun things you like to do with your friends.

- ▶ Show the My Friends page from *Reader's Notebook: Primary* or the prepared chart paper.

> Here is the My Friends page of the reader's notebook. What could I draw on this page to show something fun to do with friends?

- ▶ Sketch an adventure or fun thing to do on the page. Ask children to describe what you should draw. Then, ask for ideas about what can be written on the page about the adventure or fun thing to do, and write a sentence or two based on the children's responses. Be sure children understand the things they do with their friends do not need to be adventures.

## Have a Try

Invite the children to talk with a partner about what they will draw and write in a reader's notebook.

> Friends can do many special things together, just like Wallace and Albert like having adventures. Think about what you like to do with friends. Turn and talk with a partner about what you plan to draw and write.

▸ After time for discussion, ask a few children to share what they are going to draw and write on the My Friends page.

## Summarize and Apply

Summarize the learning and remind children to use a reader's notebook to tell about friends.

> How could you use your reader's notebook page to think about and tell something about your friends?

> Today, during independent work time, draw and write about your friends and some of the things you like to do with them. Think about what you talked about with your partner.

▸ If children are using a plain notebook, show where to label a page *My Friends*.

## Share

Following independent work time, have children sit with a partner in the meeting area to share their drawing and writing.

> Turn and talk to your partner about your drawing and writing you added to the My Friends page.

## Extend the Lesson (Optional)

After assessing children's understanding, you might decide to extend the learning over several days.

▸ Reference the My Friends page during interactive read-aloud or other instructional contexts to support children in making connections and developing opinions about characters. Have them think about what they like about their friends and if they would like to be friends with characters in books.

▸ **Drawing/Writing About Reading** Provide opportunities for children to write stories or make books about their friends during writing time or in the writing center.

**Reading Minilesson Principle**
# Draw and write about the things you like to do at home.

## Introducing a Reader's Notebook

### You Will Need

- *Reader's Notebook: Primary* or chart paper resembling the Things I Like to Do at Home page from the *Reader's Notebook: Primary*
- markers
- a text about doing things at home, such as *A Birthday Basket for Tía* by Pat Mora, from Text Set: Family
- a reader's notebook for each child

### Academic Language / Important Vocabulary

- reader's notebook

### Continuum Connection

- Draw or write about everyday actions noticed in a text: playing, making things, eating, getting dressed, bathing, cooking, shopping (p. 176)

## Goal

Draw and write about things they like to do at home in a reader's notebook.

## Rationale

When children draw and write about things they like to do at home, they begin to define their interests and preferences. This will enable them to select books they will enjoy reading.

## Assess Learning

Observe children when they use a reader's notebook. Notice if there is evidence of new learning based on the goal of this minilesson.

- ▶ Do children draw and write about things they like to do at home?
- ▶ Is there evidence they thought about the things they like to do at home and included those in their drawing and writing?
- ▶ Do they use the term *reader's notebook* in conversation?

## Minilesson

To help children think about the minilesson principle, engage them in a short discussion of using a reader's notebook to draw and write about what they like to do at home. Here is an example.

- ▶ Show the Things I Like to Do at Home page from the *Reader's Notebook: Primary* or the prepared chart paper. Show the cover of *A Birthday Basket for Tía.*

  When we read this story, we learned that Cecilia made a special birthday basket for her aunt's birthday. She gathered things they liked to do at home together.

- ▶ Revisit pages 9–10.

  This page makes me think of how much I like cooking at home. What could I draw and write in a reader's notebook if I enjoy cooking at home, like Cecilia and her aunt?

- ▶ Using children's responses, model how to draw and write on the reader's notebook page.

## Have a Try

Invite the children to talk with a partner about what they will draw and write in a reader's notebook.

▶ Revisit pages 11–12 of *A Birthday Basket for Tía*.

> Growing flowers is another thing they enjoyed doing at home. Turn and talk about the things you like to do at home you could draw and write about in your reader's notebook.

## Summarize and Apply

Summarize the learning and remind children to use a reader's notebook to tell about what they like to do at home.

> How could you use a reader's notebook page to tell about things you like to do at home?

> During independent work time, draw and write about things you like to do at home. Draw and write only on the Things I Like to Do at Home page. Bring your reader's notebook when we meet so you can share.

▶ If children are using a plain reader's notebook, show them where to label a page *Things I Like to Do at Home*.

Things I Like to Do at Home

I like to cook.
Chicken soup is my favorite.

## Share

Following independent work time, gather children together in the meeting area in a circle to share a reader's notebook.

> As we go around the circle, show your Things I Like to Do at Home page in your reader's notebook and tell what you wrote and drew on the page.

## Extend the Lesson (Optional)

After assessing children's understanding, you might decide to extend the learning over several days.

▶ Provide opportunities during writers' workshop for children to write or make books about the things they like to do at home.

▶ **Drawing/Writing About Reading** If needed, use interactive writing to demonstrate how to add writing to their pictures.

## RML 6
**WAR.U1.RML6**

### Reading Minilesson Principle
## Draw and write about the things you like to do at school.

### Introducing a Reader's Notebook

#### You Will Need

▶ a text about school, such as: *Elizabeti's School* by Stephanie Stuve-Bodeen, from Text Set: School

▶ *Reader's Notebook: Primary* or chart paper resembling the Things I Like to Do page from the *Reader's Notebook: Primary*

▶ markers

▶ a reader's notebook for each child

#### Academic Language / Important Vocabulary

▶ reader's notebook

#### Continuum Connection

▶ Draw or write about everyday actions noticed in a text: playing, making things, eating, getting dressed, bathing, cooking, shopping (p. 176)

### Goal

Draw and write about themselves at school in a reader's notebook.

### Rationale

A reader's notebook is a place for children to discover their interests and develop their reading identities. When children think and draw about what they like to do at school, they become more aware of their interests, which will help them choose books they will enjoy.

### Assess Learning

Observe children when they use a reader's notebook. Notice if there is evidence of new learning based on the goal of this minilesson.

▶ Do the children draw and write about the things they like to do at school?

▶ Are they able to explain their drawings to others?

▶ Do they use the term *reader's notebook* in conversation?

## Minilesson

To help children think about the minilesson principle, engage them in a short discussion of using a reader's notebook to draw and write about what they like to do at school. Here is an example.

▶ Revisit pages 13–14 of *Elizabeti's School*.

Elizabeti liked to play outside at recess. What things do you like to do during recess?

▶ Revisit page 15.

Elizabeti is doing math in the classroom. What are some things you like to do in the classroom?

▶ Show the Things I Like to Do at School page from *Reader's Notebook: Primary*, or the prepared chart paper.

What ideas could I write and draw about in a reader's notebook?

▶ Based on children's responses, write and draw on the page, sharing your thinking aloud as you write and draw.

## Have a Try

Invite the children to talk with a partner about what they will draw and write in a reader's notebook.

> Think about what you like to do at school. Turn and talk to a partner about what you plan to draw and write about.

▶ After time for discussion, ask a few children to share what they are going to draw and write on the Things I Like to Do at School page.

## Summarize and Apply

Summarize the learning and remind children to use a reader's notebook to tell about what they like to do at school.

> How could you use a reader's notebook page to think and tell about things you like to do at school?

> Today, during independent work time, you will draw and write about the things you like to do at school. Think about what you talked about with your partner. Use the lines below to write about your picture. Draw and write only on the Things I Like to Do at School page. Bring your reader's notebook when we meet so you can share.

▶ If children are using a plain reader's notebook, show them where to label a page *Things I Like to Do at School*.

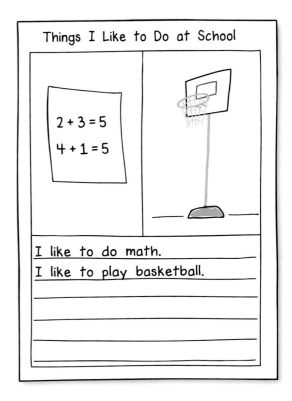

## Share

Following independent work time, gather children together in the meeting area in groups of three to share their drawing and writing.

> Show the Things I Like to Do at School page. Talk about what you wrote and drew on the page.

## Extend the Lesson (Optional)

After assessing children's understanding, you might decide to extend the learning over several days.

▶ Provide opportunities for children to continue to add to their drawing and writing about things they like to do at school in writers' workshop or in the writing center.

▶ Reference the Things I Like to Do at School page as children choose books to encourage them to choose books about their interests.

Section 4: Writing About Reading

**Reading Minilesson Principle**
## Draw and write about the places you like to go.

**Introducing a Reader's Notebook**

### You Will Need

- a book with interesting settings, such as *The Relatives Came* by Cynthia Rylant, from Text Set: Family
- *Reader's Notebook: Primary* or chart paper resembling the Places I Like to Go page from the *Reader's Notebook: Primary*
- markers
- a reader's notebook for each child

### Academic Language / Important Vocabulary

- reader's notebook

### Continuum Connection

- Draw or write about everyday actions noticed in a text: playing, making things, eating, getting dressed, bathing, cooking, shopping (p. 176)

### Goal

Draw and write about places they like to go in a reader's notebook.

### Rationale

When children share their thinking about places they like to go, they identify and record their interests. In doing so, children learn that they can choose and read about things that interest them, which supports them in choosing topics they want to draw and write about.

### Assess Learning

Observe children when they use a reader's notebook. Notice if there is evidence of new learning based on the goal of this minilesson.

- Are children able to draw and write about special places they like to go?
- Are they able to talk about their drawing and writing?
- Do they use the term *reader's notebook* in conversation?

## Minilesson

To help children think about the minilesson principle, engage them in a short discussion of using a reader's notebook to draw and write about where they like to go. Here is an example.

- Show the cover of *The Relatives Came*.

    Remember when this family drove from Virginia to visit relatives in *The Relatives Came*? Think about how the author and illustrator showed you the place this family liked to go.

- Revisit pages 5–6 and pages 9–10.

    Where does this family like to go?

    This family liked to take road trips to visit relatives.

- Show the Places I Like to Go page from *Reader's Notebook: Primary*, or the prepared chart paper.

    What ideas could I write and draw about in a reader's notebook?

- Based on children's responses, write and draw on the page, sharing your thinking aloud as you write and draw.

## Have a Try

Invite the children to talk in groups of three about what they will draw and write in a reader's notebook.

> Think about the places you like to go. What will you draw and write about? Turn and talk in groups of three about what you plan to draw and write on the Places I Like to Go page.

## Summarize and Apply

Summarize the learning and remind children to use a reader's notebook to tell about places they like to go.

> How could you use a reader's notebook page to think about and tell about places you like to go? Today, during independent work time, draw a picture of and write about the places you like to go. Draw and write only on the Places I Like to Go page of your notebook. Be ready to share your work when we meet.

▶ If children are using a plain reader's notebook, show them where to label a page *Places I Like to Go.*

## Share

Following independent work time, gather children together in the meeting area to share their drawing and writing.

> Share what you drew and wrote on the Places I Like to Go page with a partner. Remember to listen and ask each other questions about your drawings.

## Extend the Lesson (Optional)

After assessing children's understanding, you might decide to extend the learning over several days.

▶ Provide opportunities for the children to continue to add to their drawing and writing about places they like to go during writers' workshop.

▶ Reference the Places I Like to Go page of the reader's notebook when children self-select books to encourage them to choose books about their interests.

▶ **Drawing/Writing About Reading** Use interactive or shared writing to support children in adding labels or simple sentences to their reader's notebook pages.

## Assessment

After you have taught the minilessons in this umbrella, observe children as they talk and write about their reading across instructional contexts: interactive read-aloud, independent reading and literacy work, guided reading, shared reading, and book club. Use *The Literacy Continuum* (Fountas and Pinnell 2017) to observe children's reading and writing behaviors across instructional contexts.

▶ What evidence do you have of new understandings related to the All About Me section of *Reader's Notebook: Primary*?

- Are children able to draw and write about themselves, their friends, and family?

- Do they identify their interests, drawing and writing about things they like to do and places they like to go?

- Are children beginning to think about their interests when selecting books to read independently?

- Are they using the term *reader's notebook*?

▶ What other parts of the reader's notebook might you introduce to the children based on your observations?

- Are children able to distinguish between fiction and nonfiction books?

- How are they sharing their opinions about books?

- Do you see evidence that they are drawing and writing about books they read in meaningful ways?

Use your observations to determine the next umbrella you will teach. You may also consult Minilessons Across the Year (p. 51) for guidance.

## Minilessons in This Umbrella

**RML1**    Make a list of books you love.

**RML2**    Make a list of authors you love.

**RML3**    Make a list of illustrators you love.

**RML4**    Make a list of characters you love.

**RML5**    Write and draw to show things you like to read about.

**RML6**    Write and draw to show things you like to write about.

**RML7**    Collect interesting words and phrases from books.

## Before Teaching Umbrella 2 Minilessons

Before children use a reader's notebook, they should have read and discussed a variety of high-quality picture books, including several by the same author and illustrator. It would be helpful to complete several author and illustrator studies before introducing these minilessons. The minilessons in this umbrella are based on *Reader's Notebook: Primary* (Fountas and Pinnell 2014) and use the following texts from the *Fountas & Pinnell Classroom™ Interactive Read-Aloud Collection* as examples. However, select books based on your children's experiences and interests, books they have loved listening to, talking about, and sharing with one another.

**Learning and Playing Together: School**

  *David's Drawings* by Cathryn Falwell

  *Jamaica's Blue Marker* by Juanita Havill

**Mo Willems: Having Fun with Humor**

  *Knuffle Bunny: A Cautionary Tale*

  *I Am Invited to a Party!*

**Poetic Language**

  *Puddles* by Jonathan London

  *Mud* by Mary Lyn Ray

  *All the Colors of the Earth* by Sheila Hamanaka

**Living and Working Together: Community**

  *Be My Neighbor* by Maya Ajmera and J. Ivanko

**Nonfiction: Questions and Answers**

  *Best Foot Forward* by Ingo Arndt

As you read aloud and enjoy these texts together, help children

- talk about their favorite books and tell why they love them,
- think about ideas they get from books to use in their writing, and
- notice memorable and interesting words.

**School**

**Mo Willems**

**Poetic Language**

**Community**

**Questions and Answers**

**Reader's Notebook**

**Reading Minilesson Principle**
# Make a list of books you love.

### You Will Need

- *Reader's Notebook: Primary* or chart paper resembling the Books I Love page from *Reader's Notebook: Primary*

- markers

- two or three favorite books, such as the following:

  - *David's Drawings* by Cathryn Falwell, from Text Set: School

  - *Puddles* by Jonathan London, from Text Set: Poetic Texts

- basket of class favorite books

- a reader's notebook for each child

### Academic Language / Important Vocabulary

- author

- title

- cover

- reader's notebook

### Continuum Connection

- Independently record in reader's notebook the titles, authors, and illustrators of texts (p. 176)

## Goal

Make a list of favorite books in a reader's notebook.

## Rationale

When children use a reader's notebook to make a list of books they love, they think about what they like to read for future book choices. This will help develop their tastes and preferences as readers.

## Assess Learning

Observe children when they use a reader's notebook to list books they love. Notice if there is evidence of new learning based on the goal of this minilesson.

- Are children able to write the title and draw a picture on the Books I Love page?

- Can children articulate why they chose a particular book to write and draw about?

- Do they use the terms *author*, *title*, *cover*, and *reader's notebook*?

## Minilesson

To help children think about the minilesson principle, engage them in a short demonstration of listing books in a reader's notebook. Here is an example.

- Show a blank Books I Love page from *Reader's Notebook: Primary* or the blank prepared chart paper.

  > This page is from the reader's notebook. It says Books I Love. What do you think you would put on this page?

  > On this page, you write the title of books and draw the front cover of the books you read or want to read.

- Show two books the children have enjoyed, such as *David's Drawings* and *Puddles*.

  > What could you write or draw about these books on the Books I Love page?

- Ask volunteers to point to the space on the notebook page to add the title and cover sketch. Invite children to assist in the writing and drawing if appropriate.

## Have a Try

Invite the children to talk with a partner about what they will write and draw in a reader's notebook.

▶ Show the book basket of favorite class books.

> Think about what you will write and draw on the Books I Love page. These are favorite books from our class that you can choose to write and draw about, or you may choose a different one. Turn and talk to a partner about the book you plan to choose and what you will write and draw.

## Summarize and Apply

Summarize the learning and remind children to think about books they would add to the list in a reader's notebook.

▶ Hand each child *Reader's Notebook: Primary* and have the children open to the Books I Love page (or provide a plain notebook and show them where to label a page *Books I Love*).

> What can you write and draw about on this page?

> During independent work time, choose a book to write about. Choose a book from the basket or choose one of your own. Write the title of the book on the line and draw a picture of the book's cover.

## Share

Following independent work time, gather children in the meeting area in a circle to share what they wrote.

> As we go around the circle, share your Books I Love page. Talk about the book you chose and why you chose the book.

## Extend the Lesson (Optional)

After assessing children's understanding, you might decide to extend the learning.

▶ Encourage children to use their list in a reader's notebook to help them find similar books to read.

▶ Encourage children to use their list in a reader's notebook when they select a book for a book talk.

# RML2
## WAR.U2.RML2

**Reading Minilesson Principle**
## Make a list of authors you love.

### Using a Reader's Notebook

#### You Will Need

- *Reader's Notebook: Primary* or chart paper resembling the Authors I Love page from *Reader's Notebook: Primary*
- markers
- multiple text sets by the same author, such as Kevin Henkes and Mo Willems
- basket of books by favorite authors
- a reader's notebook for each child

#### Academic Language / Important Vocabulary

- author
- reader's notebook

#### Continuum Connection

- Independently record in Reader's Notebook the titles, authors, and illustrators of texts (p. 176)

### Goal

Make a list of favorite authors in a reader's notebook.

### Rationale

When children use a reader's notebook to make lists of their favorite authors, they are encouraged to think about the writing styles of authors and why they are drawn to certain books. They become articulate about their tastes as readers.

### Assess Learning

Observe children when they use a reader's notebook to list favorite authors. Notice if there is evidence of new learning based on the goal of this minilesson.

- Do children add the name of an author they love and draw a picture that connects to a book by the author in a reader's notebook?
- Can children explain something they love about the author?
- Do they use the terms *author* and *reader's notebook* correctly?

## Minilesson

To help children think about the minilesson principle, engage them in a short demonstration of how to list favorite authors in a reader's notebook. Here is an example.

- Show a blank Authors I Love page from *Reader's Notebook: Primary* or the blank prepared chart paper.

    This is another page from your reader's notebook. It says Authors I Love. What do you think you will write or draw about on this page?

- Hold up several books by a favorite author, such as Kevin Henkes. Write the name of the author on the Authors I Love page or the chart paper. Add a drawing to represent one of the book covers (e.g., *Lilly's Big Day*).

    Turn and talk about what I wrote and drew on the page.

- After time for discussion, have volunteers share their noticings. Point out that the spelling of the author's name matches the book cover and is written on the lines.

- Show multiple books by another favorite author, such as *Knuffle Bunny: A Cautionary Tale* and *I Am Invited to a Party!* by Mo Willems.

    What could we draw and write on the Authors I Love page about Mo Willems?

- If appropriate, have children assist with adding Mo Willems' name to the page and drawing a sketch that connects to a book cover.

## Have a Try

Invite the children to talk with a partner about what they will draw and write in a reader's notebook.

▶ Show the basket of books of favorite authors.

> Here are books by some of our favorite authors. You can choose an author of one of these books, or a different one. Turn and talk to a partner about which author you plan to draw and write about.

▶ After discussion, ask a few volunteers to share.

## Summarize and Apply

Summarize the learning and remind children to think about favorite authors they would like to draw and write about.

▶ Have the children open to the Authors I Love page in *Reader's Notebook: Primary* (or provide an alternative notebook and show them where to label a page *Authors I Love*).

> What did you learn about how to use this page?

> During independent work time, you will choose a book by a favorite author to write and draw about. Add the name of the author to the Authors I Love page and add a drawing of the book cover. Bring your reader's notebook when we meet so you can share.

## Share

Following independent work time, gather children in the meeting area in groups of three to share their drawing and writing.

> Show your Authors I Love page and talk about the author you chose to add to your list and the drawing you made. Tell your group why you chose the author.

## Extend the Lesson (Optional)

After assessing children's understanding, you might decide to extend the learning.

▶ Encourage children to use their list in a reader's notebook to choose other books by an author.

▶ Visit authors' websites to learn more about children's favorite authors.

Section 4: Writing About Reading

**Reading Minilesson Principle**
# Make a list of illustrators you love.

## Using a Reader's Notebook

### You Will Need

- *Reader's Notebook: Primary* or chart paper resembling the Illustrators I Love page from *Reader's Notebook: Primary*
- markers
- multiple text sets by the same illustrators, such as Kevin Henkes or Mo Willems
- sticky notes
- a reader's notebook for each child

### Academic Language / Important Vocabulary

- illustrator
- illustration
- reader's notebook

### Continuum Connection

- Understand that an illustrator created the pictures in the book (p. 36)
- Independently record in Reader's Notebook the titles, authors, and illustrators of texts (p. 176)

## Goal

Make a list of favorite illustrators in a reader's notebook.

## Rationale

When children use a reader's notebook to list illustrators they love, they are encouraged to think about the styles of different artists. This will help them to begin thinking about why they are drawn to certain illustrations and provide ideas for their own illustrations. Their aesthetic senses are enhanced.

## Assess Learning

Observe children when they use a reader's notebook to list favorite illustrators. Notice if there is evidence of new learning based on the goal of this minilesson.

- Are children able to write the name of a favorite illustrator on the Illustrators I Love page?
- Can they explain why they like an illustrator?
- Do they use the terms *illustrator*, *illustration*, and *reader's notebook*?

## Minilesson

To help children think about the minilesson principle, engage them in a short demonstration of listing favorite illustrators in a reader's notebook. Here is an example.

- Show a blank Illustrators I Love page from *Reader's Notebook: Primary* or the prepared chart paper.

    This is another page from a reader's notebook. It says Illustrators I Love. What could you write or draw on this page?

- Write the name of a favorite illustrator (e.g., Kevin Henkes) on the Illustrators I Love page or on the chart paper. Add a drawing to represent one of the book covers (e.g., *Lilly's Big Day*). Show the page or chart paper and several books by Kevin Henkes.

    Here are several books by Kevin Henkes and the Illustrators I Love page. Turn and talk to a partner about what I wrote and drew on the page.

- After time for discussion, volunteers share their noticings. Point out that the spelling of the illustrator's name matches the book cover and is written on the lines.

- Repeat the activity, having children choose an additional illustrator whose work the children know and love, such as Mo Willems.

## Have a Try

Invite the children to talk with a partner about why they like a particular illustrator.

> Turn and talk to a partner about what you like about Kevin Henkes or Mo Willems.

▶ After discussion, ask a few volunteers to say which illustrator they like best. Add each child's name to a sticky note and place on the chart next to the favorite illustrator.

## Summarize and Apply

Summarize the learning and remind children to make a list of illustrators they love in a reader's notebook.

▶ Have the children open to the Illustrators I Love page in *Reader's Notebook: Primary* (or provide an alternative notebook and show them where to label a page *Illustrators I Love*).

> Today you thought about illustrators you love and learned how to make a list of the illustrators' names in a reader's notebook. During independent work time, write about an illustrator you love in your reader's notebook. Add a drawing to show something the illustrator draws. Bring your reader's notebook when we meet so you can share.

## Share

Following independent work time, gather children in the meeting area in a circle to share their drawing and writing.

> Share your Illustrators I Love page as we go around the circle. Talk about why you chose the illustrator to add to your list.

## Extend the Lesson (Optional)

After assessing children's understanding, you might decide to extend the learning.

▶ Encourage children to add to their list in a reader's notebook as they notice books by other illustrators whose pictures they like.

▶ Visit the websites of favorite illustrators to learn more about their work.

▶ Talk about ways favorite illustrators create their drawings. Provide art materials so children can make illustrations using the same techniques.

**Reading Minilesson Principle**
# Make a list of characters you love.

## Using a Reader's Notebook

### You Will Need

- *Reader's Notebook: Primary* or chart paper resembling the Characters I Love page from *Reader's Notebook: Primary*
- markers
- several familiar books with memorable characters, such as the following:
  - *David's Drawings* by Cathryn Falwell, from Text Set: School
  - *Jamaica's Blue Marker* by Juanita Havill, from Text Set: School
  - *Knuffle Bunny: A Cautionary Tale* by Mo Willems, from Text Set: Mo Willems
- a reader's notebook for each child
- basket of books with memorable characters

### Academic Language / Important Vocabulary

- character
- reader's notebook

### Continuum Connection

- Recall important details about characters after a story is read (p. 35)
- Identify characters in a story using labels and temporary spelling (p. 176)

## Goal

Make a list of favorite characters in a reader's notebook.

## Rationale

When children develop a list of favorite characters, they think about why they connect with and enjoy certain characters in fiction books. They develop their reading interests and feel connected to the characters. The children experience empathy and enjoy humor or adventure through the character's eyes. This process deepens their understanding of the text.

## Assess Learning

Observe children when they use a reader's notebook to list favorite characters. Notice if there is evidence of new learning based on the goal of this minilesson.

- Are the children able to identify a favorite character?
- Do they write a favorite character's name on the Characters I Love page?
- Can they explain why they like a character?
- Do they use vocabulary, such as *character* and *reader's notebook*?

## Minilesson

To help children think about the minilesson principle, engage them in a short demonstration of listing favorite characters in a reader's notebook. Here is an example.

- Show the Characters I Love page from *Reader's Notebook: Primary* or the prepared chart paper with the name of a favorite character (e.g., David from *David's Drawings*). Add a quick sketch of David. Show the page to the class and the cover of *David's Drawings*.

  Why do you think I added David to the Characters I Love page in a reader's notebook?

  What special things do you remember about David?

- Show the basket of books.

  Let's think about other special characters from the books in this basket.

- Assist children with remembering favorite characters (for example, Jamaica from *Jamaica's Blue Marker*, Trixie from *Knuffle Bunny: A Cautionary Tale*).

  Where can I find the spelling of a character's name?

- Point out that some character names are on the cover, but others are in the story. Invite children to assist with writing the characters' names on the lines.

  What could I draw for each character on the page?

## Have a Try

Invite the children to talk with a partner about the character they will draw in a reader's notebook.

> Think about one of the characters you want to add to the list in your reader's notebook. Turn and talk to a partner about the character and why you like him or her.

## Summarize and Apply

Summarize the learning and remind children to think about favorite characters they would add to their list.

▶ Have the children open to the Characters I Love page in *Reader's Notebook: Primary* (or provide an alternative notebook and show them where to label a page *Characters I Love*).

> Today you learned that you can make a list of favorite characters in a reader's notebook. During independent work time, choose a favorite character to write and draw about on this page. You may choose a character from one of the books in the basket or choose another one. Bring your reader's notebook when we meet so you can share.

## Share

Following independent work time, gather children in the meeting area in groups of three to share their drawing and writing.

> Show your Characters I Love page and tell your group the name of the character you put on your list. Talk about why you chose the character.

> Did any of you choose the same character?

## Extend the Lesson (Optional)

After assessing children's understanding, you might decide to extend the learning.

▶ Encourage children to continue to add to their list in a reader's notebook as they meet new characters in their reading.

▶ As you read stories with memorable characters, invite children to talk about the things they like about the characters and what makes them interesting.

Characters I Love

David
Jamaica
Trixie

# RML5
### WAR.U2.RML5

## Reading Minilesson Principle
# Write and draw to show things you like to read about.

## Using a Reader's Notebook

### You Will Need

- *Reader's Notebook: Primary* or chart paper resembling the Things I Like to Read About page from *Reader's Notebook: Primary*
- markers
- several familiar fiction and nonfiction books, such as the following:
  - *Jamaica's Blue Marker* by Juanita Havill, from Text Set: School
  - *David's Drawings* by Cathryn Falwell, from Text Set: School
  - *Be My Neighbor* by Maya Ajmera and J. Ivanko, from Text Set: Community
  - *Best Foot Forward* by Ingo Arndt, from Text Set: Questions and Answers
- a reader's notebook for each child

### Academic Language / Important Vocabulary

- author
- title
- reader's notebook

### Continuum Connection

- Draw and write about everyday actions noticed in a text: playing, making things, eating, getting dressed, bathing, cooking, shopping (pp. 176, 178)

## Goal

Draw and write about the topics they like to read about in a reader's notebook.

## Rationale

When children tell things they like to read about, they become aware of their developing reading interests. They can use a reader's notebook as a tool to choose books they will enjoy reading.

## Assess Learning

Observe children when they use a reader's notebook to show what they like to read. Notice if there is evidence of new learning based on the goal of this minilesson.

- ▶ Are children able to make a list and draw a picture of the things they like to read about in a reader's notebook?
- ▶ Can children share their opinions with others about the things they like to read?
- ▶ Do they use the terms *author*, *title*, and *reader's notebook*?

## Minilesson

To help children think about the minilesson principle, engage them in a short demonstration of how to tell about what they like to read. Here is an example.

- ▶ Show a blank Things I Like to Read About page from *Reader's Notebook: Primary* or the prepared chart paper.

  Turn and talk about how this page can help you choose books to read.

- ▶ After time for discussion, ask a few volunteers to share.
- ▶ Show *Jamaica's Blue Marker* and *David's Drawings*.

  If I liked reading these books about Jamaica and David at school, I might write that I like books about school. Where would I write that on this page?

- ▶ As children respond, add a sentence to the first line.

  What could I draw to show I like to read books about school?

- ▶ Using children's suggestions, draw a quick sketch related to school.
- ▶ Repeat with several nonfiction books such as *Be My Neighbor* and *Best Foot Forward*. Add sentences to the list and simple, colorful sketches.

## Have a Try

Invite the children to talk with a partner to tell what they like to read about.

> Turn and talk to a partner about things you like to read about.

▶ After discussion, ask volunteers to share ideas. Record responses on the chart and review the chart.

## Summarize and Apply

Summarize the learning and remind children to list things they like to read about in a reader's notebook.

▶ Have the children open to the Things I Like to Read About page in *Reader's Notebook: Primary* (or provide an alternative notebook and show them where to label a page *Things I Like to Read About*).

> What can you draw and write about on this page?

> Choose things you like to read about and add them to your reader's notebook page. You can also draw pictures of those things. Bring your reader's notebook when we meet so you can share.

## Share

Following independent work time, gather children together in the meeting area in groups of four to share their drawing and writing.

> Show your Things I Like to Read About page and talk about things you like to read about. If you learn a new idea from someone in your group, you can add that to your list, too.

## Extend the Lesson (Optional)

After assessing children's understanding, you might decide to extend the learning.

▶ Have children meet in reading interest groups. They can suggest books they enjoyed to other members of the group.

▶ Encourage children to add to their list in a reader's notebook as they read and discover other types of books.

▶ Remind children to use their list in a reader's notebook to help them choose a book to read during independent reading time.

# RML 6
### WAR.U2.RML6

**Reading Minilesson Principle**
## Write and draw to show things you like to write about.

## Using a Reader's Notebook

### You Will Need

- *Reader's Notebook: Primary* or chart paper resembling the Things I Like to Write About page from *Reader's Notebook: Primary*
- markers
- several familiar books children have enjoyed, some by the same author or illustrator
- a reader's notebook for each child

### Academic Language / Important Vocabulary

- reader's notebook

### Continuum Connection

- Draw and write about everyday actions noticed in a text: playing, making things, eating, getting dressed, bathing, cooking, shopping (p. 176)

## Goal

Draw and write about the topics they like to write about in a reader's notebook.

## Rationale

When children use a reader's notebook to describe things they like to write about, they develop self-awareness of their interests and talents as readers and writers. They begin to think about their own voices as writers and how reading supports their learning.

## Assess Learning

Observe children when they use a reader's notebook to tell what they like to write about. Notice if there is evidence of new learning based on the goal of this minilesson.

- Are children able to make a list in a reader's notebook of things they might like to write about?
- Do they use the term *reader's notebook* in conversation?

## Minilesson

To help children think about the minilesson principle, engage them in a short demonstration of how to tell what they like to write about. Here is an example.

- Show a blank Things I Like to Write About page from *Reader's Notebook: Primary* or the prepared chart paper.

  Turn and talk about how this page can help you choose things to write about.

- After time for discussion, ask a few volunteers to share.
- Display multiple books by the same authors, such as books by Mo Willems or Kevin Henkes.

  Authors have certain things they like to write about. Look at these books by Mo Willems. What kinds of things does he like to write about?

- As children offer suggestions, add a sentence and sketch to the Things I Like to Write About page.

  Now think about Kevin Henkes. What kinds of things does he like to write about?

  Authors have things they like to write about. You might have things that you like to write about, too. You can list them on this page in your reader's notebook. When you are going to write, you will already have ideas of what to write about.

## Have a Try

Invite the children to talk with a partner about what they like to write about.

> Turn and talk to a partner about ideas you might like to add to the list on the Things I Like to Write About page.

▶ After discussion, ask a few volunteers to share. Record responses on the chart and review the chart.

## Summarize and Apply

Summarize the learning and remind children to list things they like to write about in a reader's notebook.

▶ Have the children open to the Things I Like to Write About page in *Reader's Notebook: Primary* (or provide an alternative notebook and show them where to label a page *Things I Like to Write About*).

> Today you learned how to make a list on the Things I Like to Write About page. During independent work time, choose something you would like to write about and add it to the page in your reader's notebook. You can also draw a picture.

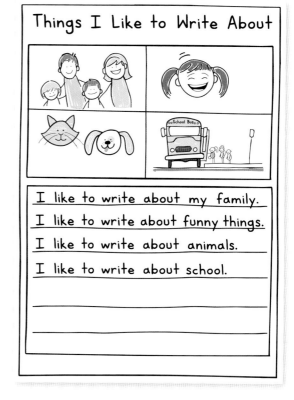

Things I Like to Write About

I like to write about my family.
I like to write about funny things.
I like to write about animals.
I like to write about school.

## Share

Following independent work time, gather children in the meeting area in a circle to share their drawing and writing.

> As we go around the circle, show your Things I Like to Write About page and share what you added. Listen to others so you can learn new ideas to add to your list.

▶ After sharing, provide time for children to add new ideas to their list.

## Extend the Lesson (Optional)

After assessing children's understanding, you might decide to extend the learning.

▶ Encourage children to add to their list in a reader's notebook as they gain new ideas from books they read and listen to.

▶ As you read new books, have children talk about new ideas of things to write about. Have them add the ideas to their list in a reader's notebook.

Section 4: Writing About Reading

**Reading Minilesson Principle**
## Collect interesting words and phrases from books.

Using a Reader's Notebook

### You Will Need

- blank page from the All About Me section of the *Reader's Notebook: Primary* or chart paper resembling a blank page from the All About Me section in *Reader's Notebook: Primary*
- markers
- three or four books with memorable language, such as the following from Text Set: Poetic Language
  - *Mud* by Mary Lyn Ray
  - *Puddles* by G. Brian Karas
  - *All the Colors of the Earth* by Sheila Hamanaka
- a reader's notebook for each child
- basket of books with memorable and interesting language

### Academic Language / Important Vocabulary

- reader's notebook
- author

### Continuum Connection

- Notice a writer's use of interesting words (p. 35)

### Goal

Recognize and record memorable and interesting language from books in a reader's notebook.

### Rationale

When children identify and record memorable and interesting language from books, they deepen their enjoyment of books and language. They begin to learn about the language choices that authors make and can think of their own writing.

### Assess Learning

Observe children when they collect memorable words in a reader's notebook. Notice if there is evidence of new learning based on the goal of this minilesson.

- Can children identify memorable words when they listen to and read books?
- Are they able to write memorable words in a reader's notebook?
- Do they use the terms *author* and *reader's notebook*?

## Minilesson

To help children think about the minilesson principle, engage them in a short discussion of memorable and interesting words to write in a reader's notebook. Here is an example.

- Show a blank page from the All About Me section of *Reader's Notebook* or a prepared chart.
- Reread pages 17–18 from *Mud*.

  What do you like about words the author uses like *squish* and *splat*?

- Using children's suggestions, write the memorable words on the blank page in the reader's notebook or the chart paper. Repeat with pages 21–24.

  You can use your reader's notebook to write special words from books. What words did you hear that you think I should write?

  Listen for words you like as I read a few pages from *Puddles*. Raise your hand when I say a word you think I should add to the reader's notebook page.

- Read pages 1–2 of *Puddles*, stopping as children raise hands to add words to the list.

## Have a Try

Invite the children to talk with a partner about interesting words in *All the Colors of the Earth.*

> ▶ Reread pages 28–29 from *All the Colors of the Earth.*
>
> Turn and talk to a partner about the words you think are special.

> ▶ After discussion, ask a few volunteers to share. Record responses on the chart and review the chart.

## Summarize and Apply

Summarize the learning and remind children to look for interesting words to list in a reader's notebook.

> ▶ Have the children open to a blank page in the All About Me section of *Reader's Notebook: Primary* (or provide an alternative reader's notebook and show them where to collect words).

> What can you learn from writing special words in a reader's notebook?

> When you read, choose a book from the basket. Add any interesting words you want to remember on a page in your reader's notebook and draw something from the book. Bring the book when we meet so you can share.

Fun Words
squish splat slurp
Stir it.  Stick it.
Ka-Boom!
buzz

## Share

Following independent work time, gather children in the meeting area in a circle to share their interesting words.

> Who found interesting words when reading today?

> ▶ Ask volunteers to share the words they added.

## Extend the Lesson (Optional)

After assessing children's understanding, you might decide to extend the learning.

> ▶ Encourage children to collect memorable words and phrases in a reader's notebook as they read other books.

> ▶ Assist children in writing poetry using the memorable words they have recorded in a reader's notebook.

## Assessment

After you have taught the minilessons in this umbrella, observe children talking and writing about their reading across instructional contexts: interactive read-aloud, independent reading and literacy work, guided reading, shared reading, and book club. Use *The Literacy Continuum* (Fountas and Pinnell 2017) to observe children's reading and writing behaviors across instructional contexts.

▶ What evidence do you have of new understandings related to using the reader's notebook?

- Do children talk about the books they love and share opinions about why they love them?
- Can children identify which authors and illustrators they love and why?
- Do they talk with others about the types of things they enjoy reading and writing about?
- Are they beginning to develop strategies for choosing books they might enjoy reading?
- Can they identify and record memorable words and phrases from the books they read?
- Do children use the terms *reader's notebook, author, illustrator,* and *title* when they talk about their writing about reading?

▶ In what other ways, beyond the scope of this umbrella, are children talking about and using a reader's notebook?

- Are they beginning to consider themselves as authors and illustrators who can decide what they will read and write about?
- Can children identify and use memorable words and phrases in their writing?
- Have they started to think about the purposes and motivations different authors have in writing stories?
- Do they talk about the different methods used by illustrators to create illustrations?

Use your observations to determine the next umbrella you will teach. You may also consult Minilessons Across the Year (p. 51) for guidance.

## Minilessons in This Umbrella

**RML1**  Tell about fiction books in your reader's notebook.

**RML2**  Make a list of your favorite fiction books.

**RML3**  Tell how a character feels.

**RML4**  Tell what a character is like.

**RML5**  Tell the story problem and how it is solved.

**RML6**  Tell where a story takes place.

**RML7**  Tell how a character changes.

**RML8**  Think about all the things you can write about fiction stories.

## Before Teaching Umbrella 3 Minilessons

These minilessons are based on *Reader's Notebook: Primary* (Fountas and Pinnell 2014), but any reader's notebook can be used. The goal is for children to have a consistent place to collect their thinking (see p. 46).

Before teaching these minilessons, introduce children to the sections of the reader's notebook and discuss the difference between fiction and nonfiction genres. As well, read and discuss a variety of high-quality fiction texts. Use the following books from the *Fountas & Pinnell Classroom™ Interactive Read-Aloud Collection* text sets or choose fiction books from your library.

**Having Fun with Language: Rhyming Texts**

  *The Giant Jam Sandwich* by John Vernon Lord

**Exploring Fiction and Nonfiction**

  *Going Places* by Peter and Paul Reynolds

**The Importance of Friendship**

  *Mr. George Baker* by Amy Hest

  *The Magic Rabbit* by Annette LeBlanc Cate

**Using Numbers: Books with Counting**

  *Handa's Hen* by Eileen Browne

**Learning and Playing Together: School**

  *First Day Jitters* by Julie Danneberg

**Living and Working Together: Community**

  *Blackout* by John Rocco

As you read aloud and enjoy these texts together, help children

- identify the book title, author's name, characters, problem, and solution,
- think about where a story takes place and why that is important to the story, and
- talk about different ways to draw and write about a fictional story.

**Rhyming Texts**

**Fiction and Nonfiction**

**Friendship**

**Using Numbers**

**School**

**Community**

**Reader's Notebook**

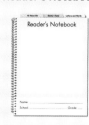

**RML1**

WAR.U3.RML1

**Reading Minilesson Principle**
## Tell about fiction books in your reader's notebook.

**Writing About Fiction Books in a Reader's Notebook**

### You Will Need

- *Reader's Notebook: Primary,* or chart paper resembling the blue Fiction page from *Reader's Notebook: Primary*
- several familiar fiction books, such as the following:
  - *Going Places* by Peter and Paul Reynolds, from Text Set: Fiction and Nonfiction
  - *Mr. George Baker* by Amy Hest, from Text Set: Friendship
- markers
- a reader's notebook for each child
- basket of class favorite books

### Academic Language / Important Vocabulary

- reader's notebook
- title
- author

### Continuum Connection

- Independently record in Reader's Notebook the titles, authors, and illustrators of texts (p. 176)
- Draw (or use other art media) independently to represent information from a text (p. 176)

### Goal

Tell about fiction books, including the title and author, when writing in a reader's notebook.

### Rationale

When children respond to fiction books through drawing and writing in a reader's notebook, they construct their ideas about the genre and their personal reading preferences. By sharing their thinking about fiction books in a dedicated notebook, they learn to keep a record to help them remember and refer back to stories they have read and enjoyed.

### Assess Learning

Observe children when they use a reader's notebook to draw and write about fiction. Notice if there is evidence of new learning based on the goal of this minilesson.

- ▶ Can children draw and write about a fiction book in a reader's notebook?
- ▶ Do children write the title and author's name on the lines?
- ▶ Do they use the terms *reader's notebook, title,* and *author*?

## Minilesson

To help children think about the minilesson principle, engage them in a short discussion of using a reader's notebook page. Here is an example.

- ▶ Show the Fiction side of the blue tab in *Reader's Notebook: Primary* or the prepared chart paper.

  The Books I Read is another section in your reader's notebook.

- ▶ Point to and read the words on the page.

  This page is for telling about fiction books you read. What do you think you can tell about on this page?

- ▶ Show the cover of *Going Places.*

  This is a fiction book. A fiction book tells a story. What was this story about?

- ▶ As children respond, write a sentence or two about the story at the bottom of the white box.

  Let's add a drawing so we can remember this book. What do you notice on the book's cover?

- ▶ Quickly sketch a go-cart.

  On the bottom of the page, are the words *Title* and *Author.* Where do I find the title and author of a book?

▶ Have volunteers come up to point to the title and author on the cover. Model writing the title and author's name on the lines.

> How could you use this reader's notebook page once you have completed it?

## Have a Try

Invite the children to talk with a partner about what they could write about a fiction story in a reader's notebook.

▶ Show the blue Fiction page or chart and the cover of *Mr. George Baker.*

> This is a fiction story. Turn and talk about what you would tell about *Mr. George Baker.*

## Summarize and Apply

Summarize the learning and remind children to use a reader's notebook to tell about fiction books.

▶ Give out *Reader's Notebook: Primary* and have the children open to the blue Fiction page, or provide an alternative reader's notebook. Show them where to label a page *Fiction.*

> What can you tell about on this page? Look at the chart to remember.

> Choose a fiction story you know or one from the basket. Draw something from the book's cover and write about the story. Look at the book to help you write the title and author's name correctly.

## Share

Following independent work time, gather children together in groups of three to share their drawing and writing.

> Share the picture and what you wrote about it. Show how you wrote the title and author on the lines.

## Extend the Lesson (Optional)

After assessing children's understanding, you might decide to extend the learning.

▶ Provide a basket of familiar fiction books. Have children work in groups to talk about what they would tell about the books in a reader's notebook.

▶ Provide groups with several fiction and nonfiction books. Ask children to determine which books are fiction, and talk about what they would write about each story.

**Fiction**
A fiction author tells a story.

This story is about two kids who build a go-cart. They want to win a race.

Title: Going Places

Author: Peter and Paul Reynolds

Section 4: Writing About Reading

## Reading Minilesson Principle
# Make a list of your favorite fiction books.

### Writing About Fiction Books in a Reader's Notebook

#### You Will Need

- *Reader's Notebook: Primary* or chart paper resembling the My Favorite Fiction Books page from *Reader's Notebook: Primary*
- several familiar fiction books, such as the following:
  - *The Magic Rabbit* by Annette LeBlanc Cate, from Text Set: Friendship
  - *Blackout* by John Rocco, from Text Set: Community
- markers
- a reader's notebook for each child
- basket of class favorite books

#### Academic Language / Important Vocabulary

- reader's notebook
- title
- author
- fiction

#### Continuum Connection

- Independently record in Reader's Notebook the titles, authors, and illustrators of texts (p. 176)

### Goal

List the names of authors and the titles of books in a reader's notebook.

### Rationale

Teaching children to identify and record the title and author of fiction books when writing about reading helps them develop organization and documentation skills. When children record their favorite books in a reader's notebook, it can serve as a useful reference tool. The list can help them choose books to write about and help them choose new books to read that are similar to books they previously enjoyed.

### Assess Learning

Observe children when they use a reader's notebook to list their favorite fiction books. Notice if there is evidence of new learning based on the goal of this minilesson.

- ▶ Do children understand the purpose of the My Favorite Fiction Books page?
- ▶ Are children able to write a title and author's name on the lines?
- ▶ Do they use the terms *reader's notebook, title, author,* and *fiction* correctly?

## Minilesson

To help children think about the minilesson principle, engage them in a short demonstration of using a reader's notebook to list favorite fiction books. Here is an example.

- ▶ Show the My Favorite Fiction Books page from *Reader's Notebook: Primary*, or the prepared chart paper. Point to the section for fiction books.

   What do you think you can write on this part of the page?

   You can make a list of your favorite fiction books.

- ▶ Show the cover of *The Magic Rabbit*.

   This is a book we read together and enjoyed, *The Magic Rabbit.* How do you know this is a fiction book?

   Since this is one of your favorite fiction books, it can be one of the books to list on this page. Who can point to the title of this book?

- ▶ Write letter by letter the book's title, checking back to the book cover to be sure each is correct. As you do, both the reader's notebook page or chart paper and the book cover should be shown.

   It is important to carefully write the title words on the line in your reader's notebook like I did.

- ▶ Repeat with the author's name.

## Have a Try

Invite the children to talk with a partner about how to fill in the My Favorite Fiction Books page.

▸ Show the My Favorite Fiction Books page or the chart. Show the cover of *Blackout*.

> Here is another favorite fiction story. Turn and talk about how you would list *Blackout* on this page.

▸ Record responses. Review the page.

## Summarize and Apply

Summarize the learning and remind children to list their favorite fiction books in a reader's notebook.

▸ Have children open to the My Favorite Fiction Books page of *Reader's Notebook: Primary* (or provide an alternative reader's notebook and show them where to label a page *My Favorite Fiction Books*).

> What will you tell about on this page?

> How will you know how to write the title and author's name?

> During independent work time, choose a favorite fiction story to read. You may pick one from the basket if you like. In your reader's notebook, write the title and author on the first line.

> My Favorite Fiction Books
>
> The Magic Rabbit by Annette LeBlanc Cate
>
> Blackout by John Rocco
>
> My Favorite Nonfiction Books

## Share

Following independent work time, gather children in groups of three to share their favorite fiction books.

> Share the page you completed today. Talk about the book. Show how you wrote the title and author. Talk about other books you might add to your list.

## Extend the Lesson (Optional)

After assessing children's understanding, you might decide to extend the learning.

▸ Have children list more favorite fiction titles on the My Favorite Fiction Books page as they listen to and read more fiction stories.

▸ Provide groups with several fiction and nonfiction books. Ask children to determine which books are fiction, and then talk about what they would write on the My Favorite Fiction Books page in a reader's notebook for each fiction story.

## Writing About Fiction Books in a Reader's Notebook

### You Will Need

- *Reader's Notebook: Primary* or chart paper resembling the Books I Read pages from *Reader's Notebook: Primary*
- several familiar fiction books depicting characters with clearly identifiable feelings, such as the following:
  - *First Day Jitters* by Julie Danneberg, from Text Set: School
  - *The Giant Jam Sandwich* by John Vernon Lord, from Text Set: Rhyming Texts
- markers
- a reader's notebook for each child
- basket of favorite fiction books depicting characters with clearly identifiable feelings

### Academic Language / Important Vocabulary

- reader's notebook
- author
- title
- character

### Continuum Connection

- Independently record in Reader's Notebook the titles, authors, and illustrators of texts (p. 176)
- Infer and describe a character's intentions, feelings, and motivations by drawing or writing (p. 177)

### Goal

Write and draw in a reader's notebook about how a character in a fiction story feels.

### Rationale

When children write and draw in a reader's notebook about characters' feelings, they learn to notice and think about characters' emotions. This deepens their comprehension of the text, helps them form connections to the characters, and develops empathy.

### Assess Learning

Observe children when they use a reader's notebook to show a character's feelings. Notice if there is evidence of new learning based on the goal of this minilesson.

- ▶ Can children draw and write in a reader's notebook about a character's feelings?
- ▶ Do children write the title and author's name on the lines?
- ▶ Do they use the terms *reader's notebook, author, title,* and *character*?

## Minilesson

To help children think about the minilesson principle, engage them in a short discussion of using a reader's notebook page to tell about characters' feelings. Here is an example.

- ▶ Show a Books I Read page in *Reader's Notebook: Primary* or the prepared chart paper.

  This page in the reader's notebook says Books I Read. What do you notice about this page?

- ▶ Show the cover of *First Day Jitters*.

  This is a fiction book we read together, *First Day Jitters*. How should I write the title and author's name on the lines?

- ▶ Model writing the title and author's name.

  Let's also add a sketch about the book so you can remember this book. What do you notice on the cover?

- ▶ As children provide suggestions, make a quick sketch.
- ▶ Show the right-hand page of blank lines or the prepared chart paper.

  This next page in the reader's notebook has lines for writing about a story. It would be interesting to write about how a character in a story feels, wouldn't it? What are you thinking about how Mrs. Hartwell feels on her first day as a teacher?

  Why is she feeling nervous?

▶ As children provide suggestions, briefly write about the character's feelings on the lines.

## Have a Try

Invite the children to talk with a partner about what to write on the Books I Read page.

▶ Show a new Books I Read page and the cover of *The Giant Jam Sandwich*.

> Here is another fiction story we read together. Turn and talk to a partner about what you would tell about *The Giant Jam Sandwich* on this page.

## Summarize and Apply

Summarize the learning and remind children to use a reader's notebook to tell how characters feel as they read.

▶ Have children open to the Books I Read page in *Reader's Notebook: Primary* (or provide an alternative reader's notebook and show them where to label a page *Books I Read*).

> What is something you learned today that you can tell about a character?

> When you read a fiction story today, think about how a character feels. Then, tell about the character in a reader's notebook. Choose a fiction story from the basket or any other fiction story you wish to read during independent work time.

## Share

Following independent work time, gather the children in the meeting area to share their drawing and writing.

> Turn and talk about the page you completed today. Talk about the picture and what you wrote about how the character feels. Show how you wrote the title and author on the lines.

## Extend the Lesson (Optional)

After assessing children's understanding, you might decide to extend the learning.

▶ During interactive read-aloud or shared reading, talk about how a character feels and why to provide an oral rehearsal for writing in a reader's notebook.

▶ **Drawing/Writing About Reading** Have children draw and write about characters' feelings after they listen to and/or read new stories.

**Books I Read**

1

Title: First Day Jitters

Author: Julie Danneberg

1

Mrs. Hartwell feels nervous about
the first of school.
I know this because she does
not want to get out of
bed or the car.

**Writing About Fiction Books in a Reader's Notebook**

### You Will Need

- *Reader's Notebook: Primary* or chart paper resembling the Books I Read pages from *Reader's Notebook: Primary*
- several familiar fiction books depicting identifiable character traits, such as these from Text Set: Friendship:
  - *The Magic Rabbit* by Annette LeBlanc Cate
  - *Mr. George Baker* by Amy Hest
- markers
- a reader's notebook for each child
- basket of class favorite fiction books

### Academic Language / Important Vocabulary

- reader's notebook
- author
- title
- character

### Continuum Connection

- Independently record in Reader's Notebook the titles, authors, and illustrators of texts (p. 176)
- Write a summary that includes important details about characters (p. 176)

## Goal

Write and draw in a reader's notebook about what a character in a fiction story is like.

## Rationale

When children begin to think about character traits, they analyze how and why characters act the way they do. Writing and drawing to show a character's traits is another way to revisit a story and helps children remember what they have read and deepens their understanding of story elements.

## Assess Learning

Observe children when they write in a reader's notebook about what a character is like. Notice if there is evidence of new learning based on the goal of this minilesson.

- Can children draw and write in a reader's notebook about what a character is like?
- Can they tell how they know what a character is like?
- Do children write the title and author's name on the lines?
- Do children use the terms *reader's notebook, author, title,* and *character*?

# Minilesson

To help children think about the minilesson principle, engage them in a short discussion of using a reader's notebook page to tell about what a character is like. Here is an example.

- Show a Books I Read page or the prepared chart paper. Show the cover of *The Magic Rabbit*.

  How do we know what to write on this page?

- Show page 4.

  Here is the magician with his rabbit. What could I draw on this page to show the magician?

- Using children's suggestions, draw a simple sketch to represent the characters.

  I want to write about what a character is like in the story. Turn and talk about what the magician is like.

- As children talk, show the lined page from Books I Read. Ask children for suggestions and write them on the page or chart paper.

- Show the first picture on page 19.

  Who is the other character in the story? Turn and talk about what the bunny is like.

- After children discuss, ask volunteers to share and add their suggestions.

## Have a Try

Invite the children to talk with a partner about what they could write on the Books I Read page.

▶ Show the Books I Read page or the chart paper from the reader's notebook and the cover of *Mr. George Baker*.

Now think about the characters George and the boy. What are they like? Turn and talk about what you could tell about George and the boy.

## Summarize and Apply

Summarize the learning and remind children to tell about what characters are like in a reader's notebook after they read.

▶ Have the children open to the Books I Read page in *Reader's Notebook: Primary* (or provide an alternative reader's notebook and show them where to label a page *Books I Read*).

What can you draw and write in your reader's notebook to show what a character is like? Look at the chart to remember.

During independent work time, read a fiction story. Then choose a character from the book to tell about. You can choose a book from the basket if you would like. Bring your reader's notebook to share when we meet.

## Share

Following independent work time, gather children together in the meeting area to share their drawing and writing.

Turn and talk about the page you completed today. Talk about the picture and what you wrote about what a character is like. Show how you wrote the title and author on the lines.

## Extend the Lesson (Optional)

After assessing children's understanding, you might decide to extend the learning.

▶ If any of the children wrote about a character from a series book, have them look at other books in the series to see if what they wrote about the character holds true.

▶ **Drawing/Writing About Reading** Have children continue to draw and write about characters they read about in fiction stories.

Books I Read

Title: The Magic Rabbit

Author: Annette LeBlanc Cate

The magician is kind.
He takes good care of the rabbit.
He shares popcorn.
He has him in his house.
The bunny loves the magician.
He found him by using a star.

# RML5
## WAR.U3.RML5

### Reading Minilesson Principle
## Tell the story problem and how it is solved.

**Writing About Fiction Books in a Reader's Notebook**

## You Will Need

- *Reader's Notebook: Primary* or chart paper resembling the Books I Read pages from *Reader's Notebook: Primary*, prepared with details of a problem and solution from a fiction story
- several familiar fiction books with clearly defined problems and solutions, such as the following:
  - *The Giant Jam Sandwich* by John Vernon Lord, from Text Set: Rhyming Texts
  - *Handa's Hen* by Eileen Browne, from Text Set: Using Numbers
- markers
- a reader's notebook for each child
- basket of class favorite fiction books

## Academic Language / Important Vocabulary

- reader's notebook
- title
- author
- character
- problem
- solved

### Continuum Connection

- Write summaries that include the story problem and how it is resolved [p. 176]

## Goal

Write and draw in a reader's notebook about the problem in a fiction story and how it is solved.

## Rationale

When children use a reader's notebook to share their thinking about a problem and solution, they demonstrate their understanding of the story's plot and can reflect on how characters handle issues. As children evaluate the problem faced by a character and recognize the solution, they make personal connections with the characters. This connection may help them as they encounter similar problems in their lives.

## Assess Learning

Observe children when they use a reader's notebook to tell about a problem and how it was solved. Notice if there is evidence of new learning based on the goal of this minilesson.

- Can children draw and write about a fiction story's problem and solution?
- Do children write the title and author's name on the lines?
- Do they use the terms *reader's notebook, title, author, character, problem,* and *solved*?

## Minilesson

To help children think about the minilesson principle, engage them in a short discussion of telling about a problem and how it was solved on a reader's notebook page. Here is an example.

- Revisit pages 8–9 of *The Giant Jam Sandwich* to prompt the conversation.

  Think about the problem that the people had in *The Giant Jam Sandwich*.

- Show pages 28–29.

  What did the people do to solve their problem?

- Show the Books I Read pages or the prepared chart paper and read the words.

  What do you notice about what I wrote and drew on these pages? Turn and talk about that.

- After time for discussion, have children share ideas.

  I wrote in a reader's notebook about the problem in the story and how it was solved, didn't I? Drawing and writing about a problem and how it was solved is another way to use a reader's notebook to help you think about what you have read.

- Repeat with *The Magic Rabbit*.

## Have a Try

Invite the children to talk with a partner about the problem and solution in *Handa's Hen*.

▶ Show the Books I Read page or the chart paper. Show the cover of *Handa's Hen*.

> Think about the problem Handa has in *Handa's Hen*. How was the problem solved? Turn and talk to your partner about what you would you tell about Handa's problem and how it was solved.

## Summarize and Apply

Summarize the learning and remind children to tell about the problem and solution in a story in a reader's notebook.

▶ Have children open to a Books I Read page in *Reader's Notebook: Primary* (or provide an alternative reader's notebook and show them where to label a page *Books I Read*).

> What did you learn about how you can write in a reader's notebook to tell the problem and solution? Look at the chart to help you remember.

> Choose a fiction story to read during independent work time. Think about the problem and how it was solved. You can choose a book from the basket. In your reader's notebook, tell about the problem and how it was solved.

## Share

Following independent work time, gather children together in the meeting area to share their drawing and writing.

> Turn and talk to your partner about the page you completed today. Talk about the picture and what you wrote about the problem and how it was solved. Show how you wrote the title and author on the lines.

## Extend the Lesson (Optional)

After assessing children's understanding, you might decide to extend the learning.

▶ During interactive read-aloud or shared reading, talk about the problem in a fiction story and its solution to provide an oral rehearsal for writing in a reader's notebook.

▶ **Drawing/Writing About Reading** Have children continue to write in a reader's notebook about fiction stories by describing the problem and its solution.

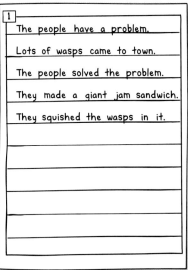

**Reading Minilesson Principle**
## Tell where a story takes place.

## Writing About Fiction Books in a Reader's Notebook

### You Will Need

- *Reader's Notebook: Primary* or chart paper resembling the Books I Read pages from *Reader's Notebook: Primary*

- several familiar fiction books, such as the following:

  - *First Day Jitters* by Julie Danneberg, from Text Set: School

  - *Blackout* by John Rocco, from Text Set: Community

- markers

- a reader's notebook for each child

- basket of class favorite fiction books

### Academic Language / Important Vocabulary

- reader's notebook
- title
- author
- place

### Continuum Connection

- Independently record in Reader's Notebook the titles, authors, and illustrators of texts (p. 176)

- Write summaries that include important details about setting (p. 177)

### Goal

Write and draw in a reader's notebook about where a story takes place in fiction books.

### Rationale

When children use a reader's notebook to draw and write about setting, they think about where the story takes place and consider location as important part of the story. This deepens their understanding of the setting's impact on the plot and characters and supports making connections to the story. Although children are talking about setting, you may wish to wait until later to introduce the term.

### Assess Learning

Observe children when they they use a reader's notebook to tell about where a story takes place. Notice if there is evidence of new learning based on the goal of this minilesson.

- ▶ Can children draw and write about where a story takes place?

- ▶ Do children write the title and author's name on the lines?

- ▶ Do they use the terms *reader's notebook*, *title*, *author*, and *place*?

## Minilesson

To help children think about the minilesson principle, engage them in a short discussion of telling about where a story takes place on a reader's notebook page. Here is an example.

- ▶ Show pages 2–3 of *First Day Jitters*.

  Think about where Sarah is at the beginning of the story.

- ▶ Show pages 24–25.

  Turn and talk about where the end of this story takes place.

  We can write in a reader's notebook about where a story takes place.

- ▶ Show a Books I Read page or the prepared chart paper. Show the cover of *First Day Jitters*. Ask children to point to the title and author as you model writing.

  What should we include on this page?

- ▶ Using children's suggestions, draw a simple sketch of Sarah's house and school.

  Where does the story take place at the beginning?

  Where else does this story take place?

- ▶ Show the lined Books I Read page. Using children's suggestions, add a few sentences about where the story takes place.

## Have a Try

Invite the children to talk with a partner about where *Blackout* takes place.

▶ Show the Books I Read page or the chart paper and page 2 of *Blackout*.

> Turn and talk about what you would tell about where *Blackout* takes place.

## Summarize and Apply

Summarize the learning and remind children to tell about where a story takes place after they read.

▶ Have children open to a Books I Read page in *Reader's Notebook: Primary* (or provide an alternative reader's notebook and show them where to label a page *Books I Read*).

> What did you learn you can write about a story in a reader's notebook? Look at the chart to remember.

> During independent work time, read a fiction book. Think about where the story takes place and write about it in a reader's notebook. You may choose a book from the basket. Bring your reader's notebook when we meet to share what you wrote.

## Share

Following independent work time, gather children together in the meeting area to share their drawing and writing.

> Turn and talk to your partner about where your story takes place. Talk about the picture and what you wrote. Show how you wrote the title and author on the lines

## Extend the Lesson (Optional)

After assessing children's understanding, you might decide to extend the learning.

▶ Create sets of familiar books with similar settings. Have children compare the settings.

▶ To deepen their thinking of the impact of setting on a story, talk during interactive read-aloud or shared reading about how a story would change if it happened in a different place.

▶ **Drawing/Writing About Reading** Have children draw and write about where stories take place as they encounter new settings when they listen to or read stories.

Books I Read

1 Title: First Day Jitters

Author: Julie Danneberg

1 She is worried about going to school. Then, she goes to school. She feels better. The story takes place at home and school.

## Writing About Fiction Books in a Reader's Notebook

### You Will Need

▶ *Reader's Notebook: Primary* or chart paper resembling the Books I Read pages from *Reader's Notebook: Primary*

▶ several familiar fiction books depicting a clear character change, such as the following:
  • *First Day Jitters* by Julie Danneberg, from Text Set: School
  • *Blackout* by John Rocco, from Text Set: Community

▶ markers

▶ a reader's notebook for each child

▶ basket of class favorite fiction books

### Academic Language / Important Vocabulary

▶ reader's notebook
▶ title
▶ author
▶ character

### Continuum Connection

▶ Independently record in Reader's Notebook the titles, authors, and illustrators of texts (p. 176)

▶ Show when characters change or learn a lesson in a story by drawing or writing (p. 177)

## Goal

Write and draw in a reader's notebook about how a character changes in the story.

## Rationale

Thinking about how a character changes helps children infer the connections between plot and character. When children think about how a character changes during a fiction story, they better understand the character's feelings and motivations. They can make connections between the character and their own lives.

## Assess Learning

Observe children when they use a reader's notebook to tell about how a character changes. Notice if there is evidence of new learning based on the goal of this minilesson.

▶ Can children draw and write about how a character changes?

▶ Do children write the title and author's name on the lines?

▶ Do they use the terms *reader's notebook, title, author,* and *character*?

## Minilesson

To help children think about the minilesson principle, engage them in a short discussion of using a reader's notebook page to tell about how a character changes. Here is an example.

▶ Show the cover of *First Day Jitters*.

  You can draw and write in a reader's notebook about how a character changes in a fiction story.

▶ Show a Books I Read page from *Reader's Notebook: Primary* or the prepared chart paper.

  How do you know what to write on this page?

▶ Ask children to point to the title and author as you model the writing, and to make a suggestion for a simple drawing, such as the school bus on the cover.

▶ Show page 14.

  How does Mrs. Hartwell feel about the first day of school?

▶ Show the last page.

  Turn and talk about how Mrs. Hartwell changes from the beginning to the end of the story.

▶ After discussion, ask volunteers to share, prompting them to include examples from the story. Using children's suggestions, write how Mrs. Hartwell changed in the story.

## Have a Try

Invite the children to talk with a partner about how the girl in *Blackout* changes.

▶ Show the Books I Read page or the chart paper. Show the girl on the front endpapers of *Blackout*.

> Think about the girl at the beginning of *Blackout*.

▶ Show the girl playing with her family on the back end pages.

> Now think about how she changed from the beginning to the end. Turn and talk about what you would you write about how the girl changes.

## Summarize and Apply

Summarize the learning and remind children to use a reader's notebook to show how a character changes.

▶ Have the children open to a Books I Read page in *Reader's Notebook: Primary* (or provide an alternative reader's notebook and show them where to label a page *Books I Read*).

> What did you learn today about what you can write in a reader's notebook? Look at the chart to help you remember.

▶ Show the cover of *Blackout*.

> Today during independent work time, write and draw in your reader's notebook about how the girl in *Blackout* changes from the beginning to the end. Think about what you and your partner talked about.

## Share

Following independent work time, gather children to share their drawing and writing.

> Show the page you completed about the girl in *Blackout*. Talk about the picture and what you wrote about how the girl changes. Show how you wrote the title and author on the lines.

## Extend the Lesson (Optional)

After assessing children's understanding, you might decide to extend the learning.

▶ During interactive read-aloud or shared reading, talk about how a character changes in the story to provide an oral rehearsal for writing in a reader's notebook.

▶ **Drawing/Writing About Reading** Have children draw and write about how a character in a fiction story changes as they meet new characters in stories.

Section 4: Writing About Reading

# RML 8
### WAR.U3.RML8

**Reading Minilesson Principle**
## Think about all the things you can write about fiction stories.

## Writing About Fiction Books in a Reader's Notebook

### You Will Need

- *Reader's Notebook: Primary* or the charts from RML3–RML7
- chart paper prepared with the heading *Ways to Write About Fiction Stories*
- markers
- fiction books used in previous minilessons in this umbrella, such as the following:
  - *First Day Jitters* by Julie Danneberg, from Text Set: School
  - *The Magic Rabbit* by Annette LeBlanc Cate, from Text Set: Friendship
  - *The Giant Jam Sandwich* by John Vernon Lord, from Text Set: Rhyming Texts
- a reader's notebook for each child
- sticky notes
- basket of class favorite fiction books

### Academic Language / Important Vocabulary

- author
- title
- character
- place
- problem
- solved

### Continuum Connection

- Independently record in Reader's Notebook the titles, authors, and illustrators of texts (p. 176)
- Draw (or use other art media) independently to represent information from a text (p. 176)

### Goal

Understand different things to write about fiction books in a reader's notebook.

### Rationale

When children review the different ways they can use a reader's notebook to write about fiction stories, their learning about a story's characters, plot, and setting is reinforced. They will begin to think deeper about the various elements of a fiction story.

### Assess Learning

Observe children when they use a reader's notebook to tell about things in a fiction story. Notice if there is evidence of new learning based on the goal of this minilesson.

- Can children talk about the different ways they can write about fiction stories?
- Are children able to choose a way to write about a fiction story?
- Do they use the terms *author, title, character, place, problem,* and *solved*?

## Minilesson

To help children think about the minilesson principle, engage them in a short discussion of the things they can tell about in fiction stories in a reader's notebook. Here is an example.

- Show the reader's notebook pages created in RML3 and show the cover of *First Day Jitters*.

  Do you remember when we worked together to write about Mrs. Hartwell on her first day of school? What do you notice on these pages of the reader's notebook?

- Begin a list on the chart paper under the prepared heading.

  These pages have writing and drawing about how Mrs. Hartwell feels, don't they? The reader's notebook can be used to write and draw about how a character feels.

- Show the reader's notebook pages created for RML4 and show the cover of *The Magic Rabbit*. Guide children to recognize that these pages have writing and drawing about what a character is like. Add to the list.

  What do you notice on these pages of the reader's notebook? What are these pages about?

- Repeat with RML5 and RML6.

## Have a Try

Invite the children to talk with a partner about what they can write about fiction stories.

▶ Show pages created for RML7 and the cover of *First Day Jitters*.

> Look at these pages from the reader's notebook. Turn and talk with your partner about what you notice and what you can add to the list.

▶ After discussion, ask volunteers to share and add to the list.

## Summarize and Apply

Summarize the learning and remind children to tell about fiction stories after they read.

▶ Read the chart of ways to write about fiction stories together with the children.

▶ Have the children open to a Books I Read page in *Reader's Notebook: Primary* (or provide an alternative reader's notebook and show them where to label a page *Books I Read*).

> Choose one of the ideas on the chart and place a sticky note with your name next to the idea. During independent work time, read a fiction book and then use the idea to draw and write about the book in a reader's notebook. You can choose a book from the basket.

## Share

Following independent work time, gather children in groups of three to share their drawing and writing.

> Share the page you completed. Talk about your picture and what you wrote about the story. Show how you wrote the title and author on the lines.

## Extend the Lesson (Optional)

After assessing children's understanding, you might decide to extend the learning.

▶ Provide a basket of familiar fiction books. In groups, have children choose a book and talk about how they would write about it using the ideas from the minilesson.

▶ **Drawing/Writing About Reading** Have children write about a book using two ideas from the minilesson's list. Ask them to compare the ideas, and talk about why it is good to have different ways to write about books.

Ways to Write About Fiction Stories

Write and draw about. . .

- how a character feels.   Dan
- what a character is like.   Jane
- the story problem and how it is solved.
- where a story takes place.   Babak
- how a character changes.   Tara

## Assessment

After you have taught the minilessons in this umbrella, observe children talking and writing about their reading across instructional contexts: interactive read-aloud, independent reading and literacy work, guided reading, shared reading, and book club. Use *The Literacy Continuum* (Fountas and Pinnell 2017) to observe children's reading and writing behaviors across instructional contexts.

▶ What evidence do you have of new understandings related to writing about fiction in a reader's notebook?

- Can children accurately identify and record book titles and authors' names?
- Are they able to make a list of favorite fiction titles?
- Can children identify, draw, and write about how characters are feeling?
- Can children identify, draw, and write about character traits?
- Can they identify, draw, and write about how a character changes from the beginning to the end of a fiction story?
- Do children identify, draw, and write about a problem and how it was solved in a fiction story?
- Do children draw and write about where a fiction story takes place and why it is important to the story?
- Do they use the terms *reader's notebook, title, author, character,* and *problem*?

▶ In what other ways, beyond the scope of this umbrella, are children talking about writing in a reader's notebook?

- Do children express opinions about what they read?
- Are they beginning to draw and write about nonfiction books?

Use your observations to determine the next umbrella you will teach. You may also consult Minilessons Across the Year (p. 51) for guidance.

## Minilessons in This Umbrella

**RML1**  Tell information about nonfiction books in your reader's notebook.

**RML2**  Make a list of your favorite nonfiction books.

**RML3**  Share information about a topic.

**RML4**  Tell something you learned about a topic.

**RML5**  Tell an interesting fact about a topic.

**RML6**  Think about all the things you can write about nonfiction books.

## Before Teaching Umbrella 4 Minilessons

While these lessons are examples of how to teach children to write about nonfiction in *Reader's Notebook: Primary* (Fountas and Pinnell 2014), any reader's notebook can be used. The goal is for children to have a consistent place to collect their thinking about reading in one place (see p. 46).

Before teaching these minilessons, it would be helpful to introduce children to the sections of the reader's notebook (see Umbrella 1: Introducing a Reader's Notebook in this section) and to help them understand the difference between fiction and nonfiction genres. (See Section Two: Literary Analysis for umbrellas on fiction and nonfiction.) Also, provide opportunities for them to read and discuss a variety of high-quality nonfiction texts with easily identified topics and facts with new and interesting information. Use the following books from the *Fountas & Pinnell Classroom™ Interactive Read-Aloud Collection* text sets or choose similar nonfiction books from your library:

**Exploring Fiction and Nonfiction**

*On the Go* by Ann Morris

**Nonfiction: Questions and Answers**

*Animals Black and White* by Phyllis Limbacher Tildes

*What Do You Do with a Tail Like This?* by Steve Jenkins and Robin Page

**Exploring Nonfiction**

*Tools* by Ann Morris

*Water: Up, Down, and All Around* by Natalie M. Rosinsky

*Surprising Sharks* by Nicola Davies

*What Do You Do When Something Wants to Eat You?* by Steve Jenkins

As you read aloud and enjoy these texts together, help children

- identify the title and author of favorite nonfiction titles,

- notice and think about the topic of a nonfiction book,

- notice new information and interesting facts from nonfiction books, and

- talk about the ways they can tell about a nonfiction book.

**Fiction and Nonfiction**

**Questions and Answers**

**Nonfiction**

**Reader's Notebook**

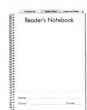

## RML1
### WAR.U4.RML1

**Reading Minilesson Principle**
# Tell information about nonfiction books in your reader's notebook.

## Writing About Nonfiction Books in a Reader's Notebook

### You Will Need

▸ *Reader's Notebook: Primary*, or chart paper resembling the blue tab (Nonfiction side) from *Reader's Notebook: Primary*

▸ several familiar nonfiction books, such as the following:

- *On the Go* by Ann Morris, from Text Set: Fiction and Nonfiction

- *Animals Black and White* by Phyllis Limbacher Tildes, from Text Set: Questions and Answers

▸ markers

▸ a reader's notebook for each child

▸ basket of class favorite nonfiction books

### Academic Language / Important Vocabulary

▸ reader's notebook

▸ title

▸ author

### Continuum Connection

▸ Record in Reader's Notebook the titles, authors, and illustrators of texts (p. 178)

▸ Tell important information about a text (p. 178)

### Goal

Understand how to share information learned in nonfiction books in a reader's notebook.

### Rationale

When children tell about nonfiction books, they share information about a topic. By sharing their thinking in a dedicated notebook, they keep a record to help them remember and refer back to books they have read and enjoyed.

### Assess Learning

Observe children when they use a reader's notebook to tell about nonfiction books. Notice if there is evidence of new learning based on the goal of this minilesson.

▸ Are children able to draw and write about a nonfiction book in a reader's notebook?

▸ Do children write the title and author's name on the lines?

▸ Do they use the terms *reader's notebook, title*, and *author*?

## Minilesson

To help children think about the minilesson principle, engage them in a demonstration of how to tell about nonfiction books in a reader's notebook. Here is an example.

▸ Show the blue Nonfiction page from the *Reader's Notebook: Primary* or the prepared chart paper. Read the words.

What do you think you could draw and Write on this page?

▸ Show the cover of *On the Go*.

What information did the author of *On the Go* write about?

▸ As children provide suggestions, write a sentence or two about the book at the bottom of the white box.

What was this book about?

Let's add a quick sketch about the book so we can remember it.

▸ As children provide suggestions, briefly sketch a key detail from the cover related to the book topic.

▸ Have volunteers come up to point to the title and author on the cover. Then model writing the title and author's name on the lines.

On the bottom of the page, I see the words *Title* and *Author*. Where do I find the title and author of a book?

## Have a Try

Invite the children to talk with a partner about *Animals Black and White*.

▶ Show the reader's notebook page or chart and the cover of *Animals Black and White*.

> Here is another nonfiction book you know. Turn and talk about what you would tell about *Animals Black and White* on this page in your reader's notebook.

## Summarize and Apply

Summarize the learning and remind children to think about what they will tell about the nonfiction book they are reading.

▶ Have children open to the blue tab in *Reader's Notebook: Primary* (or provide an alternative notebook and show them where to label a page *Nonfiction*).

> What will you draw and write about on this page?

> During independent work time, read a nonfiction book or think about one you have already read. Write about it in your reader's notebook. First, write the title and author of the book on the lines. Then, in the box, draw something about the book.

Nonfiction

A nonfiction author gives information.

This book is about the different ways people move around the world.

Title: On the Go

Author: Ann Morris

## Share

Following independent work time, gather children in the meeting area in groups of three to share their drawing and writing.

> Share the page you completed today. Talk about what you told about the book. Show how you wrote the title and author's name on the lines.

## Extend the Lesson (Optional)

After assessing children's understanding, you might decide to extend the learning.

▶ Make a class list of favorite nonfiction books based on what children have written in a reader's notebook. Post the list near the library so that children can use it to select a recommended book to read.

## RML2
### WAR.U4.RML2

# Make a list of your favorite nonfiction books.

## Writing About Nonfiction Books in a Reader's Notebook

### You Will Need

- *Reader's Notebook: Primary* or chart paper resembling the My Favorite Nonfiction Books page from *Reader's Notebook: Primary*
- several familiar nonfiction books, such as the following:
  - *Surprising Sharks* by Nicola Davies, from Text Set: Nonfiction
  - *What Do You Do with a Tail Like This?* by Steve Jenkins and Robin Page, from Text Set: Questions and Answers
- markers
- a reader's notebook for each child
- pencils

### Academic Language / Important Vocabulary

- reader's notebook
- title
- author
- nonfiction

### Continuum Connection

- Record in Reader's Notebook the titles, authors, and illustrators of texts (p. 178)

## Goal

List the names of authors and titles of nonfiction books when writing about reading in a reader's notebook.

## Rationale

Teaching children to identify and record the title and author of nonfiction books when writing about reading will help them to develop documentation skills. When children list their favorite books in a reader's notebook, the list can serve as a reference tool. The list can help them decide what books to write about and help them choose new books to read that are similar to books they previously enjoyed.

## Assess Learning

Observe children when they use a reader's notebook to list their favorite nonfiction books. Notice if there is evidence of new learning based on the goal of this minilesson.

- Do children understand the purpose of the My Favorite Nonfiction Books page?
- Do children write the title and author's name on the lines?
- Do they use the terms *reader's notebook, title, author,* and *nonfiction*?

## Minilesson

To help children think about the minilesson principle, engage them in a demonstration of how to list favorite nonfiction books in a reader's notebook. Here is an example.

- Show the My Favorite Nonfiction Books page from *Reader's Notebook: Primary* or the prepared chart paper. Point to the section for nonfiction books. Read the heading.

  What are you going to tell about on this reader's notebook page? You can make a list of your favorite nonfiction books.

- Show the cover of *Surprising Sharks*, making sure children see the title and author's name.

  How do you know this is a nonfiction book? If this is one of your favorite nonfiction books, you can list it on this page. Who can point to the title of this book?

- Ask a volunteer to come up and point to the line for the title.

  It is important to write the title words on the line, like this.

- Model writing letter by letter the title, checking the book cover to be sure each is correct. As you do, both the reader's notebook page and the book cover should be shown.

- Repeat with the author's name.

## Have a Try

Invite the children to talk with a partner about how to record the title and author on the page.

▶ Show the My Favorite Nonfiction Books page and the cover of *What Do You Do with a Tail Like This?*

Turn and talk to a partner about how you would list this book in a reader's notebook.

▶ Record responses on the reader's notebook page.

## Summarize and Apply

Summarize the learning and remind children to consider as they read whether the book is a favorite.

▶ Have the children open to the My Favorite Nonfiction Books page in *Reader's Notebook: Primary* (or provide an alternative notebook and show them where to label a page *My Favorite Nonfiction Books*).

How can you use this page?

In your reader's notebook, write the title and author of your favorite nonfiction book.

## Share

Following independent work time, gather children together in groups of three to share their favorite nonfiction books.

Share the page where you listed a nonfiction book. Talk about the book. Show how you wrote the title and author on the lines. Talk about other books you might add to your list.

## Extend the Lesson (Optional)

After assessing children's understanding, you might decide to extend the learning.

▶ Have children list other favorite nonfiction titles on the My Favorite Nonfiction Books page as they listen to and read more nonfiction books.

▶ Provide groups with several fiction and nonfiction books. Ask children to sort fiction books in one pile and nonfiction in another, and then talk about what they would write on the My Favorite Nonfiction Books page for each nonfiction book.

---

### My Favorite Fiction Books

| |
|---|
| The Magic Rabbit by Annette LeBlanc Cate |
| Blackout by John Rocco |
| |
| |
| |
| |

### My Favorite Nonfiction Books

| |
|---|
| Surprising Sharks by Nicola Davies |
| What Do You Do with a Tail Like This? |
| by Steve Jenkins and Robin Page |
| |
| |
| |

*Section 4: Writing About Reading*

**Reading Minilesson Principle**
## Share information about a topic.

### Writing About Nonfiction Books in a Reader's Notebook

## You Will Need

- *Reader's Notebook: Primary* or chart paper resembling the Books I Read pages from *Reader's Notebook: Primary*
- several familiar nonfiction books with a variety of topics, such as the following:
  - *Tools* by Ann Morris, from Text Set: Nonfiction
  - *On the Go* by Ann Morris from Text Set: Fiction and Nonfiction
- markers
- a reader's notebook for each child
- basket of class favorite nonfiction books

## Academic Language / Important Vocabulary

- reader's notebook
- title
- author
- topic

## Continuum Connection

- Record in Reader's Notebook the titles, authors, and illustrators of texts (p. 178)
- Tell important information about a text (p. 178)

## Goal

Tell about the topic of a nonfiction book in a reader's notebook.

## Rationale

When children use a reader's notebook to tell about the topic of a nonfiction book, they are given the opportunity to revisit the book and process the information differently. This increases their knowledge of the topic and helps them focus on the details the nonfiction writer includes.

## Assess Learning

Observe children when they use a reader's notebook to tell about the topic of a nonfiction book. Notice if there is evidence of new learning based on the goal of this minilesson.

- Do children draw and write in a reader's notebook about the topic of a nonfiction book?
- Do children write the title and author's name on the lines?
- Are they able to create a sketch to represent something about the topic?
- Do they use the terms *reader's notebook, title, author*, and *topic*?

## Minilesson

To help children think about the minilesson principle, engage them in a short discussion of how to draw and write about the topic of a nonfiction book. Here is an example.

- Show the cover of *Tools* and a Books I Read page or the prepared chart paper.

  Here is a page from the reader's notebook. If I want to tell what this nonfiction book is about, what could I write on this page?

- Ask children to point to the title and author as you model the writing.

  The topic is what a book is all about. What could I draw to show the topic of this book?

- Show the reader's notebook page with the lines or the prepared chart paper.

  The topic is tools and how they help us. The author chose a title that helps you know what the topic is. What could I write about the topic?

- Using children's ideas, write about the topic.

  You can share information about the topic of a book on these pages in your reader's notebook.

## Have a Try

Invite the children to talk with a partner about what *On the Go* is mostly about.

▶ Show the reader's notebook page and the cover of *On the Go*.

> Turn and talk to your partner about the topic of this book. What is this book about? What would you draw and write about the topic in your reader's notebook?

## Summarize and Apply

Summarize the learning and remind children to notice what they learn about a topic as they read.

> What is the topic of a nonfiction book? How can you tell?

> Choose a book from the nonfiction basket. When you read, think about the topic, or what the book is about. Then, in your reader's notebook, draw and write about the topic. Bring your notebook to share after independent work time.

## Share

Following independent work time, gather children together in groups of three to share their drawing and writing.

> Show the page you completed. Talk about the picture and what you wrote about the topic of your book. Show how you wrote the title and author on the lines.

## Extend the Lesson (Optional)

After assessing children's understanding, you might decide to extend the learning.

▶ Have children organize classroom nonfiction books by topics. Then, have them choose books on different topics to write and draw about in a reader's notebook.

▶ Take children to the school library and have the librarian talk about ways to find nonfiction books by topics. Have each child check out a nonfiction book to read and write about in a reader's notebook.

# RML4
## WAR.U4.RML4

**Reading Minilesson Principle**
# Tell something you learned about a topic.

## Writing About Nonfiction Books in a Reader's Notebook

### You Will Need

- *Reader's Notebook: Primary* or chart paper resembling the Books I Read pages from *Reader's Notebook: Primary*
- several familiar nonfiction books, such as the following:
  - *Surprising Sharks* by Nicola Davies, from Text Set: Nonfiction
  - *Water: Up, Down, and All Around* by Natalie M. Rosinsky, from Text Set: Nonfiction
- markers
- a reader's notebook for each child
- basket of class favorite nonfiction books

### Academic Language / Important Vocabulary

- reader's notebook
- title
- author
- topic

### Continuum Connection

- Record in Reader's Notebook the titles, authors, and illustrators of texts [p. 178]
- Reflect in writing both prior knowledge and new knowledge from a text [p. 178]

## Goal

Identify and write about new information learned from a nonfiction book in a reader's notebook.

## Rationale

When children think about the content of a nonfiction book, they need to notice what is new information and add it to their background knowledge. They learn that the purpose of reading nonfiction is to learn new information.

## Assess Learning

Observe children when they use a reader's notebook to tell about the topic of a nonfiction book. Notice if there is evidence of new learning based on the goal of this minilesson.

- Can children draw and write in a reader's notebook about new information learned from a nonfiction book?
- Do children write the title and author's name on the lines?
- Do they use the terms *reader's notebook, title, author,* and *topic*?

## Minilesson

To help children think about the minilesson principle, engage them in a short discussion of how to tell about what they learned about a topic in a nonfiction book. Here is an example.

- Show the left-hand Books I Read page or the prepared chart paper. Show the cover of *Surprising Sharks*.

  What should we include on this page?

- Ask children to point to the title and author as you model the writing.

  What do you think the picture should show?

- Ask for suggestions as you model drawing a simple sketch of a shark.

- Show the lined Books I Read page or the prepared chart paper. Show and read pages 3–4.

  What did you learn about sharks on these pages?

- Using the children's ideas, write one or two sentences about sharks.

  In your reader's notebook, you can tell about an interesting fact that you learned.

## Have a Try

Invite the children to talk with a partner about *Water: Up, Down, and All Around*.

▶ Show a blank Books I Read page and the cover of *Water: Up, Down, and All Around*. Read the title.

What information did the author tell about? Turn and talk.

## Summarize and Apply

Summarize the learning and remind children to think about the book's topic.

You can draw and write about something you learned in a nonfiction book. Look at the chart to see an example.

▶ Have the children open to a Books I Read page in *Reader's Notebook: Primary* (or provide an alternative notebook and show them where to label a page *Books I Read*).

During independent work time, choose a nonfiction book from the basket to read. Think about what you learned from the book. Write about it in your reader's notebook and then when we get together you will share what you wrote.

## Share

Following independent work time, gather children together in the meeting area to share their drawing and writing.

Turn and talk to a partner about the page that tells something you learned.

## Extend the Lesson (Optional)

After assessing children's understanding, you might decide to extend the learning.

▶ Have children share with each other new information they write about in a reader's notebook.

▶ Assist children in adding to the information learned from a nonfiction book by doing some guided online research.

▶ **Drawing/Writing About Reading** Have children continue to draw and write about information learned when they listen to or read new nonfiction books.

Books I Read

1
Title: Surprising Sharks
Author: Nicola Davies

1
I learned that the smallest shark is the dwarf lantern. It is a little bigger than a candy bar.

Section 4: Writing About Reading

## RML5
WAR.U4.RML5

**Reading Minilesson Principle**
## Tell an interesting fact about a topic.

### Writing About Nonfiction Books in a Reader's Notebook

#### You Will Need

‣ *Reader's Notebook: Primary* or chart paper resembling the Books I Read pages from *Reader's Notebook: Primary*

‣ several familiar nonfiction books with interesting facts, such as the following:

  • *What Do You Do When Something Wants to Eat You?* by Steve Jenkins, from Text Set: Nonfiction

  • *Animals Black and White* by Phyllis Limbacher Tildes, from Text Set: Questions and Answers

‣ markers

‣ a reader's notebook for each child

‣ basket of class favorite nonfiction books

#### Academic Language / Important Vocabulary

‣ reader's notebook
‣ title
‣ author
‣ fact

#### Continuum Connection

‣ Record in Reader's Notebook the titles, authors, and illustrators of texts (p. 178)

‣ Tell important information about a text (p. 178)

‣ Use a text as a resource for words, phrases and ideas for writing (p. 178)

### Goal

Tell interesting facts about the topic of a nonfiction book in a reader's notebook.

### Rationale

When children use a reader's notebook to think about interesting facts learned in a nonfiction book, they demonstrate an understanding of the information. Sharing their thinking deepens background knowledge of the topic.

### Assess Learning

Observe children when they tell about an interesting fact they learned in a nonfiction book. Notice if there is evidence of new learning based on the goal of this minilesson.

‣ Can children draw and write about an interesting fact in a reader's notebook?

‣ Do children write the title and author's name on the lines?

## Minilesson

To help children think about the minilesson principle, engage them in a short discussion of how to tell an interesting fact. Here is an example.

‣ Read pages 2–3 from *What Do You Do When Something Wants to Eat You?*

  Listen and think about a fact the author writes about. A fact is true information. You can tell some interesting facts in your reader's notebook.

‣ Show the lined Books I Read page or the prepared chart paper.

  Turn and talk about facts I could write about an octopus.

‣ After discussion, use children's suggestions to write a few sentences about the topic on the lines of the reader's notebook.

‣ Show the left-hand Books I Read page or the prepared chart. Show the cover of *What Do You Do When Something Wants to Eat You?* Ask children to point to the title and author as you model the writing.

  What facts should we tell on this Books I Read page?

‣ Show page 3. Draw a simple sketch of the octopus and ink in response to what children say.

  I will choose something about the octopus to draw since I want to show an interesting fact. What details do you think I should include in my drawing to show the interesting fact?

‣ Repeat the activity, using a fact about the puffer fish on pages 6–7.

  You can tell about an interesting fact in your reader's notebook.

## Have a Try

Invite the children to talk with a partner about a fact in *Animals Black and White*.

▶ Show and read pages 11–12 of *Animals Black and White*.

> Now turn and tell your partner a fact the author writes about. What would you tell about in your reader's notebook?

## Summarize and Apply

Summarize the learning and remind children to find an interesting fact as they read.

▶ Have the children open to a Books I Read page in *Reader's Notebook: Primary* (or provide an alternative notebook and show them where to label a page *Books I Read*).

> You can write facts in your reader's notebook. Look at the chart to see an example.

> During independent work time today, read a nonfiction book. You may choose a book from the basket. Look for an interesting fact and then write about it in your reader's notebook. Make sure you add the title, the author, and a picture. You can look in the book to find words to use in writing about an interesting fact.

## Share

Following independent work time, gather children in the meeting area to share their drawing and writing.

> Turn and talk about a fact you wrote from your nonfiction book.

## Extend the Lesson (Optional)

After assessing children's understanding, you might decide to extend the learning.

▶ Have children share the interesting facts they write about with each other, or with children from a different class.

▶ Assist children in adding to the facts they learn from a nonfiction book by doing research online or at the library.

▶ **Drawing/Writing About Reading** Have children continue to draw and write about interesting facts when they listen to or read books.

# RML 6
## WAR.U4.RML6

### Reading Minilesson Principle
### Think about all the things you can write about nonfiction books.

## You Will Need

- chart paper prepared with the heading *Ways to Write About Nonfiction Books*
- reader's notebook pages or chart paper from RML3–RML5
- nonfiction books such as the following from Text Set: Nonfiction:
  - *Tools* by Ann Morris
  - *Surprising Sharks* by Nicola Davies
  - *What Do You Do When Something Wants to Eat You?* by Steve Jenkins
- markers
- sticky notes
- a reader's notebook for each child
- basket of class favorite nonfiction books

## Academic Language / Important Vocabulary

- reader's notebook
- title
- author
- topic
- fact

## Continuum Connection

- Record in Reader's Notebook the titles, authors, and illustrators of texts (p. 178)
- Tell important information about a text (p. 178)

## Goal

Understand different ways to share information from nonfiction books in a reader's notebook.

## Rationale

When children think about the different ways to share information from nonfiction books, they will think more deeply about the topics and facts. They will begin to make connections about topics across books. This thinking will increase their background knowledge and provide a basis for their writing.

## Assess Learning

Observe children when they use a reader's notebook to tell about nonfiction books. Notice if there is evidence of new learning based on the goal of this minilesson.

- Can children talk about the things they write about nonfiction books in a reader's notebook?
- Do they write about nonfiction books in a reader's notebook?
- Do they use the terms *reader's notebook, title, author, topic,* and *fact*?

# Minilesson

To help children think about the minilesson principle, engage them in a short discussion of the different ways to use a reader's notebook to tell about nonfiction books. Here is an example.

- Show the reader's notebook pages or charts created for RML3 and show the cover of *Tools*.

  You can write about nonfiction books in different ways. What did we write about the information in *Tools*?

  You can tell about the topic of a book, or what the book is about.

- Begin a list on the prepared chart paper.
- Show the reader's notebook pages or charts created for RML4 and show the cover of *Surprising Sharks*.

  What did we write about *Surprising Sharks*?

  What does that show you about things you can write about in your reader's notebook?

- Guide children to recognize that these pages have writing and drawing about something they learned from the book. Add to the list.

## Have a Try

Invite the children to talk with a partner about what they can add to the chart.

▶ Show the reader's notebook pages or charts created for RML5 and the cover of *What Do You Do When Something Wants to Eat You?*

> Notice these pages from the reader's notebook. Turn and talk about what you notice and what we can add to the list.

▶ Record responses on the chart.

## Summarize and Apply

Summarize the learning and remind children to think about what to tell about a nonfiction book as they read.

▶ Read the chart together with the children.

▶ Have the children open to a Books I Read page in *Reader's Notebook: Primary* (or provide an alternative notebook and show them where to label a page *Books I Read*).

> Choose one idea for writing about nonfiction books from the chart and place a sticky note with your name next to it. Then, use the idea to draw and write about a book in your reader's notebook. You can choose a book from the basket to write about or choose another nonfiction book.

## Share

Following independent work time, gather children together in groups of three to share their drawing and writing.

> Share the page from your reader's notebook you completed today.

## Extend the Lesson (Optional)

After assessing children's understanding, you might decide to extend the learning.

▶ Add to the list as children think of new ways to write about nonfiction books.

▶ **Drawing/Writing About Reading** Have children write a second way about a topic from the same book. Ask them to compare the two, and talk about why it is good to have different ways to write about books.

---

**Ways to Write About Nonfiction Books**

You can write about . . .

- the topic.

  | Ari | Sam |
  | Ava | Darius |

- something you learned.

  | Leeza | Alonzo |
  | Marie | Bella |

- an interesting fact.

  | Carlos | Essel |
  | Anh | Sofia |

---

**Section 4: Writing About Reading**

## Assessment

After you have taught the minilessons in this umbrella, observe children talking and writing about their reading across instructional contexts: interactive read-aloud, independent reading and literacy work, guided reading, shared reading, and book club. Use *The Literacy Continuum* (Fountas and Pinnell 2017) to observe children's reading and writing behaviors across instructional contexts.

▶ What evidence do you have of new understandings related to writing about nonfiction in a reader's notebook?

- Can children accurately identify and record book titles and authors' names?

- Are they able to make a list of favorite nonfiction titles?

- Can children identify, draw, and write about a nonfiction book topic?

- Can children identify, draw, and write about new information learned in a nonfiction book?

- Can they identify, draw, and write about interesting facts learned in a nonfiction book?

- Do children use the terms *reader's notebook, author, title, nonfiction, topic,* and *fact*?

▶ In what other ways, beyond the scope of this umbrella, are children talking about writing in a reader's notebook?

- Are children beginning to talk and write about why authors decide to write nonfiction books and what types of things the author might be interested in based on the books he writes?

- Do they express opinions about what they read?

Use your observations to determine the next umbrella you will teach. You may also consult Minilessons Across the Year (p. 51) for guidance.

## Minilessons in This Umbrella

**RML1**   Share your opinion about a book.

**RML2**   Share your opinion about authors and illustrators you love.

**RML3**   Share your opinion about characters you love.

**RML4**   Make a book recommendation to your classmates.

**RML5**   Write a letter to share your thinking.

## Before Teaching Umbrella 5 Minilessons

This umbrella can be taught as a complete set of lessons on ways to use a reader's notebook to share opinions, or it can be taught in tandem with related umbrellas in Section Two: Literary Analysis. While these lessons are examples of how to teach children to use *Reader's Notebook: Primary* (Fountas and Pinnell 2014), any reader's notebook can be used. The goal is for children to have a consistent place to collect their thinking and have a record of their reading lives for the year (see p. 46).

Before teaching these minilessons, it would be helpful to introduce the children to the sections of the reader's notebook (see Umbrella 1: Introducing a Reader's Notebook in this section). Also, provide many opportunities for children to read and discuss a variety of high-quality picture books and complete several author and illustrator studies. Use the following books from the *Fountas & Pinnell Classroom™ Interactive Read-Aloud Collection* text sets or choose similar high-quality fiction and nonfiction books with which the children are familiar.

**Questions and Answers**

**Nicola Davies**

**Journeys**

**Diversity**

**Reader's Notebook**

**Nonfiction: Questions and Answers**

*A Cool Summer Tail* by Carrie A. Pearson

**Nicola Davies: Exploring the Animal World**

*Bat Loves the Night* by Nicola Davies

**Journeys Near and Far**

*Bailey Goes Camping* by Kevin Henkes

*Dear Juno* by Soyung Pak

**Celebrating Diversity**

*Two Eggs, Please* by Sarah Weeks

*The Name Jar* by Yangsook Choi

*Whoever You Are* by Mem Fox

As you read aloud and enjoy these texts together, help children

• share their opinions about books with supporting evidence, and

• think about the books they would recommend to others.

**Writing Opinions About Books**

### You Will Need

- *Reader's Notebook: Primary* or chart paper resembling the Books I Read page from the *Reader's Notebook: Primary*
- markers
- three or four familiar books, such as the following:
  - *Two Eggs, Please* by Sarah Weeks, from Text Set: Diversity
  - *A Cool Summer Tail* by Carrie A. Pearson, from Text Set: Questions and Answers
  - *The Name Jar* by Yangsook Choi, from Text Set: Diversity
- a reader's notebook for each child
- basket of familiar books

### Academic Language / Important Vocabulary

- author
- opinion
- reader's notebook

### Continuum Connection

- Express opinions (interesting, funny, exciting) about texts (pp. 176, 178)
- Provide evidence from the text or from personal experience to support written statements about a text (p. 176)

## Goal

Express an opinion and provide an explanation to support it.

## Rationale

When children use a reader's notebook to draw and write their opinions about books, they learn how to express their thoughts and demonstrate their understanding of texts. Expressing an opinion is the foundation for critical thinking.

## Assess Learning

Observe children when they use a reader's notebook to express an opinion. Notice if there is evidence of new learning based on the goal of this minilesson.

- ▶ Are children able to tell about their opinions on the Books I Read page?
- ▶ Can children share their opinions about a book?
- ▶ Do they use the terms *author*, *opinion*, and *reader's notebook*?

## Minilesson

To help children think about the minilesson principle, engage them in a short discussion of sharing opinions about books. Here is an example.

- ▶ Introduce the concept of an *opinion*.

  After I read a book, I think, "I like that book," or "I don't like that book." That is my opinion. Let's say the word *opinion*.

  Your opinion about a book is what you think about it. Let's say the word *opinion* again.

- ▶ Show the Books I Read page from *Reader's Notebook: Primary* or the prepared chart paper. Show the cover of *Two Eggs, Please*.

  First, I am going to write the title and author of the book.

  My opinion is that I like *Two Eggs, Please* because it is funny, so I will write that in a reader's notebook.

- ▶ Write the opinion sentence and read it aloud. Using children's suggestions, add an example from the text to support your opinion.

  Can you help me think of a funny example from the story? What could I write and draw about this funny example?

  When you say your opinion, you need to give a reason for it.

## Have a Try

Invite the children to talk with a partner about expressing an opinion about *The Name Jar*.

▶ Show the cover of *The Name Jar* and read the title.

> Turn and talk with a partner about how you could tell your opinion about this story in a reader's notebook. Include an example from the story. Your opinion is personal to you so you might have different thoughts than your partner.

## Summarize and Apply

Summarize the learning and remind children to think about their opinion of the book they read.

> What did you learn today about what to write in a reader's notebook? Look at the chart to remember.

▶ Have children open to a Books I Read page in *Reader's Notebook: Primary* (or provide an alternative notebook and show them where to label a page *Books I Read*).

▶ Show the cover of *The Name Jar*.

> You talked with your partner about expressing your opinion about *The Name Jar* in your reader's notebook. During independent work time, you will write your opinion of *The Name Jar*. First write the title and author. Then, write and draw something that shows your opinion.

## Share

Following independent work time, gather children in the meeting area to talk about their opinion of the book they read.

> Turn and talk to your partner about your opinion of your book. Show the page in your reader's notebook and describe what you wrote and drew.

## Extend the Lesson (Optional)

After assessing children's understanding, you might decide to extend the learning.

▶ Provide opportunities for children to share opinions they write and draw about in a reader's notebook.

▶ **Drawing/Writing About Reading** Have children choose a book they have listened to during interactive read-aloud or shared reading to tell about in a reader's notebook.

Books I Read

Title: Two Eggs, Please

Author: Sarah Weeks

I like this book.
It was very funny.
It was funny for a stork
to be a doctor!

## RML2

**WAR.U5.RML2**

**Reading Minilesson Principle**
# Share your opinion about authors and illustrators you love.

**Writing Opinions
About Books**

### You Will Need

- *Reader's Notebook: Primary* or chart paper resembling the Books I Read page from *Reader's Notebook: Primary*

- markers

- several books by favorite authors and illustrators, such as the following:

  - *Bat Loves the Night* by Nicola Davies, from Text Set: Nicola Davies

  - *Bailey Goes Camping* by Kevin Henkes, from Text Set: Journeys

- a reader's notebook for each child

- basket of books by favorite authors and illustrators

### Academic Language / Important Vocabulary

- author

- illustrator

- opinion

- reader's notebook

### Continuum Connection

- Formulate opinions about authors and illustrators and use writing to state why (p. 176)

- Formulate opinions about authors and illustrators and state in writing the basis for those opinions (p. 176)

## Goal

Express an opinion about an author or illustrator and provide an explanation to support it.

## Rationale

When children use a reader's notebook to tell about the authors and illustrators they love, they learn how to think about how an author and illustrator make decisions about the content. They become aware as to why they are drawn to certain books. It's important to make sure that children understand the importance of providing evidence for their opinions.

## Assess Learning

Observe children when they use a reader's notebook to express an opinion. Notice if there is evidence of new learning based on the goal of this minilesson.

- Are children able to formulate an opinion about an author or illustrator?

- Can they write that opinion and support it with evidence?

- Do they use the terms *author, illustrator, opinion,* and *reader's notebook*?

## Minilesson

To help children think about the minilesson principle, engage them in a short discussion of sharing opinions about authors and illustrators. Here is an example.

- Help them say the word *opinion* and talk about what it means.

- Show the Books I Read page from *Reader's Notebook: Primary* or the prepared chart paper. Show the cover of *Bat Loves the Night*.

   Nicola Davies is an author I love because she writes about animals, like in *Bat Loves the Night*. What could I write and draw on this page to share my opinion about Nicola Davies?

- Using children's suggestions, add to the chart. Prompt children to include a specific example from the text that supports the opinion and emphasize the importance of providing reasons for one's opinion, in this case, examples from the book.

## Have a Try

Invite the children to share their opinion of a book with a partner.

> Here's a book by another of our favorite author-illustrators, Kevin Henkes. Think about your opinions about Nicola Davies and Kevin Henkes. What do you like or not like about their writing or illustrations? Why? Turn and talk with your partner about what you would draw and write about Nicola Davies or Kevin Henkes in a reader's notebook.

▶ After time for discussion, ask volunteers to share their opinions.

## Summarize and Apply

Summarize the learning and remind children to think about their opinion of the author and illustrator as they read.

▶ Review the word *opinion* and the chart from today's minilesson.

▶ Have children open to a Books I Read page in *Reader's Notebook: Primary* (or provide an alternative notebook and show them where to label a page *Books I Read*).

> You shared with your partner your opinions about Nicola Davies and Kevin Henkes. During independent work time, you will write your opinion of either Nicola Davies or Kevin Henkes in a reader's notebook. Include an example from a book to support your opinion. Bring your reader's notebook when we meet so you can share.

## Share

Following independent work time, gather children together in the meeting area to talk about their opinions of authors and illustrators.

> Turn and talk to a partner about what you wrote in your reader's notebook. Show the page and describe what you wrote and drew.

## Extend the Lesson (Optional)

After assessing children's understanding, you might decide to extend the learning.

▶ If you used fiction books in this minilesson, repeat the lesson with nonfiction books, or vice versa.

▶ Provide opportunities, such as giving a book talk, for children to share opinions from a reader's notebook (see Umbrella 3: Giving a Book Talk in Section Two: Literary Analysis).

**Section 4: Writing About Reading**

**Reading Minilesson Principle**
## Share your opinion about characters you love.

### Writing Opinions About Books

#### You Will Need

▸ *Reader's Notebook: Primary* or chart paper resembling the Books I Read page from *Reader's Notebook: Primary*

▸ markers

▸ several books with favorite characters, such as the following:

  • *Dear Juno* by Soyung Pak, from Text Set: Journeys

▸ a reader's notebook for each child

▸ basket of books with favorite characters

#### Academic Language / Important Vocabulary

▸ character

▸ opinion

▸ reader's notebook

#### Continuum Connection

▸ Draw and write to express opinions about the characters in a story (funny, bad, silly, nice, friendly) (p. 176)

### Goal

Express an opinion about a character and provide an example to support it.

### Rationale

When children use a reader's notebook to tell about characters they love, they begin to connect the experiences characters have in books to their own lives. They also begin to think about why certain types of characters are appealing to them.

### Assess Learning

Observe children when they use a reader's notebook to share an opinion about characters. Notice if there is evidence of new learning based on the goal of this minilesson.

▸ Are children able to draw and write to show an opinion of a character?

▸ Can they support their opinions with evidence from the text?

▸ Do they use the terms *character*, *opinion*, and *reader's notebook*?

## Minilesson

To help children think about the minilesson principle, engage them in a short discussion of sharing opinions about characters. Here is an example.

> What is an opinion?

> You can tell an opinion about many parts of a book, including the characters.

▸ Show the Books I Read page from *Reader's Notebook: Primary* or the prepared chart paper. Show the cover of *Dear Juno*.

> I like the character Juno in *Dear Juno* because he sends nice letters to his grandma, just like I did when I was his age. How can I share my opinion about Juno in a reader's notebook?

▸ Using children's suggestions, add to the reader's notebook page. Model writing the title and character's name from the book. Prompt children to choose a specific example from the text to support the opinion.

### Have a Try

Invite the children to share their opinion of a character with a partner.

> Think about your opinion of Juno or another character you love from a different book. Turn and talk with a partner about what you would tell about the character in your reader's notebook.

▸ After time for discussion, ask volunteers to share their opinions.

## Summarize and Apply

Summarize the learning and remind children to think about their opinion of characters as they read.

> What is something you can write about a character in a reader's notebook? Look at the chart to help you remember.

▶ Have children open to a Books I Read page in *Reader's Notebook: Primary* (or provide an alternative notebook and show them where to label a page *Books I Read*).

> You shared with your partner your opinion about a character from a story. During independent work time, you will write your opinion of the character in a reader's notebook. Include an example from a book to support your opinion. Bring your reader's notebook when we meet so you can share.

## Share

Following independent work time, gather children together in the meeting area to talk about their opinions about a character in the book they read.

> Turn and talk to a partner about your opinions about a character. Show the page in your reader's notebook and describe what you wrote and drew.

## Extend the Lesson (Optional)

After assessing children's understanding, you might decide to extend the learning.

▶ Have children role-play scenes with their favorite characters, sharing their opinions about why they love the characters.

▶ Use shared writing to create a chart of favorite fiction book characters. Have children add drawings to illustrate the list.

▶ **Drawing/Writing About Reading** Have children write in a reader's notebook about characters in books they have listened to during interactive read-aloud or shared reading, or another book.

Books I Love

1　Title: Dear Juno

Author: Soyung Pak

2　I like Juno.
He sent letters to his grandma.
It's funny he thinks a drawing is a letter.

**Section 4: Writing About Reading**

**Reading Minilesson Principle**
# Make a book recommendation to your classmates.

## Writing Opinions About Books

### You Will Need

- *Reader's Notebook: Primary* or chart paper resembling a blank page from the end of the All About Me section in *Reader's Notebook: Primary*, two copies: one filled in with a simple book recommendation for *A Cool Summer Tail*, and the other blank
- markers
- three or four favorite books, such as the following:
  - *A Cool Summer Tail* by Carrie A. Pearson, from Text Set: Questions and Answers
  - *Two Eggs, Please* by Sarah Weeks, from Text Set: Diversity
  - *Dear Juno* by Soyung Pak, from Text Set: Journeys
- a reader's notebook for each child
- basket of class favorite books

### Academic Language / Important Vocabulary

- title
- author
- opinion
- recommend
- reader's notebook

### Continuum Connection

- Express opinions (interesting, funny, exciting) about texts (pp. 176, 178)
- Provide evidence from the text or from personal experience to support written statements about a text (p. 176)

## Goal

Understand how to make an effective book recommendation to others.

## Rationale

When children recommend books to others, they think about and articulate what makes a book enjoyable. This supports the development of critical and thoughtful reading.

## Assess Learning

Observe children when they use a reader's notebook to make a book recommendation. Notice if there is evidence of new learning based on the goal of this minilesson.

- Are children able to draw and write about a book they recommend?
- Do they support opinions with examples from the text?
- Can they use the terms *title, author, opinion, recommend,* and *reader's notebook*?

## Minilesson

To help children think about the minilesson principle, engage them in a short discussion of making a book recommendation. Here is an example.

- Show your prepared book recommendation for *A Cool Summer Tail*. Read it aloud.

  What is this writing about? What am I trying to get the reader to do?

  What I wrote is called a book recommendation. When you write a book recommendation, you are telling others what you thought about the book and why you think they should read it.

- Show the blank version of a page from the end of the All About Me section.

  Let's write a recommendation for *Two Eggs, Please*. What information should we include?

- Use children's suggestions to fill in the page, prompting as needed to include the title, author's name, and something that recommends the book. Encourage children to use a specific text example.

## Have a Try

Invite the children to talk with a partner about what to say to recommend *Dear Juno*.

▶ Show the cover of *Dear Juno*.

> If you want to recommend *Dear Juno* to a classmate, what would you tell? Turn and talk to a partner about what you would say about *Dear Juno*.

## Summarize and Apply

Summarize the learning and remind children to think about why they would recommend the book.

> What information should you include in a book recommendation? Look at the chart to help you remember.

▶ Have children open to a blank page at the end of the All About Me section in *Reader's Notebook: Primary* (or provide an alternative notebook and show them were to write).

> During independent work time today, choose one of the books we talked about today to recommend in a reader's notebook. Think about what we wrote and drew on the pages together. Bring your reader's notebook when we meet so you can share.

## Share

Following independent work time, gather children together in the meeting area to talk about their book recommendations.

> Turn and talk to a partner about your book recommendation. Show the page in your reader's notebook and describe it.

## Extend the Lesson (Optional)

After assessing children's understanding, you might decide to extend the learning.

▶ If you used fiction books in this minilesson, teach another lesson using nonfiction books, or vice versa.

▶ Provide opportunities for children to share their book recommendations with others (see Umbrella 3: Giving a Book Talk in Section Two: Literary Analysis).

▶ **Drawing/Writing About Reading** Encourage children to write book reviews on a class reading blog using the opinions they have written and drawn about in a reader's notebook.

> You will like A Cool Summer Tail
> by Carrie A. Pearson.
> It has good facts.
> One fact is bees flap their wings.

> Read Two Eggs, Please!
> by Sarah Weeks.
> It's a funny book.
> Animals talk to people.
> Animals go out to eat.
> You will laugh!

# RML5

## Reading Minilesson Principle
## Write a letter to share your thinking.

**Writing Opinions
About Books**

### You Will Need

- *Reader's Notebook: Primary* or chart paper resembling the Books I Read pages from *Reader's Notebook: Primary* with a letter written about *Two Eggs, Please*
- markers
- several familiar books children, such as the following:
  - *Two Eggs, Please* by Sarah Weeks, from Text Set: Diversity
  - *Whoever You Are* by Mem Fox, from Text Set: Diversity
- a reader's notebook for each child

### Academic Language / Important Vocabulary

- author
- title
- opinion
- letter
- reader's notebook

### Continuum Connection

- Express opinions (interesting, funny, exciting) about texts (pp. 176, 178)

### Goal

Compose a letter to share opinions about a book they love.

### Rationale

When children write letters to express their thinking about a book, they begin to think about what they read. They will become aware that their opinions have value.

### Assess Learning

Observe children when they use a reader's notebook to write a letter. Notice if there is evidence of new learning based on the goal of this minilesson.

- ▶ Do children include the title of the book and something interesting about the book?
- ▶ Do they include the recipient and the sender in the letter?
- ▶ Do they use the terms *author, title, opinion, letter,* and *reader's notebook*?

## Minilesson

To help children think about the minilesson principle, engage them in a short discussion of writing a letter. Here is an example.

- ▶ Show the Books I Love pages from *Reader's Notebook: Primary* or the prepared chart paper with the letter. Show the cover of *Two Eggs, Please*.

    I am going to read a letter I wrote to you about *Two Eggs, Please*.

- ▶ Read the letter.

    What do you notice?

- ▶ Invite a few children to share what they noticed. If necessary, guide the conversation with questions such as these: *Who am I writing this letter to? What do I write about in my letter?*

- ▶ Point out the special features of a letter: the date, the greeting, and the closing.

    One way to share your thinking about a book is by writing a letter to other readers. You can write about what you found interesting about the book.

### Have a Try

Invite the children to talk with a partner about writing a letter to recommend *Whoever You Are*.

- ▶ Show the cover of *Whoever You Are* and a few pages if necessary.

    Turn and talk with a partner about writing a letter to our class about *Whoever You Are*. What would you write about in your letter?

- ▶ Ask a few children to share their thinking.

## Summarize and Apply

Summarize the learning and remind children to think about their opinion of books as they read.

> What are some of the special features of a letter? Look at the chart to help you remember.
>
> What could you say in a letter to our class to recommend a book?

▶ Have children open to a Books I Read page in *Reader's Notebook: Primary* (or provide an alternative notebook and show them where to label a page *Books I Read*).

> During independent work time, you are going to write a letter to recommend *Whoever You Are*. Include the date, the person you are writing to, the book title, and what you found interesting. This time write the letter to our class. Think about what you told your partner. You can add a drawing if you wish. Sign your name. Bring your reader's notebook when we get together in group meeting.

## Share

Following independent work time, gather children together in the meeting area to share their letters with a partner.

> Turn and talk to a partner. Read the letter you wrote and show your drawing. How are your letters the same or different?

## Extend the Lesson (Optional)

After assessing children's understanding, you might decide to extend the learning.

▶ **Drawing/Writing About Reading** Encourage children to write letters to classmates, teachers, family, or friends about a book they love.

▶ **Drawing/Writing About Reading** Letters can be in different forms. You might extend the lesson by talking about what children could write in an e-mail, for example.

## Assessment

After you have taught the minilessons in this umbrella, observe children talking and writing about their reading across instructional contexts: interactive read-aloud, independent reading and literacy work, guided reading, shared reading, and book club. Use *The Literacy Continuum* (Fountas and Pinnell 2017) to observe children's reading and writing behaviors across instructional contexts.

▶ What evidence do you have of new understandings related to sharing opinions in a reader's notebook?

- Are children sharing opinions about books with others?
- Do children identify text evidence to support their opinions?
- Can children share opinions about authors and illustrators?
- Do they share opinions about characters?
- Do they share opinions by recommending books to classmates?
- Are children able to write a letter about a favorite book?
- Can they use the terms *reader's notebook, author, opinion, illustrator,* and *character* correctly?

▶ In what other ways, beyond the scope of this umbrella, are children sharing opinions?

- Are children beginning to think about the decisions authors and illustrators make?
- Are they willing to share their opinions with an audience by giving a book talk?

Use your observations to determine the next umbrella you will teach. You may also consult Minilessons Across the Year (p. 51) for guidance.

**alphabet book/ABC book** A book that helps children develop the concept and sequence of the alphabet by pairing alphabet letters with pictures of people, animals, or objects with labels related to the letters.

**animal fantasy** A modern fantasy text geared to a very young audience in which animals act like people and encounter human problems.

**animal story** A contemporary realistic or historical fiction or fantasy text that involves animals and that often focuses on the relationships between humans and animals.

**assessment** A means for gathering information or data that reveals what learners control, partially control, or do not yet control consistently.

**beast tale** A folktale featuring animals that talk.

**behaviors** Actions that are observable as children read or write.

**bold / boldface** Type that is heavier and darker than usual, often used for emphasis.

**book and print features** (as text characteristics) The physical attributes of a text (for example, font, layout, and length).

**character** An individual, usually a person or animal, in a text.

**chronological sequence** An underlying structural pattern used especially in nonfiction texts to describe a series of events in the order they happened in time.

**comprehension** (as in reading) The process of constructing meaning while reading text.

**conflict** In a fiction text, a central problem within the plot that is resolved near the end of the story. In literature, characters are usually in conflict with nature, with other people, with society as a whole, or with themselves. Another term for conflict is *problem.*

**cumulative tale** A story with many details repeated until the climax.

**dialogue** Spoken words, usually set off with quotation marks in text.

**directions (how-to)** A procedural nonfiction text that shows the steps involved in performing a task. A set of directions may include diagrams or drawings with labels.

**elements of fiction** Important elements of fiction include narrator, characters, plot, setting, theme, and style.

**elements of poetry** Important elements of poetry include figurative language, imagery, personification, rhythm, rhyme, repetition, alliteration, assonance, consonance, onomatopoeia, and aspects of layout.

**endpapers** The sheets of heavy paper at the front and back of a hardback book that join the book block to the hardback binding. Endpapers are sometimes printed with text, maps, or design.

**English language learners** People whose native language is not English and who are acquiring English as an additional language.

**expository text** A nonfiction text that gives the reader information about a topic. Expository texts use a variety of text structures, such as compare and contrast, cause and effect, chronological sequence, problem and solution, and temporal sequence. Seven forms of expository text are categorical text, recount, collection, interview, report, feature article, and literary essay.

**factual text** See *informational text*.

**family, friends, and school story** A contemporary realistic text focused on the everyday experiences of children of a variety of ages, including relationships with family and friends and experiences at school.

**fantasy** A fiction text that contains elements that are highly unreal. Fantasy as a category of fiction includes genres such as animal fantasy, fantasy, and science fiction.

**fiction** Invented, imaginative prose or poetry that tells a story. Fiction texts can be organized into the categories realism and fantasy. Along with nonfiction, fiction is one of two basic genres of literature.

**figurative language** Language that compares two objects or ideas to allow the reader to see something more clearly or understand something in a new way. An element of a writer's style, figurative language changes or goes beyond literal meaning. Two common types of figurative language are metaphor (a direct comparison) and simile (a comparison that uses *like* or *as*).

**fluency** In reading, this term names the ability to read continuous text with good momentum, phrasing, appropriate pausing, intonation, and stress. In word solving, this term names the ability to solve words with speed, accuracy, and flexibility.

**folktale** A traditional fiction text about a people or "folk," originally handed down orally from generation to generation. Folktales are usually simple tales and often involve talking animals. Fables, fairy tales, beast tales, trickster tales, tall tales, realistic tales, cumulative tales, noodlehead tales, and pourquoi tales are some types of folktales.

**font** In printed text, the collection of type (letters) in a particular style.

**form** A kind of text that is characterized by particular elements. Mystery, for example, is a form of writing within the realistic fiction genre. Another term for form is *subgenre*.

**genre** A category of written text that is characterized by a particular style, form, or content.

**graphic feature** In fiction texts, graphic features are usually illustrations. In nonfiction texts, graphic features include photographs, paintings and drawings, captions, charts, diagrams, tables and graphs, maps, and timelines.

**high-frequency words** Words that occur often in the spoken and written language (for example, *the*).

**humor / humor story** A realistic fiction text that is full of fun and meant to entertain.

**illustration** Graphic representation of important content (for example, art, photos, maps, graphs, charts) in a fiction or nonfiction text.

**independent writing** Children write a text independently with teacher support as needed.

**infer** (as a strategic action) To go beyond the literal meaning of a text; to think about what is not stated but is implied by the writer.

**informational text** A nonfiction text in which a purpose is to inform or give facts about a topic. Informational texts include the following genres— biography, autobiography, memoir, and narrative nonfiction, as well as expository texts, procedural texts, and persuasive texts.

**interactive read-aloud** An instructional context in which students are actively listening and responding to an oral reading of a text.

**interactive writing** A teaching context in which the teacher and students cooperatively plan, compose, and write a group text; both teacher and students act as scribes (in turn).

**intonation** The rise and fall in pitch of the voice in speech to convey meaning.

**italic (italics)** A type style that is characterized by slanted letters.

**label** A written word or phrase that names the content of an illustration.

**layout** The way the print and illustrations are arranged on a page.

**main idea** The central underlying idea, concept, or message that the author conveys in a nonfiction text. Compare to *theme, message*.

**maintaining fluency** (as a strategic action) Integrating sources of information in a smoothly operating process that results in expressive, phrased reading.

**making connections** (as a strategic action) Searching for and using connections to knowledge gained through personal experiences, learning about the world, and reading other texts.

**meaning** One of the sources of information that readers use (MSV: meaning, language structure, visual information). Meaning, the semantic system of language, refers to meaning derived from words, meaning across a text or texts, and meaning from personal experience or knowledge.

**mentor texts** Books or other texts that serve as examples of excellent writing. Mentor texts are read and reread to provide models for literature discussion and student writing.

**message** An important idea that an author conveys in a fiction or nonfiction text. See also *main idea, theme*.

**modern fantasy** Fantasy texts that have contemporary content. Unlike traditional literature, modern fantasy does not come from an oral tradition. Modern fantasy texts can be divided into four more specific genres: animal fantasy, low fantasy, high fantasy, and science fiction.

**monitoring and self-correcting** (as a strategic action) Checking whether the reading sounds right, looks right, and makes sense, and solving problems when it doesn't.

**mood** The emotional atmosphere communicated by an author in his or her work, or how a text makes readers feel. An element of a writer's style, mood is established by details, imagery, figurative language, and setting. See also *tone*.

**narrative nonfiction** Nonfiction texts that tell a story using a narrative structure and literary language to make a topic interesting and appealing to readers.

**narrative text** A category of texts in which the purpose is to tell a story. Stories and biographies are kinds of narrative.

**narrative text structure** A method of organizing a text. A simple narrative structure follows a traditional sequence that includes a beginning, a problem, a series of events, a resolution of the problem, and an ending. Alternative narrative structures may include devices, such as flashback or flash-forward, to change the sequence of events or have multiple narrators.

**nonfiction** Prose or poetry that provides factual information. According to their structures, nonfiction texts can be organized into the categories of narrative and nonnarrative. Along with fiction, nonfiction is one of the two basic genres of literature.

**nonnarrative text structure** A method of organizing a text. Nonnarrative structures are used especially in three genres of nonfiction— expository texts, procedural texts, and persuasive texts. In nonnarrative nonfiction texts, underlying structural patterns include description, cause and effect, chronological sequence, temporal sequence, categorization, compare and contrast, problem and solution, and question and answer. See also *organization, text structure,* and *narrative text structure.*

**oral tradition** The handing down of literary material—such as songs, poems, and stories—from person to person over many generations through memory and word of mouth.

**organization** The arrangement of ideas in a text according to a logical structure, either narrative or nonnarrative. Another term for organization is *text structure.*

**organizational tools and sources of information** A design feature of nonfiction texts. Organizational tools and sources of information help a reader process and understand nonfiction texts. Examples include table of contents, headings, index, glossary, appendices, about the author, and references.

**peritext** Decorative or informative illustrations and/or print outside the body of the text. Elements of the peritext add to the aesthetic appeal and may have cultural significance or symbolic meaning.

**picture book** An illustrated fiction or nonfiction text in which pictures work with the text to tell a story or provide information.

**plot** The events, actions, conflict, and resolution of a story presented in a certain order in a fiction text. A simple plot progresses chronologically from start to end, whereas more complex plots may shift back and forth in time.

**poetry** Compact, metrical writing characterized by imagination and artistry and imbued with intense meaning. Along with prose, poetry is one of the two broad categories into which all literature can be divided.

**predicting** (as a strategic action) Using what is known to think about what will follow while reading continuous text.

**principle** A generalization that is predictable.

**print feature** In nonfiction texts, print features include the color, size, style, and font of type, as well as various aspects of layout.

**problem** See *conflict.*

**problem and solution** A structural pattern used especially in nonfiction texts to define a problem and clearly propose a solution. This pattern is often used in persuasive and expository texts.

**procedural text** A nonfiction text that explains how to do something. Procedural texts are almost always organized in temporal sequence and take the form of directions (or "how-to" texts) or descriptions of a process.

**prompt** A question, direction, or statement designed to encourage the child to say more about a topic.

***Prompting Guide 1: A Tool for Literacy Teachers*** A quick reference for specific language to teach for, prompt for, or reinforce effective reading and writing behaviors. The guide is organized in categories and color-coded so that you can turn quickly to the area needed and refer to it as you teach (Fountas and Pinnell 2012).

**punctuation** Marks used in written text to clarify meaning and separate structural units. The comma and the period are common punctuation marks.

**purpose** A writer's overall intention in creating a text, or a reader's overall intention in reading a text. To tell a story is one example of a writer's purpose, and to be entertained is one example of a reader's purpose.

**question and answer** A structural pattern used especially in nonfiction texts to organize information in a series of questions with responses. Question-and-answer texts may be based on a verbal or written interview, or on frequently arising or logical questions about a topic.

**reader's notebook** A notebook or folder of bound pages in which students write about their reading. A reader's notebook is used to keep a record of texts read and to express thinking. It may have several different sections to serve a variety of purposes.

**readers' theater** A performance of literature—i.e., a story, a play, or poetry—read aloud expressively by one or more persons rather than acted.

**realistic fiction** A fiction text that takes place in contemporary or modern times about believable characters involved in events that could happen. Contemporary realistic fiction usually presents modern problems that are typical for the characters, and it may highlight social issues.

**repetition** Repeated words or phrases that help create rhythm and emphasis in poetry or prose.

**resolution / solution** The point in the plot of a fiction story when the main conflict is solved.

**rhyme** The repetition of vowel and consonant sounds in the stressed and unstressed syllables of words in verse, especially at the ends of lines.

**rhythm** The regular or ordered repetition of stressed and unstressed syllables in poetry, other writing, or speech.

**searching for and using information** (as a strategic action) Looking for and thinking about all kinds of content to make sense of a text while reading.

**self-correcting** Noticing when reading doesn't make sense, sound right, or look right, and fixing it when it doesn't.

**sequence** See *chronological sequence* and *temporal sequence.*

**setting** The place and time in which a fiction text or biographical text takes place.

**shared reading** An instructional context in which the teacher involves a group of students in the reading of a particular big book to introduce aspects of literacy (such as print conventions), develop reading strategies (such as decoding or predicting), and teach vocabulary.

**shared writing** An instructional context in which the teacher involves a group of students in the composing of a coherent text together. The teacher writes while scaffolding children's language and ideas.

**sidebar** Information that is additional to the main text, placed alongside the text and sometimes set off from the main text in a box.

**small-group reading instruction** The teacher working with children brought together because they are similar enough in reading development to teach in a small group; guided reading.

**sources of information** The various cues in a written text that combine to make meaning (for example, syntax, meaning, and the physical shape and arrangement of type).

**speech bubble** A shape, often rounded, containing the words a character or person says in a cartoon or other text. Another term for *speech bubble* is *speech balloon*.

**story** A series of events in narrative form, either fiction or nonfiction.

**story about family, friends, and school** A contemporary realistic or historical fiction text that focuses on the everyday experiences of children of a variety of ages, including relationships with family and friends and experiences at school.

**strategic action** Any one of many simultaneous, coordinated thinking activities that go on in a reader's head. See *thinking within, beyond, and about the text*.

**stress** The emphasis given to some syllables or words.

**structure** One of the sources of information that readers use (MSV: meaning, language structure, visual information). Language structure refers to the way words are put together in phrases and sentences (syntax or grammar).

**style** The way a writer chooses and arranges words to create a meaningful text. Aspects of style include sentence length, word choice, and the use of figurative language and symbolism.

**subgenre** A kind of text that is characterized by particular elements. See also *form*.

**temporal sequence** An underlying structural pattern used especially in nonfiction texts to describe the sequence in which something always or usually occurs, such as the steps in a process. See also *procedural text*, and *directions (how-to)*.

**text structure** The overall architecture or organization of a piece of writing. Another term for text structure is *organization*. See also *narrative text structure* and *nonnarrative text structure*.

**theme** The central underlying idea, concept, or message that the author conveys in a fiction text. Compare to *main idea*.

**thinking within, beyond, and about the text** Three ways of thinking about a text while reading. Thinking *within* the text involves efficiently and effectively understanding what it is on the page, the author's literal message. Thinking *beyond* the text requires making inferences and putting text ideas together in different ways to construct the text's meaning. In thinking *about* the text, readers analyze and critique the author's craft.

**thought bubble** A shape, often rounded, containing the words (or sometimes an image that suggests one or more words) a character or person thinks in a cartoon or other text. Another term for *thought bubble* is *thought balloon*.

**tone** An expression of the author's attitude or feelings toward a subject reflected in the style of writing. For instance, a reader might characterize an author's tone as ironic or earnest. Sometimes the term *tone* is used to identify the mood of a scene or a work of literature. For example, a text might be said to have a somber or carefree tone. See also *mood*.

**tools** As text characteristics, parts of a text designed to help the reader access or better understand it (tables of contents, glossary, headings). In writing, references that support the writing process (dictionary, thesaurus).

**topic** The subject of a piece of writing.

**traditional literature** Stories passed down in oral or written form through history. An integral part of world culture, traditional literature includes folktales, tall tales, fairy tales, fables, myths, legends, epics, and ballads.

**trickster tale** A folktale featuring a clever, usually physically weaker or smaller, animal who outsmarts larger or more powerful animals.

**understandings** Basic concepts that are critical to comprehending a particular area of content.

**visual information** One of three sources of information that readers use (MSV: meaning, language structure, visual information). Visual information refers to the letters that represent the sounds of language and the way they are combined (spelling patterns) to create words; visual information at the sentence level includes punctuation.

**wordless picture book** A form in which a story is told exclusively with pictures.

**writing** Children engaging in the writing process and producing pieces of their own writing in many genres.

**writing about reading** Children responding to reading a text by writing and sometimes drawing.

# Credits

Cover image from *A Birthday Basket for Tia* by Pat Mora with illustrations by Cecily Lang. Text copyright © 1992 by Pat Mora. Illustrations copyright © 1992 by Cecily Lang. Reprinted with the permission of Simon & Schuster Books for Young Readers, an imprint of Simon & Schuster Children's Publishing Division. All rights reserved.

Cover image from *A Chair for My Mother* by Vera B. Williams. Copyright © 1982 by Vera B. Williams. Used by permission of HarperCollins Publishers.

Cover image from *A Cool Summer Tail* by Carrie A. Pearson, illustrated by Christina Wald. Copyright © 2014. All rights reserved. Used with permission from Arbordale Publishing.

Cover image from *A Fine, Fine, School* by Sharon Creech. Copyright © 1998 by Sharon Creech. Jacket art copyright © 2001 by Harry Bliss. Used by permission of HarperCollins Publishers.

Cover image from *All the Colors of the Earth* by Sheila Hamanaka. Copyright © 1995 by Sheila Hamanaka. Used by permission of HarperCollins Publishers.

Cover image from *Animals Black and White* by Phyllis Limbacher Tildes. Copyright © Charlesbridge Publishing, Inc. All rights reserved. Used with permission of Charlesbridge Publishing, Inc. www.charlesbridge.com.

Cover image from *April and Esme, Tooth Fairies*. Copyright © 2010 by Bob Graham. Reproduced by permission of the publisher, Candlewick Press, Somerville, MA, on behalf of Walker Books, London.

Cover image from *Bailey Goes Camping* by Kevin Henkes. Copyright © 1985 by Kevin Henkes. Used by permission of HarperCollins Publishers.

Cover image from *Bat Loves the Night*. Text copyright © 2001 by Nicola Davies. Illustrations copyright © 2001 by Sarah Fox-Davies. Reproduced by permission of the publisher, Candlewick Press, Somerville, MA, on behalf of Walker Books, London.

Cover image from *Be My Neighbor* by Maya Ajmera and John D. Ivanko. Copyright © Charlesbridge Publishing, Inc. All rights reserved. Used with permission of Charlesbridge Publishing, Inc. www.charlesbridge.com.

Cover image from *Beatrice Doesn't Want To* by Laura Numeroff. Text Copyright © 1981, 2004 Laura Numeroff. Illustrations Copyright © 2004 Lynn Munsinger. Reproduced by permission of the publisher, Candlewick Press, Somerville, MA.

Cover image from *Best Foot Forward* by Ingo Arndt. Copyright © 2013. All rights reserved. Used with permission from Holiday House.

Cover image from *Big Blue Whale*. Text copyright © 1997 by Nicola Davies. Illustrations copyright © 1997 by Nick Maland. Reproduced by permission of the publisher, Candlewick Press, Somerville, MA, on behalf of Walker Books, London.

Cover image from *Blackout* by John Rocco. Jacket illustration © 2011 by John Rocco. Reprinted by permission of Hyperion Books for Children, an imprint of Disney Book Group, LLC. All rights reserved.

Cover image from *Born to Be a Butterfly* by Karen Wallace. Reprinted by permission of DK, a division of Penguin Random House LLC. Copyright © 2010 Dorling Kindersley Limited.

Cover image from *Brand-new Pencils, Brand-new Books* by Diane deGroat. Cover art copyright © 2005 by Diane deGroat. Used by permission of HarperCollins Publishers.

Cover image from *Can I Bring Woolly to the Library, Ms. Reeder?* by Lois Grambling, illustrated by Judy Love. Copyright © Charlesbridge Publishing, Inc. All rights reserved. Used with permission of Charlesbridge Publishing, Inc. www.charlesbridge.com.

Cover image from *Cats* by Cari Meister. Copyright © 2015 Jump! All rights reserved. Used with permission from the publisher.

Cover image from *Chrysanthemum* by Kevin Henkes. Copyright © 1991 by Kevin Henkes. Used by permission of HarperCollins Publishers.

Cover image from *David's Drawings* by Cathryn Falwell. Copyright © 2006 Cathryn Falwell. Permission arranged with Lee & Low Books, Inc., New York, NY 10016.

Cover image from *Don't Let the Pigeon Drive the Bus!* Copyright © 2003 by Mo Willems. First published by Hyperion Books for Children, an imprint of Disney Book Group, LLC. Used with permission. All rights reserved.

Cover image from *Dooby Dooby Moo* by Doreen Cronin with illustrations by Betsy Lewin. Text copyright © 2006 by Doreen Cronin. Illustrations copyright © 2006 by Betsy Lewin. Reprinted with the permission of Atheneum Books for Young Readers, an imprint of Simon & Schuster Children's Publishing Division. All rights reserved.

Cover image from *Down the Road* by Alice Schertle. Text copyright © 1995 by Alice Schertle. Illustrations copyright © 1995 by E. B. Lewis. Reprinted by permission of Houghton Mifflin Harcourt Trade Publishing.

Cover image from *Elephants Cannot Dance!* by Mo Willems. Copyright © 2009 by Mo Willems. First published by Hyperion Books for Children, an imprint of Disney Book Group, LLC. Used with permission. All rights reserved.

Cover image from *Elizabeti's School* by Stephanie Stuve-Bodeen, illustrated by Christy Hale. Copyright © 2002 Stephanie Stuve-Bodeen and Christy Hale. Permission arranged with Lee & Low Books, Inc., New York, NY 10016.

Cover image from *First Day Jitters* by Julie Danneberg, illustrated by Judith Love Dufour. Copyright © Charlesbridge Publishing, Inc. All rights reserved. Used with permission of Charlesbridge Publishing, Inc. www.charlesbridge.com.

Cover image from *Just Ducks!* Text copyright © 2012 by Nicola Davies. Illustrations copyright © 2012 by Salvatore Rubbino. Reproduced by permission of the publisher, Candlewick Press, Somerville, MA, on behalf of Walker Books, London.

Cover image from *King of the Playground* by Phyllis Reynolds Naylor with illustrations by Nola Langner Malone. Text copyright © 1991 by Phyllis Reynolds Naylor. Illustrations copyright © 1991 by Nola Langner Malone. Reprinted with the permission of Atheneum Books for Young Readers, an imprint of Simon & Schuster Children's Publishing Division. All rights reserved.

Cover image *Knuffle Bunny: A Cautionary Tale*. Copyright © 2004 by Mo Willems. First published by Hyperion Books for Children, an imprint of Disney Book Group, LLC. Used with permission. All rights reserved.

Cover image from *Leon and Bob*. Copyright © 1997 Simon James. Reproduced by permission of the publisher, Candlewick Press, Somerville, MA, on behalf of Walker Books, London.

Cover image from *"Let's Get a Pup!," Said Kate*. Copyright © 2001 by Bob Graham. Reproduced by permission of the publisher, Candlewick Press, Somerville, MA, on behalf of Walker Books, London.

Cover image from *Lilly's Big Day* by Kevin Henkes. Copyright © 2006 by Kevin Henkes. Used by permission of HarperCollins Publishers.

Cover image from *Milk: From Cow to Carton* by Aliki Brandenberg. Copyright © 1962, 1989 by Aliki Brandenberg. Used by permission of HarperCollins Publishers.

Cover image from *Mr. George Baker*. Text copyright © 2004 by Amy Hest. Illustrations copyright © 2004 by Jon J. Muth. Reproduced by permission of the publisher, Candlewick Press, Somerville, MA.

Cover images and interior spread from *Mr. Putter & Tabby Catch the Cold* by Cynthia Rylant. Copyright © 2002 by Houghton Mifflin Harcourt Trade Publishing. Reprinted by permission of the publisher.

Cover image from *Mrs. Chicken and the Hungry Crocodile* by Won-Ldy Paye and Margaret H. Lippert. Text copyright © 2003 by Won-Ldy Paye and Margaret H. Lippert. Illustrations copyright © 2003 by Julie Paschkis. Reprinted by permission of Henry Holt Books for Young Readers. All rights reserved.

Cover image from *Mrs. McNosh Hangs Up Her Wash* by Sarah Weeks, illustrated by Nadine Bernard Westcott. Copyright © 1998 by Sarah Weeks. Jacket art copyright © 1998 by Nadine Bernard Westcott. Used by permission of HarperCollins Publishers.

Cover image from *Mud* by Mary Lyn Ray. Text copyright © 1996 by Mary Lyn Ray. Illustrations copyright © 1996 by Lauren Stringer. Reprinted by permission of Houghton Mifflin Harcourt Trade Publishing.

Cover image from *Music, Music for Everyone* by Vera B. Williams. Copyright © 1984 by Vera B. Williams. Used by permission of HarperCollins Publishers.